Democracy
at the Polls

AEI'S AT THE POLLS STUDIES

The American Enterprise Institute
has initiated this series in order to promote
an understanding of the electoral process as it functions in
democracies around the world. The series will include studies
of at least two national elections in each of nineteen countries
on five continents, by scholars from the United States and
abroad who are recognized as experts in their field.
More information on the titles in this series can
be found at the back of this book.

Democracy at the Polls

A Comparative Study of Competitive National Elections

Edited by
David Butler, Howard R. Penniman,
and Austin Ranney

American Enterprise Institute for Public Policy Research
Washington and London

Library of Congress Cataloging in Publication Data
Main entry under title:

Democracy at the polls.

   (AEI studies ; 297)
   Includes index.
   1. Elections.   2. Comparative government.
I. Butler, David E.   II. Penniman, Howard Rae,
1916-   III. Ranney, Austin.   IV. Series: American
Enterprise Institute for Public Policy Research. AEI
studies ; 297.
JF1001.D45   324.6   80-22652
ISBN 0-8447-3405-5
ISBN 0-8447-3403-9 (pbk.)

AEI Studies 297

Printed in the United States of America

Contents

1

Introduction: Democratic and Nondemocratic Elections

David Butler, Howard R. Penniman, and Austin Ranney

"General elections," wrote Sir Lewis Namier, "are the locks on the stream of British democracy, controlling the flow of the river and its traffic."[1] His point can be generalized to the histories of all Western democratic nations. In each country's elections those who seek to direct its public affairs must defend their records and convince the voters that the policies they propose for the future are feasible, desirable, and best carried out by those who propose them. The office seekers try to show that their opponents' policies are ill conceived and that their past failures in office make them poor bets for managing the government in the future. The voters consider the competing cases and make their decisions. Their votes are cast and counted, the candidates elected take office, and a new government is formed or an existing one renewed.

As the election debate is fought out in the campaign and as the expectations it arouses are satisfied or disappointed after the winning candidates take office, the whole politics of a democratic nation is encapsulated. Thus the electoral process lies at the heart of democratic government, and the critical difference between democratic and nondemocratic regimes is to be found in whether or nor they hold elections and, if they do, what kind.

That, at any rate, is the major premise of the *At the Polls* volumes published by the American Enterprise Institute for Public Policy Research since 1975 on the conduct and outcomes of general elections in selected democratic nations throughout the world. By mid-1980 two volumes had been published on elections in Australia, France, and Japan and one each on elections in Canada, West Germany, India, Ireland, Israel, Italy, three of the four Scandinavian countries, New

---

[1] Sir Lewis Namier, *Avenue of History* (London: Hamish Hamilton, 1952), p. 183.

1

Zealand, the United Kingdom, and Venezuela. There were also in various stages of preparation new volumes on Belgium, Colombia, the European Parliament, Greece, the Netherlands, Spain, Switzerland, and the United States; and second-look volumes on Canada, Denmark, Germany, India, Italy, Norway, Sweden, and the United Kingdom.

These books have dealt with similar sets of concerns and have used similar research and analytical techniques. Over 200 scholars have written articles that illuminate aspects of the electoral systems and politics of the countries they have covered. However, these writers' purpose has been to concentrate on the special conditions and processes of their particular countries, not to generalize about all countries. The books are a series of single-country studies, not a comparative or cross-national study of democratic electoral processes in general.

In 1978 two of this book's editors produced the first cross-national analysis in the series, but one focusing upon another kind of democratic election—direct voting by the people on statutory and constitutional measures in referendums.[2] They found that compiling accounts of the experiences of the countries that have made the greatest use of referendums cast new light on many established generalizations. This experience encouraged the three present editors to attempt the more ambitious project undertaken in this book. We have asked our team of distinguished authors to use the information in the *At the Polls* volumes and in all the other relevant literature to see what cross-national generalizations can be made about the conduct and impact of general elections in Western democracies. Most of this book is devoted to presenting their findings.

First, however, we should explain briefly what we mean by "democratic general elections" in this book and why we have included some countries in, and excluded others from, our purview.

What Is a "Democratic General Election"?

Anyone who uses the word "democracy" in scholarly analysis, political debate, or even friendly conversation is sure to encounter the bothersome problem that the word means quite different things to different people. Some, for instance, see "democracy" as strictly a political

---

[2] David Butler and Austin Ranney, eds., *Referendums: A Comparative Study of Practice and Theory* (Washington, D.C.: American Enterprise Institute, 1978). Note that AEI had previously published a study of a particular referendum: Anthony King, *Britain Says Yes: The 1975 Referendum on the Common Market* (Washington, D.C.: American Enterprise Institute, 1977).

device, a way of making public decisions. Others see it as far more: it is also, they variously say, a certain kind of economic or social system, a particular distribution of wealth and status, and/or even a way of conducting interpersonal relations. Even among those who use the term in a strictly political sense, there is sharp disagreement: some believe that the essence of democracy is vesting in popular majorities the full power to rule, while others believe, with equal passion, that the protection of minority rights against all tyrannies, including majority tyranny, is democracy's highest value.[3]

The editors and authors of this book have no intention of plunging into this Serbonian bog where far greater minds have foundered. We are content with what we believe to be the most common usage in Western democracies. And we believe that most of those who are concerned with the subject matter of this book will agree with us that a "general election" is one in which contests are held for most or all the elected offices of a nation's central government, and that a "democratic general election" is one in which those contests largely or wholly satisfy the following six conditions:[4]

1. Substantially the entire adult population has the right to vote for candidates for office.

2. Elections take place regularly within prescribed time limits.

3. No substantial group in the adult population is denied the opportunity of forming a party and putting up candidates.

4. All the seats in the major legislative chamber can be contested and usually are.

5. Campaigns are conducted with reasonable fairness in that neither law nor violence nor intimidation bars the candidates from presenting their views and qualifications or prevents the voters from learning and discussing them.

6. Votes are cast freely and secretly; they are counted and reported honestly; and the candidates who receive the proportions required by law are duly installed in office until their terms expire and a new election is held.

---

[3] The literature on the meaning(s) of "democracy" is far too vast to be listed here. But see Robert A. Dahl, A Preface to Democratic Theory (Chicago: University of Chicago Press, 1956); Carole Pateman, Participation and Democratic Theory (New York: Cambridge University Press, 1970); Giovanni Sartori, Democratic Theory (New York: Frederick A. Praeger, 1965; and Joseph A. Schumpeter, Capitalism, Socialism, and Democracy, 3d ed. (New York: Harper Torchbooks, 1950).

[4] Cf. W. J. M. Mackenzie, Free Elections (New York: Holt, Rinehart and Winston, 1958); and Gerald M. Pomper, Elections in America (New York: Dodd, Mead & Company, 1968).

Why These Twenty-Eight Nations?

The foregoing conditions, we should be clear, add up to a *model* of democratic general elections; they are not necessarily a precise empirical description of how elections are actually conducted in every detail in any particular country. Hence actual general elections in modern nations can be arranged on a scale according to how closely they satisfy the model's conditions. At the nondemocratic end of the scale we would no doubt place the countries that do not hold elections at all. *The Europa World Book 1979* lists thirty-three countries in this class.[5] One notch nearer the democratic end of the scale perhaps come the thirty-three nations in which elections are regularly held but only one candidate is allowed for each office, and those candidates are all chosen by the nation's sole or "hegemonic" political party.[6]

Even with these sixty-six nations removed, there are still a large number we might have covered in this book. To keep the number manageable we made two further cuts: we eliminated all countries with populations of less than 3 million (which excluded such unquestionably democratic nations as Costa Rica, Iceland, Jamaica, Luxembourg, and Malta); and we eliminated all countries which were not classified as either "free" or "partly free" in the most recent world survey by Freedom House.[7]

The twenty-eight countries remaining thus do not in any sense constitute an exhaustive list of the world's democratic regimes. They do, however, provide us with a reasonable and manageable working list of nations which hold democratic general elections: Australia, Austria, Belgium, Canada, Colombia, Denmark, the Dominican Republic, Finland, France, West Germany, Greece, India, Ireland, Israel, Italy, Japan, the Netherlands, New Zealand, Norway, Portugal, Spain, Sri Lanka, Sweden, Switzerland, Turkey, the United Kingdom, the United States, and Venezuela.[8]

We asked our authors to compile all the material they could on each of these countries. Their efforts, and ours in the chapters we have written, have taught us a good deal about the practical problems of cross-national elections research. In most countries the formal rules governing the conduct of elections and the results of recent elections

---

[5] For example, Brunei, Burundi, Chad, Ecuador, Nepal, and Saudi Arabia.

[6] In addition to the Soviet Union and the other Communist "people's republics," the list includes Cameroon, Gabon, Ivory Coast, Liberia, Tunisia, and Zambia.

[7] As summarized in *U.S. News and World Report,* January 19, 1976, pp. 24-25.

[8] Freedom House also lists Upper Volta as "partly free," but most of our authors were unable to get any information on its electoral process; so we excluded it from our list.

4

are relatively easy to ascertain and in many instances are published. On the other hand, information about extralegal electoral processes is often hard to come by, and the scholarly and journalistic literature on them is large but patchy. There are a number of accounts of most aspects of elections in the countries covered by the *At the Polls* series. There are fewer accounts of electoral affairs in Finland, Portugal, and Spain. And most of our authors have found the pickings from the Dominican Republic and Sri Lanka very slim. To help those who would like to pursue the book's concerns further, we have included for each chapter a short bibliography of the most useful sources for the field it covers.

Twenty-three of our twenty-eight countries have "parliamentary" systems: that is, the voters elect all the members of the national parliament's major chamber, and the majority party or a coalition of less-than-majority parties chooses the political executive. In three nations—Colombia, France, and Venezuela—the voters directly elect the chief executive officer, and in Finland and the United States that officer is formally elected by "presidential electors" who are themselves elected by the voters and register their presidential preferences. Accordingly, the book considers national legislative elections in all twenty-eight nations and also presidential elections in the five "presidential" systems.

The Book's Objective and Strategy

Our objective in this book is nothing less than a comparative cross-national analysis of the conduct and impact of national general elections in the twenty-eight nations we have selected.

We recognize that comparative studies of political processes and institutions are often disappointing because there is so little that is truly comparable. Every country's political system is an organic whole, and cross-national analysis of the separate parts of many systems runs a serious risk of producing more confusion than illumination. The whole connotation of such key terms as "government," "cabinet," and "party" can be quite different in polities that are superficially similar. Each word has surplus meanings that are conditioned by history and current practices, and often the result is that every comparison has to be qualified so extensively by an exposition of local variations that it becomes all but meaningless.

Of all democratic institutions, however, electoral processes offer perhaps the richest possibilities for meaningful comparisons and contrasts. Elections everywhere take place under fixed rules and within finite time periods. Their outcomes in votes and seats are expressed in

5

numbers and thus lend themselves to quantitative analysis. To be sure, all statements of cause-and-effect relations must be made tentatively and cautiously, for identical or very similar formal rules and political practices may produce quite different results in different political cultures. Nevertheless, anyone seeking to draw up new electoral arrangements for a country or to modify existing ones could probably extrapolate from foreign experience with less risk of error than in dealing with almost any other aspect of democratic government.

We are well aware that we have tackled a very large subject in this book. It would be easy, without prolixity, to expand every one of these chapters to book length. Elections, as we shall see, are governed by elaborate laws and regulations designed to ensure fair play. Each campaign is conducted within a complex culture and a traditional pattern of politics that make foreign observers acutely aware of the uniqueness of each country that regularly and freely goes to the polls. The study of voting behavior, in terms of both individual psychology and political impact, has been one of the largest areas of growth in postwar political science not only in the United States but in many other countries as well. The systems by which votes are translated into legislative seats have been extraordinarily diverse, and the consequences of various forms of proportional representation and majoritarian systems have stimulated an impressive body of literature. And arching over all the technical details of the subject are many of the great problems of democratic theory—the meaning and institutionalization of choice, representation, accountability, freedom of political expression, and freedom of political action.

We believe that each of this book's chapters deals with a major element of the democratic electoral process, but we are also well aware that we have had to exclude other aspects, such as the processes by which political parties choose their national leaders, the impact of various electoral systems and outcomes on popular confidence in democratic institutions and leaders, and theories of "rational voting." For each of the elements we have chosen, however, we have asked the author to consider to what extent generalizations can be made about it that extend beyond a single polity. And since the laws and customs governing elections have far-reaching implications for the viability and flexibility of the countries' larger political systems, we conclude with a chapter on what elections decide and a chapter on the role of elections in democratic government.

2

Electoral Systems

David Butler

An electoral system is a means of translating the popular will into an elected assembly. But the "popular will" as expressed at one moment in time in a single mark on a ballot or at most a short list of preference orderings must be a blurred representation of all the complex and changing views on men and measures that coexist in a voter's mind. At their very best, elections are clumsy instruments of choice. In devising the rules for their conduct politicians have wobbled between a pragmatic acceptance of their necessary imperfections and a dream of pure fairness, of achieving a complete match between input—the voters' preferences—and output—the resultant legislature.

No two polities have come up with the same answer to the problems involved in democratic elections. In the petty details, such as the compilation of a register of voters, the timing of nominations, the arrangements for casting and counting votes, and the rules governing campaign practices and election expenses, every country has its own laws; and on the larger question, the mathematical devices for linking votes cast with seats won, there is an extraordinary variety of answers. The Parliament of the European Community is currently committed to producing a scheme under which its next election, due in 1984, can be conducted on a common system in all its member countries. But nothing is more certain than that any harmonization will be on a very limited scale, simply because the national customs surrounding elections are so deeply engrained. Bureaucratic and social traditions would make the standardization of the laws governing the franchise and registration, or behavior in campaigns and on polling day, almost impossible, at least in the short run; it is only at the level of the most general principles that consensus and common action could be agreed.

To make this point is to underline the impossibility of covering in this chapter the infinite diversity of electoral systems, in terms of either legal form or actual working.[1] But there is no reason to be defeatist; useful generalizations can be offered on the basis of a limited number of examples. Indeed there are few aspects of the political process that lend themselves more readily to comparative treatment (let alone to quantitative treatment). In dealing with elections countries have been very imitative, as the contagious movement across national frontiers of the secret ballot, women's suffrage, and proportional representation has shown.

But there has always been an ethnocentric element in this copying. The English-speaking world followed different traditions from Continental Europe. It is not just that the simplicities of the first-past-the-post system tended to survive in countries once ruled by Britain while the rest of the democratic world turned to proportional representation. It is also notable that countries which have wanted to keep single-member constituencies but to diminish the arbitrariness of the system have looked to the alternative vote in the English-speaking world, but elsewhere to the second ballot. Advocates of greater "fairness" have turned to the single transferable vote in the English-speaking world, but elsewhere to list systems of proportional representation.

An electoral system cannot be understood in isolation from the political system of which it is part. Some of the countries with the most similar voting arrangements have the most different politics. But in details of electoral rules the range is extraordinary. Other chapters in this book deal with essentials such as candidate selection, campaign finance, media access, and participation. But that is far from exhausting the catalog of comparative themes. The laws governing fair play in campaigning and in balloting, the restraints on parties and on can-

---

[1] This chapter focuses on elections to the lower or larger legislative body and not on elections to the upper chamber (which may be chosen by a similar or a different popular vote, may be elected by the lower chamber, may be nominated by the executive, may be partially hereditary, or may be nonexistent). Only in the United States, where the two houses have a similar first-past-the-post basis, is the upper chamber as important as the lower chamber. From the point of view of electoral systems, Australia provides the most interesting case study. Its Senate is chosen by the single transferable vote, in contrast to the single-member-district system of the lower house: on the whole, when House and Senate elections coincide, people vote identically, and there has been no instance in thirty years of enough voters defying the recommended order of candidates on their party's list for it to be upset. For the situation in other countries, see table 2-1.

This chapter also ignores presidential elections, which in the United States and perhaps in France, Finland, and Portugal are the most important democratic contest. (In almost all the other countries in our twenty-eight which have a president—eleven are monarchies—it is the legislature which chooses the president, who is largely a figurehead.) And it ignores the special problems of some federal systems where the rules on the franchise, party structure, and polling day arrangements vary substantially between component states—the extreme example being the elections to the European Assembly in June 1979.

didates, and the locus of responsibility for electoral administration are all matters that have been solved in different ways in different countries. Furthermore, the mere size of a legislature and the frequency of its reelection are questions that have no magic answer. Aristotle and John Stuart Mill were willing to tackle them as general problems open to general answers, but the less theoretical institutionalists of the twentieth century have been more cautious.

The Ground Rules

In the early evolution of most electoral systems, the franchise provoked most controversy. Class was the first subject of dispute: the idea of "one man, one vote" was once wildly radical; the masses could not be trusted with power—especially those in "inferior races"; at the very least, their votes must be offset by special representation for property or education. But as one nation after another showed that bourgeois control was not seriously threatened by a working-class electorate, the franchise argument turned to female suffrage. Even wilder illusions flourished about the consequences of women's voting, until they actually voted and behaved much as their menfolk did, showing no special preference for women or for handsome or frivolous men. The last franchise argument has been over age: only in the last two decades have the democratic nations settled down to a consensus on eighteen.

Associated with the broad problem of the franchise are those detailed questions of electoral registration and absentee voting. The right to vote is not enough: the administrative procedures must be adequate for its exercise. Blacks in the southern United States were for a long time denied the benefit of the Fourteenth Amendment by the action of local officials or by other pressures. But even apart from extreme cases like this, countries vary widely in the provision they make for absentee voting and in the extent to which their electoral lists are in fact coterminous with the eligible population. The development of equitable registration procedures was one of the essential elements in the development of elections.

Another battle in the evolution of electoral systems has been over the drawing of boundaries. Except where there is a single nationwide constituency, this may have a vital influence on the outcome. In proportional systems the problem is much less serious than in those with single-member seats. But in any country where there is a regional or local basis for representation, population movements inevitably render obsolete boundaries that may once have been fair, delimiting equal electorates. In general, the drift to the towns and then out to suburbs has meant that first country districts and later inner cities have become overrepresented while developing areas have become underrepresented. But the biases arising from such inevitable demographic trends have often been compounded by a deliberate policy of representing space rather than numbers—a rural loading enshrined in law or custom. In Australia until 1974 there was an explicit instruction to those drawing boundaries to give rural seats 20 percent fewer electors than urban ones—and a 10 percent loading still survives. In the United States until the *Baker v. Carr* judgment of 1962, many states deliberately overrepresented country areas. In Britain the boundary commissioners, while instructed to make constituencies as nearly equal as possible, are also told to allow for special geographical difficulties—and the two island constituencies off Scotland have electorates barely a third of the mainland average.

But even equal-sized constituencies may be "unfair," deliberately or accidentally. The gerrymandering of boundaries so that one party gets most of its seats by small margins while its rival wastes votes, piling up huge majorities in carefully designed constituencies, has been known in most parts of the world. It has been checked by the institution of neutral boundary commissioners and by increased insistence, often by the courts, on equality of numbers and other criteria of fairness.

But a party in power may still escape the losses threatened by a redrawing of boundaries by delaying action. In the United States, House seats are automatically reallocated between states every ten years, but until the 1960s state legislatures sometimes delayed the redrawing of boundaries. In Britain in 1969 the Labour government refused to give effect to a routine but disadvantageous redistribution on the ostensible ground that local government was shortly to be reorganized and that parliamentary and local boundaries should coincide.

Most countries set a limit to the life of constituency boundaries—ranging from five years in Australia and New Zealand to fifteen years in Britain. France is the only major country with single-member seats that has no statutory timetable for redistribution.

Another essential element in democratic evolution was the establishment of the secret ballot and the formulation of acceptable rules for the conduct of the polling and the counting of votes. Democratic elections demand popular acceptance. If the voters do not feel that the candidates have had a fair chance to put their case and that votes have been cast freely and counted honestly, the legislature or the government that results can hardly trade on its legitimacy. Each country has devised rules to prevent intimidation, corruption, and ballot fraud. Technical safeguards have checked abuses. But fair elections depend much more on a nation's general ethos than on any enforceable regulations. No country, for example, has developed rules or customs that remove all the advantages that go with being in power, but the campaigning benefits of incumbency for governments and for individual legislators vary widely.

To reiterate this is to stress that the mathematical side of an electoral system is not the whole story. Electoral reformers have too often emphasized arithmetic at the expense of politics. Democratic elections are in practice a matter of party competition. The electoral system may determine the number of parties—and to some extent their coherence and their structure—but many of the essential characteristics of the competing parties have nothing to do with the electoral system; they spring from a country's history and its economic and social structure. The system can make an enormous difference—but not so much as the spirit in which the democratic process is carried on. Yet the main purpose of this chapter must be to discuss the relation of votes and seats, the way in which the marks on the ballot paper are transmuted into the choice of persons.

Translating Votes into Seats

Electoral systems are seldom the stuff of campaign debate. For most of the time most people accept as fixed the rules under which they record their democratic choice. In hardly any of the elections examined in the *At the Polls* series is there serious discussion of a change in the voting system (except in a passing reference to the well-ventilated grievance of the Liberal party in Britain). Yet in every country the political outcome of the election is the product of specific rules—and in almost every country the rules have been subject to repeated modification.

The principal characteristics of the electoral system in each of the twenty-eight democratic countries we are considering in this book are shown in table 2–1. The data in the table suggest that all systems fall into a continuum that runs from a simple first-past-the-post system, based on single-member constituencies, to a purely proportional one with a national list. Before touching on the variants that lie between these poles, let us look briefly at the prime examples of the extreme cases.

Britain (or New Zealand) could be taken as the archetype of majoritarian voting; it certainly illustrates the strong appeal that the simplicity of the first-past-the-post system can have. Single-member constituencies return individual members of Parliament with a con-

TABLE 2–1
ELECTORAL SYSTEMS IN TWENTY-EIGHT DEMOCRATIC COUNTRIES

Country	Electoral System, Lower House[a]	Number of Seats	Number of Constit-uencies	Year Present Electoral System Adopted[b]	Maximum Years between Elections	Year Women's Suffrage Adopted
Australia	AV	124	124	1918	3	1902
Austria	PR	183	9	1919	4	1919
Belgium	PR	212	30	1899	4	1948
Canada	FPTP	282	264	1976	5	1920
Colombia	PR	199	26	1968	4	1957
Denmark	PR	175	17	1920	4	1915
Dominican Republic	PR	91	27	1966	4	1954
Finland	PR	199	15	1906	4	1906
France	2nd ballot	491	491	1958	5	1944
West Germany	PR & FPTP	496	248	1949	4	1919

Maximum Interval between Redistricting[c]	Venue for Disputes[d]	Other Elections[e]		Most Recent Election	
		Upper house	Head of state	Year	Seats won, by party
10 years	high court	STV	app.	1977	Lib. 67
					NCP 19
					ALP 38
set	const. court	ind. elec.	pop. elec.	1979	Soc. 95
					People's 77
					Lib. 11
10 years	leg.	mix.	her.	1978	CS 82
					Soc. 58
					Lib. 37
					other 35
10 years	leg.	app.	app.	1980	Lib. 147
					Con. 103
					NDP 32
set	elect. court	PR	pop. elec.	1978	Lib. 109
					Con. 86
					other 4
set	leg.	none	her.	1977	S. Dem. 65
					Prog. 26
					Lib. 21
					Con. 15
					other 48
set	cent. elect. board	PR	pop. elec.	1978	DRP 49
					Ref'm. 42
set	sup. court	none	pop. elec.	1979	S. Dem. 52
					Con. 47
					Cent. 36
					Comm. 35
					other 29
none	const. court	ind. elec.	pop. elec.	1978	RPF 154
					UDF 123
					Soc. 115
					Comm. 86
					other 13
each elec.	fed. court	ind. elec.	leg. elec.	1980	CDU/CSU 226
					SPD 218
					FDP 53

(Table continues)

TABLE 2–1 (continued)

Country	Electoral System, Lower House[a]	Number of Seats	Number of Constituencies	Year Present Electoral System Adopted[b]	Maximum Years between Elections	Year Women's Suffrage Adopted
Greece	PR	300	56	1975	4	1952
India	FPTP	544	542	1950	5	1919
Ireland	STV	148	42	1920	5	1918
Israel	PR	120	1	1948	4	1948
Italy	PR	630	32	1946	5	1946
Japan	[f]	511	130	1947	4	1946
Netherlands	PR	150	1	1918	4	1922
New Zealand	FPTP	92	92	1852	3	1893

Maximum Interval between Redistricting[c]	Venue for Disputes[d]	Other Elections[e]		Most Recent Election	
		Upper house	Head of state	Year	Seats won, by party
none	spec. court	ind. elec.	leg. elec.	1977	ND 173 PASOK 92 UDC 15 other 20
10 years	elect. tribs.	ind. elec.	leg. elec.	1980	Cong. I 351 Janata 31 Lok Dal 41 Comm. I 11 Comm. M 35 other 56
12 years	high court	ind. elec.	leg. elec.	1976	FF 84 FG 43 Lab. 17 other 4
sing. dist.	leg.	none	leg. elec.	1977	Likud 43 Lab. 32 DMC 15 Rel. 12 other 18
set	spec. council	PR	leg. elec.	1979	CD 262 Comm. 201 Soc. 62 other 105
set	high court	mix.	her.	1980	Lib. Dem. 284 Jap. Soc. 107 Komeito 33 Jap. Comm. 29 Dem. Soc. 32 other 26
sing. dist.	leg.	ind. elec.	her.	1977	Soc. 53 CD 49 Lib. 28 other 20
5 years	elect. court	none	app.	1978	Nat. 50 Labor 41 SC 1

(Table continues)

TABLE 2–1 (continued)

Country	Electoral System, Lower House[a]	Number of Seats	Number of Constit- uencies	Year Present Electoral System Adopted[b]	Maximum Years between Elections	Year Women's Suffrage Adopted
Norway	PR	155	20	1921	4	1909
Portugal	PR	250	22	1976	4	1975
Spain	PR	350	52	1977	4	1977
Sri Lanka	PR	168	24	1978	6	1949
Sweden	PR	349	28	1909	4	1918
Switzerland	PR	200	25	1919	4	1971
Turkey	PR	450	67	1961	4	1934
United Kingdom	FPTP	635	635	13th cent.	5	1918

Maximum Interval between Redis-tricting[e]	Venue for Disputes[d]	Other Elections[e]		Most Recent Election		
		Upper house	Head of state	Year	Seats won, by party	
set	leg.	ind. elec.	her.	1977	Lab.	76
					Con.	41
					CP	22
					Cent.	12
					other	4
set	common courts	none	pop. elec.	1979	Dem.	128
					Soc.	74
					Comm.	47
					other	1
set	cent. elect. board	PR	her.	1979	CD	168
					Soc.	121
					Comm.	23
					other	38
set	spec. court	none	pop. elec.	1977	UNP	139
					Tamil	17
					other	12
set	spec. board	none	her.	1979	S. Dem.	152
					Cent.	86
					Con.	55
					Lib.	39
					Comm.	17
set	fed. trib.	PR	leg. elec.	1979	S. Dem.	55
					Rad.	47
					CD	46
					Sw. People's	21
					other	31
set	spec. council	mostly PR	leg. elec.	1977	RPP	214
					Justice	189
					Nat. Salv.	24
					other	23
15 years	courts	her. & app.	her.	1979	Cons.	339
					Lab.	269
					Lib.	11
					other	16

(Table continues)

TABLE 2–1 (continued)

Country	Electoral System, Lower House[a]	Number of Seats	Number of Constit- uencies	Year Present Electoral System Adopted[b]	Maximum Years between Elections	Year Women's Suffrage Adopted
United States	FPTP	435	435	1788	2	1919
Venezuela	PR	199	23	1958	5	1946

[a] AV, alternative vote; PR, proportional representation; FPTP, first past the post; STV, single transferable vote.

[b] The dates entered in this column indicate when the basic rules currently in force for relating votes to seats in national elections were adopted. Many of the countries listed held democratic elections before this date; many have altered aspects of their electoral systems since; and in some, democratic rule has not been continuous. In countries where democratic government has been interrupted by a period of authoritarian rule or foreign occupation and a new constitution has been adopted since the restoration of democracy, the date of the present constitution is given, even where it reinstituted an electoral system previously used in the country (this is the case, notably, for France, Greece, Spain, and Venezuela).

scious local attachment; although the attachment may mean more to the member than to his constituents, it does guarantee that localities have their own identifiable spokesmen at the center. But the main virtues cited for the system are national ones: it usually gives clear decisions and it forces parties to be broad-based. First-past-the-post voting fosters strong parties and discourages weak ones; two parties are likely to predominate, and whichever gets a plurality in votes usually gets a clear majority in seats. Elections therefore choose governments. A single party, with a majority in the legislature, rules for a parliamentary term at the end of which it can be reendorsed or thrown out of power. The voters are sovereign, selecting not an "electoral college" out of which a coalition or a series of coalitions will emerge but a government which can be held responsible for its actions at the next election. Parties seeking to get and to retain something near to half the national vote have to be tolerant and to keep their appeal within the middle-of-the-road consensus. The way in which a small shift in votes is translated into a much larger shift in seats means that those in power have to be very sensitive to public opinion, as their backbenchers with marginal seats will always remind them. A trifling net movement between the main parties can produce a decisive switch in the balance of power, as Britain learned in 1951 and 1974.

Of course, British history also supplies instances of the anomalies that the first-past-the-post system can produce, and there are plenty of

Maximum Interval between Redistricting[e]	Venue for Disputes[d]	Other Elections[e]		Most Recent Election		
		Upper house	Head of state	Year	Seats won, by party	
10 years	leg.	FPTP	pop. elec.	1978	Dem. Rep.	276 159
set	sup. court	PR	pop. elec.	1978	COPEI AD other	86 86 27

[c] "Set," borders set; "each elec.," redistricting required for each election; "sing. dist.," single national district.

[d] "Const. court," constitutional court; "leg.," legislature; "elect. court," electoral court; "cent. elect. board," central electoral board; "sup. court," supreme court; "fed. court," federal court; "spec. court," special court; "elect. tribs.," election tribunals.

[e] STV, single transferable vote; "app.," appointed; "ind. elec.," indirect election; "pop. elec.," popular election; "her.," hereditary; "mix.," mixed selection system; PR, proportional representation; "leg. elec.," elected by legislature; FPTP, first past the post.

[f] Multimember plurality, limited vote (used only in Japan).

other examples, notably in Canada and South Africa, of its capriciousness. It does not always yield clear majorities. Most votes does not always mean most seats. Furthermore, alternation between single-party governments is not necessarily more conducive to the good of the country than the continuous compromises seen in countries whose electoral systems ensure that there will never be a clear majority.

The Netherlands (or Israel) could be taken as the archetype of proportional representation. The country is one constituency. The voters choose between any parties that put forward candidates, and seats are allocated in exact proportion to votes. With a 150-member parliament it is only necessary to get 0.67 percent of the national vote to secure one seat. The system is totally free from the statistical quirks that bedevil most proportional arrangements, let alone the anomalies of first past the post. The price of its "fairness" can be seen in the prolonged crises that regularly occur over the formation of governments. Up to six months has been spent after an election in bargaining about the composition of the coalition. The parties, and the individual politicians, assured by the electoral system of continued representation, fight doggedly to translate their share of the vote into the maximum share of power—in terms both of offices and of policies. The Dutch arrangements led to a proliferation of parties (in 1971, twenty-eight parties presented lists and fourteen secured seats). But this tendency should be kept in perspective: in 1977 four parties shared 138 of the 150 seats, while four of the other seven parties had only a single seat each.

Both the British and the Dutch systems are well entrenched in their own countries, but they have their domestic critics. In the Netherlands reforming efforts have, on the whole, focused on demands for a slightly higher threshold than 0.67 percent to secure a seat. In Britain the grievances of the Liberals and other small parties have meant that proposals to change the voting system have always excited some discussion; this increased sharply after 1974, partly because, while the Liberal votes rose to almost 20 percent, the party got only 2 percent of the seats, but also because disillusion had grown about the violent oscillations of policy that went with the alternation of single-party governments. Change was unlikely: those in a position to reform the law are usually reluctant to condemn a system that gave them power. Moreover, there is no consensus on a better alternative.

In Anglo-Saxon countries, even those with very strong party structures, there has been a reluctance to accept the central-party dominance over candidate selection that goes with list systems of proportional representation. But the single-transferable-vote system is seen as complex and, possibly, as a threat to party discipline (though it has not worked out that way in the Australian Senate or the Irish Dáil). The additional member system, insofar as it is understood, seems to involve party lists. Disagreement on alternatives offers a sturdy buttress for the status quo. The most modest of proposed changes, the alternative vote, does preserve the small single-member seat, but, though it is likely to favor a third party in the center, it offers no guarantee of greater proportionality. (It has made remarkably little difference in the Australian lower house.)

In between the British and Dutch extremes, there is a wide range of possibilities. Most of them produce results nearer to the Dutch than the British model. Italy, Germany, and the Scandinavian countries have systems guaranteeing that the proportion of seats will be very close to the proportion of votes—though in Germany and Sweden, very small parties may be excluded. But the United States, India, and Canada follow the British majoritarian pattern, with its propensity to give the largest party an exaggerated share of seats—and minor parties almost none. Fifth Republic France with the second ballot and Australia with the alternative vote have systems that are nearer the majoritarian than the proportional end of the scale. But in twenty out of our twenty-eight countries the arrangements are essentially proportional. Ireland stands in a unique middle position. It uses the single transferable vote—in theory a very pure form of PR—but its constituencies are so small, returning on average only three and a half members each, that its results can be capricious (in 1969 Fianna Fáil, with 45.7 percent of the vote, won, getting 51.7 percent of the seats, while in 1973, with 46.2 percent of the vote, it lost, getting 47.6 percent of the seats).

One essential key to judging proportional systems is the threshold which must be crossed for representation to be achieved or increased. The most common threshold is constituency size. Seats cannot be divided; so (even in the single-constituency, 150-member Dutch parliament) a party needs 1/150 of the vote to secure any representation. In Norway most constituencies have from ten to sixteen members; so a party usually needs a minimum of 6 percent of the vote in a region to secure any representation. In Ireland most constituencies have three or four members, which implies a threshold of 25 percent or 20 percent. In Italy, Germany, and Sweden there are reserve seats allotted nationally in order to make the results proportional, but in Germany a party can only qualify for these seats if it secures 5 percent of the national poll (or, which is harder, if it wins three local contests), while in Sweden there is a 4 percent threshold.

At the other extreme, proportional systems have been qualified by bonuses for the more successful parties. In Fourth Republic France in 1951 and 1956, an *apparentement* device allowed a group of allied parties to scoop up all the seats in a constituency if, together, they secured over 50 percent of the vote. In Italy in 1953 there was provision for a national bonus so that if an *apparentement* got 50 percent of the national vote it would get 66 percent of the seats (the *apparentement* just failed to reach 50 percent and the scheme was subsequently repealed).

Within established PR systems finer points of vote counting can make a difference to the allocation of seats. The largest-average method of awarding seats to votes is the simplest; but it favors the larger parties at the expense of the smaller. The d'Hondt formula, which somewhat modifies this tendency, has been more widely used. But in Denmark, Norway, and Sweden a version of the more exactly proportional Sainte-Laguë method is used. Much argument has been expended over the merits of PR systems. Politically the differences in the results are not very great; the Netherlands and Israel aside, no system is totally fair to the smaller parties, and no system diverges very far from proportionality for the major contenders. However, in the delicate business of coalition forming, the presence of one or two more minor party members or the reallocation of a single seat away from a major party can, of course, make a crucial difference.

Measures of imperfection have been drawn up by Rein Taagepera, Douglas Rae, and Arend Lijphart, among others. Taagepera shows how the point at which a party is likely to be overrepresented, not

21

underrepresented, varies from 2 percent of the vote in Denmark and Sweden to 18 percent in Ireland and Belgium and, in the non-PR systems, from 20 percent in France to 34 percent in Britain.[2]

The Effects of Electoral Systems

But it would be wrong to focus too much on the problems of proportionality and fairness. All electoral arrangements have a long-term effect on electoral behavior and on party behavior. The whole political system is colored by the electoral system, for the electoral system conditions the number of parties and the continuity of governments. It shapes individual career structures and it influences the internal cohesion and discipline of parties and the general stability of the party structure. The change from proportional representation to the second ballot is one of the larger factors (though far from the only one) explaining the difference between the Fourth and Fifth Republics. The chance consequences of the 5 percent threshold have had a prodigious effect on the history of Germany in the 1960s and 1970s. The interwar history of Britain would have been very different if the House of Commons had overruled the House of Lords on the alternative vote in 1918. The acceptance of proportional representation at the turn of the century saved the Center parties in Scandinavia and the Low Countries. And the different degrees of headquarters control over national and regional lists explain many of the differences in the behavior patterns of individual politicians.

Fear of the next election is a constant of politics. In all democracies, elections offer the final sanction against governments. But the sanction is very different in Britain or Australia, where the switch of one or two voters in every hundred can make the difference between full power and impotent opposition, and in the Netherlands or Denmark, where no party can hope for a clear-cut victory and the overwhelming majority of legislators know their election is secure.

Elections can be seen as an opportunity for an ideological census, a declaration of the voters' fundamental position on the left-right spectrum. If that is the goal, there is everything to be said for perfect proportionality: the legislature, like an opinion poll, must be an honest reflection of the views of the masses. Alternatively, elections can be seen as devices to choose viable governments and give them legitimacy. A clear answer may be better for the country than a

[2] See Rein Taagepera, "Proportionality Profiles of West European Elections" (Paper read at the annual meeting of the American Political Science Association, 1979, in Washington, D.C.); Douglas Rae, *The Political Consequences of Electoral Laws* (New Haven: Yale University Press, 1967); and Arend Lijphart and R. Gibberd, "Threshold and Payoffs in List Systems of P.R.," *European Journal of Political Research* (1977), pp. 219-44.

mathematically exact one. The conflicting appeals of fairness and of practicality have been apparent in every debate on electoral systems. The pressure toward equity has won out almost everywhere outside the English-speaking world in the acceptance of proportional representation. But pragmatic considerations have qualified the proportional triumph: the thresholds built into most proportional systems imply a recognition that too many parties may make for bad government. A legislature that is a perfect mirror of what the electorate felt on one particular polling day may not be as satisfactory a basis for effective government as one that offers a cruder but more decisive reflection of majority trends.

Glossary

Additional member system. This is exemplified by the proportional system used in Germany. Half the members are elected by first-past-the-post voting in single-member constituencies. The other half are allocated to party lists in such a way that the seats in the full assembly are proportionate to the votes cast in the country as a whole (subject to certain threshold rules).

Alternative vote. This refers to the use of preferential voting within single-member constituencies. For the Australian lower house, for example, every elector is required to number all the candidates in order of preference; the candidate with fewest first preferences is eliminated and the second preferences are counted instead; and the process continues until one candidate has a clear majority.

Apparentement. A provision in a list system of voting by which separate parties can declare themselves linked for the purposes of vote counting and seat allocation (France 1951, 1956, Italy 1953).

Constituency. This is the most common term for the geographic areas into which a country is divided for electoral purposes. A constituency may send one or several members to the legislature. Other terms include district (U.S.A.), riding (Canada), *circonscription* (France), electorate (Australia and New Zealand), and division (U.K.).

Cube law. A formula which has been used to describe the way in which first-past-the-post systems exaggerate majorities in votes into much greater majorities in seats. If votes are divided in the ratio A:B, seats are likely to be divided in the ratio $A^3:B^3$.

Cumulative voting. A rarely used system of voting in a multimember constituency in which electors can cast more than one of their votes for a single candidate.

D'Hondt system. The formula used in most list systems of proportional representation to allocate seats. It is also known as the highest-average system. Briefly, it ensures that in a constituency no reallocation of seats would reduce discrepancies in the shares of the vote received by the winners.

Droop quota. The formula used in most single-transferable-vote systems to allocate seats. It can be stated [votes/(seats + 1)] + 1.

First-past-the-post (FPTP) system. This, the oldest kind of voting arrangement, still predominates in English-speaking countries. It usually involves single-member districts. Each elector has one vote, and the candidate who gets most votes wins, even if he does not secure an absolute majority. This is also known as the relative majority or plurality system.

Gerrymandering. The drawing of constituency boundaries deliberately to secure party advantage.

Largest remainder system. The formula for allocating seats in list systems that is most favorable to smaller parties. After one seat has been distributed for every full quota (the quota being derived simply by dividing votes by seats), any remaining seats are allocated in turn to the parties with the largest residues.

Limited vote. A system of voting in multimember constituencies with a majoritarian system in which electors have fewer votes than there are seats to fill (now used only in Japan; tried in a few U.K. constituencies 1868–1880).

Panachage. A provision in a list system of proportional representation in which the elector is given the opportunity to vary the order of candidates on his party's list.

Preferential voting. A system of voting in which the elector expresses a rank order of preference between candidates. The alternative vote and the single transferable vote are systems of preferential voting.

Proportional representation (PR). This is a generic term for all the systems of election which seek, by multimember seats or reserve lists, to relate seats to votes more proportionately than is possible under a single-member-constituency system.

Redistribution. The British term for two processes distinguished in American usage: "redistricting," the redrawing of constituency boundaries, and "reapportionment," the reallocation of seats among constituencies.

Sainte-Laguë system. A formula used to allocate seats in some Scandinavian list systems of proportional representation. The use of a divisor larger than the number of seats available ensures a more proportional result than the d'Hondt system.

Second ballot. This refers to the system used in Third and Fifth Republic France, under which, in a single-member-constituency system, there is a second vote a week after the first one if no candidate has an absolute majority. It is analogous to the runoff arrangements in some American primary elections. It is sometimes known as the exhaustive ballot.

Single transferable vote (STV). This refers to the use of preferential voting in multimember constituencies. It is used in the Irish Dáil and the Australian Senate. Electors are asked to number the candidates in order of preference. Any votes surplus to a Droop quota are reallocated according to second preferences. Then the bottom candidates are successively eliminated and their preferences redistributed until all the seats are filled.

Threshold. A minimum condition for securing representation. This device limits purely proportional results, for example, by distributing seats only to parties securing a minimum of 5 percent of the vote (as in Germany) or by having constituencies with so few members that a party needs a substantial vote to have any chance of securing a seat (as in Ireland).

Bibliography

Duverger, Maurice. *Political Parties.* Translated by Barbara and Robert North. New York: Wiley, 1954.

Finer, S. E., ed. *Adversary Politics and Electoral Reform.* London: Wigram, 1975.

Haman, V. *Parliaments of the World.* London: Macmillan, 1976.

Hand, G. J.; Georgel, J.; and Sasse, C. *European Electoral Systems Handbook.* London: Butterworth, 1979.

Lakeman, Enid. *How Democracies Vote.* 3d ed. London: Faber, 1970.

Lijphart, A., and Gibberd, R. W. "Thresholds and Payoffs in List Systems of P.R." *European Journal of Political Research* 5:210–44.

Mackenzie, W. J. M. *Free Elections.* London: Allen & Unwin, 1958.

Milnor, A. J. *Elections and Political Stability.* Boston: Little, Brown, 1969.

Rae, Douglas. *The Political Consequences of Electoral Laws.* New Haven: Yale University Press, 1967.

Rokkan, S. "Elections: Electoral Systems." In *International Encyclopaedia of the Social Sciences,* 1968.

Rokkan, S., and Meyriat, J. *International Guide to Election Statistics.* The Hague: Mouton, 1969.

Taagepera, R. "Proportionality Profiles of West European Electorates." Paper read at the Annual Meeting of the American Political Science Association, 1979, in Washington, D.C.

3

Political Parties:
Ideologies and Programs

Arend Lijphart

Introduction: Ideological, Programmatic, and Pragmatic Parties

The problems and controversies concerning the definition of the term "ideology" that have plagued the political science literature may be attributed to the confusion between two different, but closely related, uses of the term: ideology as an ideal type, and ideology as a category in a dichotomous classification of ideology and pragmatism. An ideal type can serve as the polar extreme of a continuum, of which the other pole represents the complete opposite of the ideal type—and is an ideal type itself, of course. Ideology and pragmatism may be seen as two polar end points of this kind. The next step that may be taken is to divide the continuum into two or more categories; if a simple dichotomy is chosen, the category of ideology covers the entire area between ideal-type ideology and a point somewhere in the middle of the continuum which is a mixture of ideological and pragmatic elements. Within this category we can speak of different *degrees* of ideological thinking. James B. Christoph uses this distinction when he refers to two conceptual "molds": the *Weltanschauung* version of ideology, which is the equivalent of the ideal type, and ideology as an "attitude structure," which is "less likely than the 'big' world views to be intellectualized, comprehensive, systematic or consistent, and more likely to be fragmentary, limited, even inconsistent."[1]

I gratefully acknowledge the helpful comments that I received from my coauthors and from Ellen T. Comisso, Peter A. Gourevitch, and Valentine Herman.

[1] James B. Christoph, "Consensus and Cleavage in British Political Ideology," in Roy C. Macridis, ed., *Political Parties: Contemporary Trends and Ideas* (New York: Harper and Row, 1967), pp. 76-77. A further distinction may be drawn between *forensic* ideology ("the articulated, differentiated, well-developed political arguments put forward by informed and conscious Marxists or Fascists

In order to avoid the confusion between ideology as ideal type and as empirical category, Leon D. Epstein has advocated the term "programmatic" when "ideological" in the latter sense is meant.[2] In this chapter, I shall use "ideology" in this broader, more-or-less, meaning. The ideal-type conception of ideology should be retained, however, because it serves as the standard against which degrees of ideological thinking can be measured.

The questions that I shall address in this chapter are: (1) How ideological are the political parties and party systems both in contemporary democracies and in the recent history of democratic states, approximately since World War II? (2) What are the dimensions of party ideologies and programs that divide the parties from each other: socioeconomic problems, religious and cultural issues, and so on? And (3) what is the relative salience of these ideological dimensions in different countries and, in the same country, in different periods? These questions are of vital importance because they affect the mutual distance among parties and their willingness to compromise. Furthermore, divergent and uncompromising ideological positions decrease, and relatively small and less deeply felt programmatic differences increase, the chances of building coalitions among parties, constructive policy making, and the stability of the political system.

In the next section, I shall try to identify the ideological dimensions of the democratic party systems and the degree to which the party programs approximate or deviate from ideologies in the ideal-type sense. The two final sections of the chapter will analyze the strength and relative salience of the different ideological dimensions on the basis of the parties' inclinations to engage in or to abstain from durable cooperative arrangements—government coalitions and transnational party alliances. For this purpose, I shall make use of the findings of coalition theory and of analyses of party formation in the European Community.

Dimensions of Ideology

How can the contents and intensity of party ideologies and the ideological dimensions of party systems be identified? First, as

---

or liberal democrats") and *latent* ideology ("the loosely structured, unreflective statements of the common men"); see Robert E. Lane, *Political Ideology: Why the American Common Man Believes What He Does* (New York: Free Press, 1962), p. 16. See also Edward Shils, "The Concept and Function of Ideology," in David L. Sills, ed., *International Encyclopedia of the Social Sciences* (New York: Macmillan and Free Press, 1968), vol. 7, p. 66.

[2] Leon D. Epstein, *Political Parties in Western Democracies* (New York: Praeger, 1967), pp. 261-63.

Joseph LaPalombara states, "we can get some clues to a party's collective ideology by looking at party statutes, platforms, special programmatic statements, proceedings of party congresses, press releases, and speeches by the party's leading figures."[3] In addition, we can observe the actual policies pursued by a party when it is in power, or the policies promoted by a party when it shares governmental power with one or more partners in a coalition. *Ideologies and programs must be distinguished from the characteristics of the voters that parties represent.* For instance, the fact that a party receives unusually strong support from Roman Catholic voters does not automatically make it a Catholic party and does not necessarily indicate that religion is an important dimension in the party system. On the other hand, it stands to reason that there is a mutual relationship between party programs and the objective and subjective interests and needs of the party's supporters.

A second guideline for the identification of the ideological dimensions of party systems is that we should focus on the differences *between* parties rather than *within* parties. One or more ideological cleavages may divide parties internally instead of from each other, and these should not be confused with those that divide the party system itself. Third, we should restrict our analysis to the ideologies of and the ideological differences between the *significant parties*, those parties that Giovanni Sartori calls "relevant": political parties that frequently participate in cabinets and are widely recognized as acceptable coalition partners, or which are so large as to have an important impact on the system even though they are not considered acceptable governing partners. In Sartori's terminology, these are parties with either "coalition potential" or "blackmail potential."[4] Finally, we should focus on the *durable ideological dimensions* of party systems and ignore the more or less programmatic differences that may emerge in one election but fade away soon afterward.

The following ideological dimensions were present in many democratic party systems in the 1970s and are likely to continue in the 1980s:

1. socioeconomic
2. religious
3. cultural-ethnic
4. urban-rural

---

[3] Joseph LaPalombara, *Politics within Nations* (Englewood Cliffs, N.J.: Prentice-Hall, 1974), p. 534.

[4] Giovanni Sartori, *Parties and Party Systems: A Framework for Analysis*, vol. 1 (London: Cambridge University Press, 1976), pp. 121-24.

5. regime support
6. foreign policy
7. postmaterialism

The first six of these dimensions correspond quite closely with the party system cleavages identified by a number of other authors. Sartori's "four basic cleavage dimensions" are left versus right, secular versus denominational, ethnicity versus integration, and democratic versus authoritarian divisions; these are basically the same as the first, second, third, and fifth dimensions listed above.[5] Michael Taylor and Michael Laver use the equivalents of the first through the fourth and the sixth dimensions of the list above in their study of West European government coalitions.[6] Lawrence C. Dodd also uses the Taylor-Laver dimensions but adds the regime support item and drops the urban-rural division.[7] Robert Harmel and Kenneth Janda propose six ideological continua, all of which they label left-right dimensions, but only four of which correspond with the socioeconomic dimension of the list above; the other two are the secular-denominational conflict and divergent foreign policy outlooks (favoring international alignment with the "Western bloc" versus the "Eastern bloc" of nations).[8] To the dimensions identified by these various scholars I have added the cleavage between "materialists" and "postmaterialists," which Ronald Inglehart has found to be of great, and probably growing, significance in industrialized societies.[9]

The incidence of these seven ideological dimensions in the party systems of the twenty-eight countries covered by this volume is indicated in tables 3–1 and 3–2. These tables are based on my own, necessarily subjective, judgment, but I believe that the majority of

---

[5] Ibid., p. 336. However, Sartori's left-right dimension also includes the "constitutional left-right" cleavage which concerns "how equal laws relate to societal inequalities" (p. 337).

[6] Michael Taylor and Michael Laver, "Government Coalitions in Western Europe," *European Journal of Political Research*, vol. 1, no. 3 (September 1973), pp. 237-48. Their foreign policy dimension is limited to the Republic of Ireland where it refers to attitudes toward the Treaty of 1921. An additional dimension that these two authors use is the federalist versus unitarist dimension; I shall return to this point later with special reference to the Belgian party system.

[7] Lawrence C. Dodd, *Coalitions in Parliamentary Government* (Princeton, N.J.: Princeton University Press, 1976), p. 99. I have combined four of Dodd's dimensions—linguistic conflict, cultural conflict, regionalism, and German nationalism in interwar Austria—into the single cultural-ethnic dimension.

[8] Robert Harmel and Kenneth Janda, *Comparing Political Parties*, Supplementary Empirical Teaching Units in Political Science (Washington, D.C.: American Political Science Association, 1976), pp. 33-35.

[9] Ronald Inglehart, *The Silent Revolution: Changing Values and Political Styles among Western Publics* (Princeton: Princeton University Press, 1977).

TABLE 3–1

IDEOLOGICAL DIMENSIONS OF EUROPEAN PARTY SYSTEMS IN THE 1970S

Country	Socioeconomic	Religious	Cultural-Ethnic	Urban-Rural	Regime Support	Foreign Policy	Postmaterialist
Austria	X	X					
Belgium	X	X	X				
Denmark	X			X			
Finland	X		X	X	X		
France	X	X			X	X	
West Germany	X	X					
Greece	X				X	X	
Ireland	X					X	
Italy	X	X			X	X	
Netherlands	X	X					X
Norway	X	X		X			X
Portugal	X				X	X	
Spain	X				X	X	
Sweden	X			X			X
Switzerland	X	X					
United Kingdom	X						

my decisions are straightforward and noncontroversial. On the other hand, there are a number of difficult cases, and I shall point these out as I discuss each of the ideological dimensions.

1. The Socioeconomic Dimension. The four leftist versus rightist party positions on socioeconomic policy enumerated by Harmel and Janda provide a good summary of the basic components of the socio-economic dimension of ideology: (1) governmental versus private ownership of the means of production, (2) a strong versus a weak governmental role in economic planning, (3) support of versus opposition to the redistribution of wealth from the rich to the poor, and (4) the expansion of versus resistance to governmental social welfare programs.[10] The first three of these components coincide with what Martin Seliger calls the three socioeconomic "core-issues" of the left-

---

[10] Harmel and Janda, *Comparing Political Parties*, p. 35.

TABLE 3–2
IDEOLOGICAL DIMENSIONS OF NON-EUROPEAN PARTY SYSTEMS IN THE 1970s

Country	Socioeconomic	Religious	Cultural-Ethnic	Urban-Rural	Regime Support	Foreign Policy	Postmaterialist
Canada	X		X				
United States	X						
Colombia	X	X					
Dominican Republic	X						
Venezuela	X	X					
India	X		X		X	X	
Israel	X	X					
Japan	X	X			X	X	
Sri Lanka	X		X		X	X	
Turkey	X	X					
Australia	X	X		X			
New Zealand	X						

right dimension.[11] This dimension is listed first in tables 3–1 and 3–2 because it is the most important of the ideological dimensions and because it is present in all of the democratic party systems.

This conclusion appears to contradict the end-of-ideology theory, which is especially concerned with the socioeconomic ideological dimension. In fact, as Leon D. Epstein points out, it is the end of *socialist* ideology that the theory focuses on.[12] However, we can speak of the *end* of ideology only when we use the ideal-type meaning of ideology. When the term "ideology" is used in the broader sense, as an empirical category including various degrees of ideological thinking, we have to speak more modestly of a *decline* of ideology. This decline, fueled by the unprecedented growth in economic prosperity of the Western democracies in the 1950s and early 1960s, occurred particularly with regard to the question of governmental ownership

[11] Martin Seliger, *Ideology and Politics* (London: George Allen and Unwin, 1976), pp. 214-16.
[12] Epstein, *Political Parties*, p. 286.

of the means of production. In addition, the leftist positions on economic planning, income redistribution, and social welfare programs —and the rightist responses to these policy preferences—have become more moderate. Seymour M. Lipset, writing in 1964, argues that this convergence of socioeconomic ideologies marks the development of the new ideological agreement of "conservative socialism" which he calls "*the* ideology of the major parties in the developed states of Europe and America."[13]

With the advantage of hindsight, this judgment—which was partly a description and partly a prediction—appears to have been premature. For one thing, the economic problems of the 1970s have heightened left-right tensions. Moreover, even though the objective growth of the total economic pie makes its division among different groups and classes in society easier, the economic expectations of these groups inevitably remain subjective and relative. As Lipset himself emphasizes, "as long as some men are rewarded more than others by the prestige or status structure of society, men will feel *relatively* deprived."[14] There has also been a growing awareness that economic prosperity and the distribution of prosperity are to a large extent politically determined. Robert A. Dahl argues that "since any particular allotment reveals itself more and more clearly nowadays to be a product of political decisions and less and less an act of God, nature, or the inexorable operation of economic laws, conflicts over the distribution of income might, if anything, become more numerous even if less intense."[15]

The importance of political influences on economic policies and performance has been confirmed by a spate of recent studies of the political-economic nexus. It is especially interesting for the purposes of this chapter that these studies show significant differences between the socioeconomic policies pursued by leftist-oriented and rightist-oriented governments. David R. Cameron, Edward R. Tufte, Frank Castles, and Robert D. McKinlay show that leftist governments have systematically produced a higher rate of growth of the public sector of the economy, larger central government budgets, more income equalization, and higher levels of performance with regard to educa-

---

[13] Seymour Martin Lipset, "The Changing Class Structure and Contemporary European Politics," in Stephen R. Graubard, ed., *A New Europe?* (Boston: Houghton Mifflin, 1964), p. 362.

[14] Seymour Martin Lipset, *Political Man: The Social Bases of Politics* (Garden City, N.Y.: Anchor Books, 1963), pp. 444-45.

[15] Robert A. Dahl, *Political Oppositions in Western Democracies* (New Haven: Yale University Press, 1966), p. 398.

tional expenditures and public health than rightist governments.[16] Douglas A. Hibbs, Jr., finds that when a choice has to be made between price stability, favored by the parties of the right, and full employment, favored by the left, "the macroeconomic policies pursued by left-wing and right-wing governments are broadly in accordance with the objective economic interests and subjective preferences of their class-defined core political constituencies."[17] Hibbs's finding on price stability is disputed by Andrew T. Cowart, but the two authors agree on the greater sensitivity of leftist governments to the problem of unemployment. Cowart also argues that, in general, leftist governments have been considerably more interventionist in both monetary and fiscal policy making.[18] The evidence can be summarized in the following statement by Tufte: "The single most important determinant of variations in macroeconomic performance from one industrialized democracy to another is the location on the left-right spectrum of the governing political party. Party platforms and political ideology set priorities and help decide policy."[19]

Although the overall conclusion is that left-right ideological differences exist and have major policy consequences, this does not mean that these differences are the same in all countries. The distance between the political parties on the left-right ideological continuum appears to be relatively great in the United Kingdom, the Scandinavian countries, Finland, Australia, and New Zealand. Comparatively small differences on the socioeconomic dimension are found in the United States, Canada, Ireland, Turkey, India, Sri Lanka, and Colombia. In none of the countries of tables 3–1 and 3–2 is the left-right difference so small, however, that it would be justified to conclude that the socioeconomic dimension of ideology is absent or of negligible importance.

2. The Religious Dimension. The second most important ideological dimension, found in half of the democratic party systems covered in

[16] David R. Cameron, "The Expansion of the Public Economy: A Comparative Analysis," *American Political Science Review*, vol. 72, no. 4 (December 1978), pp. 1243-61; Edward R. Tufte, "Political Parties, Social Class, and Economic Policy Preferences," *Government and Opposition*, vol. 14, no. 1 (Winter 1979), pp. 18-36, esp. pp. 28-30; Frank Castles and Robert D. McKinlay, "Does Politics Matter? An Analysis of the Public Welfare Commitment in Advanced Democratic States," *European Journal of Political Research*, vol. 7, no. 2 (June 1979), pp. 169-86.

[17] Douglas A. Hibbs, Jr., "Political Parties and Macroeconomic Policy," *American Political Science Review*, vol. 71, no. 4 (December 1977), pp. 1467-87.

[18] Andrew T. Cowart, "The Economic Policies of European Governments, Part I: Monetary Policy," and "Part II: Fiscal Policy," *British Journal of Political Science*, vol. 8, nos. 3, 4 (July, October 1978), pp. 285-311, 425-39.

[19] Tufte, "Political Parties, Social Class, and Economic Policy Preferences," p. 35.

this chapter, concerns party attitudes and policies toward religion and religious values. On this dimension, too, a decline of ideology has occurred. In the Continental European countries with mixed Catholic-Protestant populations and histories of Catholic-Protestant antagonism, interreligious tensions have largely disappeared and the two groups have even tended to unite politically. The Christian Democratic Union of the Federal Republic of Germany was founded as a joint Catholic-Protestant party. In the Netherlands, the Catholic party and the two main Protestant parties presented a single list in the 1977 parliamentary elections and are planning to merge into a single party organization, the Christian Democratic Appeal. Only in Switzerland do the Christian Democrats remain an almost exclusively Catholic party. Moreover, both the explicitly religious parties and their anti-clerical opponents have moderated their claims and counterclaims to a large extent. On the other hand, the religious and secular parties are still divided on a range of moral issues, such as questions of marriage and divorce, birth control, abortion, sex education, and pornography. These issues became especially prominent in the late 1960s and 1970s.

Most of the party systems with an important religious cleavage can be found in Continental Western Europe, excluding Scandinavia, and in South America. West Germany, Italy, Austria, Switzerland, Belgium, and the Netherlands all have major Christian Democratic or Social Christian parties. In France, the original Christian Democratic party, the MRP, and its several successors have lapsed into insignificance, but the Gaullists now occupy the position of a conservative pro-church party. The Social Christian party of Venezuela, which together with the Social Democrats, Acción Democrática, increasingly dominates the country's party politics, clearly belongs to the Christian Democratic family. Colombia is a more difficult case; James L. Payne expresses skepticism about the professed ideological differences between the Liberals and the Conservatives, but he does note the "closer Conservative contact with the Catholic Church position."[20]

Spain and Portugal are also problematic cases. It would have been logical to expect the formation of Christian Democratic parties in these countries after the restoration of democracy. However, partly as a reflection of the decline of ideology along the religious dimension in the 1970s, the politicians belonging to this persuasion decided to participate in broader center-right political groupings: the Union of the Democratic Center in Spain and the Center Social Democrats in

---

[20] James L. Payne, *Patterns of Conflict in Colombia* (New Haven: Yale University Press, 1968), p. 89.

Portugal. Hence the religious cleavage affects intraparty rather than interparty relations.

The end-of-ideology proposition with regard to the religious dimension appears to be disconfirmed by the emergence of Christian Democratic parties in all of the Nordic countries, especially in the 1960s and 1970s. Such parties were founded in Finland in 1958, in Sweden in 1964, and in Denmark in 1970. The Finnish and Danish, but not the Swedish, parties have achieved parliamentary representation. However, none of these parties can be regarded as "relevant" according to Sartori's criteria. Only the older Norwegian Christian People's party, established in 1933, has played a significant political role and has participated in three cabinets.[21]

Outside Europe and Latin America we find significant religious parties, indicative of the presence of a religious-ideological dimension of the party system, in Israel, Turkey, Japan, and Australia. The National Religious party of Israel has been a crucial partner in all Israeli coalition cabinets in spite of its relatively small size, and it has been a highly effective advocate of orthodox religious policies. The Turkish National Salvation party is an Islamic party that was formed recently in order to achieve a greater role for Islam in society. It participated in cabinets from 1973 until 1977.[22] The Fair Play party (Komeito) of Japan is the political representative of the Soka Gakkai sect. Although its coalition potential is unclear and will remain so as long as the Liberal Democratic party's dominance lasts, its electoral and parliamentary strength clearly qualifies it as a significant party: it won almost 11 percent of the votes and seats in the 1976 and 1979 House of Representatives elections.

The role of the small Democratic Labor party (DLP) makes it possible to argue that the Australian party system, too, has a religious-ideological dimension. Epstein describes it as "a strongly Catholic and anti-communist breakoff" from the large Australian Labor party, and Paul J. Duffy argues that "in composition, policies and goals it seems to resemble the European-type Christian Democratic parties."[23] The DLP has never been able to win seats in the House of Representatives and therefore has no coalition potential. On the other hand, it

---

[21] John T. S. Madeley, "Scandinavian Christian Democracy: Throwback or Portent?" *European Journal of Political Research*, vol. 5, no. 3 (September 1977), pp. 267-86.

[22] See Sabri Sayari, "The Turkish Party System in Transition," *Government and Opposition*, vol. 13, no. 1 (Winter 1978), pp. 39-57.

[23] Leon D. Epstein, "A Comparative Study of Australian Parties," *British Journal of Political Science*, vol. 7, no. 1 (January 1977), p. 11; Paul J. Duffy, "The Democratic Labor Party: Profile and Prospects," in Henry Mayer, ed., *Australian Politics: A Second Reader*, rev. ed. (Melbourne: Cheshire, 1971), p. 416.

has helped the Liberals win House seats by advising its supporters to mark Liberal candidates as their second preferences, and its senators have at times provided crucial support to Liberal-Country coalition cabinets in the federal chamber, to which, as the constitutional crisis of 1975 shows, the cabinet can also be considered accountable.[24]

Finally, an explanation is due for the fact that Canada is not included among the countries with a significant religious cleavage dimension, since in Canada Protestant-Catholic identification is the best predictor of party choice. This difference between party supporters is merely a survival of past conflicts, and, as John Meisel emphasizes, religion is "of virtually no political importance in contemporary federal politics" in Canada.[25] Hence the Canadian case provides a good illustration of the fact that ideological differences between parties cannot be inferred from the characteristics of their supporters.

3. The Cultural-Ethnic Dimension. In their developmental theory of cleavage structures and party systems, Seymour M. Lipset and Stein Rokkan identify four basic sources of party system cleavages. These are, in addition to the left-right and religious dimensions, already discussed, cultural-ethnic cleavages and the divisions between rural-agrarian and urban-industrial interests.[26] The cultural-ethnic dimension does not appear as often as the religious dimension, because nineteen of the twenty-eight countries are ethnically homogeneous or contain only small and insignificant minorities. Moreover, of the remaining nine countries with potential cultural-ethnic divisions between the parties, only five have clear interparty cleavage dimensions.

Switzerland is often regarded as the plural society par excellence, but its party system reflects mainly religious and left-right differences,

---

[24] See David Butler, "Politics and the Constitution: Twenty Questions Left by Remembrance Day," in Howard R. Penniman, ed., *Australia at the Polls: The National Elections of 1975* (Washington, D.C.: American Enterprise Institute, 1977), pp. 313-36.

[25] John Meisel, *Cleavages, Parties and Values in Canada*, Sage Professional Papers in Contemporary Political Sociology, vol. 1, no. 06-003 (London and Beverly Hills: Sage, 1974), p. 9. See also Arend Lijphart, "Religious vs. Linguistic vs. Class Voting: The 'Crucial Experiment' of Comparing Belgium, Canada, South Africa, and Switzerland," *American Political Science Review*, vol. 73, no. 2 (June 1979), pp. 442-58.

[26] Seymour Martin Lipset and Stein Rokkan, "Cleavage Structures, Party Systems, and Voter Alignments: An Introduction," in Seymour M. Lipset and Stein Rokkan, eds., *Party Systems and Voter Alignments: Cross-National Perspectives* (New York: Free Press, 1967), pp. 1-64. See also Richard Rose and Derek Urwin, "Social Cohesion, Political Parties and Strains in Regimes," *Comparative Political Studies*, vol. 2, no. 1 (April 1969), pp. 7-67.

and linguistic issues are virtually absent at the national level. Even the protracted discussions concerning the Jura problem did not stimulate interparty divisions or the emergence of other linguistic controversies. In Spain, regionalist and autonomist parties won almost 10 percent of the vote in the 1979 elections, but this vote was divided among several disparate groupings; the largest ethnic party is the Catalan Convergence and Union party with only 2.7 percent of the vote and 9 out of 350 seats.[27] One or more of these parties may acquire coalition potential in the future, like the small Swedish People's party in Finland, which is a very frequent coalition partner, but they do not possess the potential to participate in government at the present time.

In the United Kingdom, similarly, the Scottish National party and other minority parties are too small to have a significant impact on national interparty relations. When the Callaghan cabinet in its last two years (1977–1979) had become a minority government, it was dependent on support from the Liberals, the SNP, and other small parties, but this unusual situation cannot be considered sufficient grounds to credit the SNP with coalition potential. No American party has an exclusive ethnic base, although it can be argued that the Democratic party has been much more representative of and sensitive to the interests of ethnic and racial minorities than the Republicans and that, to the extent that affirmative-action and other minority programs have become controversial, the Democrats tend to defend and the Republicans tend to oppose them.

At the other extreme is the Belgian party system in which the cultural-ethnic dimension has become a sharp dividing line between the two communities and their parties. During the 1960s three explicitly linguistic parties established themselves as important actors on the Belgian political scene: the Volksunie in Flanders, the Walloon Rally in Wallonia, and the Francophone Democratic Front in bilingual but mainly French-speaking Brussels. Subsequently, between 1968 and 1978, the three national parties—the Christian Social, Socialist, and Liberal parties—split into autonomous Flemish and Francophone organizations. It may also be argued that there are two different cultural-ethnic dimensions in Belgian party politics: a dimension of Flemings versus French-speakers in which the linguistic parties are at opposite ends of the scale and the older, still more nationally oriented parties take a center position, and a federalist-centralist dimension

---

[27] J. M. Maravall, "Political Cleavages in Spain and the 1979 General Election," *Government and Opposition*, vol. 14, no. 3 (Summer 1979), pp. 299-317.

with the linguistic parties on one side and the traditional parties on the other.[28]

4. The Urban-Rural Dimension. Differences between rural and urban areas occur in all democracies, but they constitute the source of party system cleavages in only a few. Even here, it is somewhat questionable whether these differences can be regarded as ideological or programmatic, although it should be remembered that they entail not only divergent industrial versus agrarian objective interests but also the subjective contrast between urban and rural styles of living.

Where agrarian parties are found, mainly in the Nordic countries, they have tended to become less exclusively rural and to appeal to urban electorates, too, prompted by the decline of the rural population. A clear indicator of this shift is that the Swedish, Norwegian, and Finnish agrarian parties all changed their names to "Center party" between 1957 and 1965. The Danish Liberal party also originated as an agrarian party but now similarly tries to portray itself as a center party.

The only other party system with an important rural party can be found in Australia. The Country party has been closely allied with the Liberals for a long time, but it would be wrong to treat it as a mere appendage of the Liberal party, because it has insisted on its independence both in elections and in Parliament. It is significant that the Country party maintains its own caucus in Parliament and has not joined the Liberal caucus—in contrast, for instance, to the Bavarian CSU, which has formed a joint caucus with the CDU in the German Bundestag.

5. The Dimension of Regime Support. This dimension occurs in democracies as a result of the presence of important parties that oppose the democratic regime or that, as in the case of the Gaullists during the French Fourth Republic, demand a drastic overhaul of the democratic form of government. In contemporary democratic systems, the dimension of regime support is significant mainly when there are sizable Communist parties: in France, Italy, Spain, Portugal, Greece, Finland, India, Sri Lanka, and Japan.

With regard to this dimension, too, a decline of ideology appears to have developed. Especially in Italy, France, and Spain, "Eurocommunism" has been adopted, signaling basic changes in Communist attitudes toward both democracy and foreign policy. However,

---

[28] André-Paul Frognier, "Parties and Cleavages in the Belgian Parliament," *Leglislative Studies Quarterly*, vol. 3, no. 1 (February 1978), pp. 109-12.

the debate about the nature of Eurocommunism is not about whether these Communist parties have changed. The crucial question is whether they have changed sufficiently and whether their new outlook can be regarded as stable and durable.[29] Tables 3–1 and 3–2 are based on the ·cautious judgment that it is still too early to be sure that a fundamental and permanent reorientation has taken place.

It may also be argued that a few of the nine party systems with a significant regime-support dimension of cleavage should be classified in this way because of antiregime challenges not only from the left but also from the right. In particular, the Italian Monarchist party and neofascist Social Movement and the Francoist parties in Spain (the Popular Alliance in the 1977 election and the Democratic Coalition in the 1979 election) are such right-wing authoritarian parties. However, these parties have been weaker than the Communists in the two countries; they have no coalition potential; and their strength is not really sufficient to give them blackmail potential.

6. The Foreign Policy Dimension. The Eurocommunism and decline-of-Communist-ideology debates also concern the question whether the Communist parties have undergone a truly fundamental shift in their traditionally pro-Soviet or pro-Chinese attitudes. Tables 3–1 and 3–2 reflect the same judgment on this dimension as on the dimension of regime support. The only exception is Finland, whose neutralism with a slight pro-Soviet tilt is broadly supported by the Communist and non-Communist parties alike as well as by the government of the Soviet Union. It should be noted that in Japan the principal foreign policy issue is the American-Japanese Security Treaty and that the main cleavage is not between Communists and non-Communists but between the Liberal Democratic party, joined by the small Democratic Socialist party, and the other parties.

The French party system is characterized by a second foreign policy dimension which concerns the parties' attitudes toward European integration. It divides both the two main parties on the left, the prointegration Socialists and the antiintegration Communists, and the two main parties on the right, the prointegration Republicans and the antiintegration Gaullists. The same cleavage has appeared in the

---

[29] See Austin Ranney and Giovanni Sartori, eds., *Eurocommunism: The Italian Case* (Washington, D.C.: American Enterprise Institute, 1978); Giuseppe Di Palma, "Eurocommunism?" *Comparative Politics*, vol. 9, no. 3 (April 1977), pp. 357-75; Robert D. Putnam, "Interdependence and the Italian Communists," *International Organization*, vol. 32, no. 2 (Spring 1978), pp. 301-49; and Ugo La Malfa, "Communism and Democracy in Italy," *Foreign Affairs*, vol. 56, no. 3 (April 1978), pp. 476-88.

three new member states of the European Community—the United Kingdom, Ireland, and Denmark—as well as in Norway, which, after a divisive referendum, declined to join. In these countries, the cleavages were often more intense within some parties, particularly the British and Norwegian Labour parties, than between the parties, but there were also clear interparty differences, such as between the British Labour party on the one hand and the Conservatives and Liberals on the other and between the Irish Labour party and the other two main parties of Ireland. Nevertheless, these divisions may be only temporary, and they are therefore not marked in tables 3–1 and 3–2. The foreign policy dimension that is indicated for Ireland in table 3–1 refers to the split between Fianna Fáil and Fine Gael on the Treaty of 1921. It is of mainly symbolic significance in contemporary Irish politics, but it does result in at least slightly different attitudes toward the Northern Ireland problem.

7. The Materialist versus Postmaterialist Dimension. One question prompted by the end-of-ideology theory is whether the ideological synthesis of "conservative socialism" represents the end of the ideological dialectic or merely a new dominant thesis which will be challenged by a new antithesis. Two elements of such an antithetical ideology emerged as a reaction to conservative socialism in the 1960s and 1970s. One is the ideology of participatory democracy, which can be seen as a reaction to the impersonality, remoteness, and centralization of bureaucratic decision making created by conservative socialism. Dahl predicted in 1966 that this rejection of the "democratic Leviathan" would be one of the new dimensions of opposition in democratic regimes.[30] The other element of a new antithetical ideology is environmentalism, a reaction to the economic growth orientation of conservative socialism.

Both participatory democracy and environmentalism fit the cluster of values of what Inglehart terms "postmaterialism." Inglehart found that especially among young middle-class people in Western democracies a high priority was accorded to goals like "seeing that the people have more say in how things get decided at work and in their communities" and "giving the people more say in important government decisions." Moreover, in the richer nations the cluster of postmaterialist values also included the objective of "trying to make our cities and countryside more beautiful."[31]

---

[30] Dahl, *Political Oppositions*, pp. 399-400.
[31] Inglehart, *The Silent Revolution*, pp. 40-50. The other postmaterialist values are much vaguer ("progress toward a less impersonal, more humane society" and "progress toward a society where ideas are more important than money") or not really new ("protecting freedom of speech").

Postmaterialism has so far not become the source of a new ideological dimension in many party systems. The only examples are Norway and Sweden, where the Center parties have made a smooth transition from old-fashioned rural to modern environmentalist values, and the Netherlands, where two new parties, Democrats '66 and Radicals, have espoused participationist ideology. The two Dutch parties are relatively small, but they were cabinet coalition partners from 1973 to 1977. The Swedish and Norwegian Center parties are larger; in fact, the Center party of Sweden was the largest non-Socialist party from 1968 until 1979, and it supplied the prime minister for the two coalition cabinets of Centrists, Conservatives, and Liberals formed in 1976 and 1979.[32] The Swedish case also shows the salience of the environmentalist dimension, because it was on the issue of nuclear energy that the first of these three-party cabinets was split from the outset and on which it disintegrated in late 1978.

The limited impact of postmaterialism is not really surprising because it is always difficult for new issue and cleavage dimensions to become represented in an established party system.[33] In addition, the postmaterialists are still only a small minority. In Inglehart's 1970, 1973, and 1976 surveys in the old Common Market countries and in Great Britain, the average proportion of postmaterialist respondents that he found was a meager 11.5 percent.[34] Another obstacle to a postmaterialist breakthrough in the party system is that the postmaterialist activists have tended to work through the leftist parties where their middle-class background has clashed with the traditional working-class orientation of these parties, and where the essentially conservative nature of the environmentalist ideology is not easily reconcilable with the leftist self-image of progressivism.[35]

The overall conclusion that may be drawn from tables 3–1 and 3–2 is that the most common ideological dimensions of democratic party systems are the socioeconomic dimension, present in all systems, and the religious dimension, found in half of the party systems. Next in importance are regime support and foreign policy, each occurring in nine of the twenty-eight countries. The cultural-ethnic, urban-rural, and postmaterialist dimensions are much rarer: they are important in

---

[32] See Neil Elder and Rolf Gooderham, "The Centre Parties of Norway and Sweden," *Government and Opposition*, vol. 13, no. 2 (Spring 1978), pp. 218-35.

[33] See Lipset and Rokkan, "Cleavage Structures," pp. 50-56; and Mogens N. Pedersen, "The Dynamics of European Party Systems: Changing Patterns of Electoral Volatility," *European Journal of Political Research*, vol. 7, no. 1 (March 1979), pp. 1-26.

[34] Inglehart, *The Silent Revolution*, p. 104.

[35] See David Wells, "Radicalism, Conservatism and Environmentalism," *Politics*, vol. 13, no. 2 (November 1978), pp. 299-306.

only five, five, and three countries respectively. Three countries have only a single salient interparty ideological dimension: the United Kingdom, the United States, and New Zealand. The maximum number of dimensions in a party system is four, and there are seven countries to which this number applies: Finland, France, Italy, Norway, India, Sri Lanka, and Japan.

Ideologies and Cabinet Coalitions

So far I have mainly tried to identify the presence or absence of party ideologies and of ideological dimensions in party systems. In doing so, however, I have frequently had to make subjective judgments concerning the strength of ideologies (particularly when confronted with doubtful cases) and concerning the relative strength of different dimensions of ideology. Is it possible to test the strength of ideologies more objectively?

One possibility is derived from the findings of coalition theory. The early coalition theories attempted to predict coalitions on the basis of the relative sizes of the possible coalition partners and the assumption that the smallest possible winning coalition would be formed. When applied to the formation of coalition cabinets in parliamentary systems, these theories predicted minimal majority coalitions, defining minimal majority as either the smallest possible coalition still capable of winning parliamentary support or as one free of unnecessary coalition partners, parties not needed to give the coalition majority support in parliament. As Eric C. Browne has pointed out, these size-based theories performed very poorly. However, the predictive power of coalition theories improved dramatically when the ideological factor was also taken into account. Different theories have defined and operationalized this crucial factor in different ways, but the underlying assumption of all of them is that parties which are ideologically close to each other are more likely to form coalitions than parties which are ideologically far apart.[36]

We can use this finding to test the relative importance of different ideological dimensions. We know that parties prefer to coalesce with other parties that have similar ideologies, and we can further assume that when ideologically compatible coalitions can be formed along two

---

[36] Eric C. Browne, *Coalition Theories: A Logical and Empirical Critique*, Sage Professional Papers in Comparative Politics, vol. 4, no. 01-043 (Beverly Hills and London: Sage, 1973). See also Taylor and Laver, "Government Coalitions in Western Europe," pp. 205-48; Dodd, *Coalitions in Parliamentary Government*; and Abram De Swaan, *Coalition Theories and Cabinet Formations: A Study of Formal Theories of Coalition Formation Applied to Nine European Parliaments after 1918* (Amsterdam: Elsevier, 1973).

FIGURE 3–1
PATTERN OF POTENTIAL CABINET COALITIONS IN BELGIUM, 1954–1958

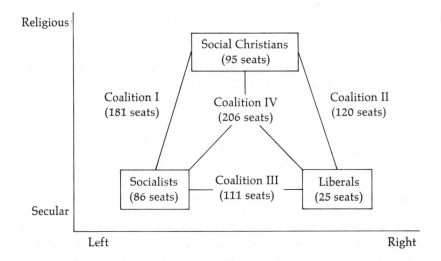

NOTE: The number of seats in the Chamber of Representatives was 212; hence the minimum parliamentary support needed by a majority coalition cabinet was 107.

or more dimensions, parties will tend to choose the dimension that is most important to them. Let us apply this test to the two most frequent ideological dimensions of party systems, the socioeconomic and religious dimensions. Figure 3–1 presents a typical situation which permits such a test: the Belgian party system following the parliamentary elections of 1954. There are three parties with coalition potential, none of which has a majority: two secular parties situated on the left and right of the socioeconomic dimension and a religious party with a center position on the socioeconomic dimension. There are four possible majority coalitions. Coalitions I and II indicate that the socioeconomic dimension is the dominant one, because they minimize the ideological distance on this dimension in spite of a maximum difference on the religious dimension. The formation of coalition III shows that the religious dimension predominates, because now the religious distance is minimized and the left-right distance maximized. Coalition IV is a grand coalition of all three parties and leaves the questions of the relative salience of the two dimensions unanswered.

Unfortunately, it is not possible to apply the test to all fourteen party systems of tables 3–1 and 3–2 that have both socioeconomic and religious dimensions. The first restriction is that the party system must operate in a parliamentary form of government with a cabinet dependent on the confidence of the legislature. This criterion excludes Colombia, Venezuela, Switzerland, and also the essentially presidential rather than parliamentary French Fifth Republic (but not the Fourth Republic). A second restriction is that no single party must have a majority of parliamentary seats. This excludes Japan, because in the period that the Fair Play party has been in parliament, from 1967 on, the Liberal Democrats have had absolute majorities. It also excludes certain periods in other countries, such as 1950–1954 in Belgium, where the Social Christian party won a majority of the seats in the 1950 elections.

A third restriction is that both types of coalition must be numerically possible from among the parties with coalition potential; that is, using the example of figure 3–1, either coalition I or coalition II (or both) *and* coalition III have to be able to be formed. This criterion eliminates Italy, because a coalition of the Liberals on the secular right with the parties of the secular non-Communist left, and not including the Christian Democrats, could never have achieved majority status. Australia has to be eliminated because the religious party (DLP) has never won seats in the House of Representatives. The third criterion also excludes a number of cabinet periods in several other countries. For instance, the antiregime oppositions on the left and the right in the French Fourth Republic were so strong that only "grand" coalitions of the proregime left, center, and right were possible, with the exception of the 1953–1956 period when the Gaullist RPF was willing to participate in cabinets and was acceptable to the other parties with coalition potential. Only Israel qualifies for our test during its entire national lifetime.[37]

Table 3–3 presents the results of the test for the relevant periods in the eight countries to which the test could be applied. When alternative coalitions could be formed, the socioeconomic dimension predominated in 82 percent of the coalition years and the religious dimension in only 15 percent. If anything, this evidence understates the strength of the socioeconomic dimension, because the assignment of the entire 1969–1976 period in West Germany to the religious category may be questioned. When the first Socialist-Liberal cabinet was formed in 1969, the Liberals (FDP) were generally perceived to be to the right

---

[37] See K. Z. Paltiel, "The Israeli Coalition System," *Government and Opposition,* vol. 10, no. 4 (Autumn 1975), pp. 397-414; and David Nachmias, "Coalition Politics in Israel," *Comparative Political Studies,* vol. 7, no. 3 (October 1974), pp. 316-33. Coalitions based mainly on the Labor and National Religious parties but also including the more left-oriented nonsocialist parties (Progressives and Independent Liberals) were counted as left-center coalitions.

TABLE 3–3

IDEOLOGICAL DIMENSIONS DOMINANT IN COALITION FORMATION IN
PARLIAMENTARY DEMOCRACIES, 1946–1979

(in coalition years)

Country and Years of Coalition	Socio-economic	Religious	Neither
	Dominant Dimension		
Austria			
1949–56	7		
1959–62	3		
1970–71		1	
Belgium			
1946–47		1	
1954–58		4	
1965–68	3		
1974–79	5		
France			
1953–54	1		
1954–55		1	
1955–56	1		
Germany			
1949–53	4		
1961–69	8		
1969–76		7	
Israel			
1949–67	18		
1967–70			3
1970–79	9		
Netherlands			
1971–79	8		
Norway			
1965–71	6		
Turkey			
1973–77	4		
Total	77	14	3
	(82%)	(15%)	(3%)

NOTE: For a discussion of method, see text.

of the CDU-CSU on the socioeconomic scale. By the time of the 1972 elections, however, partly as a result of their close alliance with the Socialists, the Liberals had moved to the center and could probably no longer be regarded as being more rightist than the CDU-CSU. Already in 1971, according to Heino Kaack, "the FDP's political platform had acquired a distinctly Socialist-Liberal slant."[38] If the years from 1972 on are excluded for this reason—instead of only the years after 1976, as table 3–3 more conservatively does—the relative strengths of the socioeconomic and the religious dimensions diverge even more: 86 versus 11 percent.

This conclusion is reinforced when we observe coalition formation in other multiparty parliamentary systems in which there is little doubt that the socioeconomic dimension is the most salient one: Denmark, Finland, Sweden, and Ireland. Here coalitions have generally united socioeconomically adjacent parties, with the exception of the Fine Gael–Labour coalition of 1973–1977 and two earlier similar coalitions in Ireland.

Upon closer inspection, however, the Irish case turns out not to be very deviant. Fianna Fáil occupies the socioeconomic center position with Fine Gael on its right and Labour on its left. The Fine Gael–Labour coalition cannot be explained by the influence of other dimensions. Although religion is not an issue in Ireland, as A. S. Cohan points out, Fine Gael has "traditionally closer links to the Church than either Fianna Fáil or Labour." On foreign policy, Fianna Fáil has tended to be more militantly nationalist than the other parties, but Fianna Fáil and Fine Gael both supported Irish entry into the European Community while Labour was opposed to it. The main motivation for the coalition between Fine Gael and Labour was that, given the usual majority or near-majority status of Fianna Fáil plus its center position and opposition to coalition government, a coalition of the two extremes presented the only chance for these two parties to take part in a cabinet. What is especially important for our analysis is that this was facilitated by the fact that the "extremes" are actually fairly close to the center position. Hence, as Cohan concludes, "a 'coalition of the extremes' is not terribly unrealistic or unworkable because the 'extremes' are not very far apart."[39]

---

[38] Heino Kaack, "The FDP in the German Party System," in Karl H. Cerny, ed., *Germany at the Polls: The Bundestag Election of 1976* (Washington, D.C.: American Enterprise Institute, 1978), pp. 83–84. It should also be pointed out that Austria 1970-1971 and France 1954-1955 are both included in the category of left-right coalitions although the Austrian Freedom party and the French Socialists served as support parties for, instead of actual partners in, the respective cabinets.

[39] A. S. Cohan, "The Open Coalition in the Closed Society: The Strange Pattern of Government Formation in Ireland," *Comparative Politics*, vol. 11, no. 3 (April 1979), pp. 331-32, 335. See also Peter Mair, "The Autonomy of the Political: The Development of the Irish Party System," *Comparative Politics*, vol. 11, no. 4 (July 1979), esp. p. 459; and Gordon Smith, *Politics in Western Europe: A Comparative Analysis* (London: Heinemann, 1972), pp. 118-19. Taylor and Laver place Fine Gael to the left of Fianna Fáil; see their "Government Coalitions in Western Europe," p. 243.

Ideologies and Transnational Alliances

A second test of the relative importance of ideologies and ideological dimensions can be based on the patterns of transnational party federations in the European Community and of the party groups in the European Parliament. These alliances provide a better test of the relative proximity or distance between national parties than the older Socialist, Christian Democratic, and Liberal "internationals" because the latter entail only a low degree of commitment. In contrast, the cooperation within the party groups of the European Parliament involves frequent and intensive interaction, and the transnational federations were formed in preparation for the first direct election of the European Parliament in June 1979.

It is worth examining the ideological controversies attending the establishment of the transnational party federations in Europe because they reveal which dimensions of ideology the member parties considered most important and, in particular, whether the socioeconomic or the religious dimension tended to receive more attention. The formation of the European People's party by the Christian Democratic parties was marred by two disputes. One was the issue of whether the conservative Bavarian CSU could be accepted as a member. Especially the Benelux Christian Democratic parties regarded the CSU as too right-wing. Because the CSU was undoubtedly a Christian party, it is clear that this controversy concerned only the socioeconomic dimension.[40]

The second problem was the relationship of the European People's party with the British Conservatives. The CDU-CSU favored close ties, but the Benelux parties were opposed. The objection was partly based on the non-Christian character of the Conservatives, but the major argument was that an alliance with the Conservatives would give the Christian Democrats too right-wing an image. Subsequently, the European Democratic Union (EDU) was formed as a vehicle for cooperation by right-of-center parties. Because it also included parties outside the European Community, it was not a rival of the European People's party, but it is significant that the EDU unites the conservative and Christian CDU-CSU with the non-Christian Conservatives from Britain and Denmark. Proximity on the socioeconomic dimension evidently outweighed distance on the religious dimension.

---

[40] The analysis in this and the following paragraphs is based on information provided by Valentine Herman and Juliet Lodge, "The Party System of the European Community: National, Transnational, and Supranational Perspectives" (Paper presented at the Annual Convention of the American Political Science Association, New York, 1978), pp. 3-20.

The main controversy besetting the formation of the transnational federation of Liberal parties—the European Liberals and Democrats—concerned the competing claims of two prospective French member parties: the right-of-center Republican party and the leftist Radical Socialist MRG. The latter was strongly supported by left-leaning parties in other countries, such as the Italian Republicans and the British Liberals. Here, too, the issue at stake had to do with the socioeconomic dimension. The traditional anticlerical or secular stance of the Liberals and the fact that the Republicans do not have historical Liberal roots hardly figured in the debate.

The main differences among the members of the Confederation of Socialist Parties are summarized by Valentine Herman and Juliet Lodge as follows: "right versus left, 'new-left' versus 'old-left,' strategy [vis-à-vis] Communists and/or Centrists, arguments with the Germans over the Berufsverbote, arguments with the French over workers' control, etc."[41] Almost all of these items are left-right issues; the religious dimension appears to be completely absent.

The three principal party groups in the European Parliament are those of the Socialists, the European People's party (known as the Christian Democrats before the 1979 European Parliament elections), and the Liberals and Democrats (formerly the Liberals and Allies). These correspond with the three transnational party federations in the European Community. In addition, there are three smaller parliamentary groups: the European Progressive Democrats, the European Democrats (formerly the European Conservatives), and the Communists and Allies. The first two, and particularly the Progressive Democrats, appear to be mainly marriages of convenience, but they also reflect a common outlook to some extent. For instance, Michael Steed points out that the Gaullists and Fianna Fáil, the two principal Progressive Democratic parties, are in close agreement on agricultural policy and that they are both "essentially nationalist parties, formed around a constitutional crisis and growing round a heroic leader."[42] The European Democrats consist mainly of Conservatives from Britain but also include the Danish Conservatives and Center Democrats.[43]

How close are these six party groups on the socioeconomic and religious dimensions of ideology? We can try to answer this question

---

[41] Ibid., p. 15.

[42] Michael Steed, "The Integration of National Parties" (Paper presented at the Tenth World Congress of the International Political Science Association, Edinburgh, 1976), p. 23. See also John Fitzmaurice, *The Party Groups in the European Parliament* (Westmead, England: Saxon House, 1975).

[43] See Juliet Lodge and Valentine Herman, *Direct Elections to the European Parliament: A Community Perspective* (London: Macmillan, 1980).

TABLE 3–4

Average Ratings and Average Deviations of the Six Party
Groups in the European Parliament on Two Ideological
Dimensions, 1978

(weighted by the size of the member parties)

Party Group	Left-Right		Clericalism	
	Average rating	Average deviation	Average rating	Average deviation
Socialists	−2.65	0.46	−0.80	0.74
Christian Democrats	+1.64	0.57	+1.79	0.37
Liberals and Allies	+1.21	1.24	−1.04	0.20
Progressive Democrats	+3.72	0.40	+1.22	0.95
Conservatives	+3.89	0.20	0.00	0.00
Communists and Allies	−4.35	0.46	−2.82	0.34
All six groups	+0.04	2.60	−0.04	1.26

NOTE: For a discussion of method, see text.
SOURCE: Calculated from data presented in Herman and Lodge, "The Party System of the European Community," pp. 44-48.

by using Herman and Lodge's ratings of the member parties of the party groups in the last indirectly elected European Parliament on a thirteen-point socioeconomic scale (from the extreme left, at −6, to the extreme right, at +6) and a thirteen-point clericalism scale (ranging between the maximum nonclerical position, −6, and the maximum clerical one, +6). Their ratings are based on interviews with members of the European Parliament, national parliaments, and party secretariats, interviews with delegates to the congresses of the transnational party federations, party manifestoes, federation documents, and so on.[44]

Table 3–4 presents the average ratings of each party group (weighted by the number of members from each national party group) and the average deviation from the mean in each party group. In addition, the mean ratings and deviations are shown for all six party groups together. The findings partly contradict our earlier conclusion about the dominance of the socioeconomic dimension. On the basis of this conclusion, we would have expected the party groups to have small mean deviations on the socioeconomic dimension and relatively large deviations on the religious dimension. In fact, only

---

[44] Herman and Lodge, "The Party System of the European Community," pp. 31-32.

the Socialists and Progressive Democrats conform to this pattern. To some extent, this result is an artifact of Herman and Lodge's general judgment that clericalism is less important than left-right differences: although both of their scales range in principle from −6 to +6, all of the parties are rated in the narrow range of −3 to +2 for clericalism but in a broader range of −5 to +6 as far as left-right ideology is concerned. Hence the surprising findings were partly built into their rating procedures. Nevertheless, the wide distance between right and left that is accepted especially in the Liberals and Allies group remains quite striking. If and when the European Parliament becomes a true legislature and if socioeconomic problems constitute its principal dimension of ideological conflict, it is likely that drastic party realignments will take place.

One other aspect of table 3–4 is worth emphasizing. In spite of the considerable deviations from the mean ideological positions in all party groups, these groups do represent definite clusters of ideology. The party group deviations are all quite small compared with the deviations from the mean for the six parties together.

Conclusion

The overall conclusions can be summarized in a few brief points:

1. In the twenty-eight democratic party systems considered here, many different ideological dimensions are of some importance, but the socioeconomic dimension occurs most frequently.

2. In party systems with both a socioeconomic ideological dimension and the second most frequent dimension—religion—the former tends to be the stronger one.

3. Party ideologies and programs do matter: they guide policy outputs, the choice of coalition partners, and the alignment with foreign parties in transnational alliances.

Bibliography

Browne, Eric C. Coalition Theories: A Logical and Empirical Critique. Sage Professional Papers in Comparative Politics, vol. 4, no. 01-043. Beverly Hills and London: Sage, 1973.

Dahl, Robert A. Political Oppositions in Western Democracies. New Haven: Yale University Press, 1966.

De Swaan, Abram. Coalition Theories and Cabinet Formations: A Study of Formal Theories of Coalition Formation Applied to Nine European Parliaments after 1918. Amsterdam: Elsevier, 1973.

Dodd, Lawrence C. *Coalitions in Parliamentary Government.* Princeton: Princeton University Press, 1976.

Epstein, Leon D. *Political Parties in Western Democracies.* New York: Praeger, 1967.

Fitzmaurice, John. *The Party Groups in the European Parliament.* Westmead, England: Saxon House, 1975.

Herman, Valentine, and Lodge, Juliet. "The Party System of the European Community: National, Transnational, and Supranational Perspectives." Paper presented at the Annual Convention of the American Political Science Association, New York, 1978.

Inglehart, Ronald. *The Silent Revolution: Changing Values and Political Styles among Western Publics.* Princeton: Princeton University Press, 1977.

Lipset, Seymour Martin, and Rokkan, Stein, eds. *Party Systems and Voter Alignments: Cross-National Perspectives.* New York: Free Press, 1967.

Mackie, Thomas T., and Rose, Richard. *The International Almanac of Electoral History.* London: Macmillan, 1974.

Sartori, Giovanni. *Parties and Party Systems: A Framework for Analysis.* Vol. 1. London: Cambridge University Press, 1976.

Seliger, Martin. *Ideology and Politics.* London: George Allen and Unwin, 1976.

Taylor, Michael, and Laver, Michael. "Government Coalition in Western Europe." *European Journal of Political Research* 1:205–48.

Tufte, Edward R. "Political Parties, Social Class, and Economic Policy Preferences." *Government and Opposition* 14:18–36.

Von Beyme, Klaus. *Die parlamentarischen Regierungssysteme in Europa* [The parliamentary systems of government in Europe]. Munich: Piper, 1970.

4

Political Parties: Organization

Leon D. Epstein

Anyone accustomed to the candidate-centered politics of the United States is impressed by the dominance of political parties in other competitive systems. The parties' dominance in mobilizing voters is almost taken for granted in the several studies of the *At the Polls* series. We no longer make the same assumption about American parties. Although they too remain important as campaign vehicles and as objects of electoral choice, their role in elections appears to have diminished relative to that of other political actors and relative to the role of parties in other nations.

During the last several decades, party organization has often struck observers as much more significant elsewhere than in the United States. The contrast was a principal theme of comparative study in the years following World War II.[1] American national parties never developed European-style programmatic mass memberships to replace the gradually declining patronage-based machines that had been the first great response to the mass franchise. Although European mass memberships may have become less impressive in the last few decades, the contrast between American and other parties was otherwise sharper than ever in the 1970s. Now the weakness of American party organizations is associated with a reduced capacity to persuade the electorate to vote by party label or even to vote at all. Thus, despite considerable diversity within the United States as well as within and between other nations, the general difference between party organizations in the United States and elsewhere looks more consequential than it did in the recent past. Understanding this difference is a major concern here, and so is the extent

---

[1] Maurice Duverger, *Political Parties*, trans. Barbara and Robert North (New York: Wiley, 1954).

to which party organizations outside the United States may be subjected to any of the forces that have reduced the role of parties in this country. Turning the question around, we may ask whether any of the forces accounting for the strength of parties elsewhere may yet affect American developments.

The Meaning of Party Organization

Party organization is a structural entity that can be distinguished from the mere aggregation of a party's regular or identifiable voters. That aggregation—the party-in-the-electorate, in American terminology—is the obvious measure of electoral strength and the subject of much of this volume. But it is not an organization in the usual sense. Beyond it, there are two distinguishable, though plainly related, levels of party organization: one to contest elections and the other to participate in government. The one that contests elections may include elected public officials, but it also enlists other political participants—perhaps only a few key persons but sometimes large numbers—who "belong" to the party even though they may never seek elected public office. They are activists by virtue of a regular contribution of time or money. Their organization is "extragovernmental." The other level of party organization consists simply of public officeholders serving under a given label. Its plainest manifestation is the legislative caucus or parliamentary party, though sometimes, as in the United States, it has an independently elected executive. Beyond elected officeholders, it includes some appointed officials who owe their positions to the electoral success of party leaders.

In competitive democratic systems, the only parties without both extragovernmental and governmental structures are those that have not succeeded in electing officeholders either because they are small or because they are new; these parties are purely extragovernmental. Except in such cases, we deal with the complication of the two kinds of organization. They relate to each other in different ways in different nations, in different parties within a nation, and at various stages of a party's development. For example, when the British Conservatives built their extragovernmental organization in the late nineteenth century, they had a large parliamentary presence of long standing. Conservative parliamentary leaders wanted the new organization to help them win elections, not to propose policies. The extraparliamentary party has not always complied, but the original intention left its mark on the structural relationship. In contrast, the

British Labour party began as an extraparliamentary organization seeking representation in the House of Commons and so developed a constitution that still provides its external membership with a large policy-making role, although it is by no means clear how effectively that role is exercised. In both cases, those in control of one organization seek to use the other for their purposes. Furthermore, those not in control of one organization may try to gain control of it through their power in the other organization. In particular, a minority faction in a parliamentary party may mobilize its extraparliamentary strength to help its cause within the party's parliamentary ranks.

Conceivably, a parliamentary party or any other "party-in-government" might try to do without an external organization to help its members win elections. In fact, however, it is characteristic of modern democratic politics that each governing party, or potential governing party, relates to a similarly labeled extragovernmental organization. The latter may be little more than a loose, skeletal entity that does very little, as is now often but not always the case in the United States; or, at the other extreme, it may be so strong as to dominate not just the electoral campaign but also the actions of its elected governing officials. European extraparliamentary membership organizations, especially those on the left, have often been charged with such domination, and so have American city machine organizations—more often in the past, but into our own times in a few conspicuous instances. Because these American organizations lacked substantial numbers of members, depended heavily on patronage, and built no participatory policy-making apparatus, their power tended to discredit parties generally in the United States. They could not claim the same democratic legitimacy that a European mass-membership organization asserts when it seeks to impose its program on candidates and officeholders. A European party organization may be unrepresentative of those who support it with their votes, but at least it often has a fairly large dues-paying membership of policy-oriented activists. American party organizations have seldom developed a regularized base of this kind even at state and local levels.

However inextricable the extragovernmental organization is from the party-in-government that has the same label and usually the same leadership, it is reasonable to concentrate attention here on the extragovernmental organization. This is the entity whose roles in selecting candidates, campaigning, and otherwise influencing electoral choices relate closely to our book's subject. How fully and effectively party organizations perform these activities is associated with the extent to which democratic elections involve choices between recognizable groups of candidates seeking power collegially rather than between individual candidates seeking office largely on their own. This is not to say that strong extragovernmental parties themselves make party-contested elections meaningful. Rather, the organizations may have become strong in response to a political environment conducive to party contests.

The Institutional Context

Prominent among the features of a nation's political environment to which party organizations respond are constitutional and other highly institutionalized legal rules for conducting electoral contests. Certain of these features are especially useful, as I shall stress, in suggesting explanations for the differences between American and other parties.

One basic institutional provision, however, underlies the development of all competitive parties: the extension of the right to vote to a mass electorate. Wherever this has taken place, even though at first well short of the universal adult franchise that we now regard as standard, party organizations have developed to mobilize the large numbers of voters, at least in national elections and usually in regional ones as well. Understandably, then, the United States, the first nation regularly to conduct elections involving large numbers of voters in the early nineteenth century, was also the first nation to have modern parties contesting these elections. Only later in the century, when American parties had reached the peak of their organizational strength, did most European parties respond to the later extension of the franchise in their nations by developing impressive extragovernmental organizations. A few social democratic party organizations had existed before many of their supporters secured the franchise—indeed, one of their purposes was to win that franchise for working men. Organizationally, they were ready for a mass electorate when it came. Their development, therefore, is consistent with the view that mass electorates—or, at any rate, potential mass electorates—have everywhere inspired party organization.

It is a fair assumption that parties perform a highly desirable, if not absolutely essential, task in simplifying choices for the mass of voters, who cannot possibly be familiar with all of the candidates for every office and what they stand for. This simplification, defenders of parties argue, makes for more meaningful choices. Especially when voters face multiple choices—as they do on the American "long ballot," used to elect about a dozen legislative and executive officials at national, state, and local levels—a party label is a most useful cue. It is printed on the ballot in many American elections in large jurisdictions—even though the party may well have only a skeletal organization and is hardly responsible, in any collective sense, for the candidates bearing its label.

Parties exist in every national legislature, helping organize its work and rewards. The members have incentives not just to win reelection themselves but to strengthen their own party's ranks within the legislature, preferably to obtain or maintain majority status for themselves. The incentives to strengthen the party, however, are not as great in the American system as they are in the parliamentary systems that characterize most of the democratic world. Under the constitutional separation of powers in the United States, congressional party majorities do not themselves provide the basis for executive authority. Unlike members of a parliamentary party, U.S. representatives and senators need not vote together in order to maintain their leaders in office or, if theirs is the minority party, to provide a credible alternative government. American legislators are thus freer to represent their constituency interests when they conflict with party interests. They do so with the knowledge that their reelection may depend significantly on such representation, rather than almost solely on the popularity of the party or its leadership, as it does in some parliamentary systems. Being chosen separately from executive leadership allows an American legislator to campaign heavily on his or her own record of service when that record is more appealing than the record of the party or of the party's candidate for executive office. Hence, the party ties of members of the U.S. Congress are not as overwhelmingly important electorally as are those of parliamentary representatives.

American legislators and legislative candidates have much more reason to be in business for themselves than do their counterparts elsewhere. Candidate-centered campaigns are understandable products of the American separation of powers. They enable candidates to add their own electoral appeal to their party's, especially when the party's appeal may be insufficient. The effect, plainly, is to reduce the importance of party organization in congressional campaigns. Candidates ordinarily find it expedient to have their own organizations even when they welcome party help.

There is another way in which the American separation of powers—really the separation of *elections* for executive and legislative offices—affects the role of party organizations. The very fact that voters are asked to choose individuals for the presidency, for governor, and for certain other state executive offices encourages personalized campaigns. Appealing to the voters' party loyalty seldom suffices, especially for a minority party's candidate. It is true that parliamentary elections are often personalized to some extent; certainly the voters realize that their ballots for parliamentary members are effectively cast in support of one leader or another. Yet in a more important sense these voters are still being asked to put a party in power, not just its particular leader. They cannot separate the two, as can American voters, who have the opportunity to choose a presidential candidate of one party and a congressional candidate of another.

However appealing a particular parliamentary party leader may be, the British voter, for example, cannot help elect that leader to executive office without also helping to give the leader's party a legislative majority and the collective power accompanying it. Therefore, in parliamentary systems a party must sell itself as well as its leader to the electorate. In such systems, there is no separate prime ministerial campaign. Anyone who wants to be prime minister must head a successful party. Even a party leader who is more appealing than his party can hardly run a campaign distinct from his party's; his own victory requires a collective party victory.

The extent to which the separate election of American executives makes for nonparty campaigning, while evident in the light of comparison with parliamentary systems, may have been obscured during much of American history by the substantial contribution that presidential elections made to the development of national parties. As the only nationally contested office, and as a most powerful office, the presidency (along with the vice-presidency) became the principal object of the only evidently national extragovernmental party organizations in the United States, the loose but persistent national committees and conventions. The organizations had their raison d'être in presidential elections, and they long influenced the conduct of presidential campaigns in ways that no national party organization influenced congressional elections. On the other hand, they were usually the instruments of particular candidates, including incumbent presidents, who found it expedient to make use of the party machinery in essentially personal campaigns. Recently, presidential candidates have sometimes established separate organizations of their own in addition to the party organizations, as election contests have become more individualized and less completely partisan.

Outside the United States, does the separate election of a powerful president have any tendency to personalize campaigns and so reduce the importance of party organization? Except possibly in Latin America and a few developing nations on other continents, it is hard to find anything close to the American separation-of-powers regime. Finland's system is similar in certain ways, but probably the

French Fifth Republic provides a more comparable and more familiar example. Its popularly elected presidency, designed by and for Charles de Gaulle, was intended to be apart from and above party politics, especially as it existed in the National Assembly. Unlike the American one, the French presidential election does not even coincide with legislative elections. De Gaulle himself and his immediate successor, supported by the largest single party, scored partly individual victories. So, in a different way, did Valéry Giscard d'Estaing in 1974; he headed a relatively small party and capitalized on his personal appeal to defeat candidates belonging to larger parties. In this respect, as in the manner of selecting candidates, French parties did not dominate the presidential election as they have parliamentary elections.[2] It remains to be seen whether they will assert such dominance in presidential contests in the future. So far, while there have not been enough contests for confident generalization, French presidential campaigns have been candidate-centered in ways reminiscent of American ones.

Another institutional feature affects party organizations more plainly than the separation of legislative and executive elections: a constitutional division between central and regional governments. Labeled "federalism," this division is established in the United States, Canada, Australia, West Germany, Switzerland, and, less familiarly and often more uncertainly, in several other nations (including India) that conduct competitive elections. On the other hand, most of the nations with which we are concerned, including Britain and France, are unitary—that is, they do not have constitutionally established regional units of government but (with exceptions) only national and local units. In these more centralized systems, party organizations are similarly centralized. Although composed of local branches that may also compete for local office, they are nationally structured and nationally oriented. In contrast, when there are substantial governments in the regions (be they called states, *Länder*, provinces, or cantons), parties organize at the regional level to compete for legislative and executive power. The national parties are then federations of the regional parties, within which local branches exist. The result is not always the relatively loose and ineffective national party organization that has characterized American politics. West German parties are strong and cohesive at the national level. Even where, as in Australia, federalism has a longer and more nearly continuous history, state party organizations are clearly crucial centers of power, but the national

[2] Jean Blondel, "The Rise of a New-Style President," in Howard R. Penniman, ed., *France at the Polls: The Presidential Election of 1974* (Washington, D.C.: American Enterprise Institute, 1975), pp. 41-69, at p. 64.

organizations are also consequential and cohesive. Canadian parties, more like the weaker American structures, seem less highly organized outside the national and regional parliamentary bodies. Yet Canadian parties, unlike American ones, dominate national and state elections much as do parties in other parliamentary democracies. In short, federalism, though it accounts for decentralized organizational structures, does not itself produce weak parties.

Another feature of what I call the institutional context, and clearly associated with the weakness of party organizations, is the legal requirement that candidates win state-operated direct primary elections in order to carry their party label on the general election ballot. Only in the United States, as the next chapter makes clear, are party organizations thus deprived of the power to select their own candidates and left only with the possibility of trying to help their "endorsed" favorites win direct primaries. Elsewhere, even in the few nations that legally regulate candidate selection, bestowal of the party label remains the business of an organized membership. At most, parties are required to observe procedures ensuring their actual members (ordinarily defined by dues paying) opportunities to participate. The direct primary is so different that foreign observers first encountering American politics find it hard to believe that ordinary voters, loosely defined as party "members," really have the power to select party candidates. Yet the direct primary has become pervasive in the United States during the twentieth century. By state law, it accounts not only for all congressional nominations but also for almost all state executive and legislative nominations. Moreover, an "indirect" variant, the presidential preference primary, is now used to select the overwhelming majority of delegates to national presidential nominating conventions. Whatever the considerable merits of direct primaries in other respects, there can be no doubt that they reduce the role of organized parties and, accordingly, the value of party membership and activity. Surely one of the reasons for belonging to a party organization is to help select its candidates. Deprived of that power as an accompaniment of membership, an individual may well calculate that his time and money can be better spent in supporting an ad hoc candidate organization, first in a primary and then in a general election.

The direct primary has added to the difficulty of developing party membership organizations in the United States. That may not have been the intention of its originators; the early twentieth-century reformers who fostered the direct primary sought primarily to deprive old-style oligarchical machines and bosses of their power over nominations. The institution itself, however, limits the power of party organizations generally, and today it is often supported on that basis. The consequences, intended or unintended, are to empower mass communication media and various nonparty organizations—candidate-centered and interest-group-dominated—to perform tasks that elsewhere belong to parties.

Even in the nations whose party organizations retain an exclusive right to bestow the party labels on candidates, however, election laws can influence the degree and the kind of activity undertaken by parties. Where parliamentary members are elected by proportional representation in large multimember districts, parties tend more completely to supersede individual candidacies than they do when elections are conducted in single-member constituencies. Israel, an extreme example, does not even list individual candidates on party ballots.[3] Other PR systems, while often providing candidate visibility and even some personal competition, do not lead to the substitution of candidate-centered organization for party organization. In Japan's multimember constituencies, greater incentives for candidate-centered campaigns exist because elections are won not by PR, but by the three to five individuals who receive the largest pluralities from voters who have cast their ballots for only one candidate. More sharply than in most PR systems, Japanese candidates may compete against others from their own party (though often from a different faction) as well as against those from other parties. Thus party domination of elections may be less complete in Japan than in countries using strict party list systems but much greater than in the United States.

Mass Memberships

Having fairly large numbers of regular dues-paying members is widely regarded, outside the United States, as characteristic of modern party organizations. We know, however, that organizations of party activists exist in certain American states and that they occasionally have a regularized dues-paying basis. We know also that membership parties are not universal elsewhere in the democratic world. For example, a well-defined way to join the major parties in Canada is not always established.[4] Moreover, not all European parties have had large membership organizations, and some that once did no longer maintain them at their old levels. Ordinarily, too, individual dues remain modest. A case, therefore, can be made that the difference with

---

[3] Avraham Brichta, "1977 Elections and the Future of Electoral Reform in Israel," in Howard R. Penniman, ed., *Israel at the Polls: The Knesset Elections of 1977* (Washington, D.C.: American Enterprise Institute, 1979), pp. 39-57, at p. 40.

[4] Allan Kornberg, Joel Smith, and Harold D. Clarke, *Citizens, Politicians—Canada* (Durham, N.C.: Carolina Academic Press, 1979), pp. 12, 57, 80.

respect to membership between American and all other parties should not be drawn too sharply.[5]

The contrast may be most apparent when we consider only a certain important type of European party in relation to the conventional American organization. That European type has usually been exemplified by socialist working-class organizations like the British Labour and the German Social Democratic parties. At one time, they were thought to provide models that middle-class parties would have to follow, in one way or another, in order to compete successfully.[6] They have had not only mass memberships but also ways for these memberships to articulate programs and policies that candidates were expected to support and, if possible, enact into law. As such, they have sought to distinguish themselves from more exclusively electoral organizations that, like earlier parliamentary parties as well as American parties, have been perceived as devoted to winning office for its own sake. That distinction, however, is difficult to sustain where middle-class parties have also developed active mass memberships interested in policy making. The British Conservatives are a case in point. Their organization cannot be written off as merely a response to the Labour party's.

In several countries, labor parties appear to have many more members than their competitors because they include affiliated trade unionists. Most of Britain's large unions, for instance, are themselves nationally integrated in the Labour party by virtue of affiliating most of their members—that is, paying from union funds a small amount for each affiliated member. This adds up to a large sum when hundreds of thousands of members are involved, and the union receives the equivalent voting power in the party's conferences. Trade unions also affiliate to local Labour parties in many constituencies. Australian and New Zealand unions are similarly affiliated at two levels, although in Australia, given its federal system, unions maintain their higher-level affiliation through state party organizations. In Sweden and Norway, trade unions affiliate with parties only at the local level but are nonetheless organizationally integrated in important ways. Before 1945, Dutch trade unions also maintained formal affiliations with a labor party. In Canada and Ireland, unions have affiliated their memberships to parties lacking, so far at any rate, major status.[7] In most other nations, unions tend to support labor or social democratic

---

[5] Jean Blondel makes a similar point more emphatically in *Political Parties: A Genuine Case for Discontent?* (London: Wildwood House, 1978), pp. 146-47.

[6] Duverger, *Political Parties*, p. xxvii.

[7] D. W. Rawson, "The Life-Span of Labour Parties," *Political Studies*, vol. 17 (September 1969), pp. 313-33.

parties, often making heavy contributions of money and time, without being formally integrated into party structures. The American pattern, it should be added, is not so different; several large unions—the United Automobile Workers in Michigan is a good example—stand in very much this relation to the Democratic party. No doubt nonaffiliated unions in various nations exercise considerable influence on party policies, although their influence is less clearly observable than that of affiliated unions entitled to blocs of votes on party executives and at party conferences.

Whether or not affiliation gives unions greater influence within political parties, it does not appear to be in decline. Instead, where unions themselves have continued to grow in membership, so often have the numbers of members they affiliate with political parties. Unions are able to maintain staunch labor party ties even when many of their members do not themselves favor those ties or the party itself.[8] There is some evidence from Sweden that white-collar unions, growing more rapidly in recent decades than the older blue-collar unions, are less likely to affiliate to the Social Democratic party,[9] but elsewhere there appears to be no strong general trend toward nonpartisan unionism.

A likelier place to look for a decline in labor and social democratic party memberships is in the number of direct individual dues payers. The data, however, are not always reliably reported; even where they are available, they may be suspected of overstatement.[10] Also, occasional surges in membership in certain parties contradict the belief in a general decline. For instance, the German Social Democratic party, while widely thought to be much less intensively organized than it was earlier in the century, nevertheless reported a growth from 650,000 in 1964 to over 900,000 in 1973.[11] The French

[8] D. W. Rawson, "The Paradox of Partisan Trade Unionism: The Australian Case," British Journal of Political Science, vol. 4 (October 1974), pp. 399-418.

[9] Rawson, "Life-Span," pp. 332-33.

[10] Impressive efforts have been made to collect membership data along with other factual descriptions of party organizations. Kenneth Janda's International Comparative Political Parties project, covering 158 parties operating in 53 countries from 1950 to 1962, is described in several of his works, including "Variations in Party Organization across Nations and Differences in Party Performance" (Paper delivered at the 1979 Annual Meeting of the American Political Science Association, Washington, D.C.). Thanks to Professor Janda's generosity, I have had the opportunity to see a computer printout of data relevant to my interests. Somewhat later membership data are presented by Stanley Henig and John Pinder, eds., European Political Parties (London: Allen & Unwin, 1969), and summarized at pp. 525-26.

[11] Kurt Sontheimer, "The Campaign of the Social Democratic Party," in Karl H. Cerny, ed., Germany at the Polls: The Bundestag Election of 1976 (Washington, D.C.: American Enterprise Institute, 1978), p. 59.

Socialist party, as it revived and reorganized in the early 1970s, evidently increased its membership from 150,000 to 300,000.[12] Scandinavian evidence, however, indicates at least slight declines.[13] And British Labour party figures show a very large decline in direct individual memberships—from about 1 million in 1953 to no more than 400,000 in the early 1970s.[14] More than ever, Labour's 6 million indirectly affiliated trade-union members constitute the bulk of the party. The Australian Labor party's trade-union affiliations are even more overwhelming: 1.5 million to about 55,000 direct dues payers.[15]

In one way or another, labor and social democratic parties retain mass memberships. Unless it is among affiliated union members, however, the numbers do not suggest continuing long-term growth. And in terms of direct memberships, labor and social democratic parties are not always much larger and more plainly participatory than middle-class parties. The British Conservative party has about twice as many direct dues-paying members as the British Labour party, and the Australian Liberals about three times as many as the Australian Labor party.[16] Moreover, the direct individual dues-paying members of labor and social democratic parties often appear to be increasingly middle-class rather than primarily working-class activists. The phenomenon is striking in the German Social Democratic party. Its growth in the late 1960s and early 1970s came heavily from student and other white-collar ranks.[17] The result in Germany and elsewhere may be a more radical, or a more socialist, program, but the organization supporting that program is hardly made up of members from the working class.

---

[12] Nancy I. Lieber, "Politics of the French Left: A Review Essay," *American Political Science Review*, vol. 69 (December 1975), pp. 1406-19, at p. 1419.

[13] E. Spencer Wellhofer, Victor J. Hanby, and Timothy M. Hennessey, "Clientele Markets, Organizational Dynamics, and Leadership Change: A Longitudinal Comparison of the Norwegian and British Labor Parties," in Louis Maisel and Paul M. Sacks, eds., *The Future of Political Parties* (Beverly Hills: Sage Publications, 1975), pp. 221-37, pp. 226-28; Steen Sauerberg and Niels Thomsen, "The Political Role of Mass Communication in Scandinavia," in Karl H. Cerny, ed., *Scandinavia at the Polls: Recent Political Trends in Denmark, Norway, and Sweden* (Washington, D.C.: American Enterprise Institute, 1977), pp. 181-216, at p. 190.

[14] Dick Leonard, "The Labour Campaign," in Howard R. Penniman, ed., *Britain at the Polls: The Parliamentary Elections of 1974* (Washington, D.C.: American Enterprise Institute, 1975), pp. 61-83, at p. 70.

[15] Lex Watson, "The Party Machines," in Henry Mayer and Helen Nelson, eds., *Australian Politics: A Third Reader* (Melbourne: Cheshire, 1974), pp. 339-65.

[16] Michelle Grattan, "The Liberal Party," in Howard R. Penniman, ed., *Australia at the Polls: The National Elections of 1975* (Washington D.C.: American Enterprise Institute, 1977), pp. 103-41, at p. 108.

[17] Sontheimer, "Social Democratic Party," p. 60.

In this respect—that is, in class status rather than ideology—developments in the membership of labor and social democratic parties may parallel developments in the leaderships of these parties. Both the British and the Australian labor parties show declining numbers of leaders with working-class backgrounds, and this tendency is believed to characterize similar parties elsewhere.[18] To be sure, enough labor party leaders still come from the working class so as to distinguish labor and social democratic parties from the liberal and conservative parties, including both major American parties, whose leadership is almost entirely middle-class, but the difference has significantly diminished. The old working-class socialist party, though still drawing its voting support heavily from the working class, is no longer so clearly a class movement as it once was.

Purposes of an Organized Membership

Three purposes of an organized membership come readily to mind: to select candidates, to conduct election campaigns, and to develop programs and policies. The first is the subject of the next chapter and should not detain us long. Yet it must be noted here that a regularized dues-paying organization is most useful for a party that selects its own candidates rather than having them selected for it by voters casting ballots in state-run direct primaries.

Internal party selection is democratically legitimized in considerable degree by the presence of a substantial organizational base of rank-and-file members—say 3,000 in a British constituency party selecting a parliamentary candidate for an electorate of around 70,000. These 3,000 members need not participate directly themselves; they may, consistently with democratic legitimacy, delegate their power to an executive committee that they have elected to choose a candidate. A less plainly legitimate result may be achieved in a major Canadian party that sometimes lacks a well-defined membership.[19] But it is not so troublesome as the results of the caucus method once widely used

---

[18] Victor J. Hanby, "A Changing Labour Elite: The National Executive Committee of the Labour Party 1900-72," in Ivor Crewe, ed., British Sociology Yearbook: Elites in Western Democracy (London: Croom Helm, 1974), pp. 126-58; R. W. Johnson, "The British Political Elite, 1955-1972," European Journal of Sociology, vol. 14 (1973), pp. 35-77; L. F. Crisp and Barbara Anderson, Australian Labour Party: Federal Personnel 1901-1975 (Canberra: Australian National University, 1975).

[19] George Perlin, "The Progressive Conservative Party in the Election of 1974," in Howard R. Penniman, ed., Canada at the Polls: The General Election of 1974 (Washington, D.C.: American Enterprise Institute, 1975), pp. 97-119, at pp. 114, 116.

in the United States. Without a regularized dues-paying criterion of membership and thus open to anyone who says he or she is a party member, an American caucus could be either poorly attended and thus transparently dominated by self-appointed leaders, or flooded by persons recruited solely for the occasion. The advantage of an established membership is apparent, and it would seem to be greater when the membership is numerous. The members need not be—and they often are not—as impressive as in the British constituency cited above, and it is certainly possible for a major party to have many of its candidates (especially those who lose subsequent elections) selected by small local memberships. On the other hand, the democratic legitimacy of the process is questioned when a party's direct dues-paying membership declines as much as that of the British Labour party has. In that situation, many constituency parties, ceasing to be mass-membership organizations in any meaningful way, begin to look like caucuses of local leaders.

Conducting election campaigns, like selecting candidates, is a purpose of political parties that a substantial regularized membership organization helps to fulfill. Parties without organized memberships, of course, have also found it possible to dominate campaigns. American parties, especially in the past, have done so through patronage networks consisting of government jobholders, and aspiring government jobholders, and that pattern is not unknown elsewhere. Parties in the United States and elsewhere may also run election campaigns with ad hoc organizations or with staff paid from funds raised outside the organization itself. Membership organizations, however, have advantages here even though they are not so crucial as they are for candidate selection. The most apparent advantage is the contribution a regularized membership can make to party activity between elections. Especially in the absence of dependable rich donors, annual dues from fairly large numbers have often provided a reliable financial basis for at least modest permanent staffing of a headquarters along with continuous communication with supporters. Furthermore, a regularized membership is particularly useful in preparing for the door-to-door canvassing that characterizes campaigns in marginal constituencies.[20] Much of that preparation, designed to identify potential party voters on electoral lists, should be accomplished before a campaign begins or at any rate very early in a campaign, before an ad hoc organization could readily be created. In this respect, the usefulness of a regularized membership is plainest in a nation, like

---

[20] The nature and importance of canvassing in different kinds of constituencies are most effectively described by John E. Turner, *Labour's Doorstep Politics in London* (London: Macmillan, 1978).

Britain, that allows elections to be called at unscheduled intervals and often at short notice.[21] But it is also plain whenever and wherever a party lacks the other resources of richer or more established rivals. Canada's left-of-center New Democratic party (NDP), for example, depends heavily on the canvassing carried out by its dues-paying membership, while its rivals, the major Canadian parties, do not always maintain such memberships either for canvassing or for the participatory policy making that interests the NDP.[22]

Nothing suggests that the major Canadian parties, or parties elsewhere that are without large dues-paying memberships, fail to mobilize canvassing efforts, especially at campaign times. Not only may they do so ad hoc from among known activists and supporters, but they may also use the efforts of closely related organizations like trade unions and church groups. Canvassing, in other words, remains a useful campaign activity in close election contests. American candidate-centered campaigns also make use of volunteer canvassers, necessarily recruited ad hoc. No doubt, the importance of canvassing is not so great as it was when there were fewer other means of reaching voters. But there is a widespread belief that canvassing remains important enough in turning out one's voters to justify the effort. The belief is fortified by a certain amount of evidence concerning the efficacy of party organizations generally.[23] Although not all of that evidence concerns dues-paying membership organizations, that kind of membership is synonymous with party organizations in most nations.

An organized party membership's third purpose, developing programs and policies, is not so clearly related to party efficacy in winning elections. Although members may propose policies that inspire enthusiasm and win votes, they may also propose policies that offend marginal voters no matter how popular they are among the party faithful. The difficulty here flows from the possibility that those willing to work regularly in a party cause, without prospect of material reward, may be more zealous ideologically or programmatically than many of the voters a party needs to attract in order to win elections. Zealous activists may be even more interested in their programs than they are in winning current elections—hoping for lasting conversions

---

[21] Michael Pinto-Duschinsky, "The Conservative Campaign," in Penniman, *Britain at the Polls*, pp. 85-107, at p. 90.

[22] Jo Surich, "Purists and Pragmatists: Canadian Democratic Socialism at the Crossroads," in Penniman, *Canada at the Polls*, pp. 121-48, at p. 141.

[23] Janda, "Variations in Party Organization," p. 8; D. T. Denver and H. T. G. Hands, "Marginality and Turnout in British General Elections," *British Journal of Political Science*, vol. 4 (January 1974), pp. 17-35.

of the electorate and indifferent to pragmatic victories that might be won in the short run. They may thus be unwilling to bend their desires to those of officeholders and aspiring officeholders, whose interest lies in policies that will be popular, appealing to the center of the political spectrum. Occasionally, therefore, party leaders may regard themselves as hampered by the organization's role in party policy making.[24] If so, however, it appears to be a price that must be paid for an organized membership's usefulness in other areas. Given the influence that leaders can exercise within their organizations, the price is seldom high, nor is it exacted often.

Potentially more important in its implications for policy making in certain parties is the claim of an organized membership to choose the leader, or leaders, of its parliamentary contingent instead of simply accepting the parliamentary party's choice of a single leader for the party generally, in and out of parliament. Thus, in the British Labour party, where the M.P.s alone elect the leader, a substantial movement has developed in the party's external organization, supported by a dissident minority of the parliamentary party, to broaden the process of selection. In the British Conservative party there have also been proposals, so far rejected, to include extraparliamentary party representatives in the party's leadership election process. The British Liberals have actually expanded their leadership election in that way, but the justification for doing so rested heavily on the very small number of Liberal M.P.s available to elect the leader. The traditional practice of the larger British parliamentary parties has been followed in both Australia and New Zealand. Even the Australian Labor party, committed historically to various radical democratic procedures, allows its parliamentary caucus to elect the national leader.

On the other hand, the Canadian parliamentary parties do not monopolize leadership election, but are only represented, along with loosely defined extraparliamentary organizations, at national party conventions that elect their leaders. Party conventions in Canada thus resemble the old American national party nominating conventions, which might have been their models. In any event, it is not clear that Canada's removal of leadership election from strictly parliamentary party hands results in the kind of transfer of power to a more programmatically zealous constituency that, it is believed, would occur were the British Labour party to take leadership selection away from the parliamentary party.

It is also unclear whether many parties in non-English-speaking nations have the same stake in the manner of leadership election

[24] Lewis Minkin, *The Labour Party Conference* (London: Allen Lane, 1978), pp. 276-77.

that the British Labour party has. The practices of Continental European parties vary considerably even within nations. Some parliamentary contingents do the electing on their own or subject to ratification by subsequent extraparliamentary congresses. In other parties, congresses actually initiate and complete the election of leaders. In still other cases, extraparliamentary organizational representatives meet with the parliamentary party to decide the leadership. There are also arrangements by which external organizations choose leaders of their own to serve as powerful counterparts to leaders chosen by parliamentary parties.[25]

Financing

Dues are only one source of party funds, and they have usually been insufficient for election campaigns even where members were numerous enough in the past to support interelection staffs. Not only in the United States, where parties and candidates have always depended on nonmembers for support, do those who seek votes also seek funds from various sources. Most parties long sought campaign contributions from outside as well as from inside their own organizations, but their incentive—indeed their need—to do so has naturally increased during a period when the expense of political communication has been growing.

One result has been greater involvement by government, both as a regulator of private contributions and expenditures and as a provider of funds from the public treasury. Although these financial arrangements are discussed extensively in chapter 7, they must be noted here for their relevance to party organization. The relationship is not entirely new. For example, Britain's longstanding legal limits on constituency campaign expenditures during the official campaign period have tended to encourage activity unaffected by those limits: interelection expenditures within a constituency, and central organization expenditure during as well as between election campaigns. And in the recent past, American legislative limits on party funding have effectively favored nonparty political organizations not similarly restricted. On the other hand, parties and their leaders, rather than individual parliamentary candidates or other political groups, benefit from governmental requirements, well established in Britain and several other European nations, that radio and television time be granted free to national party organizations.

---

[25] Henig and Pinder, *European Political Parties,* report an even greater variety of leadership election arrangements than I have noted here.

Direct public financing of political activity, though only recently adopted on a large scale, may be most consequential for the organizational prospects of political parties. Both the amount of public money and its method of distribution are crucial. So far, where public funding of national elections is most highly developed outside the United States, the money has gone mainly to the parties. West Germany, Scandinavia, Italy, and Israel are cases in point. The established parties in those nations, when their private resources no longer sufficed, were strong enough to secure government financing for themselves. For example, the West German parties received about half of their 1976 campaign funds from the public treasury and, enjoying the best of both worlds, were unrestricted by legislative limits on the totals that they could continue to raise from dues, assessments of party officeholders, and various private contributions. The amount of public money that each party received was determined by the number of votes cast in the current election for its parliamentary list of candidates, with a settling of accounts taking place after the final tally.[26] A similar formula is used in the other nations that make parties the beneficiaries of public financing, though outside Germany the amounts are usually related in part to prior electoral performance whether measured by total votes or by numbers of elected representatives, and thus the distribution favors established parties.[27] They are especially favored by Israeli and Scandinavian provisions for public money to sustain interelection activities as well as election campaigns.[28]

When public funds go directly to candidates, as they do in a few nations noted in chapter 7, parties may be substantially subsidized at the same time, as they are in Canada. In addition, parties may benefit even from the direct funding of candidates, provided that the candidates are plainly those selected by party organizations; to have the candidates they have chosen subsidized by tax revenues is to be relieved of claims on party resources. But the situation is different where candidates, as in the United States, do not regularly owe their party labels to organizational selection and often maintain their own nonparty campaign organizations. Then direct public funding of candidates would confirm, or foster, the weakness of the parties. In

---

[26] David P. Conradt, "The 1976 Campaign and Election: An Overview," in Cerny, *Germany at the Polls*, pp. 29-56, at pp. 47-48.

[27] Douglas Wertman, "The Italian Electoral Process," in Howard R. Penniman, ed., *Italy at the Polls: The Parliamentary Elections of 1976* (Washington D.C.: American Enterprise Institute, 1977), pp. 41-79, at p. 77.

[28] Leon Boim, "The Financing of Elections," in Penniman, *Israel at the Polls*, pp. 199-225; Sauerberg and Thomsen, "Mass Communication in Scandinavia," p. 191.

the United States it will make a great deal of difference whether public financing goes to candidates or to parties. Judging from the presidential campaign—so far, the only national election to be publicly financed in the United States—candidates have been the chief beneficiaries. Those seeking to be nominated by the major parties received money for their primary campaigns, and the successful party nominees then received federal funds for their general election campaigns. It is true that the latter funding could be regarded as a recognition of party and that additional smaller amounts were actually given to the national parties. Increases in these amounts are possible, and so are other forms of financial assistance for parties, but they seem unlikely to modify substantially the now established candidate-centered character of presidential politics.

Nor is Congress likely to appropriate large sums to national parties if it establishes public financing for its own election. Most if not all of such funding, it is usually believed, would go to candidates, and possibly for primaries as well as general elections. Both the Republican and the Democratic national chairmen, however, recognize their organizational stake in trying to persuade Congress to channel through parties at least some of the funds that it might provide for congressional candidates.[29] There are several American state precedents for public funding through parties. Of the seventeen states providing campaign funds in the 1970s, often in small amounts, eight gave money only to parties and one other to both parties and candidates.[30] At both state and national levels, the American argument for public funding of parties tends to be stated in terms of helping to revive the parties in an environment where candidate-centered and interest-group politics predominate. Outside the United States, party organizations simply want funds in order to maintain their status. They do have trouble raising sufficient funds from their members and other private sources, but they have not yet lost their dominant campaign roles to other kinds of political organizations.

The Challenge of the Nonparty Media

Parties elsewhere, while still in charge of election campaigns, share with American parties the problems posed by the increasingly pervasive use of the mass media for political communication. The United States is not the only nation whose parties must cope with the mass

---

29 *Washington Post*, September 21, 1979, p. A16.

30 Ruth S. Jones, "State Public Financing and the State Parties," in Michael J. Malbin, ed., *Parties, Interest Groups, and Campaign Finance Laws* (Washington, D.C.: American Enterprise Institute, 1980), pp. 283-303, at p. 293.

media, most of which—many newspapers and magazines as well as radio and television—have audiences that are undifferentiated by party. Increasingly, especially because of television, strictly party messages are likely to be overwhelmed by political news and commentary from nonparty sources.

Parties, of course, use the media themselves, either by buying advertising or by taking advantage of free radio and television time provided by the government. Through these media they reach an audience very different from the attendance at a party rally or the readership of a party newspaper in its receptivity to partisan messages. Reaching a large undifferentiated audience by means requiring specialized technical skills is hardly a conventional organizational task; yet it is a major one in political campaigns adapted to an environment in which the mass communications media are pervasive. The *At the Polls* studies show this again and again. Personal appeals, notably on television, have become prominent almost everywhere. In two weeks of the French presidential campaign of 1974, there were two dozen television broadcasts by major candidates.[31] West Germany's four party leaders, two of whom were effectively competing for the chancellorship, engaged in a televised debate that lasted almost four hours three days before the 1976 parliamentary election.[32] And the leaders of Israel's two largest party groupings, rivals for the prime ministership, debated each other on television the night before the Israeli parliamentary election of 1977.[33] To be sure, debates of this kind were special events. More commonly in national elections leaders made their personalized television appeals in the context of party presentations starring other leaders in addition to prime ministers or potential prime ministers. This was the pattern in the expensive Australian television campaign of 1975.[34] Something like it, often with publicly provided time, appears standard almost everywhere, even when debates also take place. And in a few countries besides the United States, political advertising includes brief television commercials.

But party telecasts hardly monopolize political mass communications. Not only does the press provide news and comment, but ordinarily both television and radio continue their political coverage

---

[31] Monica Charlot, "The Language of Television Campaigning," in Penniman, *France at the Polls*, pp. 227-53, at p. 234.

[32] Werner Kaltefleiter "Winning without Victory: The 1976 CDU Campaign," in Cerny, *Germany at the Polls*, pp. 111-45, at p. 138.

[33] Judith Elizur and Elihu Katz, "The Media in the Israeli Elections of 1977," in Penniman, *Israel at the Polls*, pp. 227-54, at p. 238.

[34] Grattan, "The Liberal Party," p. 134.

during election campaigns. Israel is unusual in prohibiting candidates from appearing on television news programs in the thirty days before an election and in otherwise restricting, for an even longer preelection period, the broadcast of political programs except those allocated to the established political parties;[35] reflecting fears about television's influence on elections, this policy tends to make the public more dependent not only on political parties, but also on the press for political information. Other nations are ordinarily content with less drastic measures to try to ensure fair and balanced television coverage, and their televised or broadcast political communication tends to grow and to be increasingly outside party control. The British experience is instructive. As late as the 1950s, the electronic media produced little by way of commentary or news to compete with the programs allocated to the parties. British elections did not begin to become major media events, rather than only party events, until the late 1960s. By 1974, however, both radio and television in Britain acted autonomously as political communicators. Parties alone no longer determined the agenda for campaigns. News programs, and those who decided what went into the programs, had become central.[36]

Nonparty electronic political communication may be especially significant when it begins to develop in a nation whose press remains more limited and more partisan than Britain's. Thus in the Italian election of 1976, radio and television reporting, while still incomplete by British and other Western standards, provided voters with a kind of information very different from what the parties and their supporting press had supplied.[37] Party organizations must lose some of their relative importance as communicators when the voters' exposure to other sources of political information is substantially and effectively increased, as it appears to be particularly by television.

Prospects

Little in this survey, including even the impact of television, suggests that the difference between American and other party organizations with respect to their domination of elections will diminish. That conclusion might well have been expected insofar as a principal reason for the difference was thought to be institutional; the contrasting effects of the separation of powers and the parliamentary system are

---

[35] Elizur and Katz, "The Media," p. 229.

[36] Jay G. Blumler, "Mass Media Roles and Reactions in the February Election," in Penniman, Britain at the Polls, pp. 131-62, at pp. 135-37, 143-44.

[37] William E. Porter, "The Mass Media in the Italian Election of 1976," in Penniman, Italy at the Polls, pp. 259-86, at pp. 263-65.

surely durable. So are the effects of the now firmly established American direct primary, and those of the internal party candidate-selection practices equally well established elsewhere. Only somewhat less durable is the quasi-institutional impact of the first development of modern party organizations in each nation. In the United States parties first mobilized on the basis of the subsequently discredited patronage or spoils system; in most other Western democratic nations, they developed on the basis of programmatic commitments often reinforced by class solidarity.

It is possible to treat the impact of historical party development as "somewhat less durable" not because of the occasional, and not very successful, efforts Americans have made to organize European-style mass-membership parties. Rather, as we have observed, mass-membership parties may be declining elsewhere both in size and in significance. Maintaining a large membership organization may become less relevant to electoral campaigns increasingly conducted through the mass media. Such campaigns require the technical skills of a few specialists and are less dependent on the kind of effort involved in door-to-door canvassing by party members. They also require large amounts of money beyond what can be raised from membership dues or perhaps even from any private contributions short of the scandalous. In this context, European parties, responding to financial exigencies, have secured public funds for their campaigns and even, in certain places, for the maintenance of their intercampaign activities. The result might enable a party headquarters staff to function without much of a membership base. So far, however, it must be stressed that many European parties, with or without public funds, retain much more substantial membership organizations than do the now characteristic American skeletal or cadre parties.

Even if organized membership parties elsewhere did become more like American ones, the convergence would be of limited significance as long as parties elsewhere dominated elections in a way that American parties do not. That domination need hardly end simply because party organizations lose their mass-membership character and become more fully bureaucratic and professional. Nor, of course, would American parties expect to become dominant in election contests if they should, improbably, be revived by public funding. No doubt, such funding could reinforce the professional and bureaucratic elements already impressively effective at the headquarters of certain American parties.[38] But a considerably strengthened American party staff would

---

[38] In the late 1970s, the Republican National Committee, raising money by direct mail, developed a new kind of central assistance for state parties. The development is described by John F. Bibby, "Political Parties and Federalism: The

still have to function in a political environment conducive to candidate-centered organizations that, with help from supporting interest groups, possess a formidable capacity of their own to employ professional campaign skills.

Bibliography

Duverger, Maurice. *Political Parties.* Translated by Barbara and Robert North. New York: Wiley, 1954.

Eldersveld, Samuel J. *Political Parties: A Behavioral Analysis.* Chicago: Rand McNally, 1964.

Gosnell, Harold S. *Machine Politics: Chicago Model.* Chicago: University of Chicago Press, 1937.

Henig, Stanley, and Pinder, John, eds. *European Political Parties.* London: Allen & Unwin, 1969.

McKenzie, Robert. *British Political Parties.* New York: Praeger, 1963.

Michels, Robert. *Political Parties.* Translated by Eden and Cedar Paul. Glencoe, Ill.: Free Press, 1949.

Ostrogorski, M. *Democracy and the Organization of Political Parties.* London: Macmillan, 1902.

Ozbudin, Ergun. *Party Cohesion in Western Democracies.* Beverly Hills: Sage Publications, 1970.

Sorauf, Frank J. *Party Politics in America.* Boston: Little, Brown, 1980.

Wilson, James Q. *Political Organizations.* New York: Basic Books, 1974.

Wright, William E., ed. *A Comparative Study of Party Organization.* Columbus, Ohio: Charles E. Merrill, 1971.

Republican National Committee Involvement in Gubernatorial and Legislative Elections," *Publius,* vol. 9 (Winter 1979), pp. 229-36. The increasing presence of state party staffing is noted by Malcolm E. Jewell and David M. Olson, *American State Political Parties and Elections* (Homewood, Ill.: Dorsey Press, 1978), pp. 329-30.

5

Candidate Selection

Austin Ranney

Americans often use the terms "nomination" and "candidate selection" interchangeably. In most democratic countries, however, they refer to two distinct, though related, processes. According to this more common usage, which I shall keep to in this chapter, "nomination" is the predominantly *legal* process by which election authorities certify a person as a qualified candidate for an elective public office and print his or her name on the election ballot for that office. "Candidate selection," on the other hand, is the predominantly *extralegal* process by which a political party decides which of the persons legally eligible to hold an elective public office will be designated on the ballot and in election communications as its recommended and supported candidate or list of candidates.[1]

The latter process is called candidate "selection" because it usually involves the party's choosing among several aspirants for the designation. However, in some circumstances—as, for example, when a party names a candidate for an election no one believes it can win— the process is one of searching out and persuading someone to "show the flag" in the hopeless fight. Even so, it is still called, however misleadingly, "candidate selection"; and that is what we shall call it here.

In this chapter I shall first outline the principal methods by which political parties in twenty-four democratic countries select candidates for election to the lower house of the national legislature and (in five countries only) for direct elections of the national chief executive.

My special thanks go to Charles Dodge for his diligent search for clues to candidate selection processes in countries where little has been published on the topic.

[1] Cf. Leon D. Epstein's definitions of the terms in *Political Parties in Western Democracies* (New York: Praeger, 1967), pp. 201-3.

This will be followed by a review of the qualifications that seem to be most valued in the selection of candidates. And I shall conclude by assessing the role played by candidate selection in modern democratic political parties and elections.

How Candidates Are Selected

Table 5–1 presents a summary of the machinery by which legislative candidates are chosen in twenty-four democratic nations and the aspirants' qualifications most valued by those who select the candidates.

The Rules. As the first column of table 5–1 shows, the procedures by which political parties select their parliamentary candidates are governed by public laws in only three nations—West Germany, Turkey, and the United States.

In the United States ever since the early 1900s, most aspects of the organization and operation of political parties, including their selection of candidates for the national House of Representatives and most other offices, have been closely regulated by state laws. These laws have been supplemented by a number of rules adopted by the national and state party organizations, but the only national law affecting candidate selection is the 1974 law providing for the public funding of campaigns for the parties' presidential nominations.[2]

In West Germany, Article 21 of the 1949 Basic Law (federal constitution) recognizes political parties as legitimate and necessary agencies of government and bans parties that do not accept the basic principles of democratic government. A federal law enacted in 1956 and revised in 1967 provides for generous public funding of party affairs and requires the parties to select their district candidates for the Bundestag by either of two stipulated procedures: by the direct secret vote of all the enrolled dues-paying party members in each district, or by a district nominating convention elected for the purpose by the district's party members.[3] The Political Parties Law enacted by Turkey in 1965 permits the national executive committee of any political party to select only 5 percent of the party's candidates for the

---

[2] For a more detailed description of the legal status of American parties, see Austin Ranney, *Curing the Mischiefs of Faction: Party Reform in America* (Berkeley, Los Angeles, and London: University of California Press, 1975), pp. 78-91.

[3] See ibid., pp. 77-78; and Gerhard Loewenberg in Karl H. Cerny, ed., *Germany at the Polls: The Bundestag Election of 1976* (Washington, D.C.: American Enterprise Institute, 1978), p. 25.

TABLE 5-1

CANDIDATE SELECTION IN TWENTY-FOUR DEMOCRATIC COUNTRIES

Country	Source of Rules	Selecting Agency	Supervising Agency	Traits Most Valued in Aspirants
Australia	Regional party rules	Constituency committee (local direct vote by party members)	Regional agency	Incumbency, local connections, above-average socioeconomic status and education, previous candidacy
Austria	National party rules	National committee (regional committee)	National agency (regional agency)	Incumbency, interest group affiliation, factional affiliation, above-average education, party office, local government office, previous candidacy
Belgium	National party rules	Local direct vote by party members (national committee)	National agency	Interest group affiliation, factional affiliation, ethnicity
Canada	Regional party rules	Constituency committee (local direct vote by party members, direct vote by all voters)	Regional agency	Incumbency, local connections, above-average socioeconomic status and education, local government office, ethnicity
Colombia	National party rules	National committee (regional committee)	National agency	Incumbency
Denmark	National party rules	Local direct vote by party members (constituency committee)	National agency	Incumbency, local connections, interest group affiliation

(Table continues)

TABLE 5–1 (continued)

Country	Source of Rules	Selecting Agency	Supervising Agency	Traits Most Valued in Aspirants
Finland	National party rules	Constituency committee (local direct vote by party members)	National agency	Incumbency, interest group affiliation, party office, local government office
France	National party rules	Constituency committee (local direct vote by party members)	National agency	Local connections, factional affiliation, above-average education, party office, local government office, civil service post
West Germany	National laws	Constituency committee (local direct vote by party members)	Regional agency	Incumbency, local connections, interest group affiliation, above-average socio-economic status and education, party office, local government office
India	National party rules	National committee (regional committee, constituency committee)	National agency	Local connections, factional affiliation, ethnicity
Ireland	National party rules	Constituency committee	National agency	Local connections, interest group affiliation, previous candidacy
Israel	National party rules	National committee	National agency	Incumbency, factional affiliation
Italy	National party rules	Regional committee	National agency	Local connections, factional affiliation, above-average socioeconomic status and education, party office, local government office (incumbency)

Japan	National party rules	National committee	National agency	Incumbency, local connections, factional affiliation, above-average socioeconomic status and education, party office, civil service post
Netherlands	National party rules	National committee (constituency committee)	National agency (regional agency)	Incumbency, local connections, interest group affiliation, factional affiliation, above-average socioeconomic status and education, local government office, civil service post, previous candidacy
New Zealand	National party rules	National committee, constituency committee (local direct vote by party members)	National agency	Incumbency, local connections, interest group affiliation, above-average socio-economic status and education, local government office
Norway	(National laws, national party rules)	Constituency committee	None	Local connections, interest group affiliation, above-average socioeconomic status and education, local government office
Sri Lanka	National party rules	National committee (constituency committee)	National agency	Incumbency, local connections, factional affiliation, above-average socioeconomic status and education, party office, local government office, ethnicity
Sweden	National party rules	Constituency committee (local direct vote by party members)	National agency	Incumbency, local connections, interest group affiliation, factional affiliation
Switzerland	Regional party rules	Constituency committee	Regional agency	Incumbency, local connections, interest group affiliation, ethnicity

(Table continues)

79

TABLE 5–1 (continued)

Country	Source of Rules	Selecting Agency	Supervising Agency	Traits Most Valued in Aspirants
Turkey	National laws	Local direct vote by party members (national committee)	None	Incumbency, local connections, interest group affiliation, above-average socioeconomic status and education, party office, local government office, civil service post
United Kingdom	National party rules	Constituency committee (local direct vote by party members)	National agency	Incumbency, above-average socioeconomic status and education, previous candidacy (local connections, interest group affiliation, factional affiliation)
United States	Regional laws	Direct vote by all voters	None	Incumbency, local connections, above-average socioeconomic status and education
Venezuela	National party rules	National committee (regional committee)	National agency	Local connections, interest group affiliation, factional affiliation, above-average socioeconomic status and education

NOTE: Parentheses indicate characteristics that are present but not dominant.

National Assembly and requires that all the others be selected by the direct vote of the dues-paying party members in each district.[4]

It is also worth noting that the Norwegian Nomination Act of 1921 conditionally regulates candidate selection: it urges all parties to select their candidates in each constituency or "province" by conventions of delegates elected by the parties' dues-paying members in the province's subdivisions. If the party uses this procedure, the national government will fund the provincial conventions. If it chooses not to—and the major parties in Bergen and Oslo usually so choose—it is free to use any other method it wishes, but it will not receive public funds.[5]

In all other democracies, however, candidate selection, like other party affairs, is unknown to the law. The procedures are governed by rules that are made, amended, interpreted, and enforced entirely by party agencies. In most instances, as table 5–1 shows, national party agencies have exclusive, or at least ultimate, authority over the rules, and the rules are often set forth in party constitutions, charters, or "statutes." One exception is Australia, where each major party's *state* organization adopts its own selection ("pre-selection" they call it) procedures without any supervision or control by the national organization.[6] Another exception is Canada, where each provincial organization of the Liberal, Progressive Conservative, and New Democratic parties makes the rules governing candidate selection in its province, and only the Social Credit party gives de facto control to the national party leaders.[7] The other exception is Switzerland, where only the Social Democratic party is more than a loose confederation of cantonal parties, and where the other main parties (the Free Democrats, the Christian Democrats, and the Swiss People's party) leave candidate selection, like most other matters, up to the cantonal organizations.[8]

[4] C. H. Dodd, *Politics and Government in Turkey* (Berkeley, Los Angeles, and London: University of California Press, 1969), pp. 133-34; and Frank Tachau in Kemal H. Karpat, ed., *Social Change and Politics in Turkey* (Leiden, the Netherlands: E. J. Brill, 1973), pp. 301-9.

[5] Henry Valen and Daniel Katz, *Political Parties in Norway* (Oslo: Universitetsforlaget, 1964), pp. 21-22; and Henry Valen, "The Recruitment of Parliamentary Nominees in Norway," in *Scandinavian Political Studies* (New York: Columbia University Press 1966), pp. 121-66, esp. p. 122.

[6] Leon D. Epstein in Howard R. Penniman, ed., *Australia at the Polls: The National Elections of 1975* (Washington, D.C.: American Enterprise Institute, 1977), pp. 25-27.

[7] George Perlin, Jo Surich, and Michael B. Stein in Howard R. Penniman, ed., *Canada at the Polls: The General Election of 1974* (Washington, D.C.: American Enterprise Institute, 1975), pp. 114-15, 140-42, 168-71.

[8] Jürg Steiner, *Amicable Agreement versus Majority Rule: Conflict Resolution in Switzerland*, Asger and Barbara Braendgaard, trans. (Chapel Hill: University of North Carolina Press, 1974), pp. 80, 99-100; and George A. Codding, *The Federal Government of Switzerland* (Boston: Houghton Mifflin, 1961), pp. 113, 124.

With these few exceptions, then, most parties in most modern democracies select their parliamentary candidates by procedures specified by national party rules.

Dimensions of Candidate Selection. Not surprisingly, there is a good deal of variation in candidate selection procedures from country to country and even from party to party within particular countries. Most of these differences, however, are variations in degree along several dimensions. They may be briefly summarized as follows:

1. Centralization. Almost all democratic parties maintain party agencies of some kind at the national, regional (state, province, canton, department), and local (usually parliamentary constituency or election district) levels (see chapter 4). Power over candidate selection is distributed among those levels according to one or another of the following patterns:

A. Selection by national agencies with occasional suggestions by subnational agencies: all parties in Israel and Venezuela, and the Communist parties of Austria and France.

B. Selection by national agencies after serious consideration of suggestions by subnational agencies: all parties in India, Japan, Sri Lanka, and the Netherlands; the Social Credit party of Canada; the RPR (Gaullist party) and UDF (Giscardian coalition) in France; the Communist and Socialist parties of Italy.

C. Regional selection with national supervision: the minor French parties, the Austrian Socialist party, all parties in Ireland, and the Italian Christian Democratic party.

D. Regional selection with no national supervision: all parties in Norway, and the Austrian People's party.

E. Constituency selection with national supervision: all parties in Denmark, Finland, New Zealand, Sweden, Turkey, and the United Kingdom; the Liberal and Christian Democratic parties of Belgium; the French Socialist party.

F. Constituency selection with regional supervision: all parties in Australia, West Germany, and Switzerland, and all Canadian parties except Social Credit.

G. Constituency selection with no regional or national supervision: both major parties in the United States, the Socialist party of Belgium.

Table 5–1 makes clear that the most common pattern is selection by constituency party agencies under some form of supervision by national or regional agencies, and the next most common is selection by national agencies after consideration of suggestions made by regional and constituency agencies.

By American standards (which are selection at the constituency level with no regional or national supervision), most candidate selection systems seem highly centralized. Just how centralized they are in fact, however, depends upon the kind and degree of supervision the national or regional agencies exercise over the constituency organizations' selection procedures and products. Such supervision consists of one or more of the following four devices:

A. Allocation. Some parties begin their candidate selection processes by deciding how many candidates they will put forth and in what constituencies. In Japan, for instance, each constituency elects from three to five members of the House of Representatives, but each voter can vote for only one candidate. Hence each party is forced to calculate how many candidates it should run in each constituency; too many will spread the party's votes so thin that all its candidates will lose; too few will waste the party's votes and keep it from electing as many candidates as its voting strength permits. The parties' national organizations use their power to give or withhold official endorsement for the purpose of controlling the number to be nominated in each constituency, although informal advance notice of the allotted number to the local selectors usually obviates any need later to withhold endorsement from a locally selected candidate.[9] In Ireland the single-transferable-vote system makes similar party calculations necessary, and the national executive committee of each party reserves the decision for itself.[10]

B. Placement. The national leaders of most parties have rosters, written or unwritten, of persons they would especially like to see selected as candidates—valued legislators who have lost their seats in recent elections, persons with special backgrounds and skills needed to strengthen the parliamentary party, persons with the ethnic, religious, occupational, or other traits needed to "balance" candidate slates, and so on. All national leaders have the power to suggest the selection of such persons. Some use it occasionally, although, as we shall see, it often stirs up resentment among the local selectors and does the nationally favored aspirant more harm than good. However, the national leaders of most of the principal parties in Austria, Belgium, Colombia, Ireland, and Turkey have the power to place particular persons in local candidacies whatever the local people may

---

[9] Gerald L. Curtis, *Election Campaigning Japanese Style* (New York: Columbia University Press, 1971), pp. 3-4.

[10] Basil Chubb in Howard R. Penniman, ed., *Ireland at the Polls: The Dáil Elections of 1977* (Washington, D.C.: American Enterprise Institute, 1978), p. 24.

wish. Perhaps the most striking example of such placement in recent years has been provided by the Italian Communist party. In their effort to establish a public reputation as a truly democratic and non-revolutionary organization, the party's national leaders have added to the local candidate lists a number of non-Communist, even nonparty, notables, such as a member of the European Economic Community's Commission, a former NATO deputy supreme commander, and the ex-president of the Constitutional Court.[11]

C. Positioning. In all countries with some form of party-list proportional representation, the candidates' positions on party lists are almost as important as their presence on them. In each constituency each party is entitled only to a number of seats proportional to its share of the popular votes, and those seats usually go to the candidates in sequence at the top of its list until its quota is filled. Hence each party list has some "safe" slots at the top and a few "marginal" slots just below them, and the rest are "hopeless." In most parties in most such countries, the supervisory powers of the national or regional party agencies include the power to determine the final order in which the names appear on the party's list in each constituency. In parties with strong factions that must be appropriately represented, this process plays an especially important role in keeping the factions satisfied and the parties united. The Likud party of Israel provided a good example in 1977. The party was an amalgam of three main factions, each of which had previously been an independent party with its own list: Herut, led by Menachem Begin; the Liberals, led by Simcha Ehrlich; and La'am, led by Yigal Hurvitz. The party's national leaders decided to run a full national list of 120 candidates (Israel has no subnational constituencies), and the best estimates were that 40 to 45 would be elected (in the event, 43 were elected). Hence slots 1 through 40 were considered "safe," slots 40 through 45 were considered "marginal," and slots 46 through 120 were considered "hopeless." After delicate negotiations among the three groups, the national leaders positioned the candidates thus: of the first 43 places Likud was given numbers 1 (Begin), 4, 6, 8, 11, 13, 14, 17, 19, 22, 24, 26, 27, 29, 32, 33, 35, 37, 39, and 42; the Liberals received numbers 2 (Ehrlich), 5, 7, 9, 12, 18, 20, 23, 25, 30, 34, 38, 41, and 43; and La'am was given numbers 3 (Hurvitz), 10, 15, 21, 28, 31, 36, and 40. Number 16 was allocated at the last moment to a leading member of the Independent Liberal party.[12]

---

[11] Douglas Wertman in Howard R. Penniman, ed., *Italy at the Polls: The Parliamentary Elections of 1976* (Washington, D.C.: American Enterprise Institute, 1977), pp. 65-66.

[12] Benjamin Akzin in Howard R. Penniman, ed., *Israel at the Polls: The Knesset Elections of 1977* (Washington, D.C.: American Enterprise Institute, 1979), pp. 107-10.

D. Veto. By far the most widespread supervisory device is the power of the national or regional party agencies to withhold endorsement of a locally selected candidate and thereby deny the candidate the use of the party's label if he or she chooses to remain a candidate. Only the parties in West Germany, Norway, Turkey, and the United States together with the People's party of Austria and the Socialist party of Belgium do *not* have such a veto. We should note, however, that most of the central party agencies that do possess a veto power rarely use it. They rely instead upon the local selectors' discretion to avoid choosing candidates that would have to be vetoed.[13]

2. *Inclusiveness.* A second dimension of candidate selection is "inclusiveness": how restrictive are the qualifications for participation in the process? The first thing to note is that in every country except the United States and, in some circumstances, Canada, participation is restricted to party members. Moreover, the qualifications for membership are set by each party for itself, the party enrolls (and, on rare occasions, expels) whom it wishes, and the members assume some obligation to the party (usually the payment of modest annual dues) as a condition of participating in the selection of its candidates. And people who are not willing to assume the obligations of membership cannot participate in the selection.

In these respects as in so many others, the United States is different from every other democratic country. Party candidates for the House of Representatives and for most other offices are chosen in the parties' "direct primary" elections. The term "direct primary" is sometimes applied—incorrectly and misleadingly—to especially open selection procedures in other countries; hence it might be well to set forth here the essential features of American-style direct primaries:

First, the procedures by which candidates are chosen are prescribed by law, not by party rules. Second, these laws require that each party's candidates be chosen by secret ballot in elections that are conducted like all other official elections: that is, public authorities decide what names appear on the ballots, they supervise the printing, casting, and counting of the ballots, and only the aspirants who win the legally required majorities or pluralities of the votes are certified by the public authorities as the parties' official candidates on the ballots for the subsequent general election.

Third and most important, each state's decision as to who can vote in the primary election of a particular party is made by law, not

---

[13] For a discussion of the infrequent circumstances in which candidates have been vetoed in the United Kingdom, see Austin Ranney, *Pathways to Parliament* (Madison: University of Wisconsin Press, 1965); and Michael Rush, *The Selection of Parliamentary Candidates* (London: Thomas Nelson and Sons, 1969).

by party rules, and administered by public authorities, not by party officials. Hence the leaders and organizations of the parties have no control over who participates in the selection of their candidates, and the persons who acquire that right assume no obligation whatever to the party. The state laws governing who can vote provide for one or another of five degrees of inclusiveness: (1) "Closed primaries"—in twenty-nine states participation in a given party's primary is restricted to voters who have registered with the election authorities as party members by some deadline (usually one month) prior to the primary, and they cannot change their party affiliations until after the primary. (2) "Crossover primaries"—thirteen states allow every registered voter, without any prior registration of party affiliation, to vote in whichever party's primary he publicly requests on the day of the primary. (3) "Open primaries"—six states allow every registered voter to vote in the primary of any party (but not more than one party) without any preregistration or public declaration of the party chosen. (4) "Blanket primary"—the state of Washington allows a voter to choose candidates in the primaries of *both* parties, although he cannot vote for two aspirants for the same office. (5) "Nonpartisan primary"—in the state of Louisiana all candidates for a particular office from both parties appear on the ballot with the party affiliation of each printed by his name; every registered voter can vote for any one candidate he wishes; if one candidate receives 50 percent or more of the votes, he is elected forthwith; if no one receives as much as 50 percent, a second or "runoff" election is held a week later between the two candidates who finished on top in the first election even if they have the same party affiliation; the winner in the second election wins the office.

While these variations in the form of direct primaries make some difference, the point to note is that all of them, including the nominally "closed" primaries, permit any one voter who *declares himself* to be a member of a party to vote in that party's primary. He assumes no obligation to the party to acquire this power, and the party has no power to exclude him from participation in selecting its candidates. Thus candidate selection in the United States is by far the most inclusive and the least party controlled in the world, and the number of candidate selectors runs regularly in the millions rather than in the hundreds or the thousands as in other democratic nations.

Several other countries have systems that resemble direct primaries, but none fully satisfy the criteria just mentioned. In Canada, for example, some parties in some ridings (constituencies) sometimes hold "open conventions" in which all voters in a constituency are invited to attend a meeting and help select the candidate. This may seem to be an "open primary," but the decision to hold it is made exclusively by the local party organization, not by provincial or federal law. In fact the use of open conventions has declined in recent years, and most candidates are selected by meetings restricted to or delegates chosen by local dues-paying party members.[14] Turkey comes a bit closer to the American model (or antimodel): as we have seen, the Political Parties Law of 1965 requires the parties to choose at least 95 percent of their parliamentary candidates in constituency primary elections open to all party members in the constituency. However, the qualifications for party membership are set by the parties under broad limits imposed by the law (for example, a party entrance fee may not exceed twenty pounds, and a required monthly subscription may not exceed four pounds). The parties, to be sure, are very reluctant to promulgate or enforce demanding requirements for membership; most maintain poor membership records, few require annual dues, and there is little screening of would-be members. But the fact that the parties, not the law, decide who are their members for purposes of candidate selection makes the Turkish system, at most, a near–direct primary system.[15]

Commentators sometimes mention the "de facto" or "back door" primaries that take place in the selection of candidates for the French National Assembly. In recent years the contests for both the presidency and the National Assembly have been conducted between two coalitions of parties: the left (mainly the Communists and Socialists) and the center (mainly the Gaullists and a number of non-Gaullist center parties supporting President Valéry Giscard d'Estaing). Members of the National Assembly are elected from single-member districts in a double-ballot system: if a candidate receives more than 50 percent of the vote, he is elected; if none receives that much, a second ballot is held a week later in which all the candidates who received 10 percent or more on the first ballot are eligible to run. But the practice is that on the second ballot all the parties in each coalition will support a single candidate so as not to divide their strength and forfeit the seat to the opposing coalition.

---

[14] Frederick C. Englemann and Mildred Schwartz, *Canadian Political Parties: Origin, Character, Impact* (Scarborough, Ont.: Prentice-Hall of Canada, 1975), pp. 230-31; Howard A. Scarrow, "Nomination and Local Party Organization in Canada: A Case Study," *Western Political Quarterly*, vol. 17 (March 1964), pp. 55-64; and Robert J. Williams, "Candidate Selection," in Howard R. Penniman, ed., *Canada at the Polls, 1979 and 1980* (Washington, D.C.: American Enterprise Institute, forthcoming).

[15] Dodd, *Politics and Government in Turkey*, p. 134; Sakri Sayari, "Aspects of Party Organization in Turkey," *Middle East Journal* (Spring 1976), pp. 187-99.

The perennial question becomes, which one of the coalition parties' candidates should the coalition support on the second ballot? The parties of the left have for some time answered this question by using the first ballot as a sort of "primary": the Communists and the Socialists both run candidates in each district on the first ballot and agree that whichever candidate gets the lesser vote will withdraw in favor of the other on the second ballot. Sometimes the leading parties in the center coalition have conducted similar "primaries," but more often they have agreed that only one party in the coalition will run a candidate on the first ballot. They have hoped thereby to maximize the center's chances of winning on the first ballot without having to risk a second. In recent years, however, the center has increasingly decided to have first-ballot "primaries" among some or all of its component parties: there were fifty such first-ballot contests in 1968, sixty-one in 1973, and over seventy in 1978.[16]

3. *Direct or indirect participation.* A third dimension of candidate selection procedures centers on the question of whether the party members qualified to participate do so directly by voting on the aspirants for candidacy or indirectly by electing delegates to the conventions or committees that select the candidates.

The most common practice is for candidates to be selected by conventions or committees whose members are elected by the party members, in some instances for that purpose alone and in other instances for other purposes as well. As table 5–1 shows, this is how things are done by all the parties in thirteen of the table's twenty-four countries.

At the other extreme, the United States is the only country in which all major-party candidates for the lower house of the national legislature are chosen by the votes of party "members" in direct primaries, as described above. However, the parties in Belgium and Turkey and the Socialist party in France come close. Each of the three leading Belgian parties (the Christian Social, Socialist, and Freedom and Progress parties) selects its candidates for the Chamber of Representatives by a direct vote of all the dues-paying party members in each constituency in a *poll préparatoire*. Thousands of persons regularly vote in these party-governed "primaries"; indeed, the Freedom and Progress party has a rule that if the turnout falls below 8,000 in any constituency, the national executive can set aside the results and substitute its own list of candidates. The lists selected in the

---

[16] J. R. Frears, *Political Parties and Elections in the French Fifth Republic* (New York: St. Martin's Press, 1977), p. 173.

Belgian Socialists' *polls,* on the other hand, are final and cannot be altered by any national party agency.[17] In Turkey, as we have seen, at least 95 percent of all candidates for the National Assembly must be chosen by local primary elections, and the parties' national executives can choose only 5 percent except when they must name more in order to present a full list of candidates in every district. And the French Socialists select their parliamentary candidates by votes of the party members in each constituency, although the candidates thus selected—unlike those chosen by their Belgian comrades—have to be approved by the national executive.[18]

In several countries the parties give their selecting agencies the option of using either the direct-vote or the committee/convention method. In Australia both methods have been used by the major parties, and the direct-vote method has been especially popular in the Australian Labor party, although in recent years it has been on the decline because of recurring problems of compiling valid lists of members and answering charges that the lists are "packed" to maximize the votes for particular aspirants.[19] The major parties in Canada, Denmark, Finland, West Germany, New Zealand, Sweden, and the United Kingdom allow the same option. In recent years, however, the committee/convention method has become increasingly popular, in part because of problems with direct votes similar to those experienced by the Australian Labor party, and in part because many local leaders feel that decisions made by elected committees and conventions are likely to be less divisive than those made by direct votes. In this respect as in many others, then, not only is candidate selection in the United States markedly different from its counterparts in other democracies, but the rest of the world seems to be getting less like America, not more.

Selection of Candidates for Directly Elected Presidents. In Colombia, France, and Venezuela, the nation's chief executive and head of government is directly elected by popular votes. In Finland and the United States he is formally elected by "presidential electors," who are themselves directly elected by the voters. But since the electors in both nations are almost always elected as party candidates pledged to vote for their party's presidential candidate, Finland and the United

---

[17] Jeffrey Obler, "The Role of National Party Leaders in the Selection of Parliamentary Candidates: The Belgian Case," *Comparative Politics,* vol. 5 (January 1973), pp. 157-84.

[18] Frears, *Parties in the Fifth Republic,* p. 115.

[19] Epstein in Penniman, *Australia at the Polls,* p. 26.

States have the functional equivalents of the other countries' direct-election systems.[20]

The procedures for selecting presidential candidates vary greatly among these five countries, but they all have in common the fact that political parties play a less significant role than they do in the selection of parliamentary candidates. Perhaps the best way to illustrate these points is to present a brief account of the presidential candidate selection process in each nation.

Colombia. For several decades prior to 1978, Colombian politics was dominated by a "grand coalition" between the Conservative and Liberal parties. The parties agreed, among other things, that in each presidential election they would both support the same candidate, that the parties would alternate terms in supplying the candidate, and that the candidate, when elected, would divide his appointments evenly between adherents of the two parties. When its term came, each party chose its candidate by a national convention of delegates elected by its regional organizations.

The coalition gradually broke up, and as the 1978 presidential election approached, it was clear that this time *both* parties would nominate candidates, the winner would be determined by a genuine interparty competitive election, and the new president would make his appointments exclusively from among his fellow partisans. But each party was rent by a bitter factional fight, and each feared that the faction that lost the convention fight for the presidential nomination might abstain from voting or even support the other party's candidate in the election. Each party handled its problem in a novel way.

The Liberal party's factions, under the so-called San Carlos Agreement of 1976, agreed that in the February 1978 congressional elections each faction would present its own slate of candidates, one headed by Turbay Ayala and the other by Lleras Restropo. The two slates would compete against each other as well as against Conservative candidates, and the faction whose slate won the most popular votes would have its leader accepted by the other as the party's agreed presidential candidate in the June 1978 election—a truly unique form

---

[20] Two additional situations should be mentioned. The president of Austria is directly elected, but since his powers are minimal and his functions are largely ceremonial we will not consider the selection of candidates for the office. Sri Lanka in 1978 amended its constitution to establish the direct election of its president for a six-year term (he had formerly been selected by the parliament). The president will, on the French model, serve as both chief of state and head of government and will be assisted by a prime minister whom he selects. However, the incumbent president, J. R. Jayawardene, was "deemed to have been elected for a six-year term," and so Sri Lanka will not hold its first presidential election until 1984.

of indirect presidential "primary." The Turbay Ayala slate won handily, and the party convention in March duly nominated him for president. Lleras Restropo, however, told his followers to "follow their consciences" in the June election, and many of them abstained or voted for the Conservative. Thus the "primary" device, however ingenious, failed to unite the party behind the man who "won" its nomination.

The two Conservative factions soon faced up to the fact that they were parts of a minority party and thus had to unite behind one candidate to have any chance of defeating the Liberals. They too hit upon a novel device: each faction held its own separate convention, but both conventions nominated the same candidate, Belisario Betancur.

In the June election Turbay Ayala won an unexpectedly narrow victory over Betancur, and many observers felt that the Liberal "primary" had widened, not bridged, the gap between the two Liberal factions. Even so, neither the Liberals nor the Conservatives could be sure of returning to the single national convention method that served them well in the days of the "grand coalition."

Finland. Discussing presidential candidate selection in Finland is complicated by the fact that no true interparty electoral contest for the office has been held since 1962.[21] Prior to 1962 the major Finnish parties selected their presidential candidates by national congresses of delegates elected by local party organizations. Each party then named a slate of candidates for presidential electors pledged, American-style, to the election of the party's presidential nominee. The 300 places in the electoral college were popularly elected and allocated among the parties by the same party-list system of proportional representation used for elections to the Eduskunta (parliament). That means that presidents were chosen, much as premiers were, by bargaining and coalition building among the parties' leaders and their representatives in the electoral college.

Urho Kekkonen was first elected president in 1956 by this process as the candidate of the Agrarian party. He was unusually popular and developed considerable support among adherents of several other parties. He was reelected in 1962 by interparty bargaining, most of which took place before the popular election of the electors. In 1968 he was reelected to a third six-year term, but this time he was nominated by a coalition of all the major parties with only token opposition from a few minor-party candidates.

---

[21] A useful general description is Jaako Nousiainen, *The Finnish Political System,* John H. Hodgson, trans. (Cambridge, Mass.: Harvard University Press, 1971).

In 1972 Kekkonen announced that he would not run for reelection in 1974 but would remain in office if the Finnish people so desired. The leaders of all but a few small parties of the right had come to believe that continuing him in office was essential to ensuring the continuity of Finnish foreign policy, especially good relations with the Soviet Union. Hence in 1973 their deputies in the Eduskunta passed a special law extending Kekkonen's term to 1978, and there was no 1974 election.

As 1978 approached, the leaders of the main parties announced that they were prepared to extend Kekkonen's term still further, but he reversed his earlier position and declared that he would continue in office only if he were reelected by the regular pre-1973 procedures. Accordingly, in the election of 1978 he was the joint nominee of six parties, which together held 187 of the Eduskunta's 200 seats. Candidates for presidential elector pledged to him won 82 percent of the popular votes and 260 of the 300 places, and he was duly reelected for another six-year term.

Insofar as Finland can be said to have had presidential candidate selection since 1962, the key decisions to join with other parties in support of Kekkonen in 1968 and 1978 as well as the 1972–1973 decision to extend his term have all been made by the national leaders of the leading parties, not by the party congresses and certainly not by rank-and-file party members. The selection process has thus been far more centralized and party dominated in Finland than elsewhere, but it is by no means clear what will happen when Kekkonen has left the scene.

France. Although France has directly elected its presidents since 1965, a series of circumstances have prevented the development of clear-cut and well-established party procedures for selecting presidential candidates. As Roy Pierce summarizes it:

> to the author's knowledge, no party adopted a special procedure for nominating or endorsing a presidential candidate. Both in 1965 and 1969, the endorsements of presidential candidates were made by a variety of party groups, sometimes including party congresses, but more often only involving party executive committees, somewhat larger party councils, and/or the parliamentary groups. The Socialist party was the only party to endorse presidential candidates both in 1965 and 1969 at full party congresses, although the candidate they endorsed in 1965 (Defferre) withdrew before the election and lesser party bodies, the *comité directeur* and the *conseil national,* then made the crucial decision to support Mitterrand. In all those respects, the parties' behavior

reflected their traditional organization characteristics rather than any new, common set of imperatives imposed by the new method of presidential election or even by the enhanced powers of the presidency.[22]

In 1974, presidential candidate selection by the left coalition was orderly, but the center's procedures remained ad hoc and unformed. By the death of the incumbent, Georges Pompidou, in April 1974, Francois Mitterrand had established himself beyond challenge as the leader of the left; he announced his candidacy early and was soon thereafter endorsed unanimously by the national congress of his own Socialist party and by the Communist party's national executive committee.

The center, however, was caught in considerable disarray by Pompidou's death. The Gaullist UDR had no obvious successor in the sense that Pompidou had been de Gaulle's heir apparent in the late 1960s. Jacques Chaban-Delmas, who had been prime minister under Pompidou from 1969 to 1972, felt that he was the logical successor and that the best strategy was to preempt the field by quick action. He announced his candidacy a few days after Pompidou's funeral and was quickly endorsed by the UDR's council. But other elements of the center coalition were not happy with Chaban-Delmas, and several other candidates announced their candidacies. The first was Edgar Faure, but he soon withdrew in favor of Valéry Giscard d'Estaing, the Independent Republican leader and finance minister under Pompidou. Eventually twelve persons became official candidates—Mitterrand, Chaban-Delmas, Giscard d'Estaing, three candidates from tiny far-left parties, two from equally tiny far-right parties, and four "independents."

On the first ballot Mitterrand received 43 percent of the votes, Giscard d'Estaing 33 percent, Chaban-Delmas 15 percent, and the others 9 percent. Most of Chaban-Delmas's voters and many who supported the other candidates switched to Giscard d'Estaing in the second balloting, and he won with 50.8 percent to Mitterrand's 49.2 percent.

But, as Jean Blondel points out, France was left without an established system for making presidential nominations:

> The presidential election of 1974 still did not provide the Fifth Republic with a regular nominating process. The selection was ad hoc and accidental. The Left was united by the will power of one man, Mitterrand, not because permanent

---

[22] In Howard R. Penniman, ed., *France at the Polls: The Presidential Election of 1974* (Washington, D.C.: American Enterprise Institute, 1975), pp. 38-39.

procedures and arrangements had been established. The Gaullists had found a candidate quickly, but perhaps not wisely. Self-selected candidates with strong personalities still had a field day. The UDR repeated the scenario which had proved successful in 1969, but its candidate lacked general appeal. Giscard, almost alone, basing his candidacy on sheer personal strength and an underlying mood for change, had decided to step in.[23]

Venezuela. In recent years Venezuelan politics has settled into a stable two-party system dominated by competition between the Acción Democrática party (AD) and the Christian Democratic party (COPEI).[24] COPEI has regularly selected its presidential candidate in national party conventions convened in the years just before the years of the presidential elections. Enrolled dues-paying party members in each electoral district elect delegates to provincial (state) conventions, and the provincial conventions elect delegates to the national conventions. The latter are even larger than their counterparts in the United States: there were 4,200 delegates at the 1977 COPEI national convention.

AD has sometimes used similar national conventions, but on two occasions it has conducted a national presidential "primary" in which its candidates were chosen by the direct votes of its dues-paying members. Prior to the 1968 election, AD was deeply split between two factions, one supporting Gonzalo Barrios and the other supporting Luis Beltrán Prieto Figueroa. Some party leaders believed that the presidential candidate could be selected and the party split healed by a national convention that would make suitable concessions to the losing faction. However, a powerful party leader, ex-President Rómulo Betancourt, insisted that a party primary would be much more fair and democratic. He prevailed, and the primary election was held in 1967. Prieto won a majority of the votes, but the party apparatus, largely controlled by Barrios supporters, refused to accept the result and delayed announcing Prieto as the party's official nominee. This so incensed Prieto that he left AD entirely to form his own party, and Barrios was certified as the AD nominee. In the election the AD vote was split between the two candidates, and the COPEI candidate was elected.

AD returned to the national convention method for the 1973 election. The convention nominated Carlos Andrés Pérez, and he won

---

[23] Ibid., p. 32.

[24] The discussion is drawn mainly from the chapters by David J. Myers and Donald L. Herman in Howard R. Penniman, ed., *Venezuela at the Polls* (Washington, D.C.: American Enterprise Institute, 1980).

the election over the COPEI candidate. But another major factional split soon developed between AD supporters of the Pérez administraton and its AD opponents led by Betancourt. As the 1978 election approached, Pérez pressed the cause of David Morales Bello for the AD candidacy, but Betancourt opposed Bello and instead pushed the party's secretary general, Luis Piñerúa Ordaz. As in 1967 Betancourt persuaded the 1976 party convention to schedule a presidential primary for July 1977. The Pérez faction ultimately settled on Jaime Lusinchi as their candidate, and Piñerúa was backed by the Betancourt faction. The primary elicited the impressive turnout of 732,000 voters—81 percent of the party's 900,000 dues-paying members—and Piñerúa won a majority of the votes. During the primary campaign, however, the rift between the Pérez-Lusinchi faction and the Piñerúa-Betancourt faction widened. While the administration faction did not formally secede and put up Lusinchi as a third-party candidate after they had lost the primary, their campaign efforts stressed the administration's achievements and largely ignored Piñerúa. As a result, COPEI won another unexpected victory. Even so, many in AD continue to believe that a primary is more democratic and fair than a convention, but many others believe that the 1967 and 1977 primaries led directly to the election defeats and that the convention system, which has served COPEI so well, is much better. How the issue will be resolved in selecting the AD candidate for the next presidential election remains to be seen.

The United States. There is a vast literature on the selection of presidential candidates in the United States, and we can only hit the subject's highlights here.[25] Since the advent of party-contested presidential elections in 1800, several nominating methods have been used:

1800–1824: congressional caucuses—meetings of each party's members of the Senate and House of Representatives
1828: state legislatures and state legislative party caucuses
1832–1908: national conventions of delegates elected by state and local party caucuses and conventions
1912–1968: national conventions with substantial minorities

---

25 The leading works on the selection of American presidential candidates include: Paul T. David, Ralph M. Goldman, and Richard C. Bain, *The Politics of National Party Conventions* (Washington, D.C.: Brookings Institution, 1960); James W. Davis, *Presidential Primaries: Road to the White House* (New York: Thomas Y. Crowell Co., 1967); Nelson W. Polsby and Aaron B. Wildavsky, *Presidential Elections*, 5th ed. (New York: Charles Scribner's Sons, 1980); William R. Keech and Donald R. Matthews, *The Party's Choice* (Washington, D.C.: Brookings Institution, 1976); Jeane Kirkpatrick, *The New Presidential Elite* (New York: Russell Sage Foundation and Twentieth Century Fund, 1976); and Stephen J. Wayne, *The Road to the White House* (New York: St. Martin's Press, 1980).

of the delegates chosen or bound by direct primaries

1972–: national conventions with substantial majorities of the delegates chosen or bound by direct primaries

Since 1968 a number of radical changes have been made in the presidential candidate selection processes of both parties. Some have been imposed by national laws and some by state laws, but most have come from a series of new rules ("reforms" some call them) adopted by the national parties, especially the Democrats.[26] The main changes have been the following:

First, the Democrats have adopted a number of rules governing selection of delegates to national conventions that make it harder for party organization leaders, workers, and notables to be chosen as delegates and make it easier for persons with strong commitments to the candidates and issues prominent in election years.

Second, from 1968 to 1980 the proportion of delegates elected or bound by direct primaries rose from 37 percent to 78 percent for the Democrats and from 34 percent to 77 percent for the Republicans. Hence, where primaries were one of several important elements in the nominating process from 1912 to 1968, they now monopolize most of the important decision making.

Third, a 1974 act of Congress restricts the amount of money a person or an organization can contribute to the campaign of a presidential aspirant, limits the total amount that his campaign can spend, and provides federal matching funds up to a total of $5 million for the campaign of any aspirant.

Some observers believe that these changes have made presidential candidate selection much more fair, open, honest, and democratic than it used to be. Others are skeptical of such claims, but there is little disagreement about the fact that the new rules have effectively destroyed whatever control the parties' national and state organization leaders once had over the choice of presidential candidates. As a result, both parties have become little more than passive arenas within which the real political actors—groups committed to particular candidates and to particular issue positions—contend for the nominations. The prizes are the two parties' labels, but the parties no longer control who bears them. The consequences of the new rules were immediately apparent, especially in the 1972 nomination of George McGovern and the 1976 nomination of Jimmy Carter by the Democrats. They were the first "outsiders" to take advantage of the new rules to capture the nominations despite the opposition of most established party leaders,

[26] The changes are described in detail in Austin Ranney, "The Political Parties: Reform and Decline," in Anthony King, ed., *The New American Political System* (Washington, D.C.: American Enterprise Institute, 1978), pp. 213-47.

but few observers think they will be the last. Hence, although the selection of presidential candidates in the United States appears to be much more orderly and party dominated than the process in, say, France, in reality it is equally personalistic, candidate centered, and formless.

Presidential candidate selection summarized. The foregoing accounts show that presidential candidate selection in Colombia, Finland, France, the United States, and Venezuela is generally much more fluid, changing, and ad hoc than is the selection of parliamentary candidates in those countries. Party organizations are less important, and candidate-centered organizations are much more important. The selection of controversial candidates by the victory of one faction over another is more likely to result in open party splits and secessional candidacies. Many of these differences no doubt stem mainly from the special visibility of the presidential office (which in every presidential country is far greater than that of any legislator) and from the close attention paid by the mass media to contests for presidential nominations. Indeed, the differences seem so great that relatively few of the generalizations that can be made about the kinds of persons most likely to be selected as presidential candidates apply to the persons favored as parliamentary candidates. Accordingly, we now leave presidential politics and turn to a survey of the characteristics of aspirants that seem to be most widely valued in the selection of parliamentary candidates.

The Candidates Selected

Social scientists have produced a good deal of information about the characteristics of at least one important category of parliamentary candidates: those selected for the winnable districts or the "safe" positions on the parties' lists. After all, almost every member of a national legislature begins by winning a party's candidacy in a desirable constituency or a high place on a party's list. Thus the many studies of the socioeconomic characteristics and political experience of national legislators tell us a lot about candidates as well.[27]

---

[27] Leading examples of such studies are: United Nations Educational, Scientific and Cultural Organization, *Decisions and Decision-Makers in the Modern State* (Paris: UNESCO, 1967); Donald R. Matthews, *The Social Background of Decision-Makers* (New York: Random House, 1954); Philip W. Buck, *Amateurs and Professionals in British Politics* (Chicago: University of Chicago Press, 1963); John Forster, "A Note on the Background of [New Zealand] Parliamentarians," *Political Science*, vol. 21 (1969), pp. 42-47; Klaus von Beyme, *Die politische Elite in der Bundesrepublik Deutschland* (Munich: Pioer, 1971); and Mattei Dogan, "Political Ascent in a Class Society: French Deputies, 1870-1958," in Dwaine Marvick, ed., *Political Decision-Makers* (Glencoe, Ill.: Free Press, 1961).

For a complete understanding of the traits that make for success and failure in the competition for candidacies, we would need to know not only the characteristics of the persons elected to office but also those of the defeated candidates and those of all the persons who sought candidacies but were not selected. It is plainly impossible to gather such information for even one nation let alone twenty-four. The preselection screening that eliminates most aspirants before the final selections are made almost always takes place in secret, records are rarely kept, and the few that are kept are all but impossible to collect.

Accordingly, scholars of candidate selection have followed one or both of two general strategies. One is to compare the characteristics of candidates selected for the most desirable slots—winnable constituencies or "safe" places on party lists—with those of candidates selected for less desirable slots.[28] The other is to accumulate as many firsthand accounts as possible of actual selections and make inductive generalizations about the traits most valued by those who made the selections.[29] Studies using either or both of these strategies have unearthed considerable information about those traits, and it is clear that the most widely prized are the following.

Incumbency. In most parties in most countries there is a powerful presumption that an incumbent legislator who wishes to be a candidate for reelection will be reselected, usually without much fuss. Hence where quantitative data are available, the correlation between incumbency and candidate selection for desirable slots is far higher than for any other trait. Some parties, indeed, have explicit rules requiring that, except in extraordinary circumstances incumbents *must* be reselected. Such rules are usually superfluous, however, for most selectors reselect incumbents as a matter of course.

The rationale is obvious. Other things being equal, incumbents are likely to make better candidates than nonincumbents. They are better known to the constituency's voters, it is easier to raise money for their campaigns, and they already wear the mantle of the elected public official. They are likely also to be better known by the party's selectors and to have served the party for a number of years. And

---

[28] This approach is used for the United Kingdom in Ranney, *Pathways;* for Finland in Pertti Pesonen, *Political Parties and the Finnish Eduskunta* (Tampere, Finland: University of Tampere Institute of Political Research, 1970); and for Ireland in Basil Chubb, *The Government and Politics of Ireland* (Stanford, Calif.: Stanford University Press, 1970), pp. 74-75, 94-96.

[29] This has been done for the United Kingdom in Rush, *Selection;* and for several other countries by various authors in the American Enterprise Institute's *At the Polls* series.

whatever advantages seniority may bring to a legislator and his constituents they will secure by reselecting an incumbent and lose by dropping him in favor of a newcomer. But whatever the reasons may be, the fact is that the greatest single advantage an aspirant for a candidacy can have is to hold the office already.

Local Connections. The Constitution of the United States stipulates that a member of the House of Representatives shall "when elected, be an inhabitant of that state in which he shall be chosen" (Article I, Section 2). This rather minimal local-residence requirement has given rise to a venerable and generally binding custom that a representative must be a resident of the district he represents. For most of American history this has meant longstanding residence in the district, but in recent years a small but growing number of people have sought House candidacies as admitted "carpetbaggers"—that is, persons who have only recently moved into the district and have done so in order to make themselves eligible for their party's nomination in that district.[30]

Only a handful of parties in other democratic nations have any kind of local residence rule, and most Americans, on learning how British legislators can move from one constituency to another (Sir Winston Churchill represented no fewer than five different constituencies in his long parliamentary career), conclude that strong local connections are important for legislative candidacy only in the United States.[31]

Such a conclusion would be quite wrong. Whatever the public laws and party rules may require, strong local connections—such as longstanding residence in the district, activity in local party affairs, holding local public office, or activity in local union, business, or civic affairs—is second only to incumbency as a trait widely valued by those who select parliamentary candidates. It is highly valued even in a surprising number of countries where candidate selection is conducted mainly by national party agencies—for example, Austria, France, India, Italy, Japan, the Netherlands, and Sri Lanka. And, not surprisingly, it is even more widely valued in those countries in which candidates are selected mainly by local party organizations—for ex-

---

[30] "Carpetbagger" is a term first applied to Northern opportunist politicians and confidence men who moved into the South after the Civil War, presumably to exploit the weakness of the whites and the gullibility of the newly enfranchised blacks, and who were said to be carrying all their possessions in one carpetbag (suitcase).

[31] For a description of what kinds of candidates move, in which directions, and in what circumstances in Great Britain, see Austin Ranney, "Inter-Constituency Movement of British Parliamentary Candidates," *American Political Science Review*, vol. 58 (March 1964), pp. 36-45.

ample, Canada, Ireland, Norway, and Turkey. Indeed, selecting local candidates is so often the norm that in many countries pejorative labels are commonly pinned to aspirants who seek candidacies in districts where they have no local connections: "carpetbaggers," "parachutists," "foreigners," "invaders," and the like.

There are a number of reasons for favoring aspirants with local connections. A local is likely to be better known, more trusted, more "one of us" than an outsider. He is more likely to have contributed work and money to the local party and thus to have "earned" its candidacy. Since the local's personal as well as political home is in the constituency, he is more likely to return frequently to "nurse" the voters and participate in local party functions. The voters will be more likely to vote for "one of their own" than an outsider. And a local will know and care more than an outsider about the constituency's special needs and aspirations.

Of course, there are often sufficient local reasons *not* to choose a local aspirant. If several locals are contending for the candidacy, selecting one may anger the others and perhaps split the local party activists. The local contender's deficiencies may be only too well known and thus loom much larger than the outsider's unknown or merely guessed-at faults. The local party may want the honor of having a distinguished national figure as its candidate and member. But, other things being equal, local aspirants will be chosen over outsiders more often than not.

Interest Group Affiliation. Many parties in many countries are heavily dependent upon certain interest groups for their voting support and on those groups' organizations for the bulk of their funds. The labor and social democratic parties, for one example, count on blue-collar workers for votes and on labor unions for funds. The Christian democratic parties are similarly dependent upon the votes of members of the Roman Catholic church and the funds of lay church organizations. The conservative parties need the votes of white-collar workers, managers, and professionals and the contributions of businessmen. In such parties some kind of visible affiliation with the key interest group—membership and active participation in a labor union, a religious laymen's league, a farmers' organization—is usually a necessary though not sufficient qualification for selection as a parliamentary candidate. Few parties go as far as the British Labour party in encouraging labor unions to "sponsor" candidates—an arrangement whereby a union draws up a list of people it would like to see selected as candidates and announces that if a constituency Labour party adopts a person on that list as its candidate the union will defray most of the local party's campaign and other expenses.[32]

Factional Affiliation. Just about every democratic political party contains a number of factions, each advancing the cause of a particular set of leaders or a particular line of policy or both against the competing leaders and policies of other factions. Hence every party to some degree faces the problem of keeping its major factions sufficiently happy that they will remain loyal to the party in its competition with opposing parties. One of the tactics most often used to accomplish this vital task is to see to it that the party's roster of candidates is well and truly "balanced"—that is, contains sufficient representatives of each major faction to assure all factions' leaders and members that their ideas and interests will be fairly treated and that they indeed will continue to have a voice in the party's affairs. This is an important criterion for candidate selection in almost every major party, but it appears to be crucial in such especially faction-ridden parties as the Italian Christian Democrats and all the major parties in Japan, India, and Israel.

Above-Average Socioeconomic and Educational Status. The studies of legislators' socioeconomic characteristics mentioned earlier have consistently shown that the incomes, educational levels, and occupations of legislators are generally much higher than those of the general population. It seems clear that this results not from voters' choosing upper-status over lower-status candidates in general elections, but from the strong tendency of political parties to select candidates whose socioeconomic status is well above that of the general population and, what is more, well above that of the particular party's "identifiers" in the electorate. This is not to say that the candidates of all parties are equally upper-status; they certainly are not. The social status of most conservative party candidates is generally noticeably higher than that of most labor/social democratic party candidates. The point is that conservative candidates are generally of higher status than conservative voters, and socialist candidates are generally of higher status than socialist voters.

There are a number of reasons why candidate selectors prefer aspirants of above-average status, and snobbery is the least of them (note that I do not say it plays no role whatever). Upper-status people are likely to be better educated than lower-status people. Consequently they are more likely to have acquired the personal skills that

---

[32] See Ranney, *Pathways*, pp. 225-27; and Martin Harrison, *Trade Unions and the Labour Party since 1945* (London: Allen & Unwin, 1960).

are most useful not only in fighting general elections but in facing candidate selectors. They are more likely to speak and write well, they are likely to know more about history and economics and foreign policy, they are more likely to look healthy and well dressed. They are also more likely to work in occupations with the flexible hours that permit lengthy periods of full-time concentration on getting the nomination and fighting the election. A lawyer or a university teacher can take many hours, days, or even weeks off for full-time politics and make it up later with little or no loss in income; but a lathe operator, a dockworker, or a store clerk cannot.

Other Desirable Traits. As table 5–1 shows, some parties in some countries value other traits in addition to those just mentioned. Identification with a certain race, religion, or linguistic group is important in parties in some areas in Belgium, Canada, India, Sri Lanka, Switzerland, and the United States. A record of having fought good though losing fights in earlier candidacies is well regarded in Austria, Ireland, the Netherlands, and the United Kingdom. In France, Japan, the Netherlands, and Turkey, holding or having held responsible positions in the national civil service is an asset. But the traits that are most valued in candidate selection in most parties in most democratic countries continue to be incumbency, local connections, the right interest group and factional affiliations, and above-average socioeconomic status and education.

The Role of Candidate Selection

In Political Parties. A distinguished scholar of political parties has written:

> Unless the party makes authoritative and effective nominations, it cannot stay in business, for dual or multiple party candidacies mean certain defeat. As far as elections are concerned, the united front of the party, the party concentration of numbers, can be brought about only by a binding nomination. The nominating process thus has become the crucial process of the party. The nature of the nominating procedure determines the nature of the party; he who can make the nominations is the owner of the party. This is therefore one of the best points at which to observe the distribution of power within the party.[33]

---

[33] E. E. Schattschneider, *Party Government* (New York: Farrar and Rinehart, 1942), p. 64.

Most party-watchers fully accept this dictum. Making nominations, after all, is what distinguishes political parties from pressure groups and other forms of political organization, which may support or oppose the nominees of a party but never nominate candidates of their own. Moreover, a party's candidates constitute its public face far more than its organization, its militants, or even its platform or manifesto. And as an agency of government, the core of any party is its officeholders—that is, its successful candidates.

It is therefore not surprising that the most vital and hotly contested factional disputes in any party are the struggles that take place over the choice of its candidates; for what is at stake in such a struggle, as the opposing sides well know, is nothing less than control of the core of what the party stands for and does.

In Democratic Elections. In every democratic election the number of persons legally eligible for the office or offices at stake is vastly too great for any voter, however well informed and public spirited, to consider and choose among intelligently. For example, the Constitution of the United States provides that any "natural born citizen" who is at least thirty-five years of age and who has been a resident of the nation for at least fourteen years is eligible for the presidency. In 1980 approximately 94 million Americans satisfied these requirements—obviously an impossible number for anyone to choose among knowledgeably and intelligently.

Even when the number of legal eligibles is much smaller, it is still far too large to be manageable: the Constitution requires that a member of the House of Representatives be at least twenty-five years of age, a citizen of the United States for at least seven years, and an inhabitant of the state in which his district is located. In the average district in 1980 about 285,000 persons had these qualifications—many fewer than the presidential eligibles but still far too many to permit meaningful choice.

Most of the eligibles, of course, eliminate themselves simply by making no effort to be elected. But if we accept some political scientists' estimates that about 1 percent of the voting-age population in the democratic countries are "organization activists," the pool from which most candidates are drawn, it still works out that there are hundreds of thousands of potential presidents in the nation and thousands of potential representatives in a district.[34]

Most of the activists also eliminate themselves, and no doubt some are eliminated by their spouses, employers, and friends. But the

---

[34] Cf. the estimates for various countries in Austin Ranney, *The Governing of Men*, 4th ed. (Hinsdale, Ill.: Dryden Press, 1975), pp. 174-75.

final stage of the elimination process, the one that produces the choices that appear on the ballot, is the parties' selection and naming of their candidates. The best evidence for this statement is the fact that in the general elections in all of the democratic countries we are considering in this book, very few "independent" candidates (that is, candidates with no party label on the ballot and no party support in the campaign) run; and the handful that do run are almost never elected.

The consequence is that voters in modern democratic elections do not have to choose among hundreds of thousands of eligibles or even among thousands of aspirants. In countries with first-past-the-post electoral systems, the voters' legislative ballot typically contains four or five names, only two or three of which are "serious candidates" bearing the labels of the leading parties. In the countries with multiple-member-district proportional electoral systems, the voter's ballot typically contains the candidate lists of six or seven parties. In either case the alternatives set before the voter are *party* alternatives. And in this way not only does the alternative-reduction process of candidate selection make an intelligent choice possible, but for most voters the candidates' party labels constitute the principal grounds for making choices in any particular election and the principal source for whatever meaning and continuity persist from one election to the next.

As Leon D. Epstein points out, by putting forth, labeling, and campaigning for their candidates, political parties "structure the vote"—that is, they provide a simple, easily understood, and continuing order and meaning for electoral choices. The voters do not have to be familiar with each candidate's personal qualities, political record, and issue positions. They can vote for the candidate or list of the party they prefer.[35]

The evidence strongly suggests that this is indeed the main ground on which most voters in every democratic country make their electoral choices.[36] Party-based voting may be marginally on the wane in the United States, as evidenced by the weakening of party identification, the increasing tendency to vote for congressional incumbents regardless of their party affiliations, and the rise in "split-ticket" voting. But even in the United States the voters' party preferences remain by far the most powerful single determinant of voting choice, and in most other democratic countries most voters vote for the candidate of

---

[35] For a fuller discussion of this function, see Epstein, *Parties in Western Democracies*, chap. 4, esp. p. 77.

[36] See the discussion in chapters 10 and 11 of this book.

the *party* they prefer, not the candidate whose personal qualities they most admire.[37]

So long as that continues to be the case, candidate selection by political parties will determine both the choices set before the voters in elections and the composition of the governing and opposition parties, whose interaction in parliaments and congresses is the very essence of modern democratic government.

Bibliography

General Comparative Studies. Few of the general comparative studies of politics in Western democratic countries deal with candidate selection at any length. The two most useful works are Leon D. Epstein, *Political Parties in Western Democracies* (New Brunswick, N.J.: Transaction Books, 1980), esp. chap. 8; and Stanley Henig, ed., *European Political Parties: A Handbook* (New York: Praeger, 1970), passim.

Single-Country Studies. A number of the AEI election studies have useful analyses of the procedures and politics of candidate selection. I have found the volumes on Australia, Canada, France, Italy, Israel, and Venezuela particularly helpful.

In addition, the following single-country studies have been useful:

Belgium
>Obler, Jeffrey. "The Role of National Party Leaders in the Selection of Parliamentary Candidates: The Belgian Case." *Comparative Politics* 5 (January 1973): 157–84.

Canada
>Scarrow, Howard A. "Nomination and Local Party Organization in Canada: A Case Study." *Western Political Quarterly* 17 (March 1964): 55–64.

Norway
>Valen, Henry. "The Recruitment of Parliamentary Nominees In Norway." *Scandinavian Political Studies.* New York: Columbia University Press, 1966.

Turkey
>Tachau, Frank. Pp. 301–9 in *Social Change and Politics in Turkey*, edited by Kemal H. Karpat. Leiden, the Netherlands: E. J. Brill, 1973.
>Sayari, Sakri. "Aspects of Party Organization in Turkey." *Middle East Journal* (Spring 1976), pp. 187–99.

---

[37] See Jeane Kirkpatrick in King, *New American Political System*, chap. 7; and the discussion by Donald E. Stokes in chapter 11 of this book.

United Kingdom

Ranney, Austin. *Pathways to Parliament.* Madison: University of Wisconsin Press, 1965.

Rush, Michael. *The Selection of Parliamentary Candidates.* London: Thomas Nelson and Sons, 1969.

United States

David, Paul T.; Goldman, Ralph M.; and Bain, Richard C. *The Politics of National Party Conventions.* Washington, D.C.: Brookings Institution, 1960.

Keech, William R., and Matthews, Donald R. *The Party's Choice.* Washington, D.C.: Brookings Institution, 1976.

Kirkpatrick, Jeane. *The New Presidential Elite.* New York: Russell Sage Foundation and Twentieth Century Fund, 1976.

Polsby, Nelson W., and Wildavsky, Aaron B. *Presidential Elections.* 5th ed. New York: Charles Scribner's Sons, 1980.

6
Campaign Styles and Methods

Howard R. Penniman

Two centuries ago fewer than 13,000 British voters elected more than three-fourths of the members of the House of Commons.[1] One hundred years later Parliament had enfranchised all 5.6 million male adults, provided for a secret ballot, and passed relatively stringent corrupt practices legislation. These changes in the electoral rules forced parties to give up their sometimes corrupt campaign practices[2] and sharply increase their membership in order to promote better candidates and programs, canvass voters, and ensure that voters likely to support them got to the polls.

Technological developments have had a similar power to alter campaign practices. Since 1950 they have come rapidly in most Western democracies. Computers have enabled party headquarters to gather intelligence about national political attitudes faster and more accurately than large numbers of party workers half a century ago could canvass individual constituencies. Computers have also made it possible to solicit funds from thousands of sympathizers whose support had not previously been tapped, and they have enabled candidates to send "personalized" letters to hundreds of thousands of constituents. The spread of television in many countries has allowed party leaders and candidates to speak directly to far more voters in a single telecast than disciplined mass parties could have gathered for all the rallies of an entire campaign.

New campaign technology requires smaller organizations and a new kind of political professional. No longer can a campaign manager

---

[1] Elie Halvéy, *A History of the English People in 1815* (London: Penguin Books, 1937), vol. 1, p. 192.

[2] Moisei Ostrogorski, *Democracy and the Organization of Political Parties*, vol. 1. *England*, edited and abridged by Seymour Martin Lipset (Garden City, N.Y.: Doubleday and Co., 1964), pp. 71-73 and 212.

be a full-time politician—often of low repute—who gains his liveli-
hood from his influence with elected officeholders, his insider's knowledge of government plans, his protection of petty criminals, or the
sale of favors. The new professionals include campaign directors who
have had limited experience in traditional party politics but are management specialists, hiring and directing other professionals—experts
in public opinion polling, modern fund-raising techniques, and public
relations. Edward Booth-Clibborn, chairman of the Designers and Art
Directors Association of London, organized publicity for the Labour
party during the 1979 British election campaign, while the firm of
Saatchi & Saatchi directed the advertising, radio, and television campaigns for the Conservative party.[3] Among the many professional
campaign consultants in the United States are John Deardourff, who
advises Republicans, Joseph Napolitan, who works for Democrats, and
David Garth, who has advised Democrats, Republicans, and in 1980
the independent presidential candidate John Anderson.[4] Most of these
new professionals sell their services to a single party or coalition out
of a commitment to its policies and programs, but their careers and
incomes do not depend on the spoils of electoral victory. Their talents
are eagerly sought outside the world of politics.

Television's impact on national election campaigns varies greatly
among the countries included in this study. In one-fourth of them
television receivers are too few to affect a campaign greatly. In five
of the seven countries in our sample where a majority of the workers
are employed in agriculture, television receivers are few in number and
confined to major urban centers. Sri Lanka had no television until
1970 when it was introduced on an experimental basis. In India the
ratio of receivers to the population is less than 1 to 2,000; in the
Dominican Republic 3 to 100; in Turkey 5 to 100; and in Colombia
7 to 100.[5]

Even in highly industrialized countries where almost every house-
hold owns at least one receiver, television's impact on campaigns for
the national legislature varies. Speaking of the British election in
February 1974, David Butler and Dennis Kavanagh state that "the
developments in the mass media, opinion polling and public relations
have bypassed electioneering at the local level. They have been exploited by the national campaigners in a way that has undermined

[3] David E. Butler and Dennis Kavanagh, *The British General Election of 1979*
(London: Macmillan, 1980), pp. 132-40.

[4] Both Napolitan and Garth worked for major parties in the 1978 Venezuelan
national elections, Napolitan for the Democratic Action party and Garth for the
Social Christians.

[5] William Overstreet and Michael G. Schechter, eds., *Political Handbook of the
World: 1979* (New York: McGraw-Hill, 1979), pp. 119, 145, 219, 440, 478.

the constituency campaign." And "the diminution of the relevance of local campaigning has been paralleled by the decline of local party political activity."[6]

V. O. Key, writing of the new media developments' impact on American politics, stated as early as 1958 that to "an extent startling in its degree in some jurisdictions the doorbell ringers [local party workers] have lost their function of mobilizing the vote to public relations experts, to the specialists in radio and television, and others who deal in mass communications."[7] In the United States, however, the rise of the new technology has not been accompanied by a shift of power to the national party leaders. Congressional candidates are increasingly responsible for their own nomination and election,[8] and there is no uniformity in their use of radio and television. Since they purchase their own radio and TV time, candidates in large urban centers find the cost prohibitive and telecasts of doubtful value. Each major New York City telecast, for example, can be heard by audiences of 8 million persons in fifteen or sixteen congressional districts. The cost is enormous, but no more than 6 or 7 percent of the audience is in any single congressman's district. By contrast, in smaller cities that constitute a single congressional district, a telecast is relatively inexpensive, and it is relevant to virtually the entire adult audience. In these districts even poorly financed candidates may spend at least some money for television.

The United States is not the only highly industrialized nation where television is of limited value in legislative campaigns. In Japan the ratio of receivers to population is roughly one to four; yet the nation's unusual election rules, which allow each voter to cast a ballot for only one candidate in a multimember district, combine with the rigidly regulated, highly stylized campaigns and the candidates' dependence on the support of factional leaders to minimize the importance of the few minutes allotted each candidate on television.[9]

In most developed countries with proportional representation (PR) systems, television has reduced the importance of mass organizations but has not much affected the distribution of power between a

---

[6] David Butler and Dennis Kavanagh, *The British General Election of February 1974* (New York: St. Martin's Press, 1974), p. 201.

[7] V. O. Key, Jr., *Politics, Parties, and Pressure Groups*, 5th ed. (New York: Thomas Y. Crowell Co., 1958), p. 375.

[8] Thomas E. Mann, *Unsafe at Any Margin* (Washington D.C.: American Enterprise Institute, 1979), passim.

[9] Gerald L. Curtis, *Election Campaigning Japanese Style* (New York and London: Columbia University Press, 1971), pp. 217-18. These two pages provide the only reference to television in a very interesting and complete study of a Japanese campaign for a Diet seat.

party's central organization and its local branches. Power had become centralized long before television.

Indeed, however different the new technological era feels to those who remember politics in the old days, E. J. Dionne may be right when he argues that "the most important fact is that radio, television, market research have *not* fundamentally changed the nature of politics in Western democracies. They have changed the methods of politics, and even these have not changed so radically as many would contend."[10] Whatever the importance of these changes for the political campaigns in some countries, it is probably true that the basic character of campaigns today differs from country to country and from electoral system to electoral system in many of the same ways and to about the same extent as it did in 1930. The length of campaigns, the division of campaign responsibilities between national and constituency parties, and the problems of campaign strategy are still primarily influenced by electoral laws and party systems rather than by technological developments. The new technology has tended to accentuate existing institutional relations rather than sharply change them. It is to some of these basic, often unchanged characteristics of campaigns that we now turn.

The Length of Campaigns

The time between elections is determined by law and custom. Constitutions or basic laws fix the dates for elections in about one-fourth of the countries covered in this volume. The United States, the three Latin American countries (all with presidential systems), and Norway are in that group. In Britain and most countries following the Westminster model, the prime minister may ask for dissolution of the parliament and new elections at any time during the members' term. A vote of no confidence can bring down a minority government in most parliamentary countries, while in a few the president may dissolve the legislature. In New Zealand the prime minister has the power to call for dissolution and elections but very rarely does so; all nine elections since 1951 have been on the last Saturday in November of every third year.

There are two campaigns in virtually all democratic societies. The weeks just prior to polling day usually constitute the legally recognized, official, or formal campaign period when parties put forth their

---

[10] E. J. Dionne, "What Technology Has Not Changed: Continuity and Localism in British Politics," in Louis Maisel, ed., *Changing Campaign Techniques: Elections and Values in Contemporary Democracies* (Beverly Hills and London: Sage Publications, 1976), p. 243.

maximum effort to mobilize supporters, convince the undecided, and perhaps convert some waverers in the ranks of the opposition. It is the period when the media coverage is greatest, when free radio and television time is given to candidates and party leaders in some countries, and when some governments help finance election efforts while others require the parties to account for their financial receipts and expenditures. There is also an extended campaign that is largely unrecognized by law. It is less frenetic and less publicized, but its impact on the election's outcome may be at least as great as that of the official campaign.

French law defines the official National Assembly campaign as the three weeks before the first stage of the two-step election process and the week before the second.[11] The United Kingdom provides for a minimum campaign period of seventeen days after dissolution of the House of Commons not counting Sundays, bank holidays, or the Easter or Christmas breaks.[12] After Labour's defeat in the House of Commons in 1979, James Callaghan announced on March 29 that April 7 was to be the date of dissolution and May 3 would be polling day. The parties thus actually had thirty-seven days for electioneering, although Margaret Thatcher waited until April 16, Easter Monday, to begin her Conservative campaign.[13] The British elections of February and October 1974 were called only three weeks before balloting.

Of the countries included in this study, Venezuela has the longest campaign. The law (adopted to *reduce* the length of campaigns) requires that notice of the election be given six to eight months before it is scheduled, on a Sunday during the first fortnight in December of every fifth year.[14] The December 3, 1978, election was officially announced on April 1. The incumbent Democratic Action party had held its intraparty nominating election ten months earlier, in June 1977, and with one exception, the other Venezuelan parties had selected their candidates before the end of the summer of 1977. All of the parties had been campaigning for at least seven months by the time the election date was announced. Despite all this electioneering, technically the campaign included only the last three weeks before the election.

Campaigns in most democracies are shorter than those in Venezuela but longer than those in France or Britain. Canadian rules re-

---

[11] The 1978 campaign officially opened February 20 for elections on March 12 and 19. *Facts on File*, March 3, 1980, p. 148.

[12] *Conduct of Parliamentary Elections*, 7th ed. (London: British Labour Party, 1969), pp. 80-81.

[13] In 1979 the period from March 29 to May 3 included four Sundays and the Easter break.

[14] Article 92, *Ley orgánica del sufragio* (Caracas: Consejo Supremo Electoral, 1978), p. 46.

quire that voter lists be established between the dissolution of the legislature and polling day, which allows roughly eight weeks to set up the register and conduct the campaign. Prime Minister Pierre Elliott Trudeau announced the dissolution of Parliament on March 26, 1979, and named May 22 election day. Prime Minister Joseph Clark announced the next dissolution on December 14, 1979, and set February 18, 1980, for the election.[15] In both instances the campaigns of the three major parties began immediately after the prime minister's announcement. Free television and radio time for Canadian parties is confined to the four weeks before polling.

German parties select their candidates, hold conventions, and issue their manifestoes by June of election years. They then suspend their activities until the intensive or "hot" phase of the campaign begins, some six weeks prior to the October elections. President Adolfo Suárez met the Spanish requirement of sixty days between dissolution of the Cortes and the election when he announced the dissolution on December 29, 1978, and set March 1, 1979, as the date for the country's second democratic election in less than two years. All of the parties campaigned hard from the day of the announcement, but free radio and television were available to them only during the final three weeks before the polling day.[16]

Israeli law defines several official campaign-related periods. During the 150 days prior to an election, radio and television "broadcasters are required to scrutinize their schedules to see whether any program gives undue advantage to a particular party." (In 1977 that period was shortened by eighteen days because legislators voted to dissolve the Knesset on January 5 and to hold the election May 17.) In the thirty days immediately before the election no Israeli candidate can be seen on television except during a party's allotted free time or in its advertisements. Television news reports can describe their activities, but no candidate, not even the prime minister, can be seen on the TV screen. Golda Meir's visit to the United States in 1973 was reported, but no pictures of her activities were broadcast. Scenes of the 1977 Independence Day celebrations were televised—with the candidates blotted out. During the final three weeks before the election, free radio and television time is allocated to the parties.[17]

---

15 Howard R. Penniman, ed., *Canada at the Polls, 1979 and 1980* (Washington, D.C.: American Enterprise Institute, forthcoming).

16 Howard R. Penniman, ed., *Spain at the Polls: The Cortes Elections of 1977 and 1979* (Washington, D.C.: American Enterprise Institute, forthcoming).

17 Judith Elizur and Elihu Katz, "The Media in the Israeli Elections of 1977," in Howard R. Penniman, ed., *Israel at the Polls: The Knesset Elections of 1977* (Washington, D.C.: American Enterprise Institute, 1979), pp. 228-29.

The period between dissolution and elections in India varies considerably. In 1977 Prime Minister Indira Ghandi surprised friends and critics of her regime when she called for the dissolution of the Lok Sabha on January 19 and set an election for March 16–20. By contrast, in 1979 the Lok Sabha was dissolved on August 22 and President Neelam Sanjiva Reddy insisted that new elections would be held within three months. They finally took place on January 3–6, 1980.[18]

American national law does not specify a uniform length for congressional election campaigns. They are presumed to begin after the nomination of candidates, which occurs at times set by each of the fifty states. Campaigns for a party's presidential nomination officially begin when a candidate formally names his campaign committee. The Federal Elections Commission (FEC) will match certain funds raised by a candidate's committee if the money is raised after January of the year prior to the election, that is, fourteen months before the first primary election, in New Hampshire, and twenty-two months before the election. Payment of matching FEC funds begins January 1 of the election year.[19] Presidential campaigns, which are fully funded by the national treasury, officially begin after the major party conventions in midsummer every fourth year. From that time until after the election, presidential candidates' appearances on television are limited to news broadcasts, programs paid for by the parties, and debates arranged between the major party nominees, as in 1960 and 1976.

Campaigns officially end on election eve in most countries whose political practices generally follow the British model, but Australian radio and television campaigns end at midnight on the Wednesday before the Saturday elections, and in Canada advertising in *all* media ceases two days before elections. In France and most other Continental countries, electioneering stops at midnight on the Friday before election Sunday. In Colombia a week separates the end of campaigns and the balloting—the longest period of prepolling quiet in any modern democracy. The week before the June 1978 election may have reduced the unusually high level of violence that had plagued the country for more than three months, but it may also have contributed to the abstention of 60 percent of eligible Colombian voters on election day.[20]

[18] *Facts on File*, January 18, 1977, p. 45, and January 10, 1980, p. 11. For a discussion of the 1977 election, see Myron Weiner, *India at the Polls: The Parliamentary Elections of 1977* (Washington, D.C.: American Enterprise Institute, 1978). A book by the same author on the 1980 Indian election is forthcoming.

[19] *Congressional Quarterly Weekly Reports*, November 10, 1979, p. 2529, published the amounts received by ten Republican and two Democratic candidates by October 1, 1979. Several had received more than $2 million by that date.

[20] *Facts on File*, May 5, 1978, p. 413. For a detailed discussion of the 1978 Colombian elections, see José Sorzano, *Colombia at the Polls* (Washington, D.C.: American Enterprise Institute, forthcoming).

The Extended Campaign. The long, largely unregulated, unofficial campaign is a period of continuing work by party organizations and candidates. Thomas E. Mann, after studying elections in many American congressional districts, concluded that "the outcomes of most congressional elections are determined well before the onset of active [official] campaigning." Official campaigns are not wasted effort, but electoral success often requires spending much time, energy, and money long before the few weeks of the formal campaign.[21] David B. Truman argued that "elections are not likely to be understood until they are studied as a continuous process in which the [official] campaign and balloting are at most climaxes."[22] He, too, was speaking of American elections, but his generalization applies almost equally to other democracies.

Roland Cayrol says that in 1978 in France "the unofficial campaign was longer and more intense than ever before. Indeed, it was interminable. It might even be said to have begun as early as May 1974 immediately after the presidential election with Valéry Giscard d'Estaing's narrow victory (50.8 percent to 49.2 percent) over the leftist candidate François Mitterrand."[23] The French Communist party (PCF), the Socialist party, and the Leftist Radicals spent the better part of four years working out the terms of an alliance that they hoped would finally gain them control of the National Assembly—to no avail. Writing of the same elections, Jean Charlot states, "The climax of the Gaullists' campaign was an enormous rally held in Paris at the Porte de Pantin on Saturday, February 11—'the most enormous rally ever organized in Paris by a political party,' according to *Le Monde*."[24] The "climax" by this account occurred nine days before the official campaign began.

Michael Pinto-Duschinsky in a section titled "The Permanent Campaign" says that in Britain "campaigning is almost continuous between general elections." Because the prime minister can call an election at any time during the five-year term, "party organizations— national and local—must be in a semipermanent state of readiness."

---

21 Mann, *Unsafe at Any Margin*, p. 79.

22 Quoted in Austin Ranney and Willmoore Kendall, *Democracy and the American Party System* (New York: Harcourt, Brace and Co., 1956), p. 51.

23 Roland Cayrol, "The Mass Media and the Electoral Campaign," in Howard R. Penniman, ed., *The French National Assembly Elections of 1978* (Washington, D.C.: American Enterprise Institute, 1980), pp. 144-45.

24 Jean Charlot, "The Majority," in Penniman, *French National Assembly Elections*, p. 100. Two pages earlier it was noted that Jacques Chirac "by the beginning of March 1978 had traveled 50,000 kilometers in seventy-eight departments, had held sixty-nine rallies with average audiences of 5,000-6,000, had made 292 speeches and met local officials in 112 meetings."

The fact that "four-fifths of British voters [make] up their minds" before the official campaign actually starts is another reason the parties must engage in continuous electioneering.[25] As noted earlier, even nations with fixed elections, parties, and candidates campaign from one election to the next.

The Roles of National and Constituency Parties

A nation's electoral system and its candidate selection procedures, whether established by parties or by government, determine in large measure the respective roles played by most national and constituency party organizations in national legislative campaigns. Communist and other authoritarian parties generally insist upon highly centralized control, whatever the electoral system within which they operate, in order to ensure rigid discipline and ideological purity. Authoritarian parties aside, when national leaders choose definitive lists in proportional representation systems, the likelihood of centralized control of the campaign is greatly enhanced.

Israel's PR system with definitive lists elected from a single national 120-member district offers an excellent example of centralized control. With few exceptions, national party leaders determine the candidates and their places on the party list and completely control the campaigns. For example, the Labor party, which dominated Israeli politics for fifty years prior to its defeat in 1977, traditionally appointed a small committee of its major leaders or their representatives to present a candidate list for the Central Committee's consideration. Myron J. Aronoff states that he was unable to "find a single case in which the list proposed by the nominating committee was not accepted" by the ruling Central Committee.[26] It is not surprising then that in 1977 as in previous years a few national party leaders controlled the campaign decisions, received and spent the campaign funds, and arranged the debate between Labor leader Shimon Peres and Menachem Begin of Likud.

While central party headquarters in many democracies employing party list systems match or approach the tightly centralized control of campaigns found in Israel, there are at least two structural arrangements found in some other PR systems that contribute to somewhat

[25] Michael Pinto-Duschinsky, "The Conservative Campaign: New Techniques versus Old," in Howard R. Penniman, ed., *Britain at the Polls: The Parliamentary Elections of 1974* (Washington, D.C.: American Enterprise Institute, 1975), pp. 89-90.

[26] Aronoff, "The Decline of the Israeli Labor Party: Causes and Significance," in Penniman, *Israel at the Polls*, pp. 125-29.

looser national party control. First, PR countries other than Israel and the Netherlands have more than one district. In the late 1970s the number of districts in European and Latin American PR countries ranged from nine in Austria to fifty-six in Greece. Since each district has its own list of candidates for each party, small districts increase the likelihood that some of the candidates will be local; they also enhance the role of local parties in campaigns. Second, in countries where voters may express an effective preference among the candidates on a party's list, their candidates campaign for personal support.

Belgium, Denmark, Finland, Greece, Italy, and Switzerland are among the countries where voters, after choosing a party slate, may express preferences among the candidates that may determine which of them will win seats in the national legislature. In Belgium, Denmark, and Finland voters may cast only one "preference vote"; Greek voters may express two preferences, while voters in Italy may indicate three or four choices depending on district size, and in Switzerland they may even write a ballot of their own.[27] The voters' preferences frequently coincide with the order originally established by the party, but they alter it often enough that preference voting encourages candidates within the same party to compete against each other.

In Rome, where roughly fifty seats are at stake, a candidate may advertise his name and its place on his party's list in the press, on posters, and on voter guide cards to ask for voter support. He often links his name with that of the leader or important members of the party.[28] In a small, eight-member constituency in Piraeus, in Greece, Amalia-Maria (Melina) Mercouri of *Never on Sunday* fame had second place on the Panhellenic Socialist Union (PASOK) list in the 1977 election. She "conducted a grass-roots preelection campaign by marching through the meat and vegetable markets, talking with dockers and embracing black-dressed old women." These people, she said, had helped her "cultural career" a decade earlier and "have now launched my political career. I will do everything I can to serve them." Mercouri received far more preference votes than any other PASOK candidate in Piraeus (72 percent of them from women). These preference votes lifted her to first place among the PASOK winners.[29]

---

[27] Swiss voters are given a remarkable number of choices. They may simply cross out some names on their party list or they may replace those names with names from different party lists or give a second vote to one or more preferred candidates. They may also make up their own list of candidates on blank ballots included in the packets mailed to their homes.

[28] Douglas Wertman, "The Italian Electoral Process: The Elections of June 1976," in Howard R. Penniman, ed., *Italy at the Polls: The Parliamentary Elections of 1976* (Washington, D.C.: American Enterprise Institute, 1977), p. 48.

[29] Translations on Western Europe, *Greece: The Election of November 1977—*

Whether the single-transferable-vote system encourages intra-party competition depends very largely on the role played by the parties in guiding voter decisions. In Australia each party makes clear the order it prefers and urges supporters to follow it.[30] In Ireland, by contrast, neither the national nor the constituency party organizations express a preference among their candidates. As a result, every candidate stresses his ability to aid his district—and in 1977 "thirteen of the thirty-two defeated deputies lost their seats to party colleagues."[31] Although much Irish campaigning is local, the national party headquarters produce and distribute leaflets and other propaganda to candidates for their use. Unfortunately, according to Basil Chubb, candidates have often "found the centrally prepared material more embarrassing than helpful in their districts."[32]

There is no uniformity in the roles of national and constituency parties in single-member-district countries. France, where a two-election majority system is combined with single-member districts, has seen major changes in the roles of the two levels of the parties since 1958. During the early days of the Fifth Republic, all except the authoritarian parties were candidate and constituency centered. A candidate and his substitute ("officially—if infelicitously—known as *remplaçant éventuel*"), who often represented different interests within the district, usually campaigned quite independently of the national party. At least one Gaullist candidate in 1958 refused to withdraw from the second election in spite of party orders to do so. The 1958 election "was, in fact, a candidates' campaign," and it "fell heavily on the candidates themselves. Only the Socialists and Communists, and more rarely the Gaullists and MRP, boasted significant local organizations—though even they could call on only small numbers for help."[33]

Facts, Figures and Commentary (Arlington, Virginia: U.S. Joint Publications Research Service, 1978), pp. 83 and 134, for the original PASOK list and the order of winning candidates. See *Athens News*, November 22, 1977, for the quotations on the Mercouri campaign.

[30] Howard R. Penniman, ed., *The Australian National Elections of 1977* (Washington, D.C., and Canberra: American Enterprise Institute, 1979), appendix B, pp. 347-50, reproduces advertisements and "How-to-Vote cards" prepared by the parties to guide their supporters.

[31] Basil Chubb, "The Electoral System," in Howard R. Penniman, ed., *Ireland at the Polls: The Dáil Elections of 1977* (Washington, D.C.: American Enterprise Institute, 1978), p. 31.

[32] Chubb, "Ireland, 1957," in David E. Butler, ed., *Elections Abroad* (London: Macmillan, 1958), p. 98. For a discussion of the role of the national party and the candidates, see also pp. 187, 196-97.

[33] Philip M. Williams and Martin Harrison, "France, 1958," in Butler, *Elections Abroad*, pp. 38, 57-58. For a fascinating detailed description of campaigning in constituencies around the nation, see pp. 33-72; for an account of the campaigns in the Somme and Vienne, by Jean Blondel and Merlin Thomas, see pp. 91-118 in the same volume.

By 1978, the parties that made up the two major coalitions competing for control of the National Assembly were much more firmly disciplined, national television and radio played a greater role in informing the public, and national issues had greater importance. Candidates still held meetings and discussed their constituents' problems, but a larger share of responsibility for the campaigns had shifted to national party headquarters.[34]

We noted earlier the views expressed by Butler and Kavanagh and shared by most students of British politics that the national party leaders hold the dominant position in British campaigns. This was not always so. Before 1868, when William Gladstone campaigned widely in the country, all candidates including the prime minister stayed strictly within their own districts.[35] Television, computerized voting lists, and public opinion polling have facilitated centralization and played a role in the 30 percent decline in party membership between 1952 and 1972; during the same period, the number of constituency meetings also declined and attendance fell. There are some observers, however, who agree with many members of Parliament that local campaigning and "nursing" one's constituency may still bring victory in a close election.[36]

Canadian elections follow the British model, but campaigns remain rather decentralized.[37] Control of Australian campaigns for the House of Representatives, whose members are elected from single-member districts with alternative voting, have become more and more centralized.[38] Canada and Australia are large countries with federal

---

[34] Charlot, "The Majority," and Georges Lavau and Janine Mossuz-Lavau, "The Union of the Left's Defeat: Suicide or Congenital Weakness?" in Penniman, *French National Assembly Elections*, p. 38-143.

[35] H. J. Hanham, *Elections and Party Management: Politics in the Time of Disraeli and Gladstone* (London: Longmans, 1959), p. 202. A critic of this innovation referred to it as "a sort of Ministerial Agitation which might have developed into an influence of terrorism."

[36] Dionne, "What Technology Has Not Changed," pp. 243-71, tends to emphasize the exceptions and so suggests that the efforts of the candidate and the constituency parties are sometimes important to the results. See also Butler and Kavanagh, *British General Election of 1974*, pp. 201-6 and 248-49. The same volume includes an appendix that states that "in special circumstances the British electorate is now more willing to vote for a person than a party" (p. 335).

[37] Stephen Clarkson, "Pierre Trudeau and the Liberal Party: the Jockey and the Horse," George Perlin, "The Progressive Conservative Party in the Election of 1974," and Jo Surich, "Purists and Pragmatists: Canadian Democratic Socialism at the Crossroads," in Howard R. Penniman, ed., *Canada at the Polls: The General Election of 1974* (Washington, D.C.: American Enterprise Institute, 1975), pp. 77-89, 115-16, and 135-39.

[38] Michelle Grattan, "The Liberal Party," in Howard R. Penniman, ed., *Australia at the Polls: The National Elections of 1975* (Washington, D.C.: American Enterprise Institute, 1977), pp. 131-40.

systems, relatively large populations, and a British background; yet the degree of campaign centralization is very different in the two.

If the Israeli system provides the extreme example of highly centralized control of parties and electoral campaigns, the United States offers the extreme example of national party impotence, constituency orientation, and candidate-dominated campaigns for the House of Representatives. State laws help make the legislators almost completely independent of their party, requiring that nominees for Congress be selected in state-administered primary elections where voters who assert that they are Republicans but pay no dues and have no obligations to the organization name the Republican candidates, while persons who say they are Democrats choose the Democratic candidates. In some states party organizations are even forbidden to express a preference among the persons seeking to use the party label in the general election. And at no stage of the process is the approval of national, state, or local party leaders required for a nominee to carry the party designation. This separation is encouraged by the presidential campaign financing rule that money spent on a joint appearance of presidential and congressional candidates may be charged against the president's limited budget.

The candidate builds his own organization to secure the nomination and relies on it in his general election campaign. If he publicly opposes the election of the presidential nominee of his party, he may be excluded from his party's caucus in Congress, but his right to the party label is in no way affected as long as his constituents have supported his candidacy in the primary. Some congressmen have ensured their continuance in Washington precisely by refusing to support the policies of the national party. The late Senator Harry F. Byrd, a conservative Democrat from Virginia, maintained a "golden silence" about his preferences among the presidential candidates of the major parties. In 1960, Byrd, silent as ever, allowed others to support his own candidacy for president and received fourteen Democratic electoral votes from Mississippi and Alabama that might otherwise have gone to his party's nominee, John F. Kennedy; yet he was in no way chastised by his party colleagues in the Senate, where he remained chairman of the powerful Finance Committee until his death in 1965.

Campaign Strategies

Permanent campaigning forces parties to be constantly alert for electoral opportunities and pitfalls. Generally speaking the party or coalition in power has opportunities in two areas that are unavailable to the opposition: it can enact electoral rules that favor its reelection, and

119

it can write substantive legislation or take executive action that may draw public approval and so presumably strengthen its position among the voters. In a third area, both government and opposition must make strategic decisions: they must design their actual campaigns, selecting issues, determining which votes to seek, building electoral alliances, and so on. We will consider the three strategic areas separately.

Electoral Rules. It is less common than in the past for legislative majorities in single-member-district countries to look on their own electoral success as the sole relevant criterion for drawing district boundaries. This simple but often successful stratagem is no longer available in countries where laws provide that redistricting be done by a nonpartisan or bipartisan boundary commission that is guided by other criteria. Even so, a government is not powerless to protect its interests—or to make changes it thinks will protect them. In 1970 British Prime Minister Harold Wilson postponed the effective date of the changes the boundary commission had proposed in 1969 because he felt they favored the Conservatives. This decision, though it preserved "many of the decaying constituencies" that "were largely Labour strongholds," [39] did not prevent the Conservative party from winning a clear majority in the House of Commons—and the Conservatives lost in both 1974 elections when the presumably favorable new boundaries were in force.

In 1974 the Fine Gael-Labour government of Ireland redrew a number of the Dublin area districts, replacing four-member districts with an increased number of three-member districts in the hope of gaining a half-dozen extra seats in the Dáil. This move was in the tradition of earlier governments, which had opted for smaller constituencies to make it "easier for a party which may be called upon to shoulder the responsibility of government to get sufficient seats to enable them to undertake that task with adequate parliamentary support." [40] Unfortunately from the government's point of view, the new districts helped Fianna Fáil to win a record-breaking majority in the 1977 elections.

---

[39] S. E. Finer, *The Changing British Party System, 1945-1979* (Washington, D.C.: American Enterprise Institute, 1980), pp. 34-36. No government has reduced the overrepresentation of Scotland and Wales (Finer calls the latter "Labour's rotten borough") in Parliament or increased the representation of Northern Ireland.

[40] *Dáil Debates*, vol. 108 (October 23, 1947), col. 924, quoted in Chubb, "The Electoral System," p. 33.

West Germany changed its election rules in 1953 to increase the threshold for representation in the Bundestag from 5 percent of the vote in a *Land* election to 5 percent of the vote in the entire country. The change reduced the number of parties represented from eleven after the 1949 election to only three in the elections since 1961. Indeed, there is a continuing possibility that the Free Democratic party may drop below the required minimum, thus creating a two-party system in spite of PR.[41]

A British Labour government could correctly claim to be making the suffrage more democratic while at the same time it improved its electoral chances when in 1949 Parliament abolished the plural voting privileges of university graduates and businessmen—two groups that were predominantly Conservative. Both had been entitled to vote as citizens, but the former had also voted in university constituencies and the latter in their places of business.[42]

No nation has witnessed more changes of electoral rules than France, where, Peter Campbell argues, "the electoral system has been treated as a weapon in the struggle between different political camps and between social forces for the control of the state and society." Since 1789 "only once has an electoral system survived as long as thirty consecutive years (1889–1919)."[43] At no other time from the beginning of the Third Republic in 1871 until the downfall of the Fourth Republic in 1958 did any system last even twelve years. During the Cold War period, a center government sought to weaken the Communist party on the left and the Gaullists on the right. To obtain this goal, the center parties enacted two systems of proportional representation. One applied to the eight constituencies of the Paris region where the PCF and the Gaullists both had considerable strength, while the other included all the remaining constituencies of France. In region one, the largest-remainder PR system was used to give small center

---

[41] Gerhard Loewenberg, "The Development of the German Party System," in Karl H. Cerny, ed., *Germany at the Polls: The Bundestag Election of 1976* (Washington, D.C.: American Enterprise Institute, 1978), p. 6. The presence of an environmental party in the 1980 campaign once more raised the question whether the FDP could win the required 5 percent of the vote. As it turned out, the FDP rose to 10.6 percent of the vote, and the environmentalists took only 1.5 percent.

[42] Finer, *Changing British Party System*, pp. 32-33.

[43] Peter Campbell, *French Electoral Systems and the Elections since 1789*, 2d ed. (Hamden, Conn.: Archon Books, 1972), p. 17. Phaedo Vegleris, "Greek Electoral Law," in Howard R. Penniman ed., *Greece at the Polls: The Parliamentary Elections of 1977* (Washington D.C.: American Enterprise Institute, forthcoming), states that in modern Greece no two consecutive elections have been conducted under the same electoral law. Greece, therefore, may rival France as the nation to change its electoral rules most frequently.

parties a chance to pick up at least a few marginal seats. Where center parties were strong, in region two, the rules gave them a chance to win big victories by providing that any party or coalition receiving as much as 50 percent of the vote in a department would win all of the seats— and shut out the PCF and the Gaullists in the area where they were weak. If no party or alliance received a majority of the votes, the seats were distributed under the system of highest averages, which still aided the larger center parties. In addition, the rules stated that lists winning less than 5 percent of the votes received no seats. Campbell estimates that this 1951 law "deprived the Communists of 71 seats and the RPF [Gaullists] of 26 seats" that they would have received under the old law.[44]

The Fifth Republic that de Gaulle established in 1958 returned to a two-round majority, single-member-district system. Since that date, the rules for gaining a place in the runoff election have been refined to require an increased share of the first-round vote.[45] As a result, the second round has become a series of duels between candidates of the left and of the center-right. This is the situation Charles de Gaulle long sought, believing that a majority of the French voters would never elect a coalition including the PCF. His prediction has held up for more than twenty years even in several close presidential and legislative elections.[46]

Public Policy Strategy. Ivor Crewe says that "rising living standards, full employment, and price stability are the holy grail of all governments,"[47] and David Butler and Donald E. Stokes tell us that politicians know the voters hold governments accountable "for good and bad times," a fact that "has loomed large in the minds of modern

---

[44] Campbell, *French Electoral Systems*, pp. 113-23. A somewhat comparable legal effort was made in Italy in 1953 when a new electoral law provided that if a party received 50 percent of the national vote, it would be given 65 percent of the legislative seats. The Christian Democratic party (DC) received 49.85 percent; thus it failed to profit from the rule, which was then repealed.

[45] In 1958 the law required that a candidate receive at least 5 percent of the votes cast to compete in the second round. Today a candidate must receive 12.5 percent of the number of registered voters. In some constituencies on the Left Bank in Paris, where the turnout is sometimes less than 50 percent, the current 12.5 percent threshold could require 25 to 30 percent of the votes cast.

[46] In 1974 Valéry Giscard d'Estaing won with a margin of only 1.6 percentage points, and in the 1978 legislative election the margin on the "decisive ballot" (the first ballot if it produced a winner; in other cases the second ballot) was 2.7 percentage points. See Charlot, "The Majority," p. 105.

[47] Ivor Crewe, "Why the Conservatives Won," in Howard R. Penniman, ed., *Britain at the Polls, 1979: A Study of the General Election* (Washington, D.C.: American Enterprise Institute, 1980).

prime ministers as they ponder on the timing of dissolution."[48] Whether election dates are fixed or flexible, Edward R. Tufte suggests that incumbents use the powers of their office to increase disposable income in election years as the best assurance of voter support. In nineteen of the twenty-seven countries whose policies he examined, he found "short run acceleration in real disposable income per capita [was] more likely to occur in election years than in years without elections."[49]

Whenever possible, unpopular decisions needed to fight inflation are made while the next election is still far off. None of the seven deflationary decisions in Israel between 1953 and 1973 was made within eighteen months of the next election. The eighth deflation was in 1974, three years prior to Labor's losing election of 1977,[50] and the ninth deflation, in 1980, will maintain the Israeli record unless the Begin government is unexpectedly defeated on a confidence vote. Margaret Thatcher's Conservative government enacted its relatively tough antiinflation program immediately upon assuming office. If the program succeeds, the odious early policies will be forgotten by the time the 1984 elections come round.

Incumbents do not confine their election-related policy moves to economic matters. George F. Will notes a European complaint "that during American presidential campaigns, the tail of electoral politics wags the dog of statecraft."[51] President Jimmy Carter favored American voters just before the 1980 primary election days with special news of his administration's efforts to free diplomatic personnel held hostage in Iran. Will suggests that "Valéry Giscard d'Estaing's meeting with Leonid Brezhnev in Warsaw in May 1980 was a meeting related less to Giscard's role as interlocutor than his role as candidate for reelection in 1981."[52]

Only the majority can make policy. The opposition is thus severely handicapped in election years, unless one accepts the view of an Australian journalist who argues that "once a party wins office . . . it starts losing support. It is forced by circumstances to take decisions that are unpopular, to offend powerful interests and injure voters. All

---

[48] Quoted in Edward R. Tufte, *Political Control of the Economy* (Princeton: Princeton University Press, 1978), p. 8. While prime ministers who possess the power to determine the timing of the next election have an advantage over governments whose election dates are fixed by law or custom, it is, of course, true that misjudgments may hurt their chances of victory.

[49] Tufte, *Political Control*, p. 11.

[50] Ibid., p. 13.

[51] *Washington Post*, June 1, 1980.

[52] Ibid.

that an opposition need do ... is run after the bus of government policy picking up and comforting the passengers as they fall out when it hits bumps in the road and takes corners too tightly." The description is colorful, but Colin A. Hughes correctly comments that it is an oversimplification. Only major accidents to the public policy bus are likely to produce votes for the opposition. Depressions, inflation, and unemployment are the foundations of opposition victories. And the opposition cannot force a government into these catastrophes.[53]

Strategy during the Campaign. Strategic problems during campaigns generally increase in complexity as the number of "relevant" parties increases.[54] Giovanni Sartori argues that a party is relevant if it has "coalition [or] blackmail potential." He notes that Italy's Republican party meets the criteria, though it has seldom received much more than 2 percent of the popular vote and four to six parliamentary seats, because it has been part of ruling coalitions.[55] Similarly, the tiny religious·Poalie Agudat Israel party has been part of governments in recent years although it has received no more than 2 percent of the popular vote and one or two seats in the Knesset.

New Zealand and the United States are the only democracies where two parties have consistently divided more than 98 percent of the seats in the national legislature in the last thirty years.[56] While the ideological or issue differences separating New Zealand's National and Labour parties are somewhat greater than those that divide the major American parties, all four have the characteristics of catchall parties. Their campaigns emphasize not their philosophical positions but their practical ability to solve economic, social, and foreign problems. The incumbent party justifies its policies as forwarding the country's welfare at the same time that it reminds its own voters that

---

[53] Colin A. Hughes, "The Case of the Arrested Pendulum," in Penniman, *Australian National Elections of 1977*, pp. 331-32.

[54] A stable consociational system such as we find in Switzerland may be an exception to this rule. The high level of party cooperation, the number of issues that are decided by referendum rather than parliamentary action, and the low-key campaigns may minimize the strategic problems. The same situation does not hold for all consociational political systems.

[55] See Giovanni Sartori, *Parties and Party Systems: A Framework for Analysis* (London: Cambridge University Press, 1976), pp. 121-215, for a discussion of relevance and coalition or blackmail potential.

[56] In New Zealand a Social Credit candidate won a by-election in 1977 and kept the seat in 1978. In New York state the Liberal and Conservative parties are satellites of the Democratic and Republican parties. Neither has ever won a seat in the House of Representatives; whether they support or refuse to support Democratic and Republican candidates has affected the outcome of major party contests.

it is supporting their interests. Opponents highlight the unsolved problems facing the nation while suggesting somewhat different, often vague, alternative means of curing the country's ills—without, of course, increasing taxes.[57]

The addition of a third party significantly complicates campaign strategy in a normally two-party system. Although Liberal party candidates won only eight English seats in the House of Commons in 1979, the party's presence in a majority of the constituencies of England changed campaigns in many districts very considerably. The Liberal leadership entered many unwinnable races in order to build up its share of the total national vote and give the party greater credence as a serious national contestant. This, they felt, was worth the loss of deposits in constituencies where party candidates failed to win the required minimum.

The Liberal presence forced both major parties not only to battle each other directly but also to try to persuade potential Liberal voters not to cast a "wasted vote" for a party that could not win. At the same time, there is some evidence that supporters of the smaller of the two major parties in a constituency sometimes cast "strategic" or "tactical" votes for the Liberal candidate if his chances of winning are better than those of the voters' preferred party.[58]

A brief examination of two quite different medium-sized parties, in the multiparty systems of Italy and Israel, may illustrate the extent of the strategic planning problem facing parties in some PR systems. The Italian Socialist party (PSI) is the third largest party in Italy. It received as much as 20.7 percent of the vote in the immediate post-war years but since 1972 has been limited to slightly less than 10 percent of the national vote. The Communist party (PCI) has become the leading party of the left, receiving as much as 34.2 percent of the popular vote in 1976[59] before dropping back to 30.2 percent in 1979. During the past thirty years the PSI has split frequently over ideological and strategic issues, often including the party's relations with the two big parties, the PCI to its left and the ruling Christian Democrats to its right. Studies of the political attitudes of Italian voters show that more Italians are inclined to support socialist programs than vote

[57] See Ranney and Kendall, *Democracy and the American Party System*, pp. 121-25, for a discussion of strategies of major American parties.

[58] See Michael Steed, "The Results Analyzed," in Butler and Kavanagh, *The British General Election of February 1974*, pp. 317-21. See also Bruce E. Cain, "Strategic Voting in Britain," *American Journal of Political Science* (August 1978), pp. 639-55.

[59] Joseph LaPalombara, "Italian Elections as Hobson's Choice," in Penniman, *Italy at the Polls*, p. 11.

for Socialist party candidates in elections.[60] The PSI lacks many of the advantages of the PCI, including its supporting network of unions and other organizations. In 1979, when the PCI lost votes in a national election for the first time since World War II, the dissidents went not to the Socialist party but to the Radical party, which has been described as a party of the "neobourgeoisie," supporting "divorce, abortion, women's rights, homosexuals, safe energy, disarmament and conscientious objectors."[61] The PSI can expect to recruit no supporters from the Christian Democrats or the far right; it must compete strictly within the general socialist area, along with a variety of parties that would support a government of the left if one should come to power. The PSI seeks to win over PCI supporters in the name of democratic socialism. At the same time, it insists that the PCI be brought into any coalition led by the Christian Democrats in order to legitimize a left government in the future. Yet the PSI has been criticized by others on the left for its willingness on occasion to support the DC government. The PSI leaders have yet to find solutions to the multitude of strategic problems their party faces.

The Democratic Movement for Change (DMC) in Israel faces an entirely different but almost equally complex set of strategic problems. Dissidents from the ruling Labor Alignment formed the Democratic Movement for Change not long before the Israeli elections of May 1977.[62] The founders included ambitious older Labor members who had served in the Knesset but had never gained the recognition they felt they deserved, as well as younger intellectual dissidents who wished to reform Labor to make it more internally democratic and more committed to "just" principles and less to the mundane patronage politics which they felt dominated the leadership of the party.

DMC members of whatever ilk all expected Labor to win a plurality in the May elections and confidently anticipated that the Labor leadership would have to invite them into the new Labor government. They also expected to be in a more powerful negotiating position as an independent party than as lesser members of the Labor Alignment. Some expected good cabinet posts, while others hoped to force the desired reforms—particularly reforms that would reduce the power of the party leadership, give members a voice in candidate selection

---

[60] Gianfranco Pasquino, "The Italian Socialist Party: An Irreversible Decline?" in Penniman, *Italy at the Polls*, presents a fascinating examination of the PSI and its strategic problems not only in 1976 but also in preceding years.

[61] Robert Leonardi, "The Victors: the Smaller Parties in the 1979 Italian Elections," in Howard R. Penniman, ed., *Italy at the Polls, 1979* (Washington, D.C.: American Enterprise Institute, forthcoming).

[62] For a full discussion of the DMC, see Efraim Torgovnik, "A Movement for Change in a Stable System," in Penniman, *Israel at the Polls*, pp. 147-72.

through party-conducted primary elections, and create at least some single-member districts so that some Knesset members would be directly responsible to specific electorates. In order to emphasize its commitment to reform, the DMC conducted a primary among its members to select candidates and determine their order on the ballot. Unfortunately, the DMC members chose candidates basically like themselves. The slate they selected failed to include a single Oriental Jew among the top names on the list—a matter of considerable comment from their former colleagues in Labor who had been more generous to this underrepresented group. In the election the DMC won fifteen seats, drawing most of them from Labor. But Labor failed to win a plurality in the Knesset, and the Likud under Menachem Begin was asked to form the government. Begin quickly built a majority of sixty-two before the DMC could begin serious negotiations. Three months later, just before the new cabinet was formally announced, the DMC was included but with no serious expectation of support for the reform proposals that had moved at least some of the DMC's founders. Within two years a majority of the DMC Knesset members had left the coalition with their strategy for reform in a shambles.

Political Credibility and International Credentials. New and small parties in older democracies and most parties in developing democracies have a continuing need to convince the voters that they are serious organizations worthy of attention and support. Curiously, acceptable evidence of party merit sometimes comes from foreign sources.

A Soviet connection once was enough to legitimize one party rather than another on the revolutionary left. Recognition from the Soviet Union, the acknowledged source of revolution, assured a party of standing among all revolutionaries in the country. In the 1920s this was true in both developed and developing countries, although in the former dissident groups sometimes made feeble efforts to go it alone.

In more recent years international recognition has assisted parties on the right as well as the left in their struggle for recognition and survival. When Spanish voters approved a referendum calling for the writing of a new democratic constitution in December 1976, there was still the question of which organizations could participate in the constituent assembly elections. In Spain in 1976 a Soviet connection had little of the charm that it had had for at least part of the revolutionary left four decades earlier. The Communist party of Spain (PCE) was slow to be granted the legal status it had lost at the end of the Civil War. To help the PCE overcome its past reputation of close Soviet ties, leaders of the so-called Eurocommunist parties of France and Italy met with PCE leaders in Madrid in early March 1977. The leaders of the three parties insisted that their organizations were independent of the U.S.S.R., interested only in adapting Marxist tenets to Western societies, and seeking reform by peaceful means. Among the spokesmen, Spain's Santiago Carrillo was the most critical of the absence of democracy in the U.S.S.R.[63] It cannot be established that this meeting cleared the way for recognition of the PCE as a legal party five weeks later, but it certainly demonstrated to potential supporters that the PCE was accepted as an equal by the two largest Western Communist parties.

The PCE was not the only Spanish party to profit from endorsement by other European parties. In 1972 the Spanish Socialist party (PSOE) was reorganized, and for the first time since the Civil War control of the party passed to leaders in Spain rather than in exile, a change accepted by the Socialist International.[64] By 1975 the German Social Democratic party (SPD), then in office, was giving the Spanish Socialists technical and financial assistance. These developments offered proof positive of the PSOE's legitimate place in the international socialist movement.[65]

Italy's older but much smaller Social Democratic party (PSDI) apparently faced extinction in 1979, as more and more voters dismissed it as too small or too unworthy to receive their support. The jailing of one of its leaders following the Lockheed scandals was a major blow. Robert Leonardi states that in the 1979 campaign one of the PSDI's major goals was to identify the party "in the eyes of the electorate with European Social Democratic parties and the English Labour party." This meant identifying it with the symbol of the Socialist International and such major figures of European socialism as Willy Brandt of Germany, Bruno Kreisky of Austria, and James Callaghan of Britain. Leonardi credits this strategy with the PSDI's success in increasing its vote more than any other lay centrist party. Instead of sinking into oblivion, the party returned to a position of strength within the country's center-left.[66]

---

[63] *Facts on File*, April 2, 1977, p. 242.

[64] See Eusebio Mujal-León, "The Spanish Communists and the Search for Electoral Space," in Penniman, *Spain at the Polls*.

[65] J. M. Maravall, "The Socialist Alternative: The Politics and Electoral Support of the PSOE," in Penniman, *Spain at the Polls*. See Eusebio Mujal-León, "The Spanish Left: Present Realities and Future Prospects," in William E. Griffith, ed., *The European Left: Italy, France, and Spain* (Lexington, Mass.: D. C. Heath & Co., 1979), p. 90.

[66] The PSDI's most prominent poster throughout Rome, printed in red ink on a white background, reproduced a statement signed by Willy Brandt recognizing the PSDI as part of the Socialist International and commenting on the importance of socialism in the new Parliament of Europe.

The SPD could offer more than recognition to the socialist parties it supported. It has also provided advice and financial help. Since 1969 the German government has financed parties represented in the Bundestag at a level so generous that it has made possible the development of foundations by both the SPD and the Christian Democratic Union with enough money to finance research at home and abroad and provide help in organizing and supporting foreign parties of comparable political persuasion. Their help has been useful in Europe and in developing nations where most non-Communist parties have little organization and no generally accepted program. These "parties" exist to support a charismatic leader, and disintegrate when the leader dies or is replaced. Sophisticated outside assistance in some instances has helped to provide the ingredients of permanence—organization and programs independent of a single leader.[67]

Campaign Rallies. In democratic countries a half century ago parades and monster rallies were the high points of political campaigns. Party leaders' speeches were reported in the press along with information about the size of the crowds and their response to the candidates. Turnout and audience reaction were pieces of evidence that reporters in that prepolling era used to gauge the relative public standing of the candidates.

Today there are large rallies in Western democracies—130,000 people attended the Gaullist rally in Paris mentioned earlier—but they are rare and seldom compare with those in developing democracies. Authors of essays for books in the *At the Polls* series have reported attending "massive" rallies in Wembley, England, and in a number of cities in India. In England the term referred to a meeting of 2,300 persons, while in India it described meetings that sometimes exceeded half a million.[68]

The Spanish Communist party's 1977 campaign often seemed like a trip down memory lane, a nostalgic return to the days of the left's rise to power in the 1930s, all the more poignant because of the long years of exile. The Communists had dominated the Loyalist forces in the final stages of the Civil War; then the crowds had been large and the response at a fever pitch. The PCE sought to match the crowds of yesteryear, by hard organizational work and by selecting candidates who were living legends, above all the famous Dolores Ibárruri (La Pasionaria), who had once stirred huge audiences and

---

[67] The CDU foundation, the Konrad Adenauer Stiftung, has been active in Central America and the Caribbean areas as well as in Spain and Portugal.

[68] See Weiner, *India at the Polls*, pp. 21-23; and William Livingston, "The Conservative Campaign," in Penniman, *Britain at the Polls, 1979.*

thousands of Loyalist soldiers. She returned from forty years of exile in the Soviet Union to campaign. At the 1977 rallies held in the fields outside Madrid, at least one of which reached the half-million mark, La Pasionaria was reported to have embarrassed the PCE by her sometimes fervent praise of the Soviet Union as the leader of the Communist world. Whatever the PCE's hopes, the voters responded coolly. Communist candidates received only 9.3 percent of the vote. Two years later neither the PCE nor the other parties repeated the massive rallies of 1977. Television was easier and more efficient.[69]

In Italy parties still regularly schedule rallies in the piazzas of the major cities, but the meetings are often ill attended and serve primarily as opportunities for the leaders to talk with media representatives and be photographed for television. In 1979 Enrico Berlinguer, leader of the PCI, appeared on thirty television shows—twice as many as in 1976—but attended only fourteen rallies. The same year the PSI hired a large crew of workmen to build an elaborately decorated stand for a rally in the Piazza Navona in Rome. The rally was attended by two or three hundred persons, most of whom appeared to be party workers carrying large banners from the national office a few blocks away. The party's secretary general, Bettino Craxi, was introduced and spoke vigorously for perhaps forty-five minutes. Then the program was over and the workmen began dismantling the platform.[70] In Bologna, where the beautiful central square is made available to parties for their major meetings, the results were more or less the same. There were perhaps a thousand people in the square during the major parties' rallies, but some were tourists and many others paid little attention to the speakers. This lack of response seemed to vary little with the party on the platform or the audience below.

Campaign Posters and Advertising. The use of posters, like so many other aspects of political campaigning, reflects the requirements of a nation's electoral rules and party system. A major party in single-member-district countries uses posters to familiarize voters in each constituency with the name and face of its local candidate. The United States, Britain, Canada, and Australia are among the heaviest

---

[69] In 1979 the PCE's vote rose to 10.9 percent. There is no evidence suggesting that the change in campaign method was responsible for the increased support.

[70] William E. Porter, "The Mass Media in the Italian Elections of 1979," in Penniman, *Italy at the Polls, 1979.* There were as many anti-PSI as there were Socialist distributors of books and pamphlets at the rally. The Unified New Left (NSU) rally the following night drew almost as large an audience and lasted nearly four hours. The NSU, however, received less than 1 percent of the votes on election day.

users of candidate posters.[71] Australian parties face a special problem since their candidates are not identified by party on the ballot for either the House of Representatives or the Senate. The parties therefore advertise daily in the newspapers and provide voter-guide cards at the polls telling their supporters precisely how to number the alternative vote ballot for the House and the much more complicated single-transferable-vote ballot for the Senate. In spite of their British heritage, New Zealand parties make minimal use of posters. In India, where campaign money is in short supply, graffiti on walls and fences often substitute for posters.

Ireland's single-transferable-vote system encourages candidates to tack up their own posters. The same is true in some proportional representation countries which allow voters to express their preferences among candidates. Italian candidates frequently put up posters and hand out voter cards, but most Greek candidates do not. The typical German candidate seeking district election in 1976 put up 4,000 posters in a district with roughly 165,000 voters.[72] Among countries with definitive PR lists, only Venezuela has parties that put up posters promoting candidates other than the party leaders. In some smaller Venezuelan cities and rural areas, posters featuring a local candidate on the party list are affixed to walls and telephone poles to encourage support for the whole slate.

France, of the single-member-district countries, and Spain, Italy, and Venezuela, of the PR countries, are among the heaviest users of party as opposed to candidate posters. These may serve a number of purposes. All advertise the party leaders. In Italy, Spain, and Venezuela they also announce rallies in the major cities. Posters can be instruments that provide the public with an image of the party that is sometimes at variance with the traditional view of its character. In Spain in early 1977 Communist party posters featured peasants and workers who looked like at least distant cousins of those portrayed in the "socialist realism" paintings of the 1930s. Meantime, the Socialist party posters exhibited the party symbol and pictures of their handsome young leader, Felipe González, or groups of young supporters of the party. By the end of the 1977 campaign, the PCE had dropped most of its peasant and worker pictures, at least in Madrid, in favor of posters showing younger, better dressed, middle-class party supporters. In 1979 the PCE posters in Madrid featured leaders in tweed jackets marching forward into a brighter Communist

---

[71] Livingston, "The Conservative Campaign." Livingston suggests that there seemed to be fewer posters in Britain in 1979 than in past elections.

[72] *New York Times*, September 13, 1976.

future; they projected an image of the party very different from the one projected two years earlier.

In France in 1978 the Communist party covered the country with pictures of a handsome young couple walking across the lawn of their single-family home, presumably on their way to the polls to vote for their PCF candidate. By contrast, in the Cold War period, far from reaching out for middle-class support, the PCF had sought to separate workers from others in society in order to develop and maintain class consciousness among party members.

In some countries, parties classified by Sartori as irrelevant produce the most interesting and imaginative posters. It is as if the artists and their parties recognize their political impotence and so feel free to express themselves and at the same time vent their anger against the society that rejects them. Poster after poster on display in the Bologna university area in 1976 managed to tie the Catholic church, the Christian Democratic party, and the Communists together in wild but fascinating denunciations of mainstream society. Virtually none of these reappeared in Bologna in 1979. In New Zealand the Tory party, a tiny group of young people who received only 205 votes in their Wellington districts, amused viewers with posters that were mildly satirical cartoons. A Canadian Rhinoceros party spoofed its way to fifth place among the parties in the 1979 elections, securing 62,623 votes in three provinces. Its posters supported among other things a platform proposal to repeal the law of gravity.[73]

Television advertising is common in some districts in the United States, where most stations and networks are privately owned and little free time is given candidates. Possibly one-fourth of the other democratic countries allow parties to advertise their candidates or programs on either radio or television. State-owned networks and stations provide free time, but the law often forbids the buying of further time by the parties or their supporters. Some studies in the United States suggest that short, direct television advertisements inform the less interested voter more effectively than speeches, debates, or interviews.[74] According to Michael Pinto-Duschinsky, "research in

---

[73] Gazette (Montreal), July 11, 1979. It should also be mentioned that there is an international trade in political posters. China, Cuba, and some Palestinian groups print posters in English, Spanish, French, and sometimes Arabic that are used in a wide range of countries. Though their message is necessarily general rather than geared to a particular election, they are sometimes used in electoral campaigns. Soviet posters are also used by parties in diverse countries despite the fact that the texts are printed in Russian. See Gary Yanker, Prop Art (New York: New York Graphic Society, 1972), pp. 23 and 75-77.

[74] Thomas E. Patterson and Robert D. McClure, "Television and the Less Interested Voter: The Costs of an Informed Electorate," Annals of the American Academy of Political and Social Sciences, May 1976, pp. 88-97.

Europe has apparently calculated that the most effective length for a political broadcast is four minutes"; in the light of this finding, he notes that Britain's allocation of time to the parties in ten-minute units may limit its value.[75] New Zealand is one of the few countries other than the United States that allows television advertising in units shorter than five minutes. Like the BBC, most nations' broadcasting authorities seem to insist on political messages geared to the informed viewer rather than the uninformed.

Specialized Campaigning. Nations have dealt in a number of ways with the problem of the citizens who are ill, out of the constituency, or for some other reason unable to appear at the polling place to vote. Some have simply ignored it while others have allowed early voting or voting by mail or have even assisted the voter to return to his district on election day to cast his ballot. Each of these solutions prompts a different campaign response.

The postal vote (comparable to the American absentee ballot) is available to British citizens and to citizens in most countries following the British model. Winning the postal vote may make the difference between victory and defeat in a British election. Butler and Kavanagh agree with other students of British elections that local Conservative parties "are undoubtedly better at organizing postal voting" than Labour parties. Local party workers help potential voters fill out and return their registration forms so that they will receive their ballots. This Conservative effort apparently pays off. The authors cite polling data showing that persons in marginal districts "who claim to have voted by post divided in a 5 to 3 ratio in favor of the Conservatives." The authors also list twelve districts in England and Scotland won by Conservative candidates in 1979 where the postal vote *may have* accounted for the defeat of their Labour or Scottish National opponents.[76]

Australian voters visiting or working anywhere in the country may cast ballots there for candidates of their home constituencies. They may do so in advance of the election, at the headquarters of the returning officers, or on election day at the polling place. In large cities, whole buildings are set aside for out-of-district voting. Outside such buildings all the serious parties have their information tables providing voter-guide cards and any other help to people requesting advice.[77]

---

[75] Michael Pinto-Duschinsky, "Financing the British General Election of 1979," in Penniman, *Britain at the Polls, 1979.*

[76] Butler and Kavanagh, *British General Election of 1979*, pp. 313-15.

[77] In New Zealand a section of each polling station is set aside for voters from other constituencies, who, after proper identification, may cast ballots in their home-district election.

In 1978 a new proxy law allowed French citizens living outside ·the country "to register in any town of at least 30,000 inhabitants. Surprisingly large numbers of overseas French proceeded to register in certain marginal districts" where government candidates faced the possibility of defeat. Obvious corruption was involved in at least some instances. In one of the elections invalidated by the Constitutional Council, "the decisive votes in [the winning candidate's] favor were proxies for voters in overseas France who had not personally selected the district in which their votes were cast."[78]

Italian law allows no absentee or proxy voting, but changing one's place of registration is easy, polling stations are available in hospitals and even prisons, and military personnel can vote wherever they may be in Italy at election time. Most significant is the provision that any eligible citizen away from Italy can travel free by train from the Italian border to his home town and back to the Italian border. Those living in Italy away from home may travel both ways at reduced rates. The Italian Communist party "encourages its supporters abroad to return home to vote, reaching them through letters from friends (the PCI provides a form letter for this purpose) and from the party and through electoral propaganda in the recreational facilities provided by the PCI for Italians working throughout Western Europe."[79] Needless to say, the PCI benefits from the law. Most of the people who return to vote are workers and probably inclined to support the left. Since the PCI is the party that gives attention to their needs, it can expect to gain a disproportionate share of the vote.

Fighting to Win

Leaders of "relevant" parties see winning elections as the major purpose of campaigns. They take the trouble to inform the citizens and rally them to the polls as a means of attaining this goal. Conversely, where a party sees victory as certain, its campaign is that much less intense. This is true of campaigns for the U.S. House of Representatives, which are largely personal efforts: the majority candidate in

---

[78] Pierce, "French Legislative Elections: The Historical Background," in Penniman, *French National Assembly Elections*, pp. 22-23. The proxy corruption case points up the fact that absentee voting often has been a major vehicle for corruption. With the coming of the secret ballot, only a voter marking his ballot away from the polling place could be observed. The voter could be paid off in private and the politician could examine the product. Up to 30 percent of the adult residents of three Virginia counties voted by absentee ballot for many years—until 1968, when seven local politicians were prosecuted and convicted of vote fraud.

[79] Douglas Wertman, "The Italian Electoral Process: The Election of June 1976," in Penniman, *Italy at the Polls*, pp. 43-44.

a safe district may not campaign at all, or, as Samuel J. Eldersveld suggests, he may carefully avoid clarifying his policy differences with the minority candidate, since defining them might cost him votes.[80] If Eldersveld is right, it is in competitive districts, where a candidate's propaganda is countered by opposing claims and policy statements, that the voters are most likely to be informed.

In countries where party broadcasts are forced upon the television audience, campaigns expose virtually all of the voters to political information. It is safe to say that in democracies generally, more people know more about the candidates and the issues at the end of a campaign than at the beginning. Campaigns transmit information. Since informed citizens are more likely than uninformed ones to go to the polls, campaigns may encourage people to carry out a civic duty.

Whether the political force-feeding that takes place in a campaign actually educates the voters or only dulls their appetite depends upon how the party product is presented and how interested the citizen-consumer is. In some cases there is clear evidence that the voters have been attentive. In two separate election post-mortems, Ivor Crewe and Jeane J. Kirkpatrick found that a party whose campaign platform ran counter to the views of its own sympathizers courted disaster at the polls: large numbers of people deserted their party because it took stands they disagreed with, and they noticed.[81] From Denmark another study argued, contrary to earlier generalizations, that "the changing vote in Denmark lacks the noninvolved, know-nothing character of the changing vote in some other countries."[82] Recent American work, again contrary to prevailing assumptions, places independents among the attentive electorate. Far from being ignorant or apathetic, the authors claim, self-identified independents are often people who carefully scrutinize the evidence before choosing their candidates.[83]

---

[80] Samuel J. Eldersveld, *Political Parties: A Behavioral Analysis* (Chicago: Rand McNally & Co., 1964), p. 461.

[81] Crewe, "Why the Conservatives Won"; and Jeane J. Kirkpatrick, *The New Presidential Elite: Men and Women in National Politics* (New York: Russell Sage Foundation, 1976), pp. 281-347. Crewe states, "It was issues, not organization or personalities, which won for the Conservatives."

[82] Ole Borre and Daniel Katz, "Party Identification and Its Motivational Base in a Multi-Party System: A Study of the Danish General Election of 1971," *Scandinavian Political Studies*, vol. 8 (1973), p. 109.

[83] For the research results on American independents, see Bruce Keith, David Magleby, Candice Nelson, Elizabeth Orr, Mark Westlye, and Raymond Wolfinger, *The Myth of the Independent Voter* (Washington, D.C.: American Enterprise Institute, forthcoming). Independent voters leaning to either the Republican or the Democratic party, however, are likely to be ill informed and apathetic, according to this study.

Clearly, some voters are alert to campaigns. And some voters change their minds—right up to the last minute. Candidates, campaign strategists, and pollsters alike do well to remember the lesson of the American presidential election of 1948, when Thomas Dewey's lead over Harry S. Truman in the preelection surveys was so consistent and so large that the outcome was regarded as sure. A month before the election, *Fortune* magazine smugly announced:

> Barring a major political miracle, Governor Thomas E. Dewey will be elected the thirty-fourth President of the United States. . . . So decisive are the [Roper poll] figures given here this month that FORTUNE, and Mr. Roper, plan no further detailed reports on the change of opinion in the forthcoming presidential campaign unless some development of outstanding importance occurs.[84]

The day after the election the victorious Truman was photographed waving a copy of the *Chicago Tribune* printed before the final returns were in: "Dewey Defeats Truman," ran the headline. The president's lead over Dewey was 2,135,747 votes.

Gone are the days when pollsters could assume that most voters were committed to their party's candidate even before he had been selected and that the undecided minority would fall into line soon after. More and more evidence from a variety of countries suggests that only the proximity of election day moves some reluctant voters to reach a decision.[85] If that is true, the politician who campaigns until midnight on election eve may well be the wise one.

Bibliography

Series. In addition to the *At the Polls* studies, which are listed at the back of this book, and the annual volumes of *Scandinavian Political Studies*, which describe elections in all the Scandinavian democracies, two notable series of election studies provide detailed accounts of specific campaigns: Theo-

---

[84] "The Fortune Survey," *Fortune*, October 1948, p. 29.

[85] Butler and Kavanagh, for example, concluded that in Britain "the campaign in the February 1974 election was decisive. Opinion polls suggest that more votes switched during those three weeks than in any previous election." Butler and Kavanagh, *British General Election of February 1974*, p. 112. A study of the 1973 Danish election showed that "one-third of the Danish voters changed parties" and "one-fifth to one-sixth stated that they had made up their minds in the last days before the election." Steen Sauerberg and Niels Thomsen, "The Political Role of Mass Communication in Scandinavia," in Karl H. Cerny, ed., *Scandinavia at the Polls: Recent Political Trends in Denmark, Norway, and Sweden* (Washington, D.C.: American Enterprise Institute, 1977), p. 208.

dore White's books on presidential elections in the United States and the Nuffield series on British general elections since World War II.

White, Theodore H. *The Making of the President, 1960.* New York: Atheneum, 1960.

———. *The Making of the President, 1964.* New York: Atheneum, 1965.

———. *The Making of the President, 1968.* New York: Atheneum, 1969.

———. *The Making of the President, 1972.* New York: Atheneum, 1973.

McCallum, R. B., and Readman, A. *The British General Election of 1945.* Oxford: Oxford University Press, 1947.

Nicholas, H. G. *The British General Election of 1950.* London: Macmillan, 1951.

Butler, D. E. *The British General Election of 1951.* London: Macmillan, 1952.

———. *The British General Election of 1955.* London: Macmillan, 1955.

Butler, D. E., and Rose, R. *The British General Election of 1959.* London: Macmillan, 1960.

Butler, D. E., and King, A. S. *The British General Election of 1964.* London: Macmillan, 1965.

———. *The British General Election of 1966.* London: Macmillan, 1966.

Butler, D. E., and Pinto-Duschinsky, M. *The British General Election of 1970.* London: Macmillan, 1971.

Butler, D. E., and Kavanagh, D. *The British General Election of February 1974.* London: Macmillan, 1974.

———. *The British General Election of October 1974.* London: Macmillan, 1975.

———. *The British General Election of 1979.* London: Macmillan, 1980.

Other Works

Agranoff, Robert. *The New Style in Election Campaigns.* 2d ed. Boston: Holbrook Press, 1976.

Butler, David. *Elections Abroad.* London: Macmillan, 1958.

Curtis, Gerald L. *Election Campaigning Japanese Style.* New York and London: Columbia University Press, 1971.

Epstein, Leon D. *Political Parties in Western Democracies.* New York: Praeger, 1967.

Ostrogorski, Moisei. *Democracy and the Organization of Political Parties.* Vol. 1, *England;* vol. 2, *United States.* Edited and abridged by Seymour Martin Lipset. Garden City, N.J.: Doubleday, 1964.

Rae, Douglas W. *The Political Consequences of Electoral Laws.* 2d ed. New Haven: Yale University Press, 1971.

Sartori, Giovanni. *Parties and Party Systems: A Framework for Analysis.* London: Cambridge University Press, 1976.

Tufte, Edward R. *Political Control of the Economy.* Princeton: Princeton University Press, 1978.

7

Campaign Finance:
Contrasting Practices and Reforms

Khayyam Zev Paltiel

The problem of campaign finance in the democratic electoral process
emerges from the Janus-like quality of money. Few would deny that
political parties and candidates engaged in the competitive electoral
struggle need resources beyond the goods and personal services freely
offered by their supporters. In a complex and differentiated industrial
society, electoral competitors must have access to materials and expertise which, with rare exceptions, they can only acquire in the market
at a price; these may be campaign buttons or posters, newspaper
advertising or broadcasting time, transportation or communications
facilities, office space and committee rooms, professional and clerical
staff, or the assistance of media specialists, survey researchers, and
campaign strategists. In a pecuniary society these services require
money. Money is the only resource which is readily transferable in
temporal, spatial, and interpersonal terms. With its aid, shortages of
manpower may be mastered and virtually all other deficiencies overcome—it has even been used to buy votes, though this is everywhere
illegitimate and in most countries forbidden by law. But campaign
funds are equivocal. On the one hand, contributions to party and
candidate war chests represent a sacrifice and a willingness on the
part of the givers to participate in the electoral process; on the other
hand, the great disparities in the size of donations commonly reflect
social and economic inequalities and attempts to surmount the democratic constraints of "one man, one vote" to gain disproportionate
influence on the decision-making process. The need for funds may
lead politicians to pay closer attention to the interests and claims of
their major financial backers than to those of their voting constituents.
Scandal, cost inflation, and campaign deficits have combined with the
urge for greater probity and equity to promote the reshaping of party
finance and the regulation of election expenses, a movement which has

been an outstanding feature of the legislative landscape of many democratic countries in the last two decades.

Although a detailed exposition of all the problems subsumed under the heading of political finance is beyond the scope of this short chapter, an outline of the central issues dictates some consideration of the following: the purposes and needs which party and candidate funds are intended to meet; the sources and the means employed to collect and provide the money required; the regulations and reforms which have been adopted to resolve the difficulties arising out of the traditional patterns of campaign finance; the impact of these measures; and the question of democracy and party finance.

The Need for Funds

Competitive political parties require funds for three purposes: to fight election campaigns, to maintain viable interelection organizations, and to provide research facilities and other assistance for the leadership and elected representatives of the parties at various governmental levels. Clearly, in the majority of cases primary attention is paid to the first of these, the campaign fund; but differences must be noted between the election orientation of middle-class parties of the cadre type and mass-membership parties which stress the party organization outside parliament. Yet another qualification may be noted in the case of those jurisdictions which place strict limits on campaign spending, leading to higher expenditures between elections. Attempts are made to provide maintenance funds, especially where a party enjoys the advantage of incumbency (which its parliamentary leadership often employs to reinforce its position in the party organization). Research and advisory services generally come a poor third, forced to make do with the voluntary offerings of interested individuals and groups or to rely on allied, ancillary research institutes and foundations in receipt of public and/or private support.

The foregoing may be illustrated through a comparison of party activities in Western Europe, Japan, Israel, and the Anglo-American democracies. Although some distinctions must be made between left-wing labor-oriented parties and middle-class conservative and liberal groups, little by way of direct policy research, beyond the occasional interelection and more frequent preelection public opinion poll survey, is carried out by political parties in Canada, the United Kingdom, France, Italy, Japan, Israel, or the United States. True, the social democratic New Democrats in Canada and sister parties elsewhere do make an attempt in this direction, as do PEP (now part of the Policy Studies Institute) and the Bow Group, loosely linked to the British

139

Labour and Conservative parties, or even the Brookings Institution and the American Enterprise Institute in the United States with their vague liberal and conservative orientations. Some of the Socialist and Communist parties in these countries, of course, continue to devote considerable effort to ideological debates, but the shift among social democrats from closed membership to open, consensual voters' parties has lowered the ideological temperature. And none of these activities compare with those of the elaborate educational and research foundations affiliated with political parties in the Netherlands, Austria, and West Germany. The party foundations in Austria and the Netherlands concentrate on their domestic functions, but the German foundations, supported by generous state funds, carry out many developmental and political roles in the developing world and support and foster the foundation of sister parties in Portugal, Spain, France, Scandinavia, and other European states as well as Latin America—all this in addition to performing advisory, educational, and organizational functions for their sponsors within the Federal Republic.

As noted above, the sharpest contrast in expenditures on interelection party organization lies between middle-class cadre parties and the mass parties appealing for working-class support. In contradistinction to the parliamentary orientation of the classical European (and Canadian) liberal and conservative parties, with their skeletal interelection organizations, social democratic parties in Canada, Scandinavia, and elsewhere, as exemplified by the SPD in pre- and post-Hitler Germany, have emphasized the extraparliamentary party organization and its needs; modified though it has been by the trend toward consensual politics, this tradition continues. For somewhat different reasons, the Communist parties of France and Italy have committed large resources to building mass-based parties buttressed by party-controlled parapolitical organizations covering many aspects of social life, patterned on, but going far beyond, models pioneered by the social democrats.

A somewhat different reason for high interelection spending by political parties is to be found in the United Kingdom. British electoral law stringently limits the amounts a party's candidates may spend during the formal campaign period. The emphasis therefore is on publicity and advertising in the run-up to the formal election period and on strong central and local organizations. At the local level British parties attempt to maintain a corps of salaried constituency agents; interestingly enough, however, the Conservative party, with its higher membership and stronger resources (as revealed by the Houghton Report), is better equipped on this score than the Labour party, not to mention the Liberal party and the regional nationalist groups. The central organizations of the two principal British parties spend the bulk of their funds on organization, intraparty communications, publicity, and research; it has been estimated by Richard Rose that the Conservative party devotes only about one-eighth of its expenditures to electoral preparations and campaigning; similar proportions hold true for the constituency expenditures of the major parties.[1]

Despite the exceptions discussed above, election expenses constitute the major object and item of party finance in the democratic world. However, campaign styles have evolved, and the last century has witnessed shifts in the objects of expenditure. In the earlier period, election expenses were concentrated on organizing and mobilizing the voters. Political machines engaged in widespread corruption, and large sums were expended to convey the electors to the polls; the dispensing of vast amounts of alcohol was a common feature of all campaigns, particularly on polling day. Newspapers were the chief means of communication available to the parties, and their loyalty was ensured or suborned either through outright ownership or by way of handsome printing contracts and other forms of patronage. This need to ensure the continued friendship of the press often led to the expenditure of considerable sums between elections, a burden which incumbents could shift to the public treasury through government contracts.

The broadening of the franchise, population growth, the spread of literacy with the introduction of public education, the rotary press, and cheap newspapers led to ever greater reliance on the print media. Organization at the precinct or poll and constituency levels was not neglected, but expenditures on publicity and communication became more prominent. Parallel with this development was an increasing emphasis on the immediate period of the election campaign. This pattern emerged into full view in the last generation with the advent of radio broadcasting in the 1930s, television in the 1950s, and the growing sophistication of sample survey techniques. Parties, candidates, and professional political consultants are preoccupied with image building and image projection, which draw a growing proportion of financial resources. This process has probably gone furthest in the Anglo-American democracies, but it is being emulated to an increasing degree in Western Europe. West German, French, Austrian, and Scandinavian parties and leaders on the right, center, and moderate left have adopted many of the techniques pioneered in the

---

[1] Richard Rose, *The Problem of Party Government* (London: Pelican Books, 1976), pp. 213-43.

English-speaking world, notably as closed-membership parties have given way to open voters' parties.

Special financial needs arise in the United States where the attrition of party structures and the primary system of nominations for executive and legislative offices at federal, state, and even local levels place particular burdens on political aspirants. Such persons must build personal followings to support their search for the nomination; at the presidential and state levels, this struggle can be very costly. Once built, these personal organizations rival those of the parties, diverting support and undermining their authority to enforce political cohesion. U.S. parties must also raise considerable sums to finance voter registration and get-out-the-vote drives to ensure that their supporters get to the polls.

Sources and Methods of Raising Campaign Funds

Modern systems of party and election financing are, to paraphrase what I have written elsewhere, closely linked to the structure of industrial society, the national party system, and current campaign methods.[2] Industrial society, whose features are present in most of the states under consideration, is marked by the growing prominence of three great bureaucratic sectors and their elites. The most influential and pervasive is the organized financial and industrial network and the managerial business elite. The fact that the growth of multinational enterprises means that the decision-making centers of the corporate sector are frequently located outside the borders of the respective states does not alter the substance of the problem, although it may seriously affect the behavior of parties dependent on such support and the policy outputs of governments headed by them. Next in importance is the labor bureaucracy and trade union elite, with its own cross-national ties, as in the case of Canadian and U.S. international unions or the various international federations, which present problems similar to those raised with respect to the corporate sector. Third, but not least, there is the modern bureaucratic state, with its financial resources and control of access to facilities essential to party success. Certain areas of industrial society have escaped bureaucratic penetration, but these are largely archaic, traditional, and, despite fitful upswings, of shrinking political relevance; the growing technical professions are less and less "free," more and more dependent upon and ancillary to the major sectors. The latter and their elites have with few exceptions become the main sources of

[2] Khayyam Z. Paltiel, *Political Party Financing in Canada* (Toronto: McGraw-Hill, 1970), p. 8.

funds for parties in the nations considered here. Despite repeated efforts by major parties and the occasional successes of minor parties, it has generally not been possible to acquire a regular, continuous source of funds by popular fund-raising without the assistance of one or another of these bureaucracies.

Middle-Class Parties. The transition from traditional to modern party financing techniques may perhaps best be seen through a brief comparison of the class-based parties of Europe and elsewhere. Middle-class parties like the Radicals of the French Third Republic counted on coopting the support of local notables, who formed electoral committees to organize and finance the return of their candidates; the necessary funds were raised at election time from the local elite. By contrast, working-class parties modeled themselves on trade union organization and built mass organizations of regular dues-paying members. Collected in small sums either directly from their members or indirectly through per capita levies on the membership of affiliated trade unions, these funds were used to sponsor candidates, subsidize the meager salaries of elected deputies, and maintain elaborate organizations of full-time paid officials at the local, regional, and national levels; the ordinary party activist devoted much of his time to the collection of dues and special financial campaigns to support the party press or provide additional election funds. It was not long before middle-class liberal and conservative parties attempted to emulate the organizational structure of their socialist rivals. But lacking a mass base, they continued to look to business for funds, and systematic procedures were established to procure these funds.

In Canada, for instance, the bulk of the campaign money required by the Liberal and Progressive-Conservative parties has come from essentially the same sources, the centralized corporate industrial and financial community located in Toronto and Montreal. These corporate donors numbered in the hundreds rather than in the thousands. Under this system, federal campaigns at the national and constituency levels, as well as provincial and even municipal elections, were financed from the central party funds and sources. Few people were occupied in raising these funds. The usual fund-raising apparatus was composed of finance committees in Toronto and Montreal, with the Toronto chairman being senior. Subsidiary committees were also created on occasion in other central Canadian cities; recently the party finance chairmen in the western provinces have become more prominent, reflecting a shift in the Canadian economy and the pattern of Canadian party finance. The chief solicitors have not been subject to the formal elected party organs—being responsible directly to the prime minister or party leader—nor have the lower-level solicitors usually held elective office in their parties, having in practice been coopted or having literally inherited their positions from older members of their families or business, investment, and law firms. Similar formal and informal party committees may be found in other English-speaking countries.

A different pattern is displayed by the British Conservative party, which raises considerable sums of money at the constituency level; indeed, the constituencies provide about one-quarter of the needs of the party's Central Office. At the national level the paid staff of the Central Board of Finance solicits about two-thirds of the Central Office's income. Altogether, about three-quarters of the party's national income in 1972–1973 came from business firms—a proportion paralleled by the slightly larger percentage which the Labour party received from trade union sources in the same period.[3] Organized interests also provide the funds to finance the activities of anti-nationalization lobbies and parallel action groups like Aims of Industry and British United Industrialists in the United Kingdom whose campaigns are often designed to promote the Conservative party.

Conveyors and Sponsors. The perceived threat from the left, the decline of the traditional cadre parties, and the growing concentration of the business sector helped produce the sponsor and conveyor organizations linked to the peak industrial groupings and federations of Europe and Japan.[4] Conveyor associations organized to channel and distribute funds from business associations to anti–social democratic parties appeared well before World War I in Imperial Germany. With the shift in the balance of power as between interest groups and parties during the parliamentary regime of the Weimar Republic, sponsor groups were formed by industrialists to back specific parties favorable to their needs. Similar practices were adopted and continued into the post-1945 period in Japan, Norway, France (the Conseil National du Patronat Français), the United Kingdom, and the numerous countries with strong neocorporatist traditions of functional representation. In Japan giving tends to focus on individual candidates and factions within the parties; this strong factional orientation is also noteworthy in Italy. France, Norway, and Japan also have leader maintenance organizations designed to provide financial backing for "men of talent," faction and party leaders.

---

[3] Rose, *Problem of Party Government.*

[4] Arnold J. Heidenheimer and Frank C. Langdon, *Business Associations and the Financing of Political Parties: A comparative study of the evolution of practices in Germany, Norway and Japan* (The Hague: Martinus Nijhoff, 1968), passim.

A similar phenomenon may be noted in Canada, where special funds were established with the backing of John D. Rockefeller, Jr., to provide a steady income for longtime Prime Minister W. L. Mackenzie King, and for the recent Liberal and Progressive-Conservative prime ministers, the late Lester B. Pearson and John G. Diefenbaker. And Britain's Harold Wilson received "research funds" from a group of business backers during his later period in opposition. Serving as conduits for funds raised by particular interest groups, sponsor and conveyor organizations are primarily contributor oriented, concerned with the defense or claims of their particular sector. For this reason their activities have on occasion been viewed as a threat by the very parties and factions which they purported to support, prompting demands for disclosure legislation and for public subsidies so as to free the parties from importunate demands. The history of Libertas, in Norway, is a case in point. Libertas was founded secretly in 1947 by Norwegian shipowners to raise funds for nonsocialist parties and finance efforts to influence the press and public opinion in favor of free enterprise. Itself financed by levies on shipowners, Libertas sought to affect the choice of leaders, candidates, and policies in the bourgeois parties. Its activities aroused antagonism even among the politicians the organization purported to favor, and when they were exposed in 1950 Libertas was forced to end its direct financial contributions to political parties. In Germany the excessive growth of sponsor and conveyor groups and their attempts to determine candidate lists and veto certain coalition arrangements helped promote the introduction of party and election subsidy systems in 1959 and 1967.

Parallel Action Organizations. Alongside the channels of direct financial aid to the middle-class parties, such as British United Industrialists, and sometimes replacing them, as when Libertas in Norway changed course in 1950, there have been created a host of organizations like Aims of Industry which carry out antinationalization campaigns and other propaganda efforts designed to assist a party or group of parties. By stressing or opposing policies identified with one party or another, these groups aim at influencing the outcome of elections. The mass media have provided these groups with a particularly fertile area of activity. Furthermore, in an era of increased regulation of elections and stress on civil liberties, these groups are able to escape some of the very rigid controls which have been placed on election contributions and spending, either because they can be viewed as promoting the legitimate business interest of their sponsors and contributors, or because any interference with their activities in discussing ostensibly public issues may be viewed by the public and particularly the courts as interference with the canons of free speech, a position which has been confirmed by both American and Canadian judges. Although it might seem far-fetched, the forerunners of the "political action committees" recently established by U.S. corporate interests and including such bodies as the AFL-CIO's Committee on Political Education (COPE) were the right-wing anti-socialist Wilhelmine Reichsverband gegen die Sozialdemokratie and Fridtjof Nansen's Norwegian Fedrelandslaget of the years surrounding World War I.[5] A closely related phenomenon is the campaign activity of single-issue organizations—for or against abortion, for or against capital punishment, the gun groups, the ecological movements, and so on. Taking advantage of exemptions in the election laws, concentrating their resources and efforts, groups like these can determine the success of particular candidates.

Working-Class and Socialist Parties. The German Social Democratic party in the late nineteenth century provided the model followed by most parties on the left. Mass-membership organizations of regular dues payers were organized, and funds were channeled upward from the branches to the regions and the provincial and national levels. Similar practices have been followed by socialist (and communist) parties in Canada, Norway, Finland, France, and Italy and by constituency Labour parties in the United Kingdom. In addition to direct membership, many of these parties (like the British Labour party, the Canadian Cooperative Commonwealth Federation and New Democrats, and the Swedish Social Democrats) developed the notion of indirect or affiliated membership, collecting funds through per capita levies from the membership of trade unions and cooperatives affiliated with the parties. Similar practices have been followed by agrarian parties like the erstwhile United Farmers in Canada, which exploited the channels of farm organizations. While "contracting-in," or more usually "contracting-out," arrangements gave unionists some freedom to dispute the political choices made by their leaders, few exercised this right, either out of inertia or for fear of retaliation. Critics of the indirect membership system on the right and the left have alleged that block voting and the parties' dependence on the lump sums at the disposal of their leaders have given the large trade unions undue influence on the behavior of social democratic parties, the first on the grounds that the union bosses place the interests of their organization and members above those of the nation, the second on the grounds that the unions exercise a conservative influence, converting the

---

[5] Ibid., pp. 26-30 and 97-98.

social democratic parties into instruments of class collaboration. It should be noted too that in addition to the membership and affiliation fees collected and paid by trade unions to their sister parties, they have substantial financial resources in educational and special funds which can be used in support of their political allies, not to speak of the voluntary and paid professional organizational talent and manpower which trade unions make available to parties during campaigns, either directly or through registration and get-out-the-vote campaigns.

Party Business Enterprises. Many political parties, especially in Israel and Continental Europe, are actively engaged in quasi-commercial enterprises. Some own companies, and some operate through cooperatives or partnerships subject to party control. These include anything from party newspapers to travel agencies, import-export companies, banks, consulting firms, and even lotteries. Although found largely on the left wing of the political spectrum, such enterprises include the bingo games, lotteries, and advertising yearbooks organized and published by the British Conservatives, and printing plants and economic bulletins owned and published by the German Christian Democrats and Free Democrats (Liberals). Although some party enterprises, like the daily, weekly, and periodical press, have constituted a net financial drain since World War II (albeit advancing their sponsor's cause on the ideological, communications, and propaganda fronts), most of these activities have been undertaken because they constitute net contributions to the resources of their parties; profits and surpluses can be used to replenish party coffers, and their personnel are a reservoir of manpower available for electoral campaign purposes when needed. In addition these enterprises provide a source of internal patronage and rewards to party militants and on occasion a useful means of camouflaging certain sources of funds, both foreign and domestic.

The broadest range of such parapolitical enterprises is probably found in Israel. Most Israeli parties began as settlement movements and were by necessity driven to enter into almost all facets of social and economic life even before the proclamation of the state in 1948. Parties publish daily newspapers, own their own publishing firms, have their own recreation movements and sports teams, own banks, housing projects, wholesale and retail cooperatives, control the largest sick funds including hospitals, and are the largest employers in the field of heavy industry through the trade-union-controlled industries. The cooperative and collective agrarian sector, including the famous kibbutzim, is under party control; indeed most kibbutzim must allocate as much as 20 percent of their manpower for party political purposes.

On the European continent, the most striking examples are the networks of commercial enterprises controlled by the Communist parties of Italy and France. Besides recreational activities, the Italian Communists run chains of stores, garment-manufacturing firms, travel agencies, and import-export agencies which handle a large part of the country's trade with Eastern Europe. The French Communist party according to André Campana owns no fewer than 310 enterprises, 130 in the commercial and financial sector, 28 real estate companies, 114 publishing, book-selling, and publicity firms, and 38 cooperative and mutual aid companies. The Banque Commerciale pour l'Europe du Nord, in which are deposited a large fraction of the party's funds as well as those of the Confédération Générale du Travail, which it controls, is a Soviet bank; allegedly it has acted as an important conduit for funds, and finances a large share of French trade with the Soviet bloc.[6] The French Communist party also maintains a sophisticated urban planning and consultation facility which serves municipalities under party control. The French Socialist party, for its part, has organized Urba-Conseil to perform similar services for localities and district administrations under its influence. The Bank für Gemeinwirtschaft in Germany and the Sparkasse in Austria are closely allied with those countries' Social Democrats. And the Scandinavian socialist and communist parties own travel agencies and quasi-commercial enterprises in the import-export area. Where such businesses do not exist, their absence is bitterly regretted. Some Italian Socialists, for example, are keenly aware of their party's failure to understand the importance of an organizational structure that is not strictly political—something the PCI has understood so well.[7]

Foreign Sources of Funds. No single aspect of campaign finance has aroused more controversy than the question of clandestine support of political parties from foreign sources. Generally viewed as an attaint to the integrity of the recipient's political system, such funds and their provenance have generally been concealed by all concerned. Nevertheless, parties and candidates of the left, right, and center in Bolivia,

---

[6] André Campana, *L'argent secret: le financement des partis politiques* [Secret money: political party funding] (Paris: Arthaud, 1976), pp. 152-60. See also Jean Montaldo, *Les finances du P.C.F.* [The PCF's finances] (Paris: Albin Michel, 1977), passim.

[7] In the words of Luigi Mariotti, "Pietro Nenni's greatest error was that he mistook a big speech for the importance and need to construct a consensus-building network of parapolitical groups, including commercial enterprises, in an industrial society." Interview with the author, May 2, 1977, Settignano, Florence.

Canada, Finland, France, Israel, Italy, Japan, Portugal, Spain, and even the United States, among others, have been shown to have accepted financial assistance from foreign businesses, trade unions, party organizations, and governmental bodies; all sectors of society, apparently, have been willing to support their friends abroad when necessity dictates. On the business side the most active donors are the head offices or the domestic subsidiaries of multinational corporations; this has been confirmed by the revelations concerning such doings in Canada, France, Italy, and Japan by the large chemical and oil companies, resource companies, and business machine manufacturers. Related to these have been the contributions of aircraft manufacturers and armament-makers in search of or in gratitude for contracts awarded. West German, Swedish, and American trade unions are known to have contributed to the campaign funds of French, Finnish, and Canadian parties, as have the Scandinavian and West German Social Democratic parties, either directly or through their party foundations, to fraternal parties in Italy, Spain, Portugal, and elsewhere. Similarly the West German Christian Democrats and the Free Democrats have contributed to Greek, Italian, Spanish, Portuguese, and Latin American counterparts. Nor have democratic foreign governments been loath to interfere in the democratic electoral process of particular states when threats to their military, economic, or political interests were perceived. On such occasions secret service funds have been distributed either through multinational corporations or trade unions—or, more rarely, directly through intelligence operatives; ostensibly commercial import-export transactions or advertising and publicity activities have frequently served as convenient covers for such aid.[8]

A piquant combination of the aforementioned transnational transfers involving the recent presidential elections in Bolivia was revealed by Charles Krause writing in the *Washington Post* of July 24, 1979. According to Krause, the United States, the Soviet Union, West Germany, China, Venezuela, Cuba, and Argentina were involved in financing the three major political groupings, which spent upwards of $1 million (in one case as much as $2.5 million) each. Thus the centrist National Revolutionary Alliance of Victor Paz Estenssoro, which reputedly spent $1.4 million, received $240,000 through the Bolivian Christian Democratic party from the Social Christian party of Venezuelan President Luis Herrera Campíns, a further substantial sum from a foreign firm which has a valuable import monopoly, and a smaller

---

8 For a summary overview of such clandestine support of political parties and candidates from foreign sources, see Khayyam Z. Paltiel, *Party, Candidate and Election Finance: A Background Report*, Study no. 22, Royal Commission on Corporate Concentration (Ottawa: Ministry of Supply and Services, 1977), pp. 51-96 passim.

amount from the Chinese through the Marxists-Leninists. On the other hand the Democratic Popular Union of Hernan Siles Zuazo was a recipient of West German Social Democratic party funds channeled through the Portuguese Socialists of Mario Soares. In addition the Siles coalition is reputed to have received money from the Argentine Montoneros, the Argentine ERP, the Cubans and the Libyans through the Revolutionary Left Movement, and about $400,000 through the Communist party from the Soviet Union. The rightist National Democratic Alliance of General Hugo Banzer Suárez appears to have been the direct and indirect beneficiary of the largesse of the Argentine military government.

Although Israel's political parties receive a modicum of help from fraternal parties abroad, significant aid comes from organized groups and individual supporters in the Jewish diaspora, which are affiliated to parties in Israel and contribute to them directly or through their constructive enterprises and welfare institutions.

Traditional Public Sources and Patronage. Since the rest of this chapter is devoted to a detailed discussion of the public financing of campaigns, our discussion at this point will be confined to the traditional means employed by incumbent parties to exploit the public treasury in order to replenish their campaign funds. Two of these, "toll-gating" and "macing," are related to traditional systems of political patronage; the third, the assessment of elected representatives, is more recent, arising out of the introduction of and increase in indemnities to legislators; a fourth, involving the use of secret service funds, has a long if checkered history.

The systematic assessment or "macing" of public servants for party and campaign contributions by the incumbents was a common phenomenon in the period of patronage appointments before the reform of the civil service and the introduction of the merit principle in Canada, the United States, and elsewhere. The system persists in certain parts of the English-speaking world, and it continues to flourish in those areas of southern Europe where patron-client relations are strong as well as in the nascent democracies of the developing world. Nevertheless, the elimination of the practice is generally viewed as an essential step in the creation of an impartial and efficient public service. The Commonwealth of Puerto Rico affords an excellent illustration of the practice and an imaginative step to eliminate it. Having come to power in 1940 with a promise to eliminate the influence of the sugar interests, the Popular Democratic party leader, Luis Muñoz Marin, turned to what appeared to be the only other expedient source of funds, the civil servants. From then until 1957 when a public subsidy system was introduced, the PDP's campaign funds were derived almost entirely from the regular assessment of public officials. A quota system was established whereby employees were expected to donate up to 2 percent of their salaries to the party. Certain officials were designated as collectors and made the rounds on paydays to collect; those who did not participate probably found that their careers suffered accordingly. The system achieved a high degree of efficiency and was only eliminated when public subsidies provided a satisfactory and more equitable alternative.[9]

The assessment of elected representatives differs from macing in that those required to pay are party activists whose elected status is directly dependent upon party favor. The introduction of parliamentary salaries or indemnities has permitted parties another means of access to the public purse. Generally, elected members do contribute something to their parties' campaigns. Left-wing parties, however, usually request that their representatives contribute a fixed percentage of their salaries to the party. The West German SPD has required its deputies to contribute as much as 20 percent. The Communist parties of France and Italy have gone further, compelling the members of their parliamentary factions to turn back their entire indemnities to the party and receive in exchange the equivalent of the salary of a skilled metalworker. Some, like Jasper Shannon, see this practice as antidemocratic in that the elected representative in effect grants control over his actions to an external party machine rather than to the state's representative body.

Toll-gating is the system whereby holders of government permits and concessions are required to make regular contributions to the war chests of the incumbent parties, and kickbacks (called *ristournes* in the Province of Quebec) are payments consisting of a percentage of the value of all government contracts made to the party in power. Variations of these schemes are probably the most traditional and widespread of the means used by incumbents to reinforce their financial positions. Hundreds of royal commissions and public, parliamentary, and judicial inquiries and prosecutions have detailed these processes in different jurisdictions, and there is no need to retail these stories once again. Suffice it to say that it is in reaction to the scandals arising from the use of these methods that many of the reforms discussed in the next section of this chapter were enacted.

More sinister has been the use of secret service funds to promote the reelection of incumbents. This was not uncommon in Imperial Germany. There is evidence, too, that Canada's first prime minister,

---

[9] Henry Wells, *Government Financing of Political Parties in Puerto Rico* (Princeton: Citizens' Research Foundation, 1961), passim.

Sir John A. Macdonald, used the secret funds attached to his office to advance his party's interests. There also seems to be some truth to allegations that more recently premiers in Third, Fourth, and Fifth Republic France and some chancellors in the Federal Republic of Germany have indulged in similar practices.[10]

The United States of America. To an outside observer, American campaign finance is overwhelming and confusing, both in the magnitude of the sums of money raised and spent and in the variety of means employed and groups and individuals involved in the fundraising process. The dimensions of the problem are implicit in two facts: first, that over 500,000 posts are filled by election in the United States in a four-year cycle and, second, that spending at all levels in the 1976 campaign by candidates and parties, including 6,220 political committees registered by the federal authorities, totaled about $540 million, an increase of $115 million over 1972, 80 percent more than spending in the 1968 campaign, and almost four times the outlays made a quarter-century earlier in 1952. No attempt will be made to duplicate the efforts of Alexander Heard and Herbert Alexander to summarize and analyze American party finance.[11] All we can do is indicate the constitutional imperatives determining its structural elements and the political and institutional developments which give it shape. Chief among the former are the constitutional separation of executive and legislative authority, and federalism; these have created presidential and congressional parties behind the façade of a two-party system, and a multitude of loosely linked parties at the state level. Weak articulation and the further erosion of party authority through changes in the nominating process with the spread of the direct primary system have laid stress on the individual candidate for office, with parties reduced to providing a quasi-formal framework for the official election. In the area of campaign finance the effect is the formation of hosts of ad hoc committees to raise funds for specific candidates in the prenomination and election struggles. Within and sometimes outside the bounds of the law, these bodies seek funds from

---

10 On France, see R. Kraehe, *Le financement des partis politiques* [Political party financing] (Paris: Presses Universitaires de France, 1972), pp. 28-29; see Ulrecht Duebber and Gerard Braunthal, "West Germany," in Richard Rose and Arnold J. Heidenheimer, eds., "Comparative Political Finance: A Symposium," *Journal of Politics*, vol. 25, no. 3, p. 786; for Canada, see Norman Ward, *The Public Purse: A Study in Canadian Democracy* (Toronto: University of Toronto Press, 1962), pp. 64-68.

11 Alexander Heard, *The Costs of Democracy* (Chapel Hill: University of North Carolina Press, 1960); Herbert E. Alexander, *Money in Politics* (Washington, D.C.: Public Affairs Press, 1972).

wealthy individuals, family groups, and organized interests. Navigating among these committees are the many sectional, ethnic, and ideological pressure groups, business organizations, labor unions and federations, which seek access to administrators and influence on legislation in return for lending their support. This financial system, fractured as it is among party-, candidate-, and contributor-oriented groups, further weakens intraparty cohesion and fosters the dissensus inherent in the American separation of powers.

Regulation and Reform of Campaign Finance

Scandals, a concern for equity, and rising campaign costs have precipitated the contemporary movement for the regulation of political finance and the subsidization of party and campaign costs. Controls have been introduced to "clean up" the political process, to check escalating expenditures, to reduce "unfair" competition, and to lessen any undue influence of contributors over politicians; subventions are meant to provide an alternative source of funds to lessen the dependence of parties and candidates on funds of questionable origin and to permit poor but otherwise serious participants to enter the electoral competition.

Efforts have been made in an increasing number of states to control election expenses through legislation which requires the reporting, audit, and disclosure of party and candidate finances, places ceilings on their expenditures, limits contributions beyond certain amounts, or prohibits gifts from particular sources. Income and expenditures may also be affected by statutes which restrict certain campaign activities; tax and corrupt practices laws may encourage or discourage contributions. Although the predominant means of control is statutory law, voluntary interparty agreements have also been used, as in the Federal Republic of Germany for the 1965 general election. Switzerland alone relies solely on the force of custom and public attitudes to keep expenses moderate and allow campaign contributions only from "acceptable" sources. Table 7–1 presents a summary of the statutory controls of campaign, party, and candidate finances which have been enacted in selected democratic countries.

Reporting and Disclosure. Some form of "reporting"—the requirement that parties and/or candidates make periodic financial reports to public officials—is generally viewed as an administrative necessity for the enforcement of expenditure ceilings, limitations on contributions from designated individuals and groups, and the allocation of public subsidies. Many countries in addition demand "disclosure," usually

TABLE 7–1
Statutory Control of Campaign, Party, and Candidate Finances in Selected Democratic Countries

Country	Interval	Reporting By	Reporting To	Reporting Of
Australia	Every campaign	Candidate	Electoral officer	Expenditures
Austria	Annual and every campaign	Party	Minister/ speaker of legislature	Contributions, expenditures
Canada	Annual and every campaign	Candidate and party	Electoral officer	Contributions, expenditures
Denmark	Annual	Parliamentary faction	Speaker of legislature	Accounts
Finland	Annual and every campaign	Party	Minister/ speaker of legislature	Expenditures
France	Campaign	Presidential candidates	Commission	Expenditures
West Germany	Annual and every campaign	Party	Speaker of legislature	Contributions, expenditures

Disclosure	Audit of Reports	Publicity	Limits on Contributions	Limits on Expenditures	Doctrine of Agency[a]	Sanctions
Details of expenditures		Public inspection		On total amount spent by candidates	Yes	
Amount of contributions, donor's identity, details of expenditures	Yes	Public inspection, daily press, reports to legislature		By segment		Cuts in subsidies and a tax penalty
Amount of contributions, donor's identity, details of expenditures	Yes	Public inspection, daily press, reports to legislature		On total amount and by segment spent by candidates and parties	Yes	Fines, cuts in subsidies, imprisonment, disqualification
Details of expenditures	Yes					
No	No	No	No	By segment		
Amount of contributions, donor's identity	Yes			By segment		

(Table continues)

155

TABLE 7–1 (continued)

	Reporting			
Country	Interval	By	To	Of
Ireland	Every campaign	Candidate	Electoral officer	Expenditures
Israel	Annual and every campaign	Party	Commissioner	Contributions, expenditures
Italy	Annual and every campaign	Party	Minister/ speaker of legislature	Contributions, expenditures
Japan	Annual	Constituency association	Minister/ speaker of legislature	Contributions, expenditures
Netherlands	No reporting			
New Zealand	Every campaign	Candidate	Electoral officer	Expenditures
Norway	No reporting			
Sweden	No reporting			
Switzerland	No reporting			
Turkey	No reporting			

Disclosure	Audit of Reports	Publicity	Limits on Contributions	Limits on Expenditures	Doctrine of Agency[a]	Sanctions
		Public inspection, daily press		On total amount and by segment	Yes	Fines or cuts in subsidies, imprisonment, disqualification
Amount of contributions, details of expenditures	Yes	Reports to legislature	On amount and on source	On total amount spent by parties		Fines or cuts in subsidies
Amount of contributions, donor's identity	Yes	Daily press, reports to legislature	On source			Fines or cuts in subsidies, imprisonment
Amount of contributions	Yes		On amount and on source	On total amount and by segment		
Details of expenditures				On total amount		Fines or cuts in subsidies
			On source			

(*Table continues*)

TABLE 7–1 (continued)

| Country | Reporting | | | |
	Interval	By	To	Of
United Kingdom	Every campaign	Candidate	Electoral officer	Contributions, expenditures
United States	Annual and every campaign	Candidate, party, political committee	Commission	Contributions, expenditures
Venezuela	No reporting			

NOTE: This table is intended to facilitate comparisons and should not be taken as definitive or exhaustive. The use of broadly applicable headings and short-hand entries, of course, precludes any detailed account of the arrangements peculiar to each system. A column has been left blank where the stated feature is not present in a given country, where the author was unable to ascertain whether it is present, or where an entry might be more misleading than useful (thus, though the penalties on the books for infringement of financing rules in France include fines, cuts in subsidies, and imprisonment, the "Sanctions" column

the systematic revelation of the details of party or candidate finances, which are made available to the public, including journalists and political rivals; disclosure is considered a prerequisite for any control system that relies on self-policing. A number of countries go further still, requiring that financial accounts be not only made available to the public but actually published, in some cases in the daily press.

Many reporting procedures are restricted to the official campaign period, as in the United Kingdom and older members of the English-speaking Commonwealth except Canada; these countries, too, generally ignore the existence of parties and place the legal onus only on candidates at the local level. The requirement that British (and Australian) trade unions report political gifts to the Registrar of Friendly Societies and that corporations disclose such contributions in their annual reports do make available data in addition to those voluntarily provided by the central party organizations. Canadian electoral law, on the other hand, requires all candidates and registered parties to submit audited reports following each campaign (and annually in the

Disclosure	Audit of Reports	Publicity	Limits on Contributions	Limits on Expenditures	Doctrine of Agency[a]	Sanctions
Details of expenditures		Reports to legislature	No	On total amount spent by candidates	Yes	Fines, imprisonment, disqualification
Amount of expenditure, donor's identity, details of expenditures	Yes	Public inspection, reports to legislature	On total amount and on source	On total amount if candidate accepts public funds		Fines or cuts in subsidies, imprisonment

has been left blank for France since these penalties are not generally enforced).

[a] Countries following the British tradition require that candidates and, where so provided, parties name official agents who are held responsible for the collection and expenditure of all funds in the formal campaign period. These agents must authorize all expenditures and are held legally liable and subject to fine or imprisonment for any violations of the financial provisions of the electoral laws.
SOURCE: Public documents and secondary sources available in late 1979.

case of parties) to constituency returning officers and the chief electoral officer, detailing their expenses and identifying all contributions over $100 by name, amount, and class of giver. Other jurisdictions which provide regular maintenance grants, tax benefits, or election subsidies also require annual reports from parties and groups benefiting from such aid; these countries include Austria, Finland, West Germany, Israel, and Italy.

American electoral law, which places heavy stress on the constraining value of publicity, mandates some of the most elaborate reporting procedures at both the federal and state levels. According to the 1974 Federal Election Campaign Act, candidates must establish one central campaign committee through which all contributions made on their behalf must be reported. Specific bank depositories must be designated, into and out of which all funds are to be paid. Detailed and complete declarations of contributions and expenditures must be submitted to the Federal Election Commission quarterly, and ten days prior to and thirty days following each election, unless under $1,000 has been received or spent in that period; annual reports are necessary in nonelection years. Gifts of $1,000 or more obtained within fifteen days of polling day must be divulged to the FEC within forty-eight hours. Any organization which expends funds or acts so as to influence an election must report as a political committee; also, persons who spend or contribute in excess of $100 other than through a candidate or committee must submit reports.

In sharp contrast, lawmakers in Norway and Sweden have refused to impose reporting procedures on political competitors on the grounds that these constitute a potential violation of the voters' right to privacy, the secrecy of the ballot, and the parties' right to internal autonomy and freedom from interference. The Swedish Government Commission on Party Finance of 1951 adduced additional objections: disclosure of donors' names might lead to political persecution or preferential treatment; parties relying on membership dues would be less affected than those dependent on individual or corporate contributions, thus encouraging the formation of sponsor or front organizations to conceal sources; and small parties would find the accounting costs unduly burdensome.

Limitations on Contributions. Concern for the purity of the electoral process rather than for costs has been the prime motive for imposing restrictions on the sources of party and candidate income. Ceilings on the size of contributions have been adopted in an effort to broaden the base of financial support and lessen dependence on wealthy individuals and groups. Contribution ceilings are rare but have been imposed in the United States at the federal and state levels, in Puerto Rico, the Canadian province of Ontario, New Zealand, and Japan; nevertheless, it should be noted that these limitations are easily evaded and are rarely effective in the long run. More common are the restraints placed on particular sources such as the assessment of civil servants and which include prohibitions on corporate giving in the United States, Argentina, and the Canadian provinces of Quebec and Manitoba. Austria limits donations from industrial organizations by taxing them at the rate of 35 percent. Direct contributions to parties and candidates from trade unions are also forbidden in Quebec and the United States or restricted as in the United Kingdom, where members can choose to contract out of their share of affiliation dues to the Labour party. In Italy public corporations—state holding corporations and companies in which the state holds 20 percent or more of the shares, either directly or indirectly—are prohibited from contributing to party funds. The American state of Florida prohibits campaign contributions from persons holding liquor licenses or racing franchises and those operating utilities or other public concessions. Foreign or nondomiciled interests are forbidden to donate campaign funds in Sweden, the United States, and the province of Ontario. The most far-reaching restriction has been imposed in Quebec, which allows contributions to parties and candidates only from persons qualified to vote under that province's electoral laws. However, such prohibitions are easily evaded through the use of *prêt-noms*, local subsidiaries, and fronts as the case may be. Such restrictions also encourage the formation of parallel action organizations and of voter education, registration, and get-out-the-vote campaigns designed to support particular parties or candidates.

Limits on Expenditure. Expense limitations are more common than constraints on the amounts and sources of income and have generally been adopted in an attempt to keep costs down. In most cases ceilings on party and candidate expenditures apply only to the election campaign period. The most common are statutory provisions which set the maximum amounts that parties and candidates may spend in a given period. Furthermore, certain segmental limits may be imposed through restrictions on particular activities; the latter differ from prohibitions aimed at eliminating certain electoral malpractices, which is the intent of corrupt practices legislation.

Countries which impose statutory ceilings on candidates' spending during the election period include the United Kingdom, Canada and many of its provinces, Australia, New Zealand, Japan, and the Philippines; Supreme Court decisions have in effect confined such ceilings in the United States to presidential candidates who accept public funding. British law takes no cognizance of the electoral activities of parties except where these may be attributed to the campaign effort of a particular candidate. On the other hand, the United Kingdom has imposed a drastic restriction on the election spending of local candidates. Ceilings were first imposed in 1854, and they have been revised and tightened regularly since then, in 1868, 1883, 1918, 1969, and subsequently. In the 1979 campaign each candidate was permitted a maximum expenditure of £1,750 plus 2 pence for every elector in rural or county constituencies, or 1½ pence for every elector in urban or borough constituencies, during the formal election period. Australia and New Zealand have followed the British model in this regard. However, the sad fact is that these systems have led to increasing evasion because of the lack of realism in the amounts permitted to be spent and because of the anachronistic refusal to face up to the role of parties in the election process. The Japanese system, which also focuses on the candidate,

161

is even more unrealistic. Philippine law restricts candidate spending to one year's emolument for the office sought, but the custom of "buying" votes simply makes the controls risible. Canadian federal law and numerous provincial laws impose global spending ceilings on parties and candidates during the campaign period. Permitted spending at the constituency level is determined by a sliding or fixed scale according to the number of eligible voters in the constituency; party expenditures during a national or provincial campaign are fixed at a specific sum or so many cents multiplied by the total number of voters in the aggregate of seats in which the party presents candidates. It should be noted that only parties and candidates may make election expenditures in Canada during the formal campaign period. Parties in Israel may legally spend no more than 30 percent more than the sums to which they are entitled under that country's subsidy scheme. On the other hand, France, the Scandinavian countries, and West Germany among others make no attempt to impose total spending limits on parties and candidates or parallel action groups during election campaigns. Austria has a unique scheme which requires that each party publish a projected expense budget prior to each campaign, to which it must adhere or suffer a reduction in the public grants to which it would otherwise be entitled.

Among the more important segmental limitations on expenditure are restrictions which have been placed on the use of the broadcasting and advertising media in a number of jurisdictions. Canadian federal law restricts all election advertising and limits the total amount of time which all registered parties may purchase on any one radio or television outlet to six-and-a-half hours during the last four weeks of the campaign. The province of Ontario imposes a very generous limit of twenty-five cents per voter on the sums which may be spent on all advertising during a campaign by a provincial party and by a constituency candidate. Israel has imposed limitations on the size of posters and billboards. Australia has tried an indirect approach by requiring the reporting of all newspaper advertising expenditures.

Enforcement. The effectiveness of the control measures sketched in the foregoing pages depends ultimately on the attitudes of those enforcing the laws, no matter what the formal sanctions may be. A cursory examination of the experience of the countries under review reveals that, apart from gross offenses including fraud and bribery—national scandals like the Watergate affair in the United States, the Rivard affair in Canada, or the subornation of officials by multinationals in Italy and Japan—violations of election expense laws excite only spasmodic interest. Whether this is the result of a pervading cynicism or apathy is a problem for the political psychologist; suffice it to say that the artificiality and lack of realism of some of the measures may well contribute.

Public Financing

Table 7–2 presents a summary of the various methods of public financial support adopted in a number of democratic countries. In a companion volume the author has detailed three categories of public support of campaign finances and election activities—direct subventions, specific grants or services, and indirect subsidies—which often appear in combination.[12]

Direct Subventions. Three forms of direct assistance to parties and candidates may be discerned: allocations to parliamentary caucuses, interelection maintenance grants, and campaign subsidies. In most cases this assistance goes directly to the parties, except where elections focus on local candidates or the direct election of chief executives. Eleven of the countries provide annual allocations to the parliamentary groups of the parties; in the case of Norway, Denmark, Sweden, and Finland this constitutes the principal assistance to the parties, especially in the latter two countries, which include substantial sums for organizational maintenance. Separate maintenance grants are paid annually or monthly in Argentina, Israel, Italy, Venezuela, and Quebec. Campaign subsidies by way of advances or reimbursements of permissible expenses are made in Canada and many of its provinces, West Germany, Israel, Italy, Japan, Venezuela, Puerto Rico, and Costa Rica. Canada and its provinces generally make reimbursements to candidates who achieve a certain minimum percentage of the popular vote cast in their constituencies. West Germany and Puerto Rico grant subventions to parties according to their share of the popular vote; payments are staggered over the interelection period so as to provide regular maintenance assistance as well. Some base the subsidy on the number of seats in the legislature won by the respective parties. In the United States the federal government does not subsidize congressional campaigns, but it does help defray the costs of presidential primaries and elections. Under a "matching grant" system, primary candidates who meet certain requirements receive a subsidy equal to the sum they have raised privately, up to a limit of $250 per contribution. In addition, the government grants

---

[12] Khayyam Z. Paltiel, "Public Financing Abroad: Contrasts and Effects," in Michael J. Malbin, ed., *Parties, Interest Groups, and Campaign Finance Laws* (Washington, D.C.: American Enterprise Institute, 1980), pp. 354-70.

TABLE 7-2

Public Subsidies to Parties and Candidates in Selected Democratic Countries, 1979

Country	Direct Subsidies				Indirect Subsidies
	Recipient	Interval	Basis[a]	Specific Grants or Services	
Australia	No direct subsidies			Broadcasting	
Austria	Parties, parliamentary groups		Per vote	Billposting, broadcasting, printing ballots, party foundations, press and publications, women's and youth organizations, education and information	
Canada	Candidates,[b] parliamentary groups	Election	Per vote	Broadcasting, voter registration	Tax credits
Denmark	Parliamentary groups	Annual	Per seat	Broadcasting, press and publications, women's and youth organizations	
Finland	Parties	Annual	Per seat	Billposting, broadcasting, press and publications, women's and youth organizations	
France	Presidential candidates	Election		Billposting, broadcasting, printing ballots, press and publications	Kickbacks of deputy salaries

Country	Recipients	Frequency	Basis	Uses	Indirect subsidies
West Germany	Parties, parliamentary groups	Election	Per seat, per vote	Broadcasting, party foundations, women's and youth organizations, education and information	Tax deductions, kickbacks of deputy salaries
Ireland	No direct subsidies				
Israel	Parties, parliamentary groups	Annual, every election	Per seat, per vote	Broadcasting, transportation	
Italy	Parties, parliamentary groups	Annual, every election	Per vote	Broadcasting, women's and youth organizations, education and information	Kickbacks of deputy salaries
Japan	Candidates	Every election		Billposting, broadcasting, election advertising, transportation	
Netherlands	Parliamentary groups	Annual	Per seat	Broadcasting, party foundations, women's and youth organizations	Tax deductions
Norway	Parties, parliamentary groups	Annual	Per seat	Broadcasting, nomination costs	
Sweden	Parties, parliamentary groups	Annual	Per seat, per vote	Broadcasting, press and publications, women's and youth organizations	
Switzerland	No direct subsidies				
Turkey	Parties	Annual	Per vote		

(Table continues)

TABLE 7–2 (continued)

Country	Direct Subsidies				Indirect Subsidies
	Recipient	Interval	Basis[a]	Specific Grants or Services	
United Kingdom	Parliamentary groups	Annual		Broadcasting, mailing, use of public halls	
United States	Candidates in presidential primaries and elections	Election	Matching grant in primary, fixed sum in election[c]	Nomination costs, mailing; most states pay for voter registration and ballots	Tax credits, tax deductions
Venezuela	Parties	Election	Per vote	Broadcasting, election advertising	

NOTE: This table is intended to facilitate comparisons and should not be taken as definitive or exhaustive. The use of broadly applicable headings and shorthand entries, of course, precludes any detailed account of the arrangements peculiar to each system. A column has been left blank where the stated feature is not present in a given country, where the author was unable to ascertain whether it is present, or where an entry might be more misleading than useful.

[a] "Per seat," amount of subsidy determined on the basis of seats won; "per vote," amount of subsidy determined on the basis either of votes received or of eligible voters.

[b] In Canada candidates may assign their reimbursements to their sponsoring national party organization.

[c] From funds earmarked by taxpayers.

SOURCE: Public documents and secondary sources available in late 1979.

lump sums, fixed by law and indexed to the cost of living, to the major parties for their national nominating conventions and to qualifying presidential candidates for their campaigns. The total sum available for these subsidies is determined by the taxpayers, each of whom has the option of earmarking $1 of his federal taxes for this purpose. But, as Ranney has pointed out, federal funding of presidential campaigns has further undermined the already weak U.S. party system.[13]

Specific Grants and Services. In contrast to direct general grants, specific ones are made in an attempt to meet particular needs and costs, such as broadcasting, mailing and telecommunications, billposting, paper (including ballots), meeting halls, press and information bureaus, nominations, women's groups and youth groups, party educational and research foundations, and voter registration, which is often paid for entirely by the state. In all jurisdictions where broadcasting is a public service or a state-controlled monopoly, parties and/or candidates are granted either equal or proportional time on the air. In Canada at the federal level, the state also reimburses half the cost of the broadcasting time that registered parties are permitted to purchase during the campaign period on private and public stations and networks. Four countries provide the materials and space for, or meet the costs of, billposting. Several provide ballot papers. Norway helps cover the costs of party nomination meetings if certain conditions are met, and American law provides assistance for the coverage of presidential primary campaign costs. Aside from free broadcasting time, the only assistance provided British candidates is one free mailing and free access to meeting halls in public buildings. Most countries outside the United States cover the full cost of voter registration; in Canada at the federal level and in certain provinces the payment of party-appointed enumerators provides a source of petty financial patronage to the candidates of the major parties at the local level. In Europe many states provide assistance to the sections of the established parties concerned with the press, publications, education, information, women, and youth. The most significant examples of such assistance are the vast sums of money provided by various West German ministries to the four principal foundations affiliated

---

[13] Austin Ranney, "The Impact of Campaign Finance Reforms on American Presidential Parties" (Paper prepared for the Conference on Political Money and Election Reform: Comparative Perspectives, University of Southern California, Los Angeles, December 10, 1977). The best summary of the legal arrangements for public funding in the United States is Herbert E. Alexander, *Financing Politics: Money, Elections, and Political Reform,* 2d ed. (Washington, D.C.: Congressional Quarterly Press, 1980).

with the major German parties, sums which are used for domestic and international party work.[14]

Originally established to perpetuate the memory and teachings of notable socialist, liberal, and conservative party leaders—Friedrich Ebert (SPD), Friedrich Naumann (FDP), Konrad Adenauer (CDU), and Hanns Seidel (CSU)—the foundations were transformed following the West German Constitutional Court decision of 1966 which restricted the public subvention of political parties to election costs alone. The *Stiftungen* afforded a legally acceptable channel through which government funds could continue to flow to the parties in support of their research, information, and civic education functions. The foundations serve party schools and training institutes, prepare ideological materials, and carry out surveys and other investigations for their sponsors, who can count on readily available pools of skilled manpower in planning and implementing their campaign strategies. The foundations receive some monetary support from friendly individuals, businesses, trade unions, cooperatives, and party-controlled enterprises. However, the bulk of their funds come from the budgets of the Federal Center for Political Education, the Ministry for Inner German Affairs, the Foreign Ministry, and the Ministry for Economic Cooperation; the allocations are made by interparty agreement in proportion to the number and share of the popular votes gained by their respective sponsors in the previous federal general election. On the international stage the foundations carry out community development projects in underdeveloped countries in Asia, Africa, and Latin America, organizing self-help schemes, cooperatives, and socialist or Christian trade unions where the situation is hospitable, taking care to coordinate their activities and eliminate overlap when they can. The foundations work closely with the internationals of their sponsoring parties and seek to stimulate the formation and growth of counterparts in such countries as Portugal, Spain, Greece, and Italy through assistance similar to the aid given by the German socialists to fraternal parties in France and Scandinavia. The Ebert and Adenauer foundations maintain a dense network of offices in southern Europe as well as liaison establishments in North America and elsewhere. The very salience of these efforts has aroused comment. As I have written elsewhere, "Serious questions arise, first, as to the propriety of these activities and, second, with regard to the identification of party and state as the foundations carry out projects using

---

[14] For a detailed study of the German foundations, see Henning Von Vierrege, *Parteistiftungen: Schriftenreihe zum Stiftungswesen* [Party foundations: publication series on the nature of foundations], vol. 11 (Baden-Baden: Nomos Verlagsgesellschaft, 1977).

resources subject directly and indirectly to [German] government control."[15]

Indirect Subsidies. Tax credits and tax deductions for campaign and other purposes are a form of indirect assistance to parties and candidates. These are available at the provincial and federal level in Canada, West Germany, the Netherlands, Norway, and the United States. The practice in some left-wing parties of requiring legislators to turn over part of their salaries or indemnities for party purposes may also be considered a very indirect form of public support.

Impact of Controls and Subsidies. Controls and public subventions have been enacted to stem public outrage at the more egregious financial practices of parties and candidates and in reaction to pressures from reformers wishing to reduce campaign costs and promote honesty and the liberal principles of equity and equality of opportunity. The measures have been justified on the grounds that corruption undermines the stability, integrity, and legitimacy of the political regime; that unequal access to campaign funds and dependence on clandestine sources and special interests constitute a threat to democratic values; and that high costs must be curbed or subsidized since they impede effective participation in the electoral process.

Many of the reforms reviewed in the foregoing pages have helped remove the mystery surrounding the monetary aspects of politics. But there is little evidence that costs have been restrained or reduced. Nor does it appear that subsidy schemes have promoted greater popular participation or facilitated the entry of new groups into the electoral arena. To the contrary, studies have shown that the controls have generally worked to the benefit of incumbents and established parties and have encouraged internal processes of centralization and bureaucratization. Evidence from Canada, West Germany, Sweden, Finland, Austria, and Italy indicates substantial growth in the paid staff of party organizations in the wake of the adoption of public subsidies. Campaign techniques have become increasingly sophisticated, but the growing reliance on professional expertise has downgraded middle-level party leaders and confined party militants to routine tasks. The variety and complexity of the procedures required to comply with the controls have expanded the role of paid party officials and reinforced the tendency to bureaucratization. Finnish, Italian, West German, Austrian, and Canadian experience generally demonstrates that controls and subsidies strengthen the central party organizations vis-à-vis local parties and reinforce the position of the

---

[15] Paltiel, "Public Financing Abroad," p. 363.

dominant groups within the leadership against minority factions and their leaders.

This tendency is countered where regional and local party organs have direct and independent access to sources of public funding, as they do in Sweden, or where candidates at the national or local level are in receipt of direct support independent of central party channels. Federalism also lessens the dependence of regions on the center by providing an alternative source of support from provincial or state treasuries. Provincial or local party autonomy may also be fostered by regulations such as those enacted in some Canadian provinces, which prohibit or severely restrict intraparty transfers from the federal to the provincial level or across provincial lines. In the United States the stress on individual candidates has helped erode internal party cohesion, while the growth of provincial subsidy and control schemes in Canada has weakened the already fragile links between federal and provincial parties.

The controls and the subsidies are biased in favor of incumbents and parties which have achieved representation in the legislature. In examining their effects, we find that the principal contrast is not between large and small parties or independent candidates in the electoral arena but between the "ins" and the "outs," regardless of ideological orientation. Rather than promoting openness, the legislation, the qualifications for the receipt of subventions, and the structure of the regulatory bodies tend to impose constraints on the formation of new political groups and on their participation in the electoral process; in the United States the laws clearly benefit incumbents. Their combined impact suggests that a fourth motive underlies their introduction: namely, the desire of legislators to stabilize the party system and entrench the electoral position of established groups. The result has been the crystallization of external as well as internal party relationships, growing rigidity in the party system, and lessened responsiveness to emerging social groups and changed political demands. The consequence may well be the very alienation from the virtues of the electoral process that the reforms purportedly were designed to avoid.[16]

Democracy and Party Finance

At the outset of his magisterial study of money in politics, Alexander Heard stated:

---

[16] For a fuller examination of the problems raised in this section, see Khayyam Z. Paltiel, "The Impact of Election Expenses Legislation in Canada, Western Europe, and Israel," in Herbert E. Alexander, ed. *Political Finance* (Beverly Hills and London: Sage Publications, 1979), pp. 15-39.

Like all participants in politics, those who supply and use campaign monies may, and often do, exercise political influence. Influence in its broadest sense is integral to representative government. The sensitivity of politicians to factors that affect the outcome of elections is the springhead of responsive and responsible government. Politicians are as alert to the financial contributions to their success as to other types of help. Deeper understanding of political money means deeper understanding of representative government. . . .

Political parties function as connecting organs joining government to the rest of society. They are the principal type of intermediate organization that links the citizen and his specialized groups with the forums of government decision-making. As such, political parties provide complex and sensitive channels through which interests express themselves and seek representation in government. These channels are frequently subtle and indirect transmitters of the demands, viewpoints, and ideals of affected citizens. But they serve not solely as relay pipes for political pressures; they act also as sieves separating consequential issues from those which are dispensable and arbitrating among conflicting claims.

The processes of political finance constitute one set of mechanisms through which political representation is achieved.[17]

The residue of an outdated individualistic ideology tends to obscure the fact that the flow of funds into the party system reflects the economic and social structure of society. In an increasingly complex and differentiated industrial society, there exists a constant tension between the interests of the organized groups that possess the bulk of the technical, material, and monetary resources needed by the parties, and the principle of "one man, one vote" that underlies democratic systems. Legal restrictions alone will neither eliminate group demands nor reduce the needs of the parties. The conflict is itself the very stuff of democratic politics.

Bibliography

Alexander, Herbert E. *Financing Politics: Money, Elections, and Political Reform.* 2d ed. Washington, D.C.: Congressional Quarterly Press, 1980.
————. *Financing the 1976 Election.* Washington, D.C.: Congressional Quarterly Press, 1979.

---

[17] Heard, *Costs of Democracy*, pp. 11-12.

Alexander, Herbert E., ed. *Political Finance*. Beverly Hills and London: Sage Publications, 1979.

Campana, André. *L'argent secret: le financement des partis politiques* [Secret money: political party funding]. Paris: Arthaud, 1976.

Heard, Alexander. *The Costs of Democracy*. Chapel Hill: University of North Carolina Press, 1960.

Heidenheimer, Arnold J., ed. *Comparative Political Finance: The Financing of Party Organizations and Election Campaigns*. Lexington: D.C. Heath, 1970. (Contains chapters on West Germany, Great Britain, Scandinavia, the United States, Canada, Asia, and Latin America.)

Heidenheimer, Arnold J., and Langdon, Frank C. *Business Associations and the Financing of Political Parties: A Comparative Study of the Evolution of Practices in Germany, Norway and Japan*. The Hague: Martinus Nijhoff, 1968.

The Houghton Report. *Report of the Committee on Financial Aid to Political Parties, Cmd. 6601*. London: Her Majesty's Stationery Office, 1976.

Leonard, Dick. *Paying for Party Politics: The Case for Public Subsidies*. Broadsheet vol. 41, no. 555. London: Political and Economic Planning, 1975.

Malbin, Michael J., ed. *Parties, Interest Groups, and Campaign Finance Laws*. Washington, D.C.: American Enterprise Institute, 1979.

Overracker, Louise. *Money in Elections*. New York: Macmillan, 1932.

Paltiel, Khayyam Z. "Canadian Election Expense Legislation: Recent Developments." In *Party Politics in Canada*, edited by H. G. Thorburn. 4th ed. Scarborough, Ont.: Prentice-Hall, 1979.

———. *Party, Candidate, and Election Finance: A Background Report*. Study no. 22. Royal Commission on Corporate Concentration. Ottawa: Ministry of Supply and Services, 1977.

———. *Political Party Financing in Canada*. Toronto: McGraw-Hill, 1970.

Paltiel, Khayyam Z. Committee on Election Expenses. *Studies in Canadian Party Finance*. Ottawa: Queen's Printer, 1966.

Pollock, James K. *Money and Politics Abroad*. New York: Alfred Knopf, 1932.

Report of the Committee on Election Expenses. Ottawa: Queen's Printer, 1966.

Rose, Richard, and Heidenheimer, Arnold J., eds. "Comparative Political Finance: A Symposium." A special issue of *Journal of Politics* 25:3, pp. 643–811.

Schleth, Uwe, *Partei Finanzierung* [Party funding]. Meisenheim: Hain, 1972.

Valitutti, Salvatore, and Ciaurro, Gian Franco. *Contro il finanziamento publico dei partiti* [Against the public financing of parties]. Rome: Bulzoni Editore [1975?].

Von Vierrege, Henning. *Parteistiftungen: Schriftenreihe zum Stiftungswesen* [Party foundations: publications series on the nature of foundations]. Vol. 11. Baden-Baden: Nomos Verlagsgesellschaft, 1977.

8

Mass Communications

Anthony Smith

Television and Its Predecessors

Television became the most generally available medium of mass communication in all of the developed countries in the late 1960s, and since that time political observers everywhere have been attempting to deal with the question of its influence upon the gamut of issues with which political scientists traditionally have been concerned. They ponder such problems as whether television influences the level of public participation in politics, whether it alters the types of candidates who run for election, whether it multiplies the impact of public opinion polls, whether the programs themselves have been decisive in any particular contest, whether the role of elections within the democratic body politic has been significantly changed by television. By the 1980s a wide array of countries had passed the "saturation" level of set ownership (50–60 percent of homes), and in most of these, television had become a primary means of political discourse (see table 8–1). Though its forms, together with its institutional privileges and restraints, continue to evolve, political television per se is firmly established. We of the West live in societies where mass politics and mass television have become inextricably linked.

Television's impact has not been uniform in the societies where it has assumed a major role, any more than was the impact of the popular newspaper or the cinema or radio or, for that matter, the public platform. Each society has acquired its own program formats, its own rules and restraints, and its own peculiar interactive dependencies within its political structure. In all cases, however, broadcasting assumed a political role only after national broadcasting institutions and regulatory systems had developed. In this, its evolution was different from that of the political press, which matured

TABLE 8–1
POLITICAL TELEVISION IN TWENTY-ONE DEMOCRATIC COUNTRIES

Characteristic	Australia	Austria	Belgium	Canada	Denmark	Finland	France
Television ownership P—entirely public C—entirely commercial PC—mixture of public and commercial	PC	P	P	PC	P	P	P
Year in which regular TV broadcasts began (19—)	56	56	59	52	54	56	35
TV sets per 1,000 inhabitants, 1965	172	98	163	271	227	169	133
1970	217	192	216	332	266	221	268
1976	351	236	265	428	323	363	274
Is paid political advertising permitted?	Y	N	N	Y	N	N	N
Is free TV time given to political parties?	Y	Y	Y	Y	Y	Y	Y
Is free time equal to all parties (E) or proportional to voting strength (P)?	E	P	P	P	E	E	E
Are there rules about fair balance in political programming?	—	Y	Y	Y	—	Y	Y
Is there a right of reply?	—	Y	—	—	Y	Y	Y
Have direct confrontations between party leaders been televised?	—	—	Y	Y	Y	Y	Y
Year of first election in which TV played a major role (19—)	58	56	—	53	—	—	62

NOTE: The countries included in this table are those of the twenty-eight discussed in this volume for which information was readily available. Coded entries are explained in the stub at left.

— Not ascertained or not applicable.

Y = yes; N = no.

ᵃ 1975.

SOURCE: UNESCO, *Statistical Yearbook 1977* (Paris: United Nations Educational, Scientific and Cultural Organization, 1977).

West Germany	India	Ireland	Italy	Japan	Netherlands	Norway	Spain	Sri Lanka	Sweden	Switzerland	Turkey	United Kingdom	United States
P	P	P	P	PC	P	P	P	P	P	P	P	PC	PC
52	59	61	54	53	53	57	56	78	56	58	72	36	50
193	0	114	117	183	172	131	—	—	270	104	0.1	248	362
272	0.1	152	181	219	237	220	124	—	312	203	—	293	412
311[a]	0.5	207	220	239[a]	274	270	185	—	363	285	44	317	511[a]
N	N	N	N	Y	N	N	N	N	N	N	—	N	Y
Y	—	Y	Y	Y	Y	N	Y	N	Y	Y	Y	Y	N
P	—	P	P	E	E	—	P	—	P	P	E	P	—
Y	—	Y	Y	Y	Y	Y	Y	—	Y	Y	Y	Y	Y
Y	—	N	Y	Y	Y	Y	Y	—	Y	—	Y	Y	Y
Y	—	Y	—	—	—	Y	—	—	Y	—	—	N	Y
61	—	65	—	—	—	61	77	—	—	59	—	51	52

alongside the political system of which it was a crucial element, in the late nineteenth century in most Western societies. Before the intrusion of television into their sphere, politicians already knew what they expected of the mass media and what they feared of this new medium. Television, meanwhile, had already learned the limits of political tolerance, the ways in which it had to condition its cultural growth to institutional possibilities. Every society has found it necessary to make accommodations between them, and each has done this in its own national style.

Politics was looking for a total national system of communication long before the advent of television or radio. Indeed, before we examine the specific forms which the electronic media have created for the coverage of elections, it is important to see how older media were constructed to serve evolving political systems; for television, initially at least, merely attempted to meet the expectations held of it, to continue rather than displace the kinds of communication that had preceded it into the mass electorate. Radio and television, after all, are both media of transmission primarily; they can transmit to a new and wider audience electoral communications presented in some other arena. While the process of transmission—whether of a public meeting or a debate or a selection meeting—alters the terms of the communication that is taking place, the electronic media can make it their business to alter its message as little as possible. They can also produce their own material. Or something in between can happen, as it does when the electronic media transmit communications or cover events which, though apparently independent, actually are deliberately devised for the purpose of being relayed by the electronic media to a wider public.

The interaction between established media systems and novel ones, then, is complex. Politicians bred on one form of discourse are forced into the frustrating process of adapting to another. The politician who felt at home on the platform of the mid-nineteenth century discovered that large-circulation newspapers were disseminating his statements in printed form. Later the politician found that the newspaper interview, to which he had with difficulty accustomed himself, was being transmuted into the live radio or television interview, imposing quite different constraints upon him despite the similarity of names. Small wonder that he has attempted, everywhere, to impose controls and systems of equity on media which he finds he can at least partly control. The major contrast between the media inherited by the twentieth century and those developed by it lies in this area of political control: where politicians could influence the press either individually or as parties, they have had to do so collectively—through legislation, regulation, or less formal institutionalized arrangements—in the case of radio and television.[1] Influence over the electronic media has become an occupational privilege of politicians.

It is just a century since the telegraph, the rotary printing press, and the public platform first meshed into a "total" modern political communication system. A speech made in one location could be transcribed and sent by telegraph the same day throughout the newspaper network of a nation. Politicians had acquired, for the first time, an "instant" form of communication with the voting public, which was part mechanical and part electronic. This transformation rapidly spread through all of the developing democracies. When we think of the political communication system that radio and television reshaped, we sometimes forget that it already relied on a combination of communication techniques.

Metropolis and province were drawn together into a national symbiosis, a new political geography. In the national village, the central symbolic form of political discourse was the platform, although the immediate reality for most citizens was the printed press. Through the columns of print, what the reader saw was a man making a speech to a crowd. With the addition of the microphone (at the turn of the century) the politician began to speak to larger numbers of people at the same time. His audience became an interparty gathering of adult voters, where previously he had harangued a small inner group of voting citizens surrounded by an uncomprehending, franchiseless mob. Even before the microphone, the politician aimed his words through the crowd, not at it: his real target was the reporters' bench and the rows of shorthand notebooks. The microphone made the politician aware of the vastness of the political space in which he operated and of the invisible audience to which he had to project himself. For a century the stuff of politics was tailored to the needs of the newspaper, and until a generation ago the newspaper was shaped by the requirements of politics. Out of the connection came a symbolic system of communication: the newspapers described debates, conflicts, demonstrations, activities. The innovation of television was actually to show personalities and events: to a large degree, the television coverage *is* the electoral campaign.[2]

---

[1] In the 1920s and 1930s political parties in many countries (including the United Kingdom) used the cinema for propaganda at election times. The political "commercial" designed for cinema audiences was never subject to the rules of equal time that later prevailed in radio and television. It drew on the newspaper cartoon as well as the platform for its style and content.

[2] Trevor Pateman, *Television and the February 1974 General Election*, British Film Institute Television Monograph, no. 3 (London, 1974).

177

The first decades of television are now over; the electronic media became the dominant part of the political communication system only during the 1960s. Between them, radio and television have created a fundamentally new system of political discourse, although it continues to depend entirely upon a flow of information passing through newspapers and magazines in virtually all societies. In the 1970s all of the traditional elements remained, but they performed different functions within the whole and at different levels of importance.

The newspaper-dominated system emphasized the continuity of voters' political affiliations. The audience was divided into partisan groupings, each of whom received information from the parties themselves and from the printed media organizationally connected with them or supporting them as a matter of editorial policy. Party loyalty entailed newspaper loyalty and normally also membership in a defined social and economic group. The strength of these identifications in turn reinforced the stability of the party system. But television works differently on all of these scores. Because it aspires to impartiality and because its audience is less differentiated, less often self-selected, than the readership of the political press, television exposes more of the people more of the time to views different from those they already hold. By showing both sides of an argument, it tends to erode the stability of people's political views and party identification and even the stability of the party system. It has this effect all the more where it gives equal time to all parties, encouraging new factions to fight elections. Thus, in many countries (Denmark and Israel, for example) the pollsters found evidence of increasing percentages of voters changing their minds during election campaigns in the 1970s. While newspapers are still a force for mobilizing voters of a given persuasion to support their leaders, television encourages discussion, not commitment.

In its coverage of elections, television aspires not only to impartiality but also to completeness. For the last three general elections one of the commercial companies in Britain has assembled a group of 500 voters from a single constituency, segregated them for a period of days, and permitted them to be fed with a balanced diet of party propaganda, ending up with speeches given by the main party leaders and a straw poll, to see how their views have shifted as a result of a concentrated, balanced, but isolated dose of propaganda. For another program, used in the British EEC referendum and the second 1974 general election, two recently retired politicians were sent on a nationwide filmed tour as "everyman" commentators. The notion behind these endeavors was that it was possible to find and bring to the screen a comprehensive reality of "voterdom," a balanced, fair, irrefutable representation of the body politic. The British Broadcasting Corporation's series "Election Forum," broadcast during the general elections of 1964 through 1974, enabled each party leader to answer viewers' questions selected, from the tens of thousands sent in, by a panel of nationally known interviewers; however meretricious the formula in scientific terms, the intention was to pursue and secure the *ipsissima verba* of the "true" voter, the "ordinary" man who inhabits social reality as conceived by television. Into this reality, mediated by its image on the screen, the viewer was invited to enter. And he consented to enter in the belief that he was being shown the whole—where his newspaper-reading forebears found reassurance in identifying only with part.

It is not surprising, therefore, that the widespread decline in the intensity of partisanship among voters is ascribed to the influence of television.[3] There may well be other factors which have produced this new mood among voters—a distrust of "argy-bargy" among politicians, a sense of classlessness, the feeling that no single party can have a monopoly on "truth"—but these, too, may be affected by the manner in which politics is presented by television. Here again, the inextricability of causes and effects is the greatest lesson taught by the attempt to study the meaning of television in society.

Political Bias in the Media

The whole basis of the ownership and control of television is entirely different from that of the press, even in societies such as Australia where most of the metropolitan TV stations are owned by the same four empires that control most of the press. Television everywhere is socially owned or socially controlled or both. Newspapers won the economic fruits of the battle for freedom of expression as well as the moral advantages, but in many societies they handed their influence over to political parties, with which they became affiliated. Newspapers were partisan; they had a known bias about which their readers did not complain. Television has increased the expectation of impartiality in all media and has made the bias of newspapers appear increasingly improper. In a climate thus altered, the journalists of Australia actually instigated industrial action against newspaper owners who appeared to be forcing them to be "unfair" to one side during the political upheaval and election of 1975.

---

[3] Jay G. Blumler, Michael Gurevitch, and Julian Ives, *The Challenge of Election Broadcasting* (Leeds: Centre for TV Research, Leeds University, 1977).

Even today, an almost perfect example of the traditional system of political communications survives in Norway: 152 newspapers are shared by 4 million people, nearly every one of whom lives within reach of a group of politically competing dailies. At election time their attention is divided between a paper that presents clear party information emanating from national party news agencies, and television, which presents the classic noncommercial media campaign, with equal time for all contending parties. Norway is in this sense unique—and even in Norway a tendency toward concentration has set in. In Sweden and Denmark it has gone further, and the old party papers have turned themselves into independent or nonpolitical tabloids in order to retain their reader appeal.[4] Tabloids, as we can see clearly in Britain and Germany, may remain politically very active during election campaigns, supporting one party leader and excoriating the others; however, the quality of their political information clearly declines; they boil down policies and analyses to slogans or smears. In such circumstances radio and television increase in importance as media of information and arguably play a greater role than ever in helping the undecided voters to reach their voting decisions (while at the same time helping to increase the numbers who become undecided).

The whole question of bias has become a key political issue, likely to become more vexatious in the 1980s than in the 1970s. Immediately after the 1979 election in Britain, the Labour party began to discuss more intensely than before the need for a popular printed press which was not biased in favor of their opponents; the campaign of 1979 had been marked by extreme political polarization among the popular tabloids (including several launched since the elections of 1974), which had supported Thatcher against Callaghan four to one, while the "quality" newspapers had been neutral or pro-Conservative (or, in the case of the *Times*, temporarily nonexistent). The left again felt betrayed by the press, as the Labor party of Australia had after the debacle of 1975—and it felt so partly because television's model of fairness had turned the "bias" of the press from a civil right into a vexation, a social wrong. At the Labor party conference of October 1979, the party—not for the first time in its history—discussed launching a new popular daily. The example of Norway's and Sweden's social democratic press is a source of permanent admiration and frustration to the British Labour party.

The accusation of bias is made frequently against television and radio, but in conditions which are quite different, since the

---

[4] Anthony Smith, *Subsidies and the Press in Europe* (London: Political and Economic Planning, 1977).

electronic media are expected to be completely neutral politically. France is an interesting exception. De Gaulle in the Fifth Republic insisted on taking control of the television services of the ORTF precisely because he believed the press had always been biased against him; under the Fourth Republic the progovernment bias of the ORTF (and its predecessor, RTF) had been disguised and softened somewhat because of the frequent changes of administration. Under the Fifth Republic the ORTF was reformed and later abolished, but it was replaced by a series of separate channels whose senior appointments were all still made by the president of the republic, thus increasing the frustration of those French voters who wanted television to be a neutral source of political information. The politically aligned newspapers of France, meanwhile, have taken a battering under the Fifth Republic, one by one falling either into insolvency or into the hands of a few newspaper giants (the *papivores* of Henri Grandmaison's celebrated *roman à clef*). Thus France has been left with a fascinating dilemma, rather different from that of the other nations of Europe: it has a journalistic profession bred in a world of active political dissension, trained by history to take part in political polemics both on television and in the printed press, but operating in an environment where increasingly the press is controlled by individuals who do not respect the right of journalists to write as they wish, while television has lost its stomach for political propaganda, avoiding debate altogether between elections.

What France has bequeathed the world, in *Le Monde*, is a new model of collective control in journalism, in which policy is decided after a certain degree of internal debate among the senior personnel. Newspapers in Germany and Scandinavia have moved with some enthusiasm to discuss such systems, while one or two smaller Italian papers have been turned into cooperative enterprises; if they succeed as well as *Le Monde*, these may, in time, open up a new avenue of development within Europe's journalistic political culture. For the moment, however, each major national election in Europe has merely served to emphasize the frustrations of voters, politicians of minority parties, and journalists, all of whom feel acutely that a structural unfairness has crept into the system of political communication. This has happened in an era when no one is in practice free to take an initiative. It is economically impossible (or almost so) to start new papers. It is legally impossible to take control of a broadcasting outlet—except in Italy, where the chaotic profusion of radio and television stations provides the audience with entertainment but deprives the politician of clear and easy access to the electorate.

The end of the corporatist connections between parties, news-papers, and mass organizations (which are still of great importance in the Scandinavian societies) has meant that a certain cohesiveness has evaporated from the communication system of many democracies; where political, social, and economic elites formerly pursued basically consensus goals, today they find themselves in conflict with the professionalist ideology of journalists. It is harder than it used to be to mold citizens into some kind of collective national unity; they pursue individual goals and tastes or give their loyalty to participatory subgroups. Thus the age of television has come to be an age of declining hierarchy; indeed, all the *forms* of television (round tables, interviews, confrontations, speeches on the hustings) symbolize the supplanting of political paternalism by participation at the grass roots, and the substitution of social egalitarianism for the more tra-ditional *de haut en bas* conduct of political discussion.

In the United States, with its myriad local monopoly newspapers, the question of partisanship in the press crops up in quite different forms. Every local monopoly newspaper retains, of course, its complete editorial freedom, but it feels very strong social pressure not to support one candidate while freezing out all others from public exposure. There are some interesting exceptions to this (the McGoff papers of Michigan, for example), but on the whole American news-papers strongly hold the doctrine of party impartiality, although many continue to endorse candidates in editorials. Print media monopolies feel pressures similar to those that affect the publicly regulated media, although they have no juridical compulsion to be impartial even in reporting the news.

The decline of partisan newspapers has sent politicians hunting for other means of mobilizing their core supporters. In several societies (Canada and Australia are two) advertising has become in-creasingly important, provoking new tensions between publishers and journalists. In Italy the arrival of "free" radio and television stations in their hundreds has created complex new opportunities for party managers with enough cash to buy broadcasting time; but when it comes to the press, widespread changes in the structure of owner-ship have taken place, and journalists' committees have gained considerable power in more and more papers (even where ownership itself is not cooperative). Since advertising directly affects a paper's economic viability, these committees have frequently preferred to exercise their influence over their publishers through their power to accept or reject advertisers, rather than through their decisions about news content or editorial stance. Many, for example, have refused to sell space to the MSI, the party of the extreme right.

Political advertising has several advantages over the political broadcasts the parties air in the free time available to them in most countries. Prepared party broadcasts are transmitted simultaneously on all channels in many places, and everywhere they are subject to rules and regulations designed to equalize the advantage offered to all the major parties. While the candidates' prepared broadcasts can bore a politically sated electorate, advertisements can seek out the voter unawares, when he is watching television for entertainment or reading nonpolitical material in his newspaper or magazine. A slogan that reaches him this way will not be immediately counteracted by a competing party's different message. In most of the countries of Western Europe, however, political advertising is banned on television (even where television commercials are permitted for ordinary goods and services; see table 8–1), and it is subject to expenditure limitations in the majority of countries during the campaign itself.

One of the principal problems presented to campaign managers in most modern mass media systems is making headlines. The parties must capture the vast majority of their media exposure by doing and saying what the media will deem worth covering. Campaign managers, with an eye to press deadlines, must produce not argument but stories, not policies but personalities. In today's consumer society the politician's right to state his case in the media is more circumscribed than it once was—and he does not always like what he has to do to obtain the projection he needs. Nor can he avoid unfavorable coverage: permanently on show wherever he goes, he cannot afford mistakes or second thoughts. In these circumstances it is not surprising that campaign managers and political leaders virtually everywhere are showing ever greater interest in decision making within the television and newspaper organizations that now mediate political communication.

The Role of Television in Election Campaigns

To understand the propagandistic and educative function of television in campaigns one must first grasp the importance of television as a new element in the institutional structure of the modern state. Because the "natural" audience of television and the "natural" audience of the statesman coincide, the conduct of political life as a whole has been greatly altered by its arrival. Television has tested the foundations of political systems, as well as introducing a crucial new factor into the formation of opinion. Thus, the story of the painful stages by which Fifth Republic France developed a system of equity for granting free television time to candidates during major elections is a case study in Gaullism's coming to terms with pluralism: it was television that eventually forced Gaullism to confront the problem of limiting the personal power of the president in a political system created to suit one man.[5]

In the television era, voters learn to read the system as well as watch the programs—to see not with but through the eye, as William Blake put it. The voter sees whether communists or fascists or fringe groups are permitted air time, whether the opposition is given exposure, whether a remote political elite is merely conducting a dialogue with itself; he sees what is not there as acutely as what is. The gradual evolution of the forms of television coverage of elections in Western societies, by forcing changes in representation on the screen, has forced changes in the nature of the political systems themselves; France, after de Gaulle, provides a good example. If election campaigns, in Elihu Katz's phrase, are the major learning experiences of democratic politics, then campaigns as seen on television are the most vivid expression of the modern democratic system.[6]

The formats for political coverage adopted by television producers (after long debate within the world of political management and broadcasting administration) reveal some of the deeper meanings of the political system as a whole. Politicians can perform four basic functions on television: they can answer questions, they can debate among themselves, they can face sections of the electorate on public platforms or in studios, and they can walk campaigning through the streets. The fact that these functions exist for the purpose of being portrayed to the wider electorate renders the functions themselves symbolic. But symbolic of what? The electorate is choosing a politician not to answer questions but to govern. The unspoken proposition underlying the formats television has adopted (with the assent of the politicians and parties concerned) is that an individual who performs these four functions well is likely to become a good head of government or minister or representative. Television viewers watching a politician inquiring the price of an apple in a store understand that the individual wishes to be thought of as concerned about the price and quality of food, familiar with the problems of daily life, and able to get along with storekeepers. We know from a wealth of literature concerning American presidential

---

[5] Roger Errera, *Les libertés à l'abandon* (Paris: Le Seuil, 1975); Ruth Thomas, *Broadcasting and Democracy in France* (Bradford, England: Bradford University Press, 1976).

[6] Elihu Katz, "Platforms and Windows—Broadcasting's Role in Election Campaigns," in Denis McQuail, ed., *Sociology of Mass Communications* (Harmondsworth, England: Penguin Books, 1972).

elections of the enormous expertise that goes into packaging the images of senior politicians in the United States; similar cosmetic attention to the image of leaders takes place elsewhere, though perhaps less frenetically and with less belief in its efficacy. But everywhere the values with which politicians seek to associate themselves in fashioning their media images reflect the underlying political culture. In portraying acts and projecting images that express those values, television performs its main teaching function.

At the high point of the French presidential campaign of 1974, the two main candidates debated each other on the screen. Unlike the Kennedy-Nixon debates—the only previous face-to-face encounter between the major contenders in a national election—the Giscard-Mitterrand discussions were a direct confrontation, with scarcely any intervention by the presiding interviewers. In the United States the reporter-questioner symbolized the sovereignty of the viewing audience over the combatants. In France the contenders fought alone, without seconds—as did representatives of the main competing groups in dozens of local radio debates throughout France. The nation was being taught that the Fifth Republic was capable of contemplating and surviving an internal shift of social power, that a candidate of the left could legitimately compete for power through intellectual struggle.

The television age has introduced the notion that direct debate (or debate through third-party questioning) is the natural climax of an election campaign and that without it the electorate has been denied some essential proving of the candidates. In Britain, no such confrontation has ever taken place, but in each of the last five elections a challenge has been made by one of the party leaders, and the importance attached to it has brought out the latent "presidentialism" of Britain's electoral system. The broadcasters' attempts to coax the party leaders into the studio have become a major source of tension between the parties and the media. The candidates have felt this pressure to be an intrusion into their campaigns by a nonparticipant, all the more unwelcome when it has made them appear to refuse a challenge from two quarters—from a rival and from the broadcasters. But whether the candidates like it or not, the ability to offer challenges and parry them has itself become a necessary political skill.

In the 1970s most Western societies overcame the fundamental diffidence of politicians toward television and accepted the new medium as an essential element in electoral campaigning. Today what tensions arise between broadcasters and parties tend to occur in situations in which each side understands the imperatives behind the attitudes of the other. Each has its own canon, its own code,

TABLE 8–2

AUDIENCE OPINIONS OF THE AMOUNT OF TIME DEVOTED TO
ELECTIONS IN GREAT BRITAIN, 1970–1974

(in percentages)

The Amount of Time Devoted to the Election Was:	1970	February 1974	October 1974			
			BBC TV	ITV	BBC radio	Commercial radio
Far too much	17	31	28	27	14	20
A bit too much	30	36	35	32	16	13
About right	45	30	34	28	43	35
Not enough	3	1	1	1	4	4
Can't say	5	2	1	7	13	15
Not stated	—	—	1	5	10	13
Total	100	100	100	100	100	100

SOURCE: BBC Audience Research Report, "The Coverage of the October 1974 Election Campaign on Television and Radio," June 1976.

within which it needs to be seen to be operating: the politician needs to control the issues over which the campaign is fought, yet to be seen to be responding to the concerns of the electorate; the broadcaster needs to be seen to be asking his or her own questions on the public's behalf. Both sides are committed to democracy, which they know to be frail and vulnerable; both broadcasters and politicians, by their participation in their joint activity, proclaim their dependence upon parliamentary and electoral institutions. The broadcaster claims to be maintaining the credibility of democracy, by keeping it interesting, by engaging the attention of the voters in the process. The politician claims to be keeping it alive despite the depredations of the other.

The greatest fear of both is that the electorate will simply go away—switch off the programs and tune out the election; and indeed, the problem of nonvoting has on the whole been on the increase during the period that television coverage of politics has developed. Television management in Britain feels that television has a duty to keep viewers watching the election—which means, among other things, not boring them with saturation coverage. Great anxiety arose in media circles when a large number of voters in Britain expressed the view that the television coverage of the February 1974 British general election had been excessive (see table 8–2), and coverage of the election that came the following October was reorganized so as not to intrude so noticeably into peak-hour viewing. The pursuit of new forms, new ways of wooing the audience, continues as part of the pursuit of a compromise between the requirements of representative government and those of a medium of public entertainment. It is not only the broadcaster who needs high ratings; it is the politician too.

Rules Governing the Allocation of Broadcasting Time

In the United States television has greatly reinforced the competitive aspects of the electoral contest, epitomized in the debates between Nixon and Kennedy and between Carter and Ford. In the "presidential debate," the U.S. television system (three competing commercial networks and a public network, all nationwide) has conjoined its own needs, predilections, and perspective on the American audience with those of the political system. This mortal combat requires of the candidates a tremendous act of humility toward the judgment of the public; more clearly than any other television form, it reinforces the idea of the electorate as sovereign.

The appeal of the debate, which excludes the minor candidates, is strong enough that Congress has been willing to suspend the equal-time provisions of the Federal Communications Act in order to make the debates legally possible. Section 315 of the act was designed to prevent unfair discrimination by the politically strong against the politically weak on television and radio. By thrusting it aside, Congress in a sense acknowledged the needs of television over the rights of the political minority. The television debate, and Congress's indulgence toward it, have become a permanent addition to the paraphernalia of American electoral life.

In Britain too, television has introduced an institutional novelty: the Committee on Party Political Broadcasting, which came into existence with formal sanction neither from Parliament nor from public or broadcasting bodies. Ever since the war a group of party representatives has met from time to time with representatives of the two national broadcasters, the BBC and the Independent Broadcasting Authority (IBA, known originally as ITA when its purview covered commercial television only), under the chairmanship of the president of the council, a senior minister, to agree on the allocation of inter-election party broadcasts. These broadcasts are additional to the special programs, arranged by the same committee, which take place during campaigns. Under the BBC charter and the independent television legislation, no party is permitted to buy radio or television time, and free time is provided according to an allotment agreed on by broad-

187

casters and parties, normally in the proportion of 5:5:3 for Labour, Conservative, and Liberal, with small additional allocations in Scotland, Wales, and Northern Ireland for the smaller nationalist parties and very short broadcasts for the Communists and the far-right parties when these contest more than fifty seats in a general election. The same committee allocated time to the rival sides during the 1975 referendum campaign to decide Britain's membership in the EEC.

The purview of the Committee on Party Political Broadcasting shifts with circumstance; its privilege is immense—the broadcasts it authorizes occur simultaneously on all three national TV channels (as well as at different times on the radio), so that viewers have no escape. The broadcasting bodies themselves participate in the discussions and sometimes initiate them, but their representatives are outnumbered on the committee, whose members include ministers and shadow ministers of very considerable authority, as well as the chief whips of the main parties. The committee does not, of course, have power over any other aspect of radio or television and does not oversee television's coverage of the campaign. Nevertheless, its control over the important instrument of the special election broadcasts means that in one important way the television election is fought out on the parties' ground.

Canada is another country with free, officially allocated air time. In addition, the commercial stations have voluntarily adopted the practice of the national Canadian Broadcasting Corporation (CBC) and allocate free time among all competing parties according to the number of seats they are contesting for the House of Commons. The commercial stations, however, also accept political advertising. Canada thus has acquired two syles of campaigning on television: in CBC's free time and the commercial stations' equivalent, one sees rather staid statements made to the camera by party leaders, while more expensive and sophisticated techniques of visual presentation are used in the commercials. Under Canada's diverse media system, political leaders have to be both teachers and preachers in the European manner and packaged politicians American-style.

Most instructive are the changes that have taken place in Italian electioneering. In 1975 Radiotelevisione Italiana (RAI) suddenly lost its monopoly over broadcasting. Hundreds of radio and TV stations sprang up, and the possibility of purchasing time on the new free radio stations in the 1976 election forced Italian politicians to see campaigning in a new light. Making themselves understood by the mass of voters became more important than winning arguments against opponents or querulous journalists. Meanwhile RAI, with its two nationwide channels, continued to run free party broadcasts. Time is allocated to the parties by a parliamentary commission, which also selects the journalists to take part in a Tribuna Elettorale, carried on both channels simultaneously. Every party has two forty-five-minute programs to itself and participates in an interparty program at the end of the campaign. Italy arrived at this "modern" formula for television campaigning later than most other democratic countries and in doing so made a more striking break with previous practice. Where in the past politicians appeared on television rather stiffly responding to journalists who acted as their stooges, they now field unanticipated questions.[7] The parliamentary commission has become an independent arbiter, like the broadcasting authorities or broadcast election committees in other European countries, acting almost as a manager of the television campaign.

Even in France, where the government of the day has much more power over the rules by which time is distributed, the three networks have tended to arrange a balance between the parties during elections. Moreover, the parties themselves now recognize the need to conform to the requirements of television, and this means, where possible, choosing leaders who are already known to the viewing public. No longer content to wait for invitations from the networks to participate in interviews and debates that will make its leaders' faces known, each group of parties tries to ensure that it has at least one major spokesman who is familiar to the television public and effective in appearances on television. Thus, television has become a catalyst of political change in the Fifth Republic, forcing the party groupings to make internal reforms consistent with the special needs of the dominant campaign medium. From the standpoint of societies that have already undergone the change, this looks like "modernization"; in fact, it is another example of the ubiquitous shaping power of television.

Nature and Consequences of TV Campaign Coverage

Looking back over the development of election broadcasting since its nervous beginnings in the 1960s, one can discern a fundamental change in the post-television era: despite the increasing variety of formats for campaign coverage and the increasing freedom of broadcast journalists in their reporting, and despite the power of broadcast journalism, between elections, to raise and emphasize issues, it is the politicians who define what a given election is about. In the era

---

[7] Giovanni Cesare, *Televisione sprecata: verso una quarta fase dei sistema communicazioni di massa?* [The misuse of television: toward a fourth phase of the mass communication system?] (Milan: Feltrinelli, 1974).

dominated by the mass newspaper, the platform, and radio, politicians by and large responded to great upheavals in society. They were subject to heckling, demonstrations, even violence. They confronted the voters, willingly or unwillingly. In the era of television, party managers mediate with the public through formal party broadcasts, while the politicians are presented to the electorate interacting with the public in facsimile, as it were. They are seen walking the streets, casting their own votes, and engaged in the now essential symbolic activities. They are often subjected to questions from ordinary voters on radio and television programs in Britain, Scandinavia, Italy, and other countries, but the whole apparatus of equity constructed by television authorities everywhere has precluded the unforeseen interjection of fresh issues by unauthorized individuals, which do not fit the formats of debate and discussion constructed by the producers.

In a paper advocating reform of television's election coverage in Britain, Jay Blumler, Michael Gurevitch, and Julian Ives list four main "dilemmas" which they think illustrate the extent to which the politician's view has been permitted to dominate elections.[8] First there is the dilemma of political advocacy, how best to enable the parties to address the voters. This, say the writers, "deserves pride of place in a public broadcasting system." Second comes the dilemma of news values, revolving around the question whether there are "normal" news values which are sacrificed during an election in favor of a special set of priorities designed to guarantee parties and leaders coverage on the basis of "fairness" rather than of "newsworthiness." Third comes the national/regional dilemma, the difficulty of striking a balance between national and regional issues. Finally, the writers list what they call the campaign dilemma, the problem of whether or how to separate the campaign activity of the contenders from the coverage it receives. Can broadcasters any longer act as if the campaign is something taking place elsewhere, out of their control, and merely reported by them?

These four major issues are not capable of permanent solution; they are likely to confront all Western societies in the 1980s. What is significant about them is that they all presuppose the dominance, as of right, of the politicians. It can be argued that in an election the contenders should be obliged to confront issues raised elsewhere within press or society. Television, by the nature of the arrangements it makes with the politicians, tends to present elections as if they were consultations with the electorate on an agenda set by those desiring power, rather than opportunities to raise new issues or reformulate

---

[8] Blumler, Gurevitch, and Ives, *Challenge.*

existing ones. The forms television has adopted for its electoral coverage reflect this bias.

Jay Blumler's earlier studies of the coverage of British elections revealed a discontent among television journalists springing from the feeling that reporters in all media should be telling the politicians what the electorate was thinking—and telling the voters what the politicians were omitting to mention.[9] The problem in performing this role on television, through either reports or interviews, lies in the difficulty of legitimizing any initiative taken by television. The broadcasters have not been "elected" by anyone to perform the mission of adding heat where the situation has not generated heat of itself.

Nevertheless, of all the powers attributed to the mass media twenty years ago, it is the agenda-setting function that has best survived. Choosing, emphasizing, and formulating the principal long-term concerns of an electorate appear to be the most enduring powers of the media, as well as their most significant contribution to the political scene. Nevertheless, this remains, for institutional reasons, the hardest role for television to perform, because it is the most difficult to legitimize, especially in the context of elections. The broadcast coverage of elections becomes more ingenious, more varied, even more entertaining than in the past but carries far less weight in *political* terms than might be supposed from the effort, money, and time expended on it. Elihu Katz writes of the importance of seeing a campaign "from the point of view of the society."[10] Certainly in countries where party broadcasts are carried on all channels simultaneously or in countries with only one channel, television does perform the function of exposing most citizens to arguments other than those they might choose to receive. It also forces them to reflect, though perhaps at the cost of a certain resentment. But society is seldom exposed to arguments not given attention by the principal participants in the campaign.

It is possible to perceive a pattern of development common to most of the democratic societies that have taken the path of large-scale television coverage of elections. In the first period there emerges a set of problems affecting the principal politicians, which can take several elections to overcome. The broadcasting authority—or some committee on which it is represented—is obliged to find a way to share time between the parties and to lay down the basic rules of operation: whether independent or "loyal" journalists may be used, what style of questioning may be adopted, what share of time must

---

[9] Jay G. Blumler and Denis McQuail, "The Audience for Election Television," in Jeremy Tunsall, ed., *Media Sociology: A Reader* (London: Constable, 1970).
[10] Katz, "Platforms and Windows."

be given to minority or extremist parties, how parties previously engaged in a political coalition are to be treated, and so on. A host of quasi-constitutional and sometimes explicitly legal problems are covered and formulas developed by which party leaders are projected to the electorate.

However, when the broadcasting institution has acquired enough independence to perform these tasks, it begins to look again at the model of the body politic in which it is now participating. It notices how great a gap between candidates and electorate is opened up when television viewing replaces attendance at political rallies and other forms of direct personal involvement. To fill this gap the producers and the broadcasting authority try to work out appropriate new program formats. Phone-ins develop on the radio and sometimes on television too. Devices are created by which viewers may write in to the candidates and have some of their questions answered on the air. Occasionally politicians agree to attend televised meetings of randomly selected voters who put questions to them. In Britain it has been extremely difficult to get politicians to participate in such programs, except at the local level. The radio phone-in has become a great success in a string of countries, but politicians seldom wish to confront on television voters who have not been selected by party headquarters. As the years pass and the telecommunications systems mature, however, new generations of politicians become less apprehensive of doing before the cameras what they do every week in their constituencies.

Within the Western democracies, there exist two quite different models by which television mediates election campaigns. The United States, Canada, and Australia are societies in which both press and broadcasting function with little regulation; the campaigners' first endeavor in such societies is to capture the attention of reporters and editors, rather than to extract favorable opportunities from them for addressing the electorate or being displayed before it. In the democracies of Western Europe, where the level of national regulation and intervention in the broadcasting systems is high, politicians have prescribed rights to air time, even where there remains difficulty in agreeing on an equitable distribution among parties. Even in these societies the press usually remains unlicensed and unregulated and has built up a set of expectations among politicians, reporters, and, not least, the public itself about what constitutes newsworthy, reportable behavior on the part of contenders for power. Radio and television inherit these assumptions but are prevented by the fairness regulations from implementing them freely. Television in particular is obliged to adopt standards quite different from those of either a neutral press or a party-oriented press, and the resulting frustrations are greatest among those political activists who do not qualify for equal or proportional treatment. In countries where the allocation of broadcasting time and the overall "status" accorded to politicians within news and public affairs coverage are clearly defined by statute and agreement, a great deal of political activity, especially among weak or excluded groups and parties, is dedicated to claiming broadcasting time. With every election campaign, the question of fair exposure in the mass media is reopened.

The Connoisseurship of the Viewer

For the audience a new kind of connoisseurship, as Katz calls it, is born of election television. The voter uses the screen to inform himself and to make judgments about the relative success of a wide range of candidates. With the help of the polls he can assess their rising and falling fortunes almost day by day throughout the campaign and reach a highly textured decision about whom to support. Perhaps this is one of the factors making for the growing volatility among voters that has been noted in the era of television. Voters absorb a large part of the information on which they base their voting judgments in the privacy of their homes; more often than in the past, their decisions are specific to a given race, and they are less often formed as a result of attendance at public meetings. The whole orchestration of a modern campaign is centered on television, and those least ready to make up their minds are not encouraged by the system to do so until the last moment. Television keeps the voter feeling that something more may yet happen to influence his decision. It is little wonder that, as has often been noted, more voters leave their decision until the last moment than ever before, and more switch between elections (though there may well be other reasons for this change).

The newspaper has also found new ways to support this growing connoisseurship; the contrast between tabloids and "quality" papers in several countries has grown more pronounced during the television era, and an interesting division of labor has tended to occur between the different kinds of papers. In Germany, for example, the four papers with national coverage tend to emphasize their role as intermediaries between the politicians and the people, their partisanship being of a loftier and more "in-group" kind than that of the local and tabloid press.[11] Their aloofness is the key to their role in political life, a role

[11] Elisabeth Noelle-Neumann, "Der getarnte Elefant: uber die Wirkung des Fernsehens" [The camouflaged elephant: the effects of television], in *Offentlichkeit als Bedrohung, Alber Broschur Kommunikation*, Vol. 6 (Freiburg-Munich: Verlag Karl Alber, 1977).

that is enhanced by television's inability to play it. The print media can exercise an influence upon a campaign out of proportion to their readership simply through the skillful representation of issues as they perceive them, either on behalf of a party or in the interests of the electorate.

In addition, print media of high credibility can exercise considerable influence as a yardstick against which television's agenda can be measured. The press has a far wider range of input than television: it simply draws on more information from more sources, and it has more columnists of attested experience and judgment. Television producers and reporters require a standard for the salience of issues, on a day-to-day basis, and they cannot create this within the confines of their own very special world. To a great extent they find it in the press. While so many of the traditional functions of the press have faded in the age of television, it is important to observe that some have increased in importance. In elections, and between them, information flows through all of a nation's media, and it is judged at the intersections for salience, urgency, general relevance; the repertoire of technologies now available to politicians and party managers means that they need a much greater range of skills than they once did to put those technologies to good use. In the last decade the procedures were laid down—in the next, perhaps, the skills will come.

Bibliography

Blumler, Jay G., and McQuail, Denis. "The Audience for Election Television." In *Media Sociology: A Reader*, edited by Jeremy Tunstall. London: Constable, 1970.

———. *Television and Politics—Its Uses and Influences*. London: Faber & Faber, 1968.

Blumler, Jay C.; Gurevitch, Michael; and Ives, Julian. *The Challenge of Election Broadcasting*. Leeds: Centre for TV Research, Leeds University, July 1977.

Cesare, Giovanni. *Televisione sprecata: verso una quarta fase dei sistema communicazioni di massa?* [The misuse of television: toward a fourth phase of the mass communication system?] Milan: Feltrinelli, 1974.

Errera, Roger. *Les libertés à l'abandon*. Paris: Le Seuil, 1975.

Katz, Elihu. "Platforms and Windows—Broadcasting's Role in Election Campaigns." In *Sociology of Mass Communications*, edited by Denis McQuail. Harmondsworth, England: Penguin Books, 1972.

Lehr, Wolfgang, and Berg, Klaus. *Rundfunk und Presse in Deutschland* [Radio and press in Germany]. Mainz: Hase & Koehler, 1976.

McGinnis, Joe. *The Selling of the President 1968*. New York: Trident Press, 1971.

Noelle-Neumann, Elisabeth. "Der getarnte Elefant: uber die Wirkung des Fernsehens" [The camouflaged elephant: the effects of television]. In *Offentlichkeit als Bedrohung, Alber Broschur Kommunikation.* Vol. 6. Freiburg-Munich: Verlag Karl Alber, 1977.

Pateman, Trevor. *Television and the February 1974 General Election.* British Film Institute Television Monograph, no. 3. London, 1974.

Ploman, Edward W. *Broadcasting in Sweden.* London: Routledge & Kegan Paul and IIC, 1976.

Seymour-Ure, Colin. *The Political Impact of Mass Media.* London: Constable, 1974.

Smith, Anthony. *Subsidies and the Press in Europe.* London: Political and Economic Planning, 1977.

Smith, Anthony, ed. *Television and Political Life—Studies in Six European Countries.* London: Macmillan, 1979.

Suleiman, E. *Politics, Power and Bureaucracy in France.* Princeton: Princeton University Press, 1974.

Thomas, Ruth. *Broadcasting and Democracy in France.* Bradford, England: Bradford University Press, 1976.

Weiss, Hans Jurgen. *Wahlkampf im Fernsehen* [Elections on television]. Berlin: V. Spiess, 1976.

Wember, Bernard. *Wie informiert das Fernsehen?* [How does television inform?]. Munich: List, 1976.

Williams, Arthur. *Broadcasting and Democracy in West Germany.* Bradford, England: Bradford University Press, 1976.

Windlesham, Lord David. *Communication and Political Power.* London: Jonathan Cape, 1966.

9

Public Opinion Polls

Dennis Kavanagh

Election campaigning has of late become increasingly professional. Candidates and party organizers have devised more elaborate strategies; they have spent more money; and they have relied on new mass media techniques. The emergence of public opinion polling on a regular and systematic basis has coincided with all three of these developments.

Parties and candidates have long relied on intuition and impressions for interpreting the mood of voters and explaining election outcomes. But opinion polls, based on the questioning of a representative, systematically drawn sample of the electorate, date from the 1930s. A key date is 1936, when the Gallup poll and the Elmo Roper polls correctly predicted the outcome of the Roosevelt-Landon presidential election in the United States. In 1937 and 1938 Gallup affiliates were established in Great Britain (the British Institute of Public Opinion) and France (the Institut Français d'Opinion Publique, generally known as IFOP) to use similar methods for assessing public opinion. But it was only in the 1960s that polls were widely used by the mass media and parties for election purposes. Since then the use of polls has grown almost exponentially. There are more polls and competition among them has stiffened. Thirty years ago Gallup and its affiliates were dominant in Britain, Australia, and the United States. Now there are at least half a dozen large and specialized firms in these and most other countries.

An easily overlooked condition for the activity of market and opinion research is the freedom to interview people and publish the

For comments on an earlier version of this paper I would like to thank Hugh Berrington of Newcastle University, Seymour M. Lipset of Stanford University, Humphrey Taylor of Louis Harris and Associates, Inc., and Robert Worcester of MORI, London.

findings of polls on political views and voting intentions. This freedom is found mainly in the Western European and Anglo-American societies. In a number of third world states in Africa, the Middle East, and Southeast Asia there are opinion polls, but they usually avoid questions on national politics. In Spain the liberalization since Franco's death has seen a growth of polling activity, and the polls now report voting intentions. Some political and media authorities remain uneasy about the influence which the findings of opinion polls may have on the actual vote. In France, West Germany, Brazil, and South Africa opinion polls freely report between election campaigns, but for the duration of the official campaign, or in its later stages, these countries ban reports of the polls' findings or, as in West Germany, their forecasts.

This overview of public opinion polling in a dozen Western countries concentrates on the following five areas: the background to the polls' development; their uses during elections; the role of the private polls; objections to the polls; and, finally, an assessment of their significance for modern democratic elections.

Background

There are broadly three categories of polling in Western countries. First there are the *public polls*, conducted by national public opinion firms or research institutes. Their findings on the standing of parties and personalities and on attitudes on issues are presented for public consumption. A handful of these organizations, like the George Gallup, Louis Harris, and Daniel Yankelovich firms in the United States, the Swedish Institute of Public Opinion Research (SIFO) in Sweden, and IFOP or the Société Française d'Enquêtes par Sondages (SOFRES) in France, dominate. Their main clients are the press and major television networks, although some of these companies also do private work for parties and candidates. Notwithstanding the publicity which attends their voting surveys, these major market research companies derive only a small fraction of their incomes from political surveys.

Second, there are *private polls*, conducted by commercial firms. For example, in the United States the Opinion Research Center was associated with the Republicans between 1960 and 1972; Market & Opinion Research International (MORI) has worked with the British Labour party since 1969; and the Institut für Demoskopie (IFD) has worked with the German Christian Democrats off and on over thirty years. Some of this material eventually finds its way into the public domain. There are also polling organizations which are formally linked to or founded by political parties. For example, in West Germany, Intermartel is linked to the Free Democrats, and the Social Democratic party has a share in the Infratest organization. In Britain, the Opinion Research Centre was established with the encouragement of the Conservatives, and the firm has conducted surveys for the party in every election since 1966. In France it is usual for the commercial polling firms to hive off the sections that deal with private polls for political parties. It is also interesting to note the ways in which some opinion polls become "reserved" for a particular political party simply by tradition: for example, the Louis Harris, Oliver Quayle, and Pat Caddell firms work for the U.S. Democratic party, IFD for the West German Christian Democrats. In France SOFRES and IFOP are remarkable in working for all political parties. Parties in West Germany, Austria, and the Netherlands also have their own well-funded research institutes which provide a polling capability. The Konrad Adenauer Stiftung regularly conducts independent survey research for the Christian Democrats.

Third, there are polls conducted for what might be termed *scientific purposes*. These differ from the commercial polls in three respects. Their primary purpose is to promote understanding of electoral behavior rather than to provide an up-to-the-moment reading of current opinion or to predict the winner of a particular election. In France, for example, important surveys have been conducted by the Fondation Nationale des Sciences Politiques. The second difference is that they are usually financed by the government or by academic agencies. In the United States, for example, the National Science Foundation funds studies of presidential and congressional elections by the University of Michigan's Center for Political Studies. In Britain funds for academic surveys are provided by the Social Science Research Council. In Sweden the government sponsors two kinds of academic surveys: annual omnibus surveys conducted by the National Bureau of Statistics; and national election studies, begun in 1956 and now jointly conducted by the National Bureau of Statistics and academic political scientists. The final difference is the fact that, whereas the media polls and private polls are analyzed and reported in a matter of days after the interviews are conducted, academic research is usually reported several months or even years after the interviews. Scholarly testing of hypotheses imposes costs in terms of elaborate statistical analysis and careful presentation, as well as delays in publication in learned journals. The content of academic surveys is, understandably, more detailed than that of the faster and cheaper commercial polls.

There are different clients for opinion polls. All, presumably, have a common interest in understanding public opinion, but their purposes differ. A newspaper editor, for example, is interested in a good story; polls appear to be a growing source of journalistic copy during elections. A pressure group wants to get its issue position on the agenda or to change public opinion. Political parties are mainly interested in affecting electoral behavior. Some voters may use poll information about other voters' electoral preferences to make their own decisions.

Polls appear to be used as frequently by parties of the right as of the left. But to what extent is it easier for pollsters to work with right-wing parties than with the left-wing ones? Arguably, the former will be more sympathetic to free enterprise and commercial considerations. But in Sweden and Germany, at least, this does not hold; there the Social Democrats are avid users of polls. More important than a left/right division may be the extent to which a party's orientation is determined by ideology or pragmatism. Some leaders on the right as well as the left may believe that the polls simply "take the poetry out of politics," as Aneurin Bevan once complained. Insofar as public opinion on issues is clustered in the ideological middle, then poll findings are likely to disillusion politicians on the extreme left and right and reinforce centrists. The findings of polls therefore have consequences for factional fights in parties. The spokesman for a minority viewpoint can either disbelieve or ignore inconvenient information; alternatively, he may also regard it as an indicator of how much ground he has to make up in overturning the dominant views.

What Opinion Polls Do

In a short chapter such as this, one can only generalize about the polls' activities across a range of countries. Their electoral role varies in part according to the nature of the particular political and electoral system. In two-ballot electoral systems, such as that in France, knowledge of the second preferences of voters is important. In presidential systems key questions will focus on the personalities and the strengths and weaknesses of the candidates. By contrast, parliamentary elections in Britain and West Germany have shown that the popularity of a leader may be relatively poorly correlated with support for his party. In federations or decentralized party systems there are more local polls. This obviously applies in the United States, where candidates are the main users of polls and a single congressional district may contain as many as a half-million voters. Mayors in France are also major users of polls. Where there are sharp regional differences in party lineups or the strengths of the parties, a national poll has to be used cautiously for understanding the mood of voters or predicting the outcome. This is the case with opinion polls in Canada where, according to one authority, "regional climates of opinion are frequently at variance with national patterns."[1]

The American example might be distinguished from the others. Parties in most parliamentary countries are largely national, have large central offices, and do not hold direct primary elections. In the decentralized American system, on the other hand, the national committees of two main parties do relatively little polling. Pollsters work directly for candidates in the primary elections and then in the general election. There are a myriad of pollsters working for state, congressional, and local candidates. Since the organizations and the data do not belong to parties per se, there is little cumulation of knowledge. In Germany, Sweden, Britain, and other countries where the same pollsters work regularly and systematically for the central party office, they can do research, relate current results to past ones, and advise on strategies to improve the party situation over a five- or ten-year period.

Prediction. Most public attention is paid to public polls as tools for prediction. "Getting it right" in the polls, however, may variously refer to predicting the winner or predicting the gap between the main parties or, most difficult of all, predicting the main parties' shares of the votes. Collating the findings of the *At the Polls* series shows variations in the polls' success in predicting election outcomes. In Australia the Morgan Gallup poll's average error in forecasting the gap between the two main parties in eight House elections between 1958 and 1975 was 3.6 percentage points. Only in 1972 and 1975 was the margin of error less than 4 points, when it was 1 and 0.4 points respectively.[2] In British elections between 1964 and 1979, the mean error of the public polls' final forecasts of the gap between the two leading parties was 3.5 points. Only in 1964 and 1979 was it less than 2 points, and in 1970 it was as high as 6.7 points.[3] In France, in both presidential and parliamentary elections, and in the United

---

[1] Lawrence Le Duc, "The Measurement of Public Opinion," in Howard R. Penniman, ed., *Canada at the Polls: The General Election of 1974* (Washington, D.C.: American Enterprise Institute, 1975), p. 210.

[2] Terence Beed, "Opinion Polling and the Elections," in Howard R. Penniman, ed., *Australia at the Polls: The National Elections of 1975* (Washington, D.C.: American Enterprise Institute, 1977), p. 222.

[3] See Richard Rose, "The Polls and Election Forecasting in February 1974," in Howard R. Penniman, ed., *Britain at the Polls: The Parliamentary Elections of 1974* (Washington, D.C.: American Enterprise Institute, 1975), p. 119.

States, the public polls have been remarkably close to the final gap, even in such close elections as 1960, 1968, and 1976 in the United States and 1974 and 1978 in France. Lancelot has referred to the French polls' "incontestable accuracy."[4] The predictions of SIFO in Sweden, which are made three days before election day, proved remarkably accurate in the 1970s.[5] The average deviation between the polls' forecast and each party's share of the vote was 0.62 percentage points in 1970 (for seven parties), 0.68 points in 1973 (for eight parties), 0.78 points in 1976 (for seven parties), and 0.65 points in 1979 (for five parties). Doing better than predicted may confer a moral victory on the loser. In American primary elections this interpretation has sometimes been important in giving "momentum" to a candidate.

Prediction is a hazardous occupation for pollsters. In view of the difficulties, it is surprising that they do as well as they do. The normal sampling-error margin of about 3 percentage points (at the 95 percent confidence level) may be too wide for predicting a closely contested election correctly. Another problem lies in the translation of votes (which are what the polls measure) into seats (which usually decide elections in parliamentary systems). Electoral systems do not always work proportionately or predictably. In Britain there have been two occasions since 1950 (1951 and February 1974) when the party with the most votes "lost" the election in that it had only the second-largest number of seats. In 1979 the Canadian Liberals suffered the same fate, and in 1979 the Japanese Liberals increased their share of votes but lost seats. In Ireland in 1973 the ruling party, Fianna Fáil, gained first-preference votes but lost seats and lost control of the government. The differing regional strengths of the Canadian parties make Gallup's record there all the more impressive. In only two of the twelve general elections between 1945 and 1974 did it fail to get within 2 percentage points of the Liberal and Conservative share of the votes.[6] In Italy, the accuracy of the polls has traditionally been hampered by the reluctance of Communist supporters to reveal their political sympathies to interviewers. Recently, however, it is voters on the right who seem to be wary; in 1976 the polls overestimated the Socialist vote by 4 points on the average and

[4] Alain Lancelot, "Opinion Polls and the Presidential Election, May 1974," in Howard R. Penniman, ed., France at the Polls: The Presidential Election of 1974 (Washington, D.C.: American Enterprise Institute, 1975), p. 175.

[5] In contrast to the monthly Swedish Institute of Public Opinion Research poll sample, the sample used for the prediction consists largely of people who were interviewed at the election three years earlier, though it is stratified by previous vote.

[6] Le Duc, "The Measurement of Public Opinion," p. 217.

understated the Christian Democrats' strength by 5.2 points.[7] Pollsters are usually careful to poll to the last day in order to avoid a repetition of the polls' disastrous failure to forecast correctly the outcome of the 1948 American presidential election. But the allocation of the undecided voters and adjustments for differential voting turnout are matters for subjective, not scientific, judgment.

Fairly or unfairly, opinion polls are widely judged by the accuracy of their forecasts. In Ireland in 1977 the opinion polls defied the conventional wisdom: they correctly anticipated the handsome victory of Fianna Fáil against the predictions of the mass media, pundits, and bookmakers. The result greatly improved the polls' standing. According to Garret FitzGerald, the new leader of the opposition party, "Perhaps the result of the election will encourage all concerned to take these polls more seriously in the future."

Candidate visibility and support. A good rating in the polls may promote a person's candidacy even if he is not officially in the race. For reasons mentioned above, the best illustrations are found in the United States. Eisenhower before 1952 and Edward Kennedy in 1979 are obvious examples of this effect. Nelson Rockefeller tried to exploit his favorable standing in the polls in 1968 to persuade Republican convention delegates that he would be a more successful standard-bearer than Richard Nixon. A good standing in the polls is also useful to show electoral appeal, gain endorsements, and raise funds. It may help persuade contributors that a declared candidate can win a nomination or an election. American private and public polls are concerned to find out which candidate is in the lead and how different candidates or combinations of candidates run against others.[8] In France opponents of François Mitterrand in the Socialist party used and abused opinion polls to promote the rival candidacy of Michel Rocard. In the United States polls can be used to kill a candidacy; this is what happened to George Romney, who withdrew from the race before the primaries in 1968, and to Walter Mondale before the primaries in 1976. Hubert Humphrey's campaign in the California primary in 1972 was seriously damaged by the California Field poll showing him twenty points behind McGovern a week before the election—which he actually lost by a margin of only five points.

Election timing. Where prime ministers have discretion in calling or not calling an election for a particular date, they usually take

---

[7] See Giacomo Sani, "The Italian Electorate in the Mid-1970s: Beyond Tradition?" in Howard R. Penniman, ed., *Italy at the Polls: The Parliamentary Elections of 1976* (Washington, D.C.: American Enterprise Institute, 1977), p. 88.

[8] In 1968 Nixon commissioned polls to see how he would fare with different vice-presidential running mates in eighteen key states.

account of polls and other portents. Lord Hailsham has suggested that it is rare for governments in Britain to lose elections; by timing economic booms to coincide with the run-up to an election and reading the opinion polls, the prime minister has a formidable set of advantages.[9] In fact, however, in Great Britain since 1945 the parties in power have won only five of the ten general elections, and in 1951, 1970, and February 1974 they clearly got the dates wrong. The Conservatives' private pollsters advised an early dissolution in January 1974; Edward Heath's decision to delay the election by three weeks to February 28 probably cost him the victory. There is still some dispute about the attention James Callaghan paid to public and private polls in deciding not to call the expected election in the autumn of 1978. The recent volatility of voters, especially in Britain, makes leaders more wary about reading too much into the polls. However, the Irish government's voluntary dissolution in 1977 was taken in defiance of the polling evidence, and the government was resoundingly defeated.

Presentation. Survey findings influence campaign presentation in various spheres.

1. Presenting policy. In most countries polls are extensively used to test campaign slogans, posters, and themes, but it is difficult to pin down actual cases of polls' influencing policy. According to Humphrey Taylor, who was a pollster with the Conservative party in Britain for four general elections, his task was "communication of already decided policies and the presentation of the party itself." He claimed "only a marginal influence on the Conservative party."[10] The difficulty in discerning the influence is that it is probably wise for a pollster who wishes to have a long-term relationship with a party not to emphasize his influence on politicians. He may be blamed if things go wrong subsequently. The politicians also will not wish to publicize the relationship. Taylor's private polls certainly contributed to the Conservative government's decisions after 1970 to boost old-age pensions and to introduce pensions for people over eighty, to sell council houses to tenants, and to accept comprehensive education in spite of the opposition of many party activists.

2. The personal style of candidates. With elections now being fought more than ever before through the mass media, in particular television, which is a "low intensity" medium, personality is im-

---

[9] "Elective Dictatorship," *Listener*, October 21, 1977.

[10] Humphrey Taylor, "The Use of Survey Research in Britain by Political Parties and the Government," *Policy Analysis* (Winter 1977), p. 78. Few pollsters have achieved the influence and intimacy which Pat Caddell has with President Carter.

portant.[11] Polls are now extensively used to monitor the impact of broadcasts on television. It is difficult to generalize in this area, for the kind of television image desired is probably a cultural variable, even though the same tool—the opinion poll—is used to measure it.

3. The use of more direct and colloquial language in communications. Politicians are more concerned than in the past to speak in everyday language to the public, and polls may help by showing them whether the language they use is having the desired effect.

Manipulation. All parties and candidates want to guard against the impression that they will suffer a landslide defeat or score a landslide victory. The temptation is to misuse the polls, particularly private polls, where methods and findings are rarely open to public scrutiny. But there have been surprisingly few scandals concerning opinion polls and elections—cases of "doctored" data or misleading reports; two such affairs may have taken place in the United States in 1978 in the campaigns of Senator Dick Clark in Iowa and Governor Lamar Alexander in Tennessee.[12] More common is the selective release of private polls. The best safeguards against these abuses are comformity with an approved code of practice and competition from public polls.

Another problem is the possibility that a candidate, by timing and targeting his campaign efforts, can influence the polls' findings. It has been claimed that President Nixon in 1972, knowing in advance the pollsters' sampling areas and interview schedules, made it a point to concentrate his advertising and workers in those areas in time for the poll.[13] A campaign organization may also play back purported findings about public opinion in the hope of influencing voters. In Britain in 1979, Tommy Thompson, former chairman of ORC, raised funds from industry to carry out a series of polls in marginal constituencies on the issue of nationalization. They showed that the majority of Labour voters were hostile to further nationalization, in contrast to official Labour policy. Similar polls on attitudes to trade unions were sponsored but, following protests from trade union leaders and the Conservative party, publication of the results was delayed until after the election.[14]

Information. Parties conduct "quickie" private polls during elections to check voters' reactions to issues, speeches, broadcasts, and

11 Marshall McLuhan, *Understanding Media* (New York: McGraw-Hill, 1964).

12 "Polls Watcher Wanted," *Economist*, January 13, 1979.

13 Michael Wheeler, *Lies, Damned Lies and Statistics* (New York: Dell, 1976), p. 131.

14 David Butler and Dennis Kavanagh, *The British General Election of 1979* (London: Macmillan, 1980).

themes. Speed is essential for this research to have any impact; because of the pace of events in an election campaign a survey can be out of date within a day or two. The information can reassure the party or candidate about new developments and help them decide whether or not to react. In 1960 Kennedy was encouraged by the polls to confront directly the worries some voters felt about his Catholicism, and in 1968 Nixon decided to ignore rather than attack the candidacy of George Wallace, who attracted many voters sympathetic to Nixon's point of view on many issues. In the first 1974 election in Britain the Labour party was reassured as the "Conservative" issues declined in salience and Labour's preferred issues became more important. The changes in the agenda of the campaign presaged a shift in voting intentions, to Labour's advantage.

Targeting voters. Targeting voters is particularly important for campaign advertising and broadcasts. This aspect of campaigning is usually left to market specialists, who commission voter surveys in elections as they do consumer surveys in their nonpolitical work. Rarely, however, are the target voters homogeneous, and rarely are they receptive to a single issue or appeal. The "target voter" tends to differ across countries and elections. In the United States he usually is to be found in large states and key social groups. In Britain target voters are found in the hundred or so marginal constituencies and, again, in particular social groups; both parties emphasized the skilled working-class or blue-collar voters (32 percent of all voters) in 1979. In France the main parties focus on the support for the "proximate" candidates who were eliminated in the first ballot. In general the target voters are those who would seem to be likely to defect from one's own side or likely to be attracted from the opposition.

Affecting voting. The foregoing features deal with the effects of polls on campaign managers and candidates. But what about the mass electorate? Terms like "bandwagon," "backlash," and "boomerang" are increasingly used to describe those effects, but the fact is that there are no conclusive findings on the impact of polls on voters. Several possible effects suggest themselves:

1. The polls may help small parties gain momentum; for example, the Progress party in Denmark or the British Liberals in the Orpington by-election in 1962.

2. They may encourage tactical voting; for example, where the polls forecast a close result, there may be a shift from the smaller to the bigger parties.

3. They may tell voters something about the effectiveness of their votes; for example, poll results may encourage voters to vote for

a minor party if they are committed to it or, alternatively, discourage them if they are only temporary protesters against the major parties. Thus the Liberals in the February 1974 British election saw their share of the votes increase considerably as the campaign proceeded.

Explanation of electoral change. This is most effectively done through panel studies. By interviewing the same group of voters at successive stages, a panel measures changes in individual voters' attitudes. In Sweden and West Germany panel studies are conducted between elections. In France, Britain, the United States, and Australia they are held during the campaign for both political and scholarly purposes.

The Influence of Private Polls

Private polls want not only to convey information to their clients but also to ensure that it is absorbed and understood. Though they will deny it, most private pollsters want to have some influence on campaign strategies. In general the private pollsters' influence seems to depend on such variables as the following:

Whether the party or client is in government or opposition. Not only are ministers busy but they are usually more concerned to implement and justify existing programs than to test new policies for their electoral acceptability. In Britain, the closeness of the private pollsters to a party's strategic thinking has varied with the party's position as government or opposition; a party's position in office usually downgrades its professional organizers as well. The incumbents' attention usually turns more readily to electoral strategy as the election date nears. With the shorter electoral cycle and the proliferation of primaries and general elections in the United States, it is not surprising that American presidents are attentive to the polls.

The pollsters' involvement with the party. The more the pollster knows about the party's plans, policy options, and priorities, the more he is likely to exercise influence. A useful guideline here is the extent to which politicians involve themselves in selecting the areas for research or leave the initiative to the pollsters. Wolfgang Ernst used to have monthly meetings with Chancellor Willy Brandt to discuss his survey findings. In Britain and the United States the private pollsters regularly attend campaign strategy sessions of the main parties or candidates. The British Labour party keeps its pollsters more at arms length than the Conservatives when it comes to the formulation of strategy. Questions of the structure of the campaign organization, personalities, and political values affect this relationship.

Some pollsters identify very closely with the politics of the parties and the party leaders for whom they are working. Indeed, they may well be strongly identified with a particular ideological position or a power group within the party. Others retain a much more distant, professional relationship. In general, pollsters who get too closely identified with a particular leader or faction or point of view tend to lose their relationship with the party when those with whom they have been associated lose power in the party. This seems to have been the case with Mark Abrams, who was closely associated with the Gaitskellite faction of the Labour party in the early 1960s.

The salience of the issue and the extent of disagreement within the party. It is almost impossible for a pollster to sell a course of action where the party leadership is set on a different policy. Where the leadership is divided, polling information is a tool which a faction may use in intraparty debates on policy or personality. Again, where an issue is relatively "open" from the viewpoint of the party's ideology, the pollster may have more influence. The important question is, What is the partisan self-confidence and determination of the leaders? According to Bob Worcester, the Labour party's pollster: "I characterize the responsibility I have as one of bringing witness to the ripples, the waves and the tides. If the Labour party leadership wants to swim against the tide of public opinion, that is their responsibility. I see my role as telling them which way the tide is running and how strongly, and then I stop."[15]

Consonance with other cues. Polls are only one sort of information for campaigners. To be influential, the import of the polls has to be consistent with other information and pressures. Survey material in the late 1950s coincided with electoral setbacks and social and economic change to help the revisionists in the Social Democratic party in West Germany and the British Labour party. In an effort to adapt to social change and reach out to the less politically oriented floating voters, both parties reversed their traditional emphasis on public ownership and made appeals to all social classes.

Whether the party is programmatic or not. Attention to the polls is also affected by the nature of the party. Parties do have interests,

---

[15] "Rasmussen interview with Robert Worcester," *British Politics Newsletter,* no. 8 (Spring 1977), p. 8. For discussion of relations between the parties and private pollsters, see David Butler and Dennis Kavanagh, *The British General Election of October 1974* (London: Macmillan, 1975), chap. 8, and *The British General Election of 1979,* chap. 13. For a full discussion of the role of private polls in British politics, see my "Political Parties and Private Polls," to be published in R. Worcester, ed., *Political Communications and the 1979 General Election* (London: Macmillan, 1981).

traditions, and widely shared values which they are reluctant to abandon. Again, the useful if crude distinction seems to be between the United States and Western Europe. Western European parties are generally regarded as having a more programmatic function than American parties. The American parties are more decentralized, less disciplined, have less control over the recruitment of candidates, and, at the national level, may be taken over by a new candidate for the presidency every four years. Accordingly, because American parties are less institutionalized and have less ideological baggage, the private pollster may have a larger role in suggesting and refining policy positions. For all the opportunism and development of "catchall" trends in pursuing voters in recent years, the main Western European parties, by comparison, still appear less flexible.[16]

Reasons why the private polls have little or no impact on a party's strategy are not hard to find. Much of the information offered by the polls prompts the candidate to ask the question, So what? Surveys may show that voters want apparently inconsistent policies— less unemployment and less inflation, or lower taxes and more state services. Slight alterations in question wording on a substantive issue produce notable differences in responses. In Britain, this has been true when questions substitute "public ownership" for "nationalization," "the EEC" for "the Common Market," and "devolution" for "a separate Scottish Assembly." The data may point to actions or to policies which a party considers to. be "politically impossible," in the short term anyway; for example, a left-wing party getting tough with trade unions or a party promising the restoration of capital punishment in Britain. Alternatively, the party may lack the organization and will to use survey research; in 1963 Mark Abrams commented that survey findings would not lead anywhere in the Labour party because there was no effective machinery to shape political propaganda.[17]

Polls are not the only source of information or pressure operating on a candidate. The candidate has to appeal to activists who may have very different interests and issue preferences from those of less involved voters. In 1972 one reason why McGovern felt that he had to

---

[16] On the concept of "catchall" parties, see Otto Kirchheimer, "The Transformation of the Western European Party Systems," in Joseph LaPalombara and Myron Weiner, eds., Political Parties and Political Development (Princeton: Princeton University Press, 1965).

[17] Mark Abrams, "Public Opinion Polls and Political Parties," Public Opinion Quarterly, vol. 27 (1963), pp. 9-18. After Labour's electoral defeat in 1959, the party's National Executive refused to sponsor a survey into the reasons for defeat; it was financed instead by a magazine, Social Commentary. See Mark Abrams et al., Must Labour Lose? (London: Penguin, 1960).

make further speeches on the Vietnam issue (on which Democratic voters were split) was its usefulness in raising money from activists.[18] In 1968, Humphrey, though urged by pollsters and advisers to protect himself against charges of being "soft" on the law-and-order issue, found it personally embarrassing to be seen to deviate from his traditional stance. The growing importance of the "purist" outlook in the United States has been reflected in the campaigns of Barry Goldwater (1964), Eugene McCarthy (1968), and George McGovern (1972). This approach emphasizes the importance of the candidate's sticking to his principles, regardless of electoral consequences. The purist is more interested in moral crusades than in compromise or conciliation of the opposition; compared with the traditional "professional" politician, he is less oriented toward winning the election. The supporters of Goldwater and McGovern were able to capture their party machines, but their presidential candidates were routed in the general elections.[19]

There is also a tendency for politicians to dismiss the polls when their tidings are gloomy or fail to show what practical steps can be taken to reverse the likelihood of electoral defeat. In Britain and France the private pollsters tend, quite undeservedly, to be enveloped in the sense of failure that follows a party's defeat. In the United States in mid-October 1964, Dean Burch, the Republican National chairman, canceled the ORC polls for Goldwater. The last straw for the campaign teams was the pollsters' failure to find the latent or "secret" support for Goldwater that the team believed was there. They had hoped, paradoxically, that the polls would confirm their belief in a "hidden vote" waiting to be mobilized. McGovern, by contrast, continued to rely heavily on Pat Caddell in 1972 in spite of his depressing reports.

Finally, poll findings may be compatible with quite different interpretations. If a party's strong issue is of less salience than others, strategists may as readily interpret this finding as a basis for emphasizing as for ignoring it. And, as politicians are quick to complain, information about the grievances and concerns of voters is rather dispiriting without suggestions for what to do about the situation. "Polls are not very good on the 'what to do' consequences of their research," was a revealing, if unfair, comment made by one British politician.

In some countries—for example West Germany, Japan, and the United States—enormous sums are spent on private polls. It would

---

[18] On the McGovern campaign, see Theodore H. White, *The Making of the President, 1972* (New York: Atheneum, 1973).

[19] Nelson Polsby and Aaron Wildavsky, *Presidential Elections*, 4th ed. (New York: Scribners, 1976).

be surprising if much of this was not, literally, "wasted," if considered in terms of how much of the pollsters' data were absorbed and acted on by campaign strategists. A party or politician should have a clear idea of what is wanted from the polls. John Kennedy and Harold Wilson were reputed to be particularly shrewd and critical readers of polls. But some polling is commissioned simply because others are doing it, because people like information for its own sake, and because it just might prompt an election-winning idea or theme.

There is another value in having the private pollsters in close and regular contact with party strategists. They do bring some objectivity to what is essentially an in-group and partisan gathering. Because they also work for commercial clients, they provide other perspectives during the election. They are professionals at gathering evidence, and they are trained to assess it calmly.

Objections to the Polls

Most complaints center on the claim that polls have undue influence on elections. According to the Australians Murray Goot and Terence Beed, because polls are reported frequently and help the media to portray an election as a horse race, candidates spend more time reacting to the latest headlines, trends, and forecasts.[20] Between the 1966 and 1970 general elections in Britain the number of lead stories in the British press during the three-week campaign periods which dealt with the polls increased from a tenth to a third.

Polls may also affect campaign workers' morale, particularly when they forecast victory by a large margin for one side or the other. The polls certainly had this effect on the Goldwater and McGovern organizations, the British Conservatives in October 1974, and the Australian Labor party in 1975. Polls which report a large lead for one side over the other make the outcome appear inevitable, and the media may switch their attention to the consequences of defeat for the losing party.

More debatably, it is sometimes claimed that the publication of polls affects the outcome. Claims of bias or unfairness by the media and pollsters are a staple of campaign exchanges. An IFOP "quickie" poll conducted immediately after the first TV debate between Giscard d'Estaing and Mitterrand in the French presidential election of 1974 was very favorable to Giscard and prompted an official complaint from

---

[20] Murray Goot and Terence W. Beed, "The Polls, the Public, and the Reelection of the Fraser Government," in Howard R. Penniman, ed., *The Australian National Elections of 1977* (Washington, D.C.: American Enterprise Institute, 1979), pp. 141-84.

Mitterrand. In 1974 also, the French polls and papers observed a self-denying ordinance against publishing poll results in the last week of the election. It was later made a statutory rule, and during the 1979 campaign for the European Parliament in France, the polls were barred by law from publishing their findings in the latter stages of the campaign. In West Germany in 1969 the pollsters did not publish their findings in the last week, but the London *Times* commissioned a poll by Marplan and broke the ban. A similar ban is still in force today whereby the polls report the current strength of the German parties without making forecasts. As Max Kaase notes, the pollsters' distinction between presenting their findings and not making forecasts escapes most of the public.[21] In New Zealand until 1978 the Heylen organization did not publish its election polls, fearing that they would influence voters. In the 1978 election, Labour accused Heylen of attempting to mislead the public by not publishing a poll taken a week before the election that showed the National and Labour parties evenly matched. Heylen intended to release the poll after the election, but Labour went ahead and leaked it to the media on the eve of the election.[22]

There is probably no easy way to accommodate the sensitivities and allay the disappointment of politicians; they are interested parties. But there is no good evidence bearing on how, if at all, the polls influence voting behavior. In order to believe that polls do have an influence, one must assume that voters (1) are aware of other voters' first and second preferences, (2) know how other voters will react on election day in the light of poll findings, and (3) assume that the net changes will not cancel out. It is possible that some voters calculate how they can most effectively cast their votes in the light of poll findings, but, as far as I know, it has not been clearly demonstrated that in fact they do so. In the 1964 American presidential election, the National Broadcasting Company commissioned a study by Market Dynamics of the effects on voting in the West of computer forecasts that were based on New York returns and released before the polls closed in the west-

---

[21] Max Kaase, "Public Opinion Polling in the Federal Republic of Germany," in Karl Cerny, ed., *Germany at the Polls: The Bundestag Election of 1976* (Washington, D.C.: American Enterprise Institute, 1978), p. 210. Some countries deliberately restrict the publicity given to the findings of opinion polls. In Australia there is an embargo on radio and television coverage of them after midnight on the final Wednesday prior to the Sunday general election. In Britain the broadcasting authorities are forbidden to carry election news on polling day.

[22] See Howard R. Penniman, "Preface," in Howard R. Penniman, ed., *New Zealand at the Polls: The General Election of 1978* (Washington, D.C.: American Enterprise Institute, 1980), p. x.

ern time zone. Comparisons of the behavior of groups who saw the forecasts and groups who did not showed only slight differences.[23]

In Britain there is some circumstantial evidence that polls may affect voting behavior. In four successive general elections between 1966 and 1974, the party that was ahead in the immediate preelection polls did less well than predicted in the election itself. Some observers attribute this to the "reverse bandwagon effect" of the opinion polls' findings: voters wavering in their support for the party in the lead, or fearing that it might receive too large a majority, voted for the party said to be behind.

In the 1979 British general election, the polls again reported a narrowing of the Conservative lead until the weekend before the election. In the last few days, however, there was a boomerang effect, and the Conservative lead increased again. Observers speculated that this time the voters had reacted to the prospect of a deadlocked parliament. There is clearly no general or consistent effect of the polls on voting behavior. Any hypothetical effects need to be set against the impact on voters of events and political activities reported by the media in the last days of the campaign: the polls may be merely reflecting these changes. If many voters decided to vote tactically, the result of their separate calculations might be an indeterminate election. Moreover, voters may be influenced in different ways without voting tactically. But, insofar as the polls provide more information for the voters and enhance their awareness of the significance of their votes, they are surely no bad thing.

Banning polls or their publication hardly seems an effective answer to the problem—if there is one. An obvious check against abuse is competition between independent polling organizations. Parties or interest groups are self-interested users of poll findings. In West Germany, for example, the willingness of the mass media to commission polls means that the voters are no longer exposed to selective leaks by the parties; the public polls act as an external check. It is also difficult to ban polls effectively in a free society. As the German case shows, if foreign media commission polls and publish them overseas, the results will be transmitted back.

A different complaint is that where the mass media are the main suppliers of the polls and are bitterly partisan, this may lead to doubts about the status of the polls—even when the pollsters have little con-

---

[23] For a useful discussion, see Harold Mendelsohn and Irving Crespi, *Polls, Television and the New Politics* (Scranton, Pa.: Chandler, 1970), chap. 5. For an earlier study, see Donald Campbell, "On the Possibility of Experimenting with the Bandwagon Effect," *International Journal of Opinion and Attitude Research*, vol. 5 (1951).

trol over colorful and misleading press coverage. In Australia in 1975, the Murdoch papers conducted such a vitriolic press war against the Labor party that the impartiality of the polls they commissioned was questioned.[24]

Conclusion

There are several common trends in campaigning across the industrialized liberal democratic countries. The growth of opinion polls is only one factor to set beside the role of the electronic media, the spending of large sums of money, and the declining importance of traditional party campaign activities. It is possible to suggest a number of consequences of the growth of the opinion polls.

First, the polls have probably led to more informed reporting and analysis of campaigns, issues, and personalities. One can now use evidence where once one relied on hearsay or other impressions. Sustained exposure to public and private polls has improved the capacity of politicians and campaign managers to read the evidence with a discerning eye.

Second, the polls may influence the political agenda. By asking voters to indicate which issues *are* important and which *should be* important, the polls may spotlight issues that are neglected by elites but bother voters. It is understandable that much attention is paid to the polls as tools for predicting voters' behavior. This, we have seen, is a risky enterprise. A more important role of opinion polls, between as well as during elections, is to tell politicians what people think and what issues concern them.

Surveys are also indispensable for evaluating a winning party's claim to have a mandate for a general program or a particular policy. Public polls carry much of this information, showing issue preferences broken down by party or social class. In fact, the number of issues that decisively affect voting behavior are few; parties are, for one thing, cautious about taking clear-cut positions.

But sophisticated analysis of elaborate surveys invariably takes time to filter through. Later interpretations of Eugene McCarthy's good showing in the New Hampshire primary in 1968 revealed that his was not, after all, primarily an antiwar vote.[25] Analysis of McGovern's defeat in the 1972 presidential election shows that it had as much to do with voters' assessments of the candidate's competence

---

[24] Beed, "Opinion Polling and Elections," p. 234.

[25] Philip Converse et al., "Continuity and Change in American Politics: Parties and Issues in the 1968 Election," *American Political Science Review*, vol. 63 (1969), pp. 1083-1105.

and personality as with his issue stands.[26] Academic analysis of Labour's two 1974 election victories shows that they were gained in spite of the electorate's growing hostility to major planks of the party's platform.[27] Again one can contrast the more complex analyses that students of electoral behavior now offer with the rather simple judgments which were made of election outcomes in the not too distant past.

There is no clear relation between the growth of opinion polls and the decomposition of parties (a largely American phenomenon, anyway) and the trend away from programmatic parties to catchall parties. It can be argued that opinion polls, insofar as they report a lack of ideology and partisanship, do provide evidence against the ideological elements in political parties and weaken the role of the local activist as an opinion former in the party. These trends have been noticed in the main parties in West Germany, Austria, Italy, and France, affecting even the large Communist parties in the last two countries. But in Britain (since 1970) and the United States the patterns are more complex. In Britain, the Labour and Conservative parties have reacted to electoral defeat by adopting a more ideological stance in opposition (in Labour's case, the extraparliamentary wing is important in exerting this pressure). In the United States the parties appear to be decaying as organizations, while changes in issues and in the formal structure of the parties have enhanced the role of the ideologue. The rise or decline of partisanship or of attachment to political parties probably has little to do with the increasing use of polls.

Polls are regularly attacked and praised as surrogates for direct democracy. They may offer a check on the mediating or representative claims of parties, pressure groups, and mass media. It is also the case that where they are centrally commissioned, local candidates resent them as yet another instance of the centralization and nationalization of campaigning. They may therefore strengthen the position of leaders within the parliamentary parties, and the parliamentary parties against the mass members. Such claims may invite a skeptical "So what?" Used with care, however, opinion polls remain an important feedback device for decision makers and citizens between and during elections.

---

26 Warren Miller and Teresa Levitin, *Leadership and Change* (Cambridge: Winthrop, 1976).

27 Ivor Crewe et al., "Partisan Dealignment in Britain, 1964-1974," *British Journal of Political Science*, vol. 7, no. 2 (1977), pp. 129-90.

Bibliography

I have drawn heavily on the *At the Polls* series for information about polling operations in various countries. Other useful sources include:

Berrington, Hugh. *Public Opinion Polls, British Politics, and the 1970 General Election.* Political Studies Association paper, Edinburgh, 1972.

Hodder-Williams, Richard. *Public Opinion Polls and British Politics.* London: Routledge & Kegan Paul, 1970.

Mendelsohn, Harold, and Crespi, Irving. *Polls, Television and the New Politics.* Scranton, Pa.: Chandler, 1970.

Noelle-Neumann, Elisabeth. "Uses of Survey Research for Decision-Makers in the Social-Political Sphere: A Case Study, The German General Election 1976." Mimeographed.

Taylor, Humphrey. "The Use of Survey Research in Britain by Political Parties and the Government." *Policy Analysis,* Winter 1977, pp. 75–84.

Teer, F., and Spence, J. D. *Political Opinion Polls.* London: Hutchinson, 1973.

Stoetzel, Jean, and Girard, André. *Les sondages d'opinion publique* [Public opinion polls]. Paris: Presses Universitaires de France, 1973.

Webb, Norman. "The Democracy of Opinion Polls." Unpublished paper, Social Surveys (Gallup Poll) Limited, 1979.

10

Electoral Participation

Ivor Crewe

Voting as a Form of Participation

The subject of this chapter is "turnout"—the extent to which the adult populations of the world's major liberal democracies exercise the most basic of democratic rights, the right to vote. It will seek answers to two pairs of questions: How—and why—does national turnout differ so markedly between countries? And how and why have turnout rates changed, or in many cases not changed, over the last thirty or so years?

It hardly needs saying that the simple act of voting is just one of many forms of participation open to the ordinary citizen. Elections and modern parties provide other, more demanding, opportunities, such as active membership or office in a local party, helping in a campaign, or standing as a candidate. And, of course, participation encompasses more than the electoral process. Quite apart from illegal activity or direct action, it includes nonpartisan activity such as work on behalf of a community pressure group, and the individual contacting of officials and elected representatives on personal matters.

But although voting is far from synonymous with participation, there are good reasons for giving it special attention. First, there are *historical reasons*. In the conflicts over the widening of the franchise to workers, then women, and finally, in the United States, to blacks, the right to vote came to represent—both to those seeking it and to those in a position to concede or withhold it—not simply the legal right to engage in an additional (and in reality, a marginal) means of political influence. It became the symbol of citizenship itself: the right to participate in public affairs in general. Hence the intensity which struggles over suffrage extension have historically had. Second, there are reasons provided by *democratic theory*. Elections based on a full adult franchise encapsulate more directly than any other means of participation the two core democratic principles of universality and equality—that every individual, whatever his social or economic circumstances, should have an equal say. The study of turnout allows us to examine whether any departures from these principles occur in practice. And finally, there are *technical reasons*. Turnout figures constitute the only reliable information about electoral participation, or indeed participation in general, that is available for the large majority of liberal democracies, over a long enough period to discern trends, and that is also roughly equivalent in "meaning" across nations.[1]

If the act of voting is only one form of participation, what *kind* of participation does it typically involve? Nie and Verba have distinguished four major dimensions of participation:[2] (1) the degree of *initiative* required of the participant; (2) the degree of *conflict* incurred with others; (3) the *type of influence* exercised upon officials and politicians, that is, the amount of information imparted and pressure exerted; and (4) whether the *outcome* affects the community (or part of it) or the individual only. Let us examine the act of voting in the light of each of these dimensions in turn.

Initiative. It is clear that voting normally demands only the minimum of individual initiative or effort. It requires neither skill nor money and rarely takes more than a few minutes' time. Polling stations are usually numerous and within near distance of almost all electors. The party organizations and media determine the issues and candidates for the elector. The postwar emergence of television as a major source of political information in all but a handful of democracies provides the elector with information that is greater in volume and easier to digest than ever before. The only institutional disincentives to vote arise from problems of mobility and registration (still

---

I am grateful to Anthony King, Arend Lijphart, Howard Penniman, and Bo Särlvik for spotting inaccuracies in the first draft, and also for their general comments.

[1] This last assumption has recently been queried by Norman Nie and Sidney Verba, who argue that the act of voting is part of a "participant syndrome" in some countries (such as the United States, Japan, and Nigeria) reflecting an involvement in politics and commitment to participation, but not in others, such as Austria and India, where it registers a partisan allegiance that does not entail a willingness to participate in any other sense. See Norman H. Nie and Sidney Verba, "Political Participation," in Fred I. Greenstein and Nelson W. Polsby, eds., *Handbook of Political Science*, vol. 4 (Reading, Mass.: Addison-Wesley, 1975), p. 20.

[2] These were first proposed in *Participation in America* (New York: Harper & Row, 1972), chap. 3, and have recently been shown to apply equally well to nations of very different political systems and levels of economic development in Sidney Verba, Norman H. Nie, and Jae-on Kim, *Participation and Political Equality* (Cambridge: Cambridge University Press, 1978), chap. 3.

an important consideration in the United States, about which more later) and, to a lesser extent, the complexity of the ballot in some countries. But by and large voting is easy.

Conflict. Here the position seems equally clear. The secrecy of the ballot protects the voter from the sanctions of employers, superiors, officials, or indeed those of equal status such as members of the family or fellow workers (although the election campaign, which is an institutionalization of partisan conflict, may well bring the elector into contention with others). Indeed, such is the value put on voting in most democracies that failure to vote is as likely to precipitate recrimination from those to whom it becomes known, especially in the voter's immediate circles of family, neighborhood, and work (this is even more true in many Communist countries, of course, where severe sanctions against nonvoters are sometimes imposed). Voting is also a peculiarly *individual* act. If it does not involve conflict, it does not require *cooperation* with others either. Most participation is organized collective activity, demanding from the individual the skills of interpersonal cooperation and management. Even contacts with officials require a readiness and ability to enter at least one such relationship. The act of voting does not even demand that. Again, it is an easy act.

Influence and outcome. These two dimensions concern the benefits rather than the costs of participation. And in this respect voting is a discouraging and "difficult" act. The individual's vote imparts little information or pressure. Compared with directly communicating with an official or elected representative, or with working for an organized pressure group, casting a ballot provides no immediate or tangible benefit to the elector, either exclusively or as a member of a group. A general election result can, of course, have a direct bearing on the material circumstances of individuals. But the chance that an election result in a constituency, let alone the whole country, will rest on *one individual's* decision to vote is minute; thus the benefits seen as likely to accrue from voting rather than abstaining seem equally minute.

Voting usually involves, therefore, both negligible costs *and* negligible benefits. The traditional emphasis on the former has led political scientists to take high turnout for granted and ask, Why do the few not vote? The more recent emphasis on the latter, notably by rational choice theorists, has prompted the question, Why do the many bother? Each approach on its own is flawed by concentrating on only one side of the cost-benefit equation. The joint consideration of both sides, however, leads to two propositions. First, so long as both costs and benefits remain minimal, the act of voting will be, so

218

to speak, beyond the reach of any cost-benefit calculus, and instead subject to nonrational factors. These would include the intrinsic value attached to voting, the strength of identification with a political party or social group, and the degree of mobilization by party organizations. But, second, turnout should be sensitive to even a small change in the cost-benefit ratio. A modest raising of the inconvenience of voting should sharply reduce turnout;[3] likewise a modest rise in the perceived benefits should sharply increase it. We shall find both propositions useful in the course of this chapter.

Who Is Entitled to Vote?

To begin at the very beginning, Who is entitled to vote in the world's major democracies? In an important sense the answer is provided by definition: a necessary (but not sufficient) condition for a country's inclusion in this book is universal adult suffrage. None of the eligible twenty-seven countries denies its citizens the vote on grounds of income, sex, race, religion, ethnicity, politics, or literacy; in none is plural voting allowed; in all, the vast majority of the adult population are entitled to vote.[4]

But there are a number of qualifications to make to this apparently uniform provision of full adult suffrage. To begin with, even among those countries with an uninterrupted record of democracy since World War II, the universal franchise is a remarkably recent provision. In the United States the legal basis for the disfranchisement of blacks in federal elections was not finally removed until the Voting Rights Act of 1965; in Australia aborigines were not fully enfranchised until 1967. Women were not granted the vote on equal terms with men until 1944 in France, 1946 in Italy, Japan, and Venezuela, 1948 in Belgium, and, most notorious of all, 1971 in Switzerland.[5]

Second, there is no such thing as true or pure universal adult suffrage. As table 10–1 shows, all democracies deny the vote to a

[3] This is persuasively argued in Brian Barry, *Sociologists, Economists and Democracy* (London: Collier, Macmillan, 1970), pp. 13-23.

[4] I do not consider the Dominican Republic in this chapter, for lack of data. Some of Sri Lanka's Indian Tamil minority may be considered disfranchised. The Indian Tamils living in what was then Ceylon were denied citizenship under the citizenship law passed in 1948; since then, some have been voluntarily repatriated and others granted citizenship. Though there remain Indian Tamils in Sri Lanka who are not citizens and therefore cannot vote, many others participate in political life. The major parliamentary opposition is the Tamil United Liberation Front, and an Indian Tamil sits in the current cabinet.

[5] And this is at the federal level only. There still remains one canton where women do not have the right to a local vote. See Jurg Steiner, *Amicable Agreement versus Majority Rule* (Chapel Hill: University of North Carolina Press, 1974), p. 109. Portugal gave women the vote only in 1975.

TABLE 10–1
ELIGIBILITY FOR THE VOTE

Country	Voting Age	Residence Requirement[a]	Categories of Persons Disqualified			
			Recognized as mentally deficient	Criminals	Holders of certain public office	Other
Australia[b]	18	Minimum of 1 month in constituency, 6 months in country	Yes	Yes (if sentence longer than 12 months)	No	Holders of temporary entrance permits; prohibited immigrants
Austria	19	Yes, in constituency	Yes	Yes	No	Persons confined to work house; parents who have lost rights over their children
Belgium	21	Minimum of 6 months in constituency	Yes	Yes (also if convicted of electoral offenses)	No	Conscientious objectors, deserters; prostitutes, vagabonds, undischarged bankrupts, parents who have lost rights over their children
Canada[c]	18[d]	Yes, in constituency	Yes	Yes (also if convicted of electoral offenses)	Chief and assistant electoral officer; returning officers; judges	No

					Police, armed forces	
Colombia	18	n.a.	n.a.	n.a.	n.a.	n.a.
Denmark	18	Yes, in country	Yes	No	No	No
Finland	18	Inclusion on census register	No	Yes (if convicted of electoral offenses)	No	Vagrants
France	18	Minimum of 6 months in constituency	Yes	Yes	No	Undischarged bankrupts
West Germany	18	Minimum of 3 months in country	Yes	Yes	No	No
Greece	20	n.a.	Yes	Yes (including those on bail)	No	Conscientious objectors, deserters
India	21	Yes, in constituency	Yes	Yes (also if convicted of electoral offenses)	No	No
Ireland	18	Yes, in constituency	No	No	No	No
Israel	18	No	No	No	No	No
Italy	18	Yes, in country	No	Yes	No	Offenders against morality codes
Japan	20	Yes, in constituency	No	Yes (also if convicted of electoral offenses)	No	No

(Table continues)

TABLE 10–1 (continued)

Country	Voting Age	Residence Requirement[a]	Categories of Persons Disqualified			
			Recognized as mentally deficient	Criminals	Holders of certain public office	Other
Netherlands	18	Yes, in country	Yes	Yes (if sentence longer than 12 months)[e]	No	Vagrants, drunkards; parents who have lost their rights over their children
New Zealand[f]	20	Minimum of 3 months in constituency and 1 year in country	Yes	Yes	No	Persons on Corrupt Practices List
Norway	18	No	Yes	Yes (also if convicted of electoral offenses)	No	No
Portugal	n.a.	n.a.	n.a.	n.a.	n.a.	n.a.
Spain	21	n.a.	n.a.	n.a.	n.a.	n.a.
Sri Lanka	18	Yes, in constituency	Yes	Yes (also if convicted of electoral offenses)	No	Some Indian Tamils denied citizenship
Sweden	18	Yes, in country for at least some time in last 7 years	Yes, if placed under tutelage by a court	No	No	No

Switzerland[g]	20	Yes, in country	Yes	Yes	No	No
Turkey	18	n.a.	n.a.	Yes	n.a.	n.a.
United Kingdom[h]	18	Yes, in constituency on qualifying date[i]	Yes	Yes (also for electoral offenses)	No	Peers
United States	18	Yes, in state	Yes[j]	Yes[k]	No	Offenders against morality codes[l]
Venezuela	18	n.a.	Yes	Yes	Armed forces	No

NOTE: n.a. = information not available.

[a] See also table 10-3 for provisions for citizens working abroad.

[b] All British subjects meeting residence requirements are entitled to vote.

[c] All British subjects meeting residence requirements are entitled to vote.

[d] Under eighteen if active member of armed forces.

[e] Also debarred from voting three years after the end of the term of imprisonment.

[f] All British subjects meeting residence requirements are entitled to vote.

[g] There are variations from canton to canton.

[h] All British subjects (which includes citizens of all Commonwealth nations) and citizens of the Republic of Ireland meeting residence requirements are entitled to vote.

[i] In Northern Ireland, for three months prior to the qualifying date.

[j] In forty-six states.

[k] Forty-five states and the District of Columbia disqualify voters after conviction of a felony.

[l] These vary from state to state.

SOURCES: Inter-Parliamentary Union, *Parliaments of the World* (London: Macmillan, 1976); Inter-Parliamentary Union, *Chronicle of Parliamentary Elections and Developments*, vols. 10-12, 1975/76, 1976/77, 1977/78; *Keesing's Contemporary Archives*; Geoffrey Hand et al., eds., *European Systems Handbook* (London: Butterworths, 1979).

small proportion of their adult populations by imposing minimum requirements or specific exemptions. And the requirements and exemptions vary: there is no universal definition of an "elector." All but four democracies restrict the vote to citizens by birth or naturalization, and the noncitizens entitled to vote in the four exceptions are a limited category: British citizens (who satisfy residence requirements) in Australia, Canada,[6] and New Zealand, and Commonwealth and Eire citizens in the United Kingdom. All but Israel have requirements of residence in the constituency or country, often for a minimum period of months and sometimes longer (a year, in New Zealand). As regards disqualifications, the majority of democracies exclude from the franchise convicted criminals (in some cases only for serious offenses), those convicted of electoral corruption, and those certified as mentally deficient. But there are exceptions: prisoners may vote in Israel, Ireland, Denmark, and Sweden (where special polling booths are provided); the mentally ill are not excluded from the polls in Finland, Ireland, Israel, Italy, or Japan. And then there are a variety of additional categories of disfranchised: undischarged bankrupts in Belgium and France; members of the armed forces in Colombia and Venezuela; judges and election officers in Canada; life and hereditary peers in Britain; vagrants and drunkards in Finland and the Netherlands; prostitutes in Italy and Belgium. Finally, the minimum voting age differs from country to country: in the majority it is now down to eighteen, but in Greece, Japan, New Zealand, and Switzerland it is twenty, and in Belgium, India, and Spain it remains at twenty-one.

These departures from the principle of full adult suffrage do not of course account for more than a few percent of the adult population. But two in particular should not be dismissed as mere curiosities. The requirement of citizenship denies the right to vote to foreign workers, who are beginning to form a not insignificant proportion of the population in some countries—North Africans and Spaniards in France, Italians in Switzerland, Pakistanis in Britain, polyglot *Gastarbeiter* in Germany, and so on. The size of foreign communities like these will probably grow, as will those created by the free labor market within the European Economic Community, a trend which will be reinforced if the EEC comes to incorporate the labor-exporting nations of Spain, Portugal, and Greece. Second, the combination of residency requirements and arrangements for updating the electoral roll periodically rather than cumulatively (the case in most countries) is likely to result in the de facto disfranchisement of a nontrivial segment of the population as geographical mobility increases—a

---

[6] Except for those in Australia on temporary entrance permits, and for those in Canada who did not qualify as electors before June 29, 1968.

trend common to all industrialized democracies. Thus there is still scope for modest extensions of the suffrage.

On What Occasions Are People Entitled to Vote?

A useful distinction can be drawn between who may vote and what may be voted upon, between the *right* to electoral participation and the *range* of electoral participation. The range of voting opportunities in any country depends on four factors (in order of importance): (1) the *type of office* subject to direct popular election, such as the presidency, the upper chamber of the legislature, a party's candidate for office; and the *type of decision*, for example, major constitutional proposals, any contentious issue raised by a popular initiative; (2) the *levels of elected government,* including state government in a federal system and supranational legislatures like the European Assembly; (3) the *frequency of elections*, whether determined by constitutional stipulation or by political contingency; and (4) the *number of votes* the ballot format puts at the elector's disposal in any one election—whether voting is ordinal as opposed to categorical, whether there are runoff ballots or mechanisms for choosing candidates within party lists, and so on (this should be distinguished from plural voting, which is now virtually extinct in our twenty-seven democracies.)

Table 10–2 displays the range of voting opportunities for each of our twenty-seven democracies and provides a marked contrast with table 10–1. Who may vote differs only slightly from country to country; what they vote about, and how often, varies enormously.

Consider each of the components of the range of participation in turn. First, the offices and issues subject to election. In seven of our twenty-seven countries—Colombia, Finland, France, Portugal, Sri Lanka, the United States, and Venezuela—the president is popularly elected; the remainder have hereditary monarchs or presidents indirectly elected by the legislature or an electoral college. In ten of our twenty-seven countries—Australia, Belgium, Colombia, Italy, Japan, Spain, Switzerland, Turkey, the United States, and Venezuela—the upper chamber of the legislature is popularly elected; the remainder are unicameral or have indirectly elected or appointed upper chambers. Three countries—Belgium, Turkey, and the United States—hold party "primaries" (see chapter 5). One country, Switzerland, has frequent national referendums; a few others, such as Australia, Denmark, Ireland, and New Zealand, have had about half a dozen since 1945;[7] ten have had none at all, including the United States, which does, however, have numerous state and local referendums. Moreover,

---

[7] This refers to the *occasions* of a national referendum. In Australia a variety of issues have usually been put to the electorate on each occasion.

TABLE 10–2
NUMBER AND TYPE OF ELECTIONS

Country	Frequency of Elections (in months)[a]	Can Voters Choose between Candidates of Same Party?[b]	Popular Election of Upper House?	Popular Election of President?	Number of Levels of Subnational Elections	Supranational Elections?	National Referendums since 1945[c]	Other
Australia	28.8	No (but STV system for Senate elections)	Yes	No: monarchy	Two	No	7 (18)	—
Austria	39.9	Yes	No: indirect	No: indirect	Two	No	1	—
Belgium	35.8	Yes	Yes (mainly)	No: monarchy	Two	Yes: EEC	1	Party primaries
Canada	37.1	No	No: appointed	No: monarchy	Two	No	0	—
Colombia	not app.	n.a.	Yes	Yes	n.a.	No	1	—
Denmark	29.0	Yes	No upper house	No: monarchy	One	Yes: EEC	7 (10)	—
Finland	40.7	Yes	No upper house	Yes	n.a.	No	0	—

Country								Runoff ballots
France	38.9	No	No: indirect	Yes	Two	Yes: EEC	8	—
West Germany	46.6	Yes	No: indirect	No: indirect	Two	Yes: EEC	0	—
Greece	not app.	Yes	No upper house	No: monarchy until 1968, then indirect	n.a.	No	4	—
India	60.0	No	No: indirect	No: indirect	Two	No	0	—
Ireland	44.0	Yes (STV electoral system)[d]	No: indirect	No: indirect	One	Yes: EEC	4 (6)	—
Israel	42.5	No	No upper house	No: indirect	One	No	0	—
Italy	46.4	Yes	Yes	No: indirect	One	Yes: EEC	3 (4)	—
Japan	30.6	No	Yes	No	n.a.	No	0	—
Netherlands	41.3	Yes	No: indirect	No: monarchy	Two[e]	Yes: EEC	0	—
New Zealand	34.9	No	No upper house	No: monarchy	One	No	5[f]	—

(Table continues)

227

TABLE 10–2 (continued)

Country	Frequency of Elections (in months)[a]	Can Voters Choose between Candidates of Same Party?[b]	Popular Election of Upper House?	Popular Election of President?	Number of Levels of Subnational Elections	Supra-national Elections?	National Referendums since 1945[c]	Other
Norway	47.9	No	No: indirect	No: monarchy	One	No	1	—
Portugal	not app.	No	No upper house	Yes	One	No	0	—
Spain	not app.	No	Yes (mainly)	No: monarchy	One	No	3	—
Sri Lanka	60.4	No	No upper house	Yes	n.a.	No	0	—
Sweden	37.3	Yes	No upper house	No: monarchy	One	No	2	—
Switzerland	48.0	Yes (in most cantons)	Yes	No: indirect	One	No	160+	—
Turkey	41.2	No	Yes	No: indirect	n.a.	No	1	Party primaries

United Kingdom	40.6	No	No: appointed/ hereditary	No: monarchy	Two	Yes: EEC	1	—
United States	Presidential: 48.0 Congressional: 24.0	No	Yes	Yes	Two	No	0	Party primaries (all states)
Venezuela	not app.	No	Yes	Yes	Two	No	1	—

Note: n.a. = information not available; not app. = information not applicable—democracy not continuous since 1940s.

a Refers to lower house elections only. Calculated for the period from the first postwar election to the present day.

b Refers to lower house only. A "yes" in this column means that the voter has some opportunity to express preferences between candidates of the same party, usually as a result of a special provision within the constraints of the list system. A "no" means there is no such opportunity, because the electoral system is a strict list system or a strict individual vote.

c Local and regional referendums are excluded. Figures outside parentheses refer to the number of referendum *occasions*, figures inside to the number of referendum issues.

d Under Ireland's single transferable vote, two or more candidates of the same party run in most districts. They do not run on a party list but as individual candidates with a party affiliation, and the voter is free to give his first, second, and lower-order preferences to candidates of different parties.

e There are also elections for a few "regions" between the provincial and municipal levels.

f In addition, a referendum on liquor licensing hours has been held in conjunction with all general elections since 1908.

Sources: As for table 10-1; also Thomas T. Mackie and Richard Rose, *The International Almanac of Electoral History* (London: Macmillan, 1974); and David Butler and Austin Ranney, eds., *Referendums: A Comparative Study of Practice and Theory* (Washington, D.C.: American Enterprise Institute, 1978).

there is no pattern or clustering to this variety: of the ten democracies with popularly elected upper chambers, only three—Colombia, the United States, and Venezuela—also have popularly elected presidents.

Not surprisingly, our second component—the levels of elected government—varies less than the first. The range is largely between two levels (Denmark, Israel, and New Zealand) and three (Australia, West Germany, the Netherlands, and the United Kingdom), although in some large federal states such as the United States it is reasonable to talk of four (federal, state, and two local levels: county and municipal). But our third component, the frequency of elections, does range widely. Table 10–2 displays the average (mean) interval in months between general elections to the lower house for each of the twenty-two countries with an uninterrupted record of democracy since the 1940s. On average the elector votes in such general elections once every three-and-a-bit years (40.7 months), but some get the chance to vote more than others: the citizens of the United States (24.0 months), Australia (28.8 months), and Denmark (29.0 months) have had twice as many opportunities, if they could be bothered to exercise them, as Indians (60.0 months) or Sri Lankans (60.4 months).

Our final component of voting opportunities encompasses the number and nature of choices that the electoral system affords the individual voter in a single election. I refer here not to the relationship between the distribution of votes and that of seats or of cabinet portfolios, or to the comparative size of constituencies—matters for another chapter in this book—but to the choices afforded in the act of voting itself. For example, at each Bundestag election the German elector has two votes, one for a statewide party list, the other for a candidate in his local constituency. In presidential and legislative elections the French have one vote, but they actually cast ballots twice, on each of two Sundays a week apart (a fortnight for presidential elections), the second Sunday being the occasion for a runoff between two or sometimes three of the many candidates standing in the first round.[8] In elections to the Irish Dáil voters cast only one ballot, but the single-transferable-vote electoral system allows them to rank order the candidates of all the parties. And in most of the sixteen countries with a party-list PR electoral system, there are provisions for recording a candidate preference or altering the order of candidates on a party list

---

[8] In legislative elections any candidate securing an absolute majority of the votes cast in the first round is elected and no runoff is held; this rarely occurs in more than 15 percent of the constituencies. In legislative elections, to be eligible for the runoff a candidate must win the support of at least 12.5 percent of the registered voters; in presidential elections, the runoff is between the two candidates who received the most votes at the first ballot among those candidates who do not choose to withdraw from the race.

in addition to choosing a party. In none of these countries do many voters appear to take full or indeed any advantage of such options (only about 10 percent rank order candidates to the Irish Dáil other than by party, for example, and very few alter the order of candidates on party lists). Nor should one exaggerate the extra amount of participation put into the hands of a voter by even the most elaborate of electoral systems: a single vote always represents an infinitesimally small particle of power. Nonetheless, electors in a categorical-ballot, simple-majority, single-member electoral system such as Britain's could claim with reason that one of their votes involved a more limited form of choice of representatives than the vote of a Frenchman or an Irishman. In terms of participation it is worth less.

Taken separately, each of these four components produces only minor differences in the range of voting opportunities across countries; taken together the differences can be substantial. Consider, for example, the case of Australia and New Zealand, two countries often yoked together in cross-national analysis for reasons of geography and culture. Since World War II the typical Australian (for whom voting is compulsory) has trooped off to the polls every twenty-nine months to elect the House of Representatives, the New Zealander (for whom voting is voluntary) once every thirty-five months. Australians also directly elect their upper chamber, the Senate (but, unlike in the United States, not always at the same time as the House of Representatives); New Zealand's Parliament is unicameral. Australia has two levels of popularly elected subnational government, state and local; New Zealand has only one. Moreover, Australian state legislatures consist of two chambers, each of which is popularly elected.[9] Australia has had seven nationwide referendums (on eighteen different issues, of which only two were held on the same day as a general election); New Zealand has had five, in addition to a three-choice question on liquor licensing in conjunction with every election. To put it simply, Australians engage in a great deal more electing than New Zealanders do.

In theory one could quantify the overall amount of voting to which citizens of different countries were entitled; in practice such estimates would be a Herculean task. There would be insoluble problems of weighting. Does a vote in a nationwide referendum count more or less than a vote for a president? Is a vote for a state legislature worth more than a vote for a county council? And also problems of definition: do multilevel elections held on the same day (as in the United States) count as one or many elections?

---

[9] Except for Queensland, which is unicameral, and for the upper chamber of New South Wales, which is indirectly elected.

However, one does not need a computer to know which country would emerge top of the league. No country can approach the United States in the frequency and variety of elections, and thus in the amount of electoral participation to which its citizens have a right. No other country elects its lower house as often as every two years, or its president as frequently as every four years. No other country popularly elects its state governors *and* town mayors; no other has as wide a variety of nonrepresentative offices (judges, sheriffs, attorneys general, city treasurers, and so on) subject to election. Only one other country (Switzerland) can compete in the number and variety of local referendums; only two others (Belgium and Turkey) hold party "primaries" in most parts of the country. The average American is entitled to do far more electing—probably by a factor of three or four—than the citizen of any other democracy. The degree to which he exercises that right is another matter, however, as will become plain in the next section.

National Turnout Rates since 1945

Unlike national ranges of electoral participation, national turnout rates can be estimated with some precision. But before the national turnout figures are examined, a technical caveat is in order. Quite apart from the occasional discrepancy between apparently authoritative sources[10] —an interesting reflection of the difficulty of compiling even the simplest and most basic of electoral statistics—the accuracy of the turnout figures depends on the efficiency of the electoral registers on which they are all based (except for the United States). To the extent that registers include the names of persons for whom voting is impossible (the dead, the double-counted) or very inconvenient (emigrants, those temporarily abroad, or, in some countries, those who have moved out of the constituency for which they are registered), the turnout figure will be artificially depressed. But to the extent that the registers omit those unlikely to exercise their right to the vote (the homeless, tenants of single rooms, immigrants), turnout figures will be artificially inflated. (In the United States the registration laws result in the temporary exclusion from the rolls of such large numbers that turnout is based on a "voting age population" figure provided by the Bureau of the Census.)

The efficiency of the register undoubtedly varies from country to country. Where it is continuously revised on the basis of a municipally

[10] In particular between *Keesing's Contemporary Archives* and the Inter-Parliamentary Union's annual *Chronicles of Parliamentary Elections and Developments*; fortunately the discrepancies are never serious.

maintained population register, as in Austria, Germany, the Netherlands, Switzerland, and Norway, it contains fewer surplus names than where it is compiled at a fixed point of the year, as in Britain and France. Countries with concentrations of poor and polyglot populations in the overcrowded parts of large cities (such as Australia, Canada, France, and Britain) are more likely than those without (Ireland, New Zealand, Norway) to underregister electorally apathetic citizens and thus obtain slightly inflated turnout figures. The accuracy of registers will also vary over time within any one country. In Britain, for example, it is increasingly common for political scientists to adjust the official turnout figure to the age of the register at the time of the election. One formula is +3.4 percent (not registered) —1.0 percent (registered twice) —.15m percent (effect of deaths) —0.67m percent (effect of removals), where m = months from the date of the register's compilation.[11] Applying the formula can make a difference: thus the official statistics show quite sharply fluctuating turnout in Britain's last three general elections (78.1 percent, 72.8 percent, 76.0 percent), while the adjusted figures suggest serene stability (79.1 percent, 78.7 percent, 78.6 percent). The formula itself, however, probably needs renewing from time to time. It is generally agreed, for example, that the electoral register in Britain has declined in accuracy over the last ten years.[12]

The precise impact of the register's efficiency in each country is impossible to assess, but in many cases the error is likely to amount to three or four percentage points. This means that small fluctuations in turnout both between and within countries should be treated with caution (at least as an indicator of commitment to vote) and reliance should be confined to substantial differences and to averages based on a series of elections.

Table 10–3 rank orders the mean national turnout for general elections to the lower house of the legislature for all twenty-seven countries since 1945. (For the United States, turnout in presidential elections is used since turnout figures for congressional elections are unobtainable. Apart from its historical significance, 1945 is a suitable cutoff point because before that date women were denied the vote in a

---

[11] See Richard Rose, "Britain: Simple Abstractions and Complex Realities," in Richard Rose, ed., *Electoral Behaviour: A Comparative Handbook* (London: Collier, Macmillan, 1974), p. 494.

[12] For a recent, detailed analysis of the efficiency of the British electoral register, see David Butler and Colm O'Muircheartaigh, "What Is 40%? A Note on the Eligible Electorate," mimeo, February 1979. It concludes that the conventional view that 4 percent of the qualified electorate is left off the register is now out of date and that "a figure of 6 percent would probably still err on the side of caution."

TABLE 10–3

TURNOUT STATISTICS

Country	Number of Elections since 1945	Compulsory Voting?	Mean Turnout since 1945[a]	Rank Order	Postwar Trend: 1940/50s to 1970s (in percentage points)	Turnout Volatility (mean inter-election changes, in percentage points)	% Vote Invalid (postwar mean)
1. Australia	14	Yes[b]	95.4	1	Down: −0.6	0.6	2.2
2. Netherlands 1945–67	7	Yes	94.7	2	not app.	0.5	2.7
3. (Venezuela)	(5)	(Yes: if aged 21–65)	(94.4)[c]	(—)	(not app.)	(not app.)	(4.7)
4. Austria	10	3 provinces only	94.2	3	Down: −3.2	1.0	1.2
5. Italy	9	Almost, but not formally	92.6	4	Up: +1.0	0.8	3.1
6. Belgium	12	Yes	92.5	5	Up: +0.2	1.7	5.9
7. New Zealand	12	No	90.4[d]	6	Down: −6.6	2.9	0.6
8. (Portugal)	(2)	(No)	(87.6)	(—)	(not app.)	(not app.)	(5.2)

9. West Germany	8	No	86.9	7	*Up:* +6.9	2.6	2.1
10. Denmark	14	No	85.8	8	*Up:* +5.0	1.5	0.4
11. Sweden	10	No	84.9	9	*Up:* +10.6	3.0	0.4
12. (Netherlands 1970 +)	(3)	(No)	(83.5)	(—)	(not app.)	(4.5)	(0.6)
13. (Sri Lanka)	(6)	(No)	(82.2)[e]	(—)	(not app.)	(not app.)	(n.a.)
14. Israel	9	No	81.4	10	*Down:* −2.6	4.1	1.9
15. Norway	9	No	80.8	11	*Up:* +2.5	3.0	0.4
16. France	11	No	79.3	12	*Up:* +2.0	3.9	1.9
17. (Greece)	(11)	(Yes: if aged 21–70 and within 200 km of constituency)	(79.1)[f]	(—)	(n.a.)	(not app.)	(n.a.)
18. Finland	10	No	79.0	13	*Up:* +2.7	4.3	0.4
19. United Kingdom	11	No	76.9	14	*Down:* −3.9	4.1	n.a. (negligible)
20. Canada	12	No	76.4[g]	15	*Up:* +2.9[h]	3.1	0.9
21. Ireland	9	No	74.7	16	*Up:* +2.2	1.9	0.7
22. Japan	13	No	73.1	17	*Down:* −1.3	3.1	0.9

(Table continues)

TABLE 10–3 (continued)

Country	Number of Elections since 1945	Compulsory Voting?	Mean Turnout since 1945[a]	Rank Order	Postwar Trend: 1940/50s to 1970s (in percentage points)	Turnout Volatility (mean inter-election changes, in percentage points)	% Vote Invalid (postwar mean)
23. (Spain)	(2)	(No)	(72.7)	(—)	(not app.)	(not app.)	(n.a.)
24. (Turkey)	(10)	(No)	(67.4)[i]	(—)	(not app.)	(3.3)	(n.a.)
25. Switzerland	8	No (except 4 small cantons)	64.5	18	Down: −15.1	2.8	1.1
26. India	6	No	58.7[j]	19	not app.	4.5	n.a.
27. United States (presidential)[k]	8	No	58.5[a]	20	Down: −2.2	3.5	n.a.
28. (Colombia)	(5)	(No)	(46.6)[l]	(—)	(not app.)	(not app.)	(n.a.)
Average, ranked countries only	10	—	81.0	—	Up: +0.02	2.7	1.5
Average, all countries	9	—	78.6	—	—	2.8	1.8

NOTE: The figures for countries without a continuous record of democracy since the late 1940s are placed in parentheses and excluded from the rank order, as are those for which exact figures are not available for a sufficient number of elections; n.a. = data not available; not app. = not applicable—too few observations.

a Except for the United States, turnout is defined as votes cast (including invalid and blank votes) as a percentage of registered voters. The figure for the United States refers to valid votes only, as a percentage of the voting age population.

b Voting compulsory for all registered voters; registration optional for Aborigines.

c Based on 1968 and 1973 elections only; data for 1947, 1953, and 1963 elections unreliable or not available.

d Excludes 1978 election, for which no turnout data are yet available.

e Based on estimates of total electorate for 1960, 1965, and 1970 elections; turnout data not available for 1952, 1956, and 1977 elections.

f Based on elections of 1956, 1958, 1974, and 1977 only; turnout data for eight other postwar elections not available or unreliable.

g Based on ten elections, 1945–1972; turnout figures for the 1947 and 1979 elections not available.

h Based on difference between 1940s/1950s and 1960s/1970s.

i Based on last four elections (1965, 1969, 1973, 1977) only; turnout data for six other postwar elections not available or unreliable.

j Based on five out of six elections since independence (no turnout data available for 1967 election).

k Figures for the House of Representatives unobtainable.

l Based on most recent three elections only (1968, 1970, 1974); turnout data for 1946 and 1949 elections not available.

SOURCES: Inter-Parliamentary Union, Parliaments of the World, Inter-Parliamentary Union, Chronicle of Parliamentary Elections and Developments, 1965+; Keesing's Contemporary Archives; Mackie and Rose, International Almanac of Electoral History (also supplements in the European Journal of Political Research, vol. 2 (3), September 1974; vol. 4 (3), September 1976; vol. 5 (3), September 1977; vol. 6 (3), September 1978); Rose, Electoral Behaviour: A Comparative Handbook (London: Collier, Macmillan, 1974).

number of countries.) Except for the United States, turnout includes invalid and blank votes (a more than negligible proportion in a few countries) on the grounds that a sufficient condition of electoral participation is simply to turn up at the polling station. The figures for countries without a continuous record of democracy since the late 1940s—Colombia, Greece, Portugal, Spain, and Venezuela—are placed in parentheses, as are those for Sri Lanka and Turkey, for which exact figures are not available for a sufficient number of elections. For purposes of analysis the Netherlands is treated as two countries: (1) the Netherlands 1945–1967, when voting was compulsory, and (2) the Netherlands after 1970, when it became voluntary.

Table 10–3 contains a number of features worth noting. The first is that, despite its strict irrationality in terms of individual benefits received, four out of five citizens in the world's major democracies do in fact vote. Only in such precarious and recently reestablished democracies as Colombia do nonvoters outnumber voters.[13] But the second feature is the spectacular *range* in national turnouts, despite the common assumption that voting is a universally simple act. National turnouts vary from 95 percent in Australia and the Netherlands 1945–1967 to under half as much in Colombia (47 percent). This range goes well beyond the fluctuating inaccuracies of electoral registers, of course, and suggests that there are real and major national differences in people's willingness to participate in elections.[14]

This conclusion is reinforced by a third feature of the figures: the remarkable stability of most countries' turnout since the war. In the twenty-one countries for which calculations are valid, turnout has moved by an average of only 2.7 percentage points between elections, part of which, for reasons already explained, can be attributed to changes in the accuracy of the register. Moreover, with only a few exceptions, these changes in turnout have not cumulated into a discernible trend but have fluctuated around a mean of almost rocklike stability. By and large, countries with unusually high or unusually low turnouts in the immediate postwar period had similarly high or

---

[13] This is also true of the American South.

[14] A conclusion strengthened by the wide disparities of turnout between the nine members of the EEC at the first direct elections to the European Parliament in June 1979. The national turnout figures (including blank and invalid votes) were: Belgium 91.3 percent, Luxembourg 88.9 percent, Italy 84.7 percent, Germany 65.8 percent, Ireland 63.6 percent, France 60.8 percent, the Netherlands 57.8 percent, Denmark 47.1 percent, the United Kingdom 32.3 percent. This rank ordering is only partly parallel with that for elections to the national legislatures: Ireland ranks higher, and the Netherlands and Denmark considerably lower, than expected. The relatively high turnout in Belgium, Italy, and Germany is true to national form, however, as is the United Kingdom's bottom place.

low turnouts in the 1970s: the rank-order correlation between these two periods emerges as 0.9. As table 10–3 shows, of the eighteen countries for which comparisons are possible, only five show a movement up or down of more than 4 points: Sweden (up 10.6 points), Germany (up 6.9 points), Denmark (up 5.0 points), New Zealand (down 6.6 points), and Switzerland (down 15.1 points). These movements, it should be added, have occurred when average turnout across all eighteen countries shows no trend at all: it was 81.21 percent in the 1940s and 1950s, 81.23 percent in the 1970s. In summary, then, we find major variations between countries, little variation within countries. Clearly there is something to be explained.

Explanations of Variations in National Turnout

Where does one search for these explanations? An obvious answer is the voluminous literature on factors underlying variations in turnout within national populations.[15] Summarizing drastically, one can distinguish between macroexplanations, which focus on the attributes of the elector's environment, and microexplanations, which concentrate on the attributes of individual electors. Among microexplanations one can further distinguish between the elector's *capacities and resources,* such as income, private transportation, and education, and the elector's *psychological orientation* to politics, such as his sense of civic duty, attachment to a party, and feeling of involvement in political affairs. Macroexplanations cannot be categorized as neatly, but three in particular should be kept in mind: (1) the legal and administrative facilitation of voting, as reflected in registration regulations, provisions for absentee voters, and so on; (2) the degree to which the vote is institutionally mobilized, the amount of dragooning by parties and by organizations attached to parties like trade unions and churches; and (3) the incentive to vote provided by the closeness of the contest and other aspects of the party and electoral system. Needless to say, in the real world these factors tend to be related to each other in complicated ways. Moreover, for none of these factors do satisfactory measures exist for more than a few countries. Precise explanations based on refined techniques of multivariate analysis are therefore not possible; nonetheless, these factors do provide a framework of explanation or, as the case may be, speculation.

Let us begin with the macroexplanations.

---

[15] Still useful, if somewhat dated, summaries of the literature can be found in Lester W. Milbraith, *Political Participation* (Chicago: Rand McNally, 1965), and Robert E. Lane, *Political Life* (New York: Free Press, 1959).

The Legal and Administrative Facilitation of Voting. Four countries—Australia, Belgium, Greece, and Venezuela—take the legal facilitation of voting to its logical conclusion: they make it compulsory for all or most of their electorate.[16] A common criticism of compulsion is that if the sanctions are light or only nominal they will be ineffective; if severe, intolerable. In reality, in the countries where voting is compulsory, both convictions and sanctions against nonvoters appear to be negligible, except perhaps in Venezuela. Australian abstainers are liable to a fine if they cannot provide the local electoral officer with a satisfactory explanation, but by all accounts most are imaginative enough to escape prosecution. The same can be said of Belgium: less than a quarter of 1 percent are prosecuted, let alone convicted.[17] But the law-abidingness of most citizens does make compulsion effective: Australia tops the postwar turnout league with 95.4 percent, and Belgium's turnout averages 92.5 percent. The most compelling evidence of its effectiveness comes from the Netherlands, which abandoned compulsion after the 1967 election. Until 1967 average turnout was 94.7 percent; since 1967 it has been 83.5 percent. Admittedly, not all of the extra voters press-ganged into the polling stations comply: the rate of invalid voting is higher in Belgium (5.9 percent on average, and rising) and Venezuela (4.7 percent) than in any other country (but is only 2.2 percent in Australia). Nonetheless, these proportions are well below the ten-percentage-point gain in turnout which, on the evidence from the Netherlands, appears to be the minimum increment produced by compulsion.[18]

There is no clear-cut distinction between compulsory and voluntary voting. In Italy, where the constitution stipulates that voting is a duty, "DID NOT VOTE" is stamped on the identification papers of abstainers. As Galli and Prandi put it: "no specific penalties are attached to this entry . . . but such a procedure in a country with a long tradition of bureaucratic control helps to spread the conviction that voting is not only a right but a public duty and that failure to exercise the right might have unfortunate consequences."[19] But this

---

[16] In Venezuela compulsion is restricted to those aged twenty-one to sixty-five, in Greece to those aged twenty-one to seventy and living within 200 kilometers of the constituency where they are registered. Voting is compulsory in three states of Austria and four small cantons of Switzerland; in both countries the proportion of the national electorate affected is under 10 percent.

[17] See Keith Hill, "Belgium: Political Change in a Segmented Society," in Rose, *Electoral Behaviour*, p. 59.

[18] If the increment in turnout resulting from compulsion is estimated to be the difference between the average postwar turnout for all "compulsory" states and that for all "voluntary" states, it rises to seventeen points.

[19] Giorgio Galli and Alfonso Prandi, *Patterns of Political Participation in Italy* (New Haven and London: Yale University Press, 1970), p. 28.

is not the only reason for Italy's exceptionally high postwar turnout (92.6 percent on average). Extraordinary care is taken to make it convenient to vote: the polling stations are open for *two* days, and for long hours on the first (6:00 A.M. to 10:00 P.M.); election days are public holidays; and community organizations, not only the parties, ferry the old and infirm to the polls. Moreover, a provision unique to Italy makes generous concessions on train fares available to those who have to return to their home constituency to vote, a real benefit to migrant workers in the North or beyond Italy's frontiers who wish to spend a few days with their families in Sicily and the South.

Table 10–4 arrays the various ways voting is legally and administratively encouraged in our set of twenty-seven countries. Five hold their election over more than one day (as a concession to strict sabbatarians in Finland and Norway), including India, whose first election after independence was held over a period of four months and whose more recent elections are still spread over five days. A majority of countries hold elections on a rest day, which presumably raises turnout by a fraction.

More important are the provisions for absentee voting. Electoral law needs to keep a balance between maintaining the vote as a personal act, free from duress and fraud, and ensuring that no one is prevented from voting through unavoidable absence on election day. The result is a complex medley of provisions, which can be placed into five categories:

Advance voting (seven countries). This is the opening of polling stations (usually a municipal or government office) before the date of the election for those who know they will be unable to vote on the day. Canada, Finland, Sweden, and New Zealand allow any elector to vote in advance, although the period available for doing so varies; in Sweden it is any time in the preceding twenty-four days, but only the seventh or ninth day in advance in Canada. The other three countries, however, restrict advance voting to narrowly specified categories: those absent through their job (Japan and Norway) or sailors only (Israel).

Postal voting (fifteen countries). This too is voting in advance, but is permissible by post as well as in person. The regulations differ considerably in the categories of elector to whom postal voting is made available. Australia, Belgium, Switzerland, and Germany make no restrictions (which in the first two cases is only consistent with voting's being compulsory). Ireland obliges its police and armed forces to vote by post (as does Switzerland) but allows no other elector to do so. Other eligible categories include those in the hospital, the ill and

241

TABLE 10–4
THE FACILITATION OF VOTING

Country	Number of Days Polling Booths Open	Work Day or Rest Day?	Postal Voting	Proxy Voting	Polling Booths in Special Institutions?	Constituency Transfer?	Advance Voting?
Australia	1	Rest day	Absentees, ill, pregnant	No	Embassies	Yes, within state	No
Austria	1	Rest day	No	No	Hospitals, old age homes	By application in advance	No
Belgium	1	Rest day	Absentees, hospital patients, public service officials	Restricted to those abroad and in itinerant occupations	No	No	No
Canada	1	Work day	No	Students, ill, those at sea, prospectors	No	No	Yes, for elderly, infirm, pregnant, armed forces, hospital patients, those absent through their job, on religious grounds
Colombia	1	Rest day	n.a.	n.a.	n.a.	n.a.	n.a.

Denmark	1	Work day	Prisoners, hospital patients, those on diplomatic missions, on isolated islands, ships, lighthouses, & in national register offices	No	No	No	No
Finland	2	Both: Sunday & Monday	No	No	Diplomatic missions abroad, ships, hospitals (in advance)	No	Yes
France	1	Rest day	(Abolished 1975)	Sailors, armed forces (some), civil servants, those abroad, invalids, disabled	No	No	No
West Germany	1	Rest day	Absentees from country or constituency, ill and infirm	No	No	Yes	No

(Table continues)

243

TABLE 10-4 (continued)

Country	Number of Days Polling Booths Open	Work Day or Rest Day?	Postal Voting	Proxy Voting	Polling Booths in Special Institutions?	Constituency Transfer?	Advance Voting?
Greece	1	Rest day	No	n.a.	n.a.	n.a.	n.a.
India	5	Both	Higher federal/state officials, armed forces, police serving in another state, election officials, prisoners, government employees abroad	No	No	No	No
Ireland	1	Work day	Obligatory for armed forces and police	No	No	No	No
Israel	1	Work day	No	No	Soldiers	For nomads	Yes, for sailors
Italy	2	Both: Sunday & Monday	No	No	No	For armed forces only	No

Country							
Japan	1	Rest day	No	For illiterate and ill, 2 proxy voters required, appointed by election official	No	No	Yes, for those away on business
Netherlands	1	Work day	Government employees abroad	Yes, within strict limits	No	On advance application	No
New Zealand	1	Rest day	Yes	No	No	Yes	For all absentees, ill, infirm, pregnant, lighthouse keepers
Norway	2 (in most areas)	Both: Sunday & Monday	Yes	No	On ships and in diplomatic missions abroad	No	For hospital patients and those absent through job
Portugal	1	Rest day	Yes	n.a.	n.a.	Yes	n.a.
Spain	1	Work day	n.a.	n.a.	n.a.	n.a.	n.a.
Sri Lanka	1	Work day	Election officials, those absent through job	No	No	No	No

(Table continues)

TABLE 10–4 (continued)

Country	Number of Days Polling Booths Open	Work Day or Rest Day?	Postal Voting	Proxy Voting	Polling Booths in Special Institutions?	Constituency Transfer?	Advance Voting
Sweden	1	Rest day	Yes	Use of spouse & relatives as "messengers" before witness	Hospitals, ships, old age homes, embassies, prisons	Postal votes may be cast at any post office on election day, without advance notice or special registration	Yes, for any elector
Switzerland	2 (3)	Both	Automatic for armed forces, otherwise by application 4 days before voting; varies by canton	Varies by canton	No	No	No
Turkey	1	Rest day	n.a.	n.a.	n.a.	n.a.	n.a.

United Kingdom	1	Work day	On application, for: disability, removal to another constituency, isolated residence, candidates, constables, returning officers, religious reasons, absence through job	On application, for armed forces, crown servants abroad, those abroad through job (& spouses)	No	No	No
United States	1	Work day	By application, for armed forces & government employees in most states	In some states, for blind and disabled	No	No	No
Venezuela	1	Rest day	No	No, but "assisted" voting for blind and disabled	Prisons, hospitals, old age homes	No	No

NOTE: n.a. = information not available.

SOURCES: Inter-Parliamentary Union, *Parliaments of the World*; and Inter-Parliamentary Union, *Chronicle of Parliamentary Elections and Developments*.

infirm, those who have moved out of the constituency for which they are registered, those absent through their jobs, election officials, prisoners, those in diplomatic missions abroad, and those living in very isolated areas. Britain is the only country to accept religious grounds for postal voting.

Proxy voting (eight countries). This is the appointment of one person, usually the spouse or a close relative, to vote on behalf of another. Strictly speaking, proxy voting should be distinguished from *assisted voting* (where one elector helps another who is blind or disabled to mark the ballot in the polling station) and from *messenger voting* (where, in front of a formal witness, an elector completes a ballot at home and allows another person to deliver it to the polling station). Proxy voting carries a real risk of fraud or intimidation and is therefore always subject to careful scrutiny and confined to a few strictly defined categories such as the disabled, those working abroad, and members of the armed forces. Japan grants proxy voting to the illiterate, but only under the supervision of two proxies appointed by the election officer.

Special polling stations (eight countries). Some countries provide special polling stations in hospitals and old age homes, ships, barracks, prisons, and embassies abroad. Finland, Norway, and Sweden have gone furthest in establishing polling stations in such institutions. In New Zealand in recent years polling stations serving a number of constituencies have been installed at race tracks, Saturday shopping malls, and other places where there are likely to be large crowds. There is even a floating polling station which visits each small settlement in the Marlborough Sounds in the week before polling day.

Constituency transfer (seven countries). Some countries provide for an elector to vote in a different polling station or constituency from that for which he is registered. Once again, this is a provision that varies in its eligibility requirements (it is only available to nomadic Bedouin in Israel, for example, and to the armed forces in Italy) and convenience (advance application is required in Austria and the Netherlands). The most flexible arrangements are in Australia and New Zealand, where an elector can turn up unannounced at *any* polling station (so long as it is within the same state in Australia) and vote.[20]

---

[20] In the United States, the rural midwestern state of North Dakota has no voter registration, and in some rural areas of Wisconsin voters are not required to register. Even in these states, however, an individual can vote only in his own district.

But whether these various arrangements make a noticeable difference to the turnout rate is doubtful. Austria and Italy make little use of them and yet have the highest turnout rates of the countries without compulsory voting. Most of the provisions affect only small numbers (some of whom, like prisoners and the bedridden, would be unlikely to vote anyway) and are accompanied by enough red tape to put off all but the most eager. Postal voting, the provision that can probably make the most difference, accounts for only between 1.5 percent and 2.0 percent of the votes in Britain (where it is available to all absentees other than those on holidays), and of course an unknown number of these would have been cast in the absence of postal voting provisions.[21] Added together the different provisions could make a more substantial impact; they might account for the higher turnout in Australia than in other countries with compulsory voting and for some of the significant postwar growth in turnout in Sweden. But as table 10–4 shows, these are the only two countries to have adopted most of these arrangements.

What clearly can make a substantial difference, however, are administrative *disincentives* to vote, and in one country at least, these remained serious until the mid-1960s. The United States, true to its liberal and Protestant tradition, is the only country where the individual elector is not automatically registered by the authorities but must take the initiative himself; part of voting is the civic duty of getting oneself onto the register. Two notorious obstacles to registration, the poll tax and literacy tests, systematically used to disfranchise blacks in the rural South, were abolished by the Twenty-Fourth Amendment, ratified in 1964, and the 1970 Voting Rights Act Amendments. The requirement to reregister regularly—often at intervals of as little as one year—has now almost completely died out, but it was still common in the early 1960s. So, too, was a one-year residency requirement, which the 1970 Voting Rights Act Amendments effectively reduced to a maximum of thirty days, at least for federal elections.

Nonetheless, in all but four states preregistration is still required, and the expenditure of energy and time it demands remains a discouragement, especially for the mobile, who are subject to residency requirements and confusing variations in state regulations. There are closing dates for registration, and these differ between states (usually thirty days before the election, sometimes fifty days). Registration

---

[21] However, it was the postal vote, counted separately, which gave the center-right coalition in Sweden a crucial one-seat margin in the closely fought election of September 1979. The Conservatives' narrow victory in the British general election of 1951 can also be attributed to the postal vote in a small number of key marginal seats.

offices are not necessarily open out of working hours, or indeed for more than a restricted period within them. Only a few states have provision for neighborhood registration; in others potential voters have to register in the county seat. And most states do not allow ordinary citizens (in effect party workers) to register potential voters. In the most systematic study of registration laws and turnout to date, Rosenstone and Wolfinger calculated that:

> depending on one's probability of otherwise voting, a 30-day closing date decreased the likelihood of voting by 3 to 9 percentage points. A 50-day closing date . . . lowered the probability of voting by about 17 percent for those with a 40 to 60 percent chance of going to the polls. . . . Irregular registration office hours (less than 40 hours a week) lowered by 2 to 4 percentage points the probability that a person would vote. Offices closed on Saturdays and in the evenings decreased by 2 to 6 percent the probability of voting. In states that did not allow any form of absentee registration the chances of voting were 2 to 4 percent lower.[22]

They conclude that if all states had adopted registration laws as permissive as those in the most permissive states, turnout would have risen by about nine percentage points (more than 12 million votes) overall, and by an even higher percentage within some subgroups—14.5 points among southern blacks. This study, it should be noted, was based on the 1972 presidential election, well after the most stringent registration regulations had been eliminated. As the authors put it, compared with voting, registration "may require a longer journey, at a less convenient hour, to complete a more complicated procedure—and at a time when interest in the campaign is far from its peak."[23] It is as if the elector had to vote twice.

But current registration requirements can account for only part of the low rate of turnout in the United States. Even if it were raised by the nine-point decrement, average U.S. turnout in the 1970s would still be only 64 percent, placing the United States second to last of the eighteen countries we can rank. Moreover, during the period that these barriers to registration have been being dismantled, turnout in presidential elections has been steadily *falling*—from 61.6 percent in 1960 to 54.4 percent in 1976. Thus there must be other factors at work, one of which is suggested in the next section.

---

[22] Steven J. Rosenstone and Raymond E. Wolfinger, "The Effect of Registration Laws on Voter Turnout," *American Political Science Review*, vol. 72 (1978), p. 31.
[23] Ibid., p. 22.

The Organizational Mobilization of the Vote. An obvious possible source of national differences in turnout rates is the relative intensity of the efforts made by parties and affiliated organizations such as trade unions and churches to get citizens to the polls. The extensiveness and effectiveness of these efforts do, presumably, vary across countries; the difficulty lies in finding indicators and measurements which are both valid and truly comparable.

One admittedly crude indicator would be the strength of the links between a country's party system and its established social divisions, such as class, religion, language, and race. Why should such links raise turnout? First, voters are more likely to find a meaning and benefit in their vote if they can think of a party as representing "their" group interests. This is particularly true of those electors with only a limited interest in politics—the very ones most likely to abstain—whom surveys have shown to be more likely to perceive the world of politics in terms of group interests rather than issues or ideology.[24] Second, such links make it easier for parties to identify and organize their support. People of the same class, religion, or ethnic group tend to live together, and, quite apart from the mobilizing effects of residential concentration per se, this allows party organizations to make use of community leaders, channel their resources, "target" their propaganda, and so forth. Moreover, long-established social groups develop an infrastructure of exclusive organizations for the promotion of their interests, values, traditions, and enjoyment—trade unions, professional bodies, cultural societies, social clubs, newspapers and broadcasting stations, schools and colleges—which also play a part in persuading their members to vote.

There are two aspects to the link between party system and social cleavages. One is its *breadth*—the proportion of the electorate whose party allegiance arises from membership in a close-knit social group. The other is its *depth*—the degree of interpenetration between the party organization and the network of institutions serving its "client" social group. No precise measure of depth of linkage is available, although it is possible to apply broad categories—to identify, say, those countries characterized by a system of *verzuiling* or "segmented pluralism" (Austria, Belgium, the Netherlands, and Switzerland, for example). But two reasonably up-to-date and comparative estimates of *breadth* of linkage are available: (1) in *Electoral Behaviour: A Comparative Handbook*, Rose gives the proportion of variance in

---

[24] See Philip Converse, "The Nature of Belief Systems in Mass Publics," in David Apter, ed., *Ideology and Discontent* (New York: Free Press, 1964), pp. 206-61; and Norman Nie, Sidney Verba, and John R. Petrocik, *The Changing American Voter* (Cambridge, Mass.: Harvard University Press, 1976), p. 121.

partisan allegiance in each of fifteen democracies that can be explained by a combination of class, religion, and region; and (2) in an unpublished paper Bingham Powell calculates "Alford" indexes of class voting and religious voting based on Rose's data for ten countries as well as recent election surveys for another ten.[25] The index with the higher value—indicated for each country in table 10-5 by a circle—may be taken as a measure of the breadth of linkage between party allegiance and social cleavage for that country.

Table 10-5 presents these two measures for each of fourteen and nineteen countries respectively; it reveals a strong, positive association between a country's turnout rate on the one hand and, on the other, the closeness of fit between its party system and major social cleavages. The correlations using the Rose data are +0.64 with overall postwar turnout and +0.52 with turnout in the 1970s; using Bingham Powell's index, which has less face validity but is available for more countries, they are +0.46 with overall postwar turnout and +0.30 with turnout in the 1970s. If the three countries with compulsory voting are added—Australia, Belgium, and the Netherlands 1945-1967—the correlations look very similar.[26] Despite the small number of cases, the first three of these correlations are significant at the 5 percent level. Crude though these indicators are, they do suggest that a country's turnout partially depends upon the degree to which party allegiance aligns with rather than across class, religious, and ethnic affiliations.

Two further observations on these figures are worth making. First, depth of linkage—the degree of organizational integration between party system and social cleavages—does appear to make an extra difference.[27] The two "noncompulsory" countries with the high-

---

[25] G. Bingham Powell, "Voting Turnout in Thirty-One Democracies: Effects of the Socio-Economic, Legal and Partisan Environments," mimeo, University of Rochester, August 1977. A substantially revised version will appear in Richard Rose, ed., *Party and Electoral Systems* (Beverly Hills, Calif.: Sage Publications, 1980). I am indebted to Powell's imaginative paper for the idea of taking Rose's data as a measure of the link between party system and social cleavages.

[26] In the same order, they were +0.62, +0.43, +0.52, and +0.31; again, only the last is not significant at the 5 percent level.

[27] Although it appears to have made less difference in the United States of the nineteenth century when turnout was higher (exceeding 80 percent on three occasions). Walter Dean Burnham attributes most of the post-1900 decline in turnout to personal-registration barriers, but also to the growth of an urban and industrialized working class unaccompanied by a socialist party or an exclusively labor political movement. See Walter Dean Burnham, "The United States: The Politics of Heterogeneity," in Rose, *Electoral Behaviour*, p. 698. See also Walter Dean Burnham, "The Changing Shape of the American Political Universe," *American Political Science Review*, vol. 59 (1965), pp. 7-28; and his *Critical Elections and the Mainsprings of American Politics* (New York: Norton, 1970), especially chap. 4.

est postwar turnout—Austria and Italy—are also two of the best-known examples of countries in which the church and the labor movement between them "share out" society by comprehensively mobilizing their members into a network of separate unions, professional bodies, educational and cultural associations—and, of course, political parties. It is noticeable, incidentally, that in Denmark, Sweden, and Norway, where only one sector—labor—has penetrated its membership in this way, turnout levels are above average but well below those in Austria and Italy.

Second, there is clearly a connection between a country's overall turnout and the electoral strength of those of its parties established to represent the working class.[28] The correlation between average turnout since 1945 and the average share of the vote taken by labor, social democratic, and communist parties combined over the same period is +0.55. The connection is even more compellingly demonstrated by the weak or nonexistent state of workers' parties in the six countries at the bottom of the turnout league: the United States, India, Switzerland, Ireland, Japan, and Canada. Whether it is low turnout that keeps workers' parties weak or the absence of strong workers' parties that keeps turnout low is impossible to settle without a complex analysis, but the well-documented stability of party systems in democracies strongly suggests the latter.[29]

The Impact of Electoral and Party Systems. Can electoral and party systems affect turnout levels independently of the social bases and ideology of the parties by making voting seem less or more worthwhile to the ordinary elector? It is occasionally claimed that proportional representation based on multimember constituencies (PR) produces a higher turnout than simple-majority electoral systems based on single-member constituencies (hereafter SM-SM).[30] The reasoning is, first, that whereas most single-member seats in a normal election are impregnable, almost all multimember constituencies are marginal in the sense that the total distribution of seats between the parties cannot be predicted; and second, that the distorted party-vote/party-seats

---

[28] There is an honored place in election folklore for the view that the share of the vote going to workers' parties fluctuates in tandem with turnout. I know of no academic study which has demonstrated this to be true for any country.

[29] On the "freezing" of party cleavages since the 1920s, see Seymour M. Lipset and Stein Rokkan's introduction to their *Party Systems and Voter Alignments* (New York: Free Press, 1967); for an analysis of trends since 1945, see Richard Rose and Derek Urwin, "Persistence and Change in Western Party Systems since 1945," *Political Studies*, vol. 18 (1970), pp. 287-319.

[30] See, for example, Enid Lakeman, *How Democracies Vote*, 2d ed. (London: Faber & Faber, 1974), pp. 163-64.

TABLE 10–5

Party Systems, Social Cleavages, and Turnout

Country (in order of postwar turnout)	Mean Turnout since 1945[a]	% Variance in Partisan Allegiance Explained (Rose data)[b]	Index of Class Voting (Powell data)[c]	Index of Religious Voting (Powell data)[c]	Share of Vote Going to Workers' Parties (postwar mean)[d]
Australia	95.4[e]	14.6	33	16	50.5
Netherlands	94.7 (1945–67)[e] / 83.5 (1971–77)	51.2	17	68	34.8 (1945–67) / 36.6 (1971–77)
Austria	94.2	46.0	44	43	47.9
Italy	92.6	28.3	17	43	42.7
Belgium	92.5[e]	34.5	27	48	36.3
New Zealand	90.4	n.a.	43	n.a.	45.3
West Germany	86.9	19.7	26	33	38.1
Sweden	84.9	37.9	45	23	50.6
Israel	81.4	n.a.	35	33	45.7
Norway	80.8	37.9	39	n.a.	50.5
France	79.3	34.4 (4th Rep.) / 18.7 (5th Rep.)	21	35	42.7

Finland	79.0	33.2	(54)	n.a.	46.2
United Kingdom	76.9	12.0	(35)	13	44.0
Canada	76.4	15.0	4	(29)	14.1
Ireland	74.7	3.1	(16)	n.a.	12.8
Japan	73.1	n.a.	(27)	n.a.	33.9
Switzerland	64.5	n.a.	21	(63)	28.3
India	58.7	n.a.	−6	n.a.	n.a.
United States	58.5	12.8	(18)	(18)	not app.

NOTE: For an explanation of method, see text. Turnout figures and rank order are from table 10-3; n.a. = data not available; not app. = not applicable.

a See notes to table 10-3.

b Obtained from Rose, *Electoral Behaviour*, p 17.

c The circle is used to indicate for each country which of the two indexes, class voting or religious voting, is the higher. Data obtained from Powell, "Voting Turnout in Thirty-One Democracies," table 3. See the footnotes to Powell's table for a description of his sources and definitions. In a revised version of the paper, to appear in Rose, *Party and Electoral Systems*, Powell slightly alters the basis of both indexes. As he only provides the revised figure for the higher of the two indexes for any one country, and as differences between the original and revised figures turn out to be small (where comparisons can be made), I have reproduced the figures from the original paper.

d Calculated from figures provided in Mackie and Rose, *International Almanac of Electoral History*, and from the supplements in the *European Journal of Political Research* (for precise references, see note to table 10-3). For definition of workers' parties, apply to author.

e Voting compulsory.

ratio inevitably manufactured by SM-SM will discourage some electors from voting, especially supporters of minor parties. Survey evidence certainly suggests that it is the electors expecting a close finish who are the most likely to vote;[31] the below-average turnout for presidential and congressional elections (but not for Democratic primaries) in the solidly Democratic South, and the modest but consistent turnout differences between safe and marginal seats in Britain, back that up.[32] But equally plausible counterarguments are at hand: that single-member constituencies encourage a closer relationship between representative and constituents, which in turn raises turnout; that the possibility of alternating single-party governments usually produced by SM-SM but precluded by PR raises the temperature of the campaign and thus the turnout. These are murky waters. All that can be reported here is that, excluding the countries where voting is compulsory, in the nine countries with SM-SM, average turnout since the war has been 76.0 percent; in the fourteen with PR it has been 80.5 percent.[33] But one should forgo the obvious inference, for all but two of the PR systems (Japan and France) have strong links between party and social allegiances, whereas all but one of the SM-SM systems (New Zealand) have weak links. With too few cases for more refined analysis, the most sensible conclusion is that countries with both PR *and* closely aligned party and social cleavages tend to have high turnout; countries with neither tend to have low turnout.

The feeling that an election will be close-run or a romp-home, and that much or little is at stake in the result, can also arise simply from the balance of partisan forces and the circumstances in which the election is held. Other things being equal, one would expect turnout to be high when the chances of the opposition's supplanting the government seem strong, to be low when the chances seem slim. It is certainly easy to think of hard-fought, dramatic elections in which turnout surged: Ireland in 1932, Sweden in 1948, Britain in February 1974, and India in 1977. But it is also possible to find examples of similarly dramatic elections in which turnout stayed the same or fell back: the United States in 1968, France in 1958, Britain in 1964. Systematic

---

[31] See Angus Campbell et al., *The American Voter* (New York: John Wiley, 1960), p. 99, who show this for medium and strong partisans.

[32] On Britain, see Michael Steed's appendix in David Butler and Dennis Kavanagh, *The British General Election of October 1974* (London: Macmillan, 1975), and his appendixes to earlier books in the Nuffield series. The 1979 election was true to form: turnout was 4 points higher in marginal seats (defined as vulnerable to a 2.5-point swing) than in safe seats.

[33] If countries with compulsory voting are counted, the figures are 77.9 percent and 82.8 percent.

testing is impossible; as Sartori shows, it is extraordinarily difficult to categorize the competitiveness of party systems, never mind single elections. Suffice it to say that no substantial difference can be found between the average turnouts of the seven countries which have most claim to be considered two-party systems and the seven which have most claim to be considered predominant-party systems.[34]

The absence of competitiveness in a party system can help us, however, to explain one puzzle: the deviant case of Switzerland.[35] To almost every generalization about the determinants of national turnout, Switzerland proves the exception. It operates PR with multimember constituencies; its multiparty system has an exceptionally close fit with its religious, linguistic, and class divisions; it even has compulsory voting in four cantons. In addition, it is geographically compact and small in population (indeed, it is divided into cantons representing small valley communities); and, of course, it is unusually prosperous. Yet its postwar turnout (64.5 percent) is the third lowest of those ranked here, and the second lowest in any industralized country. Moreover, no other country, not even the United States, has seen its turnout *decline* so remorselessly: in the 1940s and 1950s it averaged 69.7 percent; by the 1970s it had fallen in successive steps to 52.4 percent.[36] This cannot be attributed to the potentially dampening effect of enfranchising women in 1971, for turnout was already low beforehand and has declined in the *three* elections since. A plausible explanation has been suggested by G. Bingham Powell:

> The most likely explanation is . . . the deliberate demobilization of party competition by the major national parties themselves. Since the late 1930s, the four major parties, each linked to a cleavage group, have guaranteed themselves roughly equal place in the shared collective national executive (which has a rotating chairmanship). Unless a new party should suddenly break into the big four, the party electoral outcomes at the national level are virtually mean-

---

[34] See Giovanni Sartori, *Parties and Party Systems* (Cambridge: Cambridge University Press, 1976), chaps. 5 and 6. The seven two-party systems were Austria, Canada, Germany, Ireland, New Zealand, the United Kingdom, and the United States. The seven predominant-party systems were France, India, Israel, Italy, Japan, Norway, and Sweden. This corresponds to Sartori's definition for the two types of party systems but not exactly to his actual classification of countries!

[35] I am heavily indebted to G. Bingham Powell, "Voting Turnout in Thirty-One Democracies," p. 23, for some of the points made in this paragraph.

[36] And in the federal election of October 1979 (as this chapter was going to press) it fell again, to 48.5 percent. Moreover, at the numerous referendums, turnout is even lower: in the six held in 1977 and 1978, it averaged 47.2 percent.

ingless . . . there is little incentive for the voters to go to the polls, or for the major parties to try to mobilize them.[37]

Microexplanations: Personal Resources and Capacities. We can now turn to microexplanations of electoral participation as a possible source of cross-national variations. In a comprehensive survey of research in the 1950s, Seymour Lipset identified the following "social characteristics correlated with voting turnout":[38]

High Turnout	*Low Turnout*
High income	Low income
High education	Low education
Occupational groups:	Occupational groups:
Businessmen	Unskilled workers
White-collar employees	Servants
Government employees	Service workers
Commercial crop farmers	Peasants, subsistence farmers
Miners	
Whites	Negroes
Men	Women
Middle-aged people (35–55)	Young people (under 35)
Older people (over 55)	
Old residents in community	Newcomers in community
Married people	Single people
Members of organizations	Isolated individuals

By and large this summary has stood the test of both time and international comparison. Later studies of the United States and other industrial democracies find a very similar pattern of relationships, the only major revisions resulting from the "controlled" findings produced by multivariate analyses, notably:

---

[37] G. Bingham Powell, "Voting Participation in Thirty Democracies," in Rose, *Party and Electoral Systems*, p. 17. Against this argument it can be pointed out that although a similar all-party "cartelization" of government occurred under the Grand Coalitions in Austria from 1945 to 1966, turnout was consistently high. However, in contrast to outcomes in Switzerland, the election outcome in Austria did affect both the overall distribution of ministries and their specific allocation between parties and thus the direction of government policy. Moreover, the two-party system of Austria allowed every election result to be interpreted in terms of a party's winning or losing, and thus provided an edge which is impossible in Switzerland's evenly balanced four-party system.

[38] Seymour M. Lipset, *Political Man* (London: Mercury Books, 1963), p. 184. Lipset's table included two other correlates of higher turnout/lower turnout: crisis situations/normal situations and workers in Western Europe/workers in the United States.

1. the disappearance, even reversal, of the differences between whites and blacks after controlling for socioeconomic background[39]

2. the elimination of sex differences in turnout within new cohorts and among the better educated and those with a higher occupational status; and thus the steady narrowing of such differences within the electorate as a whole

3. the "aging" of the point in the life cycle at which turnout appears to dip, from fifty-five in the 1950s to seventy in the 1970s, which suggests a generational rather than an age difference[40]

4. the robustness of the association between education and turnout. In a recent study based on a Bureau of the Census sample of *90,000,* Wolfinger and Rosenstone, summarizing their elaborate multivariate analysis, refer to the "transcendent importance of education," emphasizing that "the turnout differences associated with education are vastly greater than those produced by other variables" and that "most of the other variables related to turnout seemed to reflect surrogates of education."[41]

Not all of these demographic factors could be converted into national differences in turnout rates. For example, sex ratios, age profiles, and distributions of marital status do not vary sufficiently from country to country and anyway are related to only slender differences of turnout. But one might expect the greater electoral diligence of the better educated and better remunerated in most countries to have an aggregate impact at the national level. Other things being equal, the wealthier a country and the more extensive its educational provisions—in other words, the more economically developed a country—the higher its turnout should be.

The merest glance at the rank order and long-term stability of national turnout rates in table 10–3 suggests otherwise. Poverty-ridden India nestles between Switzerland and the United States at the bottom of the ladder; Italy and New Zealand—two of the poorer industrialized democracies—stand near the top. In almost all countries trends in turnout have stayed unswervingly flat during a period of unprecedented economic growth and educational advance. The statistics confirm these impressions: the correlation between mean

---

39 Verba and Nie, *Participation in America,* chap. 10.

40 On this and the preceding revision see Richard Brody, "The Puzzle of Political Participation in America," in Anthony King, ed., *The New American Political System* (Washington, D.C.: American Enterprise Institute, 1978), pp. 291-99.

41 Raymond E. Wolfinger and Steven J. Rosenstone, "Who Votes?" (Paper presented to the 1977 annual meeting of the American Political Science Association, Washington, D.C., September 1977), pp. 59-60.

postwar turnout and 1976 GNP per capita is +0.05; between turnout and percentage of the relevant age group in tertiary education it is —0.09; and between turnout trend and 1960–1976 growth in GNP per capita it is —0.04.[42] However, the correlation between turnout trend and annual percentage rise in enrollment in tertiary education is +0.36, which would be consistent with the increase in turnout in Sweden and Denmark, although not with its decline in the United States.[43] This last finding aside, we have a puzzle: at the individual level income and education are related to turnout; on the aggregate level they are not.

One is faced with a similar puzzle on investigating the possibility that national differences in turnout rates reflect variations in the psychological orientation to politics—the political culture—from country to country. The best known (and still most useful) comparative study of such orientations, *The Civic Culture*, found that interest in politics, attention to political affairs in the media, feelings of civic duty and of individual political efficacy, and trust in political as opposed to other solutions to individual and communal problems, were consistently highest in the United States, followed by Britain, then Germany, and finally Italy—exactly the reverse of their rank order for postwar turnout![44]

What might account for this paradox? A possible explanation is indirectly suggested by Verba, Nie, and Kim, who found that the relationship between "socio-economic resource level" and participation varied from negligible to substantial across the seven countries they studied, yet all but disappeared once they controlled for different levels of organizational mobilization.[45] This was especially true of low-cost, low-benefit forms of participation like turning out to vote. This suggests the plausible, albeit still speculative, explanation that national rates of turnout rest on a *combination* of individual-level factors and institutional factors of the kind we have described. In the presence of such institutional incentives to vote as a close alignment between partisan and social divisions, automatic registration, a PR electoral system, a competitive party system, and the administrative facilitation of voting, individual-level factors will be overridden. They will therefore be

---

[42] Data on per capita GNP and enrollment in tertiary (postsecondary) education were taken from the *United Nations Statistical Yearbook*, 1978. The correlations are for countries with voluntary voting; the addition of those with required voting makes virtually no difference to the coefficients.

[43] The annual percentage rise in tertiary education was higher in the United States (1.7 percent) than in any other country in the analysis.

[44] Gabriel Almond and Sidney Verba, *The Civic Culture* (Princeton: Princeton University Press, 1963); the study also included Mexico.

[45] See Verba, Nie, and Kim, *Participation and Political Equality*, pp. 119-24.

unable to account for variations in turnout either within or between the countries that have such arrangements (Austria, Italy, the Netherlands, and so on). Likewise, in the absence of institutional incentives, or the presence of *dis*incentives such as complex registration laws, individual-level factors will have freer rein, explaining the different propensity to vote both within countries like Canada and the United States and, again, between them.

Final Thoughts

But does turnout matter? There are arguments "in defense of apathy":[46] to abstain is no less precious a right than to vote; moreover, a low national turnout might reflect quiet satisfaction, not hostility or sullen resignation, among electors. Why should one compare turnout levels across countries and over time and be disturbed if a country's turnout is below the international average or declining over the years? After all, in all but two of our twenty-seven democracies the majority of citizens go to the polls, in most cases the overwhelming number. Is it worth worrying about whether that majority consists of 60 percent rather than 90 percent?

There are two reasons for *not* worrying—too much. The first is that it is difficult to see what more could be done in most countries to raise levels of turnout substantially: registration rules, residence requirements, and facilities for absentee voting could all no doubt be improved, but except in the United States it is hard to believe that they could make more than a marginal difference. A deliberate reduction in the number of safe seats, through a change in the electoral system or of the constituency boundaries, might raise turnout, although the analysis earlier suggested that the impact would probably be small. The more powerful determinants of turnout levels, such as the breadth and depth of party mobilization, are usually too deeply rooted in a country's social and political arrangements to be made either the subject or the instrument of social engineering.

The second is that turnout rates alone provide only a limited perspective on the amount of electoral, let alone political, participation in which a country's citizens engage. This is partly because there is more to electoral participation than marking a ballot paper. A small minority will be actively involved in various aspects of party campaigning; the majority will follow politics in the press and on tele-

---

46 W. H. Morris-Jones, "In Defence of Apathy: Some Doubts on the Duty to Vote," *Political Studies*, vol. 2 (1954), pp. 25-37; see also Bernard Berelson, Paul F. Lazarsfield, and William N. McPhee, *Voting* (Chicago: University of Chicago Press, 1954), chap. 14.

vision and occasionally talk about it with friends and family. But it is also because turnout rates do not indicate the amount of electing—the frequency of occasion, the range of offices and decisions, the "value" of the vote—to which a country's citizens are entitled. Thus, although the turnout rate in the United States is below that of most other democracies, American citizens do not necessarily do less voting than other citizens; most probably, they do more.

But in another sense turnout levels and trends have a serious claim on our attention: they constitute essential data for a political sociology of power in liberal democracies. Countless single-country studies in the past have demonstrated that it is the more privileged sectors of the community, not the more deprived, who tend to make most use of the vote and the political influence it bestows. The cross-national study of turnout rates reinforces that conclusion. In countries with universal or near-universal turnout there must be as much or nearly as much electoral participation on the part of the poor and uneducated as among the prosperous and privileged; what the generally disadvantaged lack in resources they can partly make up in numbers. In countries with relatively low turnout rates, however, it is those who most need the vote who tend to use it least, and universal suffrage fails to provide the political counterweight to the power of property and wealth in the way that was intended by its more radical proponents.

Bibliography

Almond, Gabriel, and Verba, Sidney. *The Civic Culture*. Princeton: Princeton University Press, 1963.

Brody, Richard. "The Puzzle of Political Participation in America." In *The New American Political System*, edited by Anthony King. Washington, D.C.: American Enterprise Institute, 1978.

Crewe, Ivor; Fox, Tony; and Alt, James E. "Non-voting in British General Elections, 1966–October 1974." In *The British Political Sociology Yearbook*, vol. 3, edited by Colin Crouch. London: Croom Helm, 1977.

Lipset, Seymour M. "Elections: Who Votes and Who Doesn't?" In Seymour M. Lipset, *Political Man*. London: Heinemann, 1960.

Mackie, Thomas T., and Rose, Richard. *The International Almanac of Electoral History*. London: Macmillan, 1974.

Milbraith, Lester W. *Political Participation*. Chicago: Rand McNally, 1965.

Nie, Norman H., and Verba, Sidney. "Political Participation." In *Handbook of Political Science*, vol. 4, edited by Fred I. Greenstein and Nelson W. Polsby. Reading, Mass.: Addison-Wesley, 1975.

Powell, G. Bingham. "Voting Participation in Thirty Democracies: Effects of Socio-Economic, Legal and Partisan Environments." In *Party and Electoral Systems*, edited by Richard Rose. Beverly Hills, Calif.: Sage Publications, 1980.

Rokkhan, Stein. *Citizens, Elections, Parties.* Oslo: Universitetsforlaget, 1970.

Rose, Richard, ed. *Electoral Behaviour: A Comparative Handbook.* London: Collier, Macmillan, 1974.

Rosenstone, Steven J., and Wolfinger, Raymond E. "The Effect of Registration Laws on Voter Turnout." *American Political Science Review* 72: 22–45.

Verba, Sidney, and Nie, Norman H. *Participation in America.* New York: Harper & Row, 1972.

Verba, Sidney; Nie, Norman H.; and Kim, Jae-on. *Participation and Political Equality.* Cambridge: Cambridge University Press, 1978.

Wolfinger, Raymond E., and Rosenstone, Steven J. "Who Votes?" Paper presented to the 1977 annual meeting of the American Political Science Association, Washington, D.C.

11

What Decides Elections?

Donald E. Stokes

The evolution of liberal democracy could be said to have assigned popular elections three closely related roles:

1. They provide a way for the people to intervene effectively in the affairs of state, especially by saying who should govern.
2. This intervention helps to realize symbolic or material values that enjoy wide popular support.
3. The realization of these values helps to legitimize the political system and those who exercise the authority of government.

This normative vision of the role of elections poses a dilemma for this chapter and the next. All of these roles in a sense belong to the assessment of what elections decide that is reserved for the following chapter. But the first two are so obviously relevant to what decides elections that they should enter the analysis here. Where democracy is well established, the decisions rendered by the electorate will be shaped by its desire to intervene in behalf of the goals it values, just as the actions taken by political leaders will be shaped by their awareness of the electorate's power to intervene. The strength of this reciprocal relationship is one of democracy's vital signs.

This sketch of the role of popular elections may seem overdrawn to those who are steeped in the literature of voting research. Electoral studies over several decades have tended to reinforce the view that elections are routine events dominated by traditional alignments and cut off from the major issues facing the societies in which they are held. But this impression is almost certainly mistaken. One of the themes of my account is that recent elections in the democratic world have involved an interaction of leaders and led high in political content.

The analysis draws extensively on the remarkable series that provides the backdrop to this book. The volumes of the *At the Polls* series are a fresh and important attempt to examine the sources of election outcomes in a comparative setting. This chapter will describe the nature of this attempt in the context of several traditions of analytic work, marshal the evidence to be drawn from the series in a more generalized form, and offer at the end some thoughts on how this continuing venture could be given a sharper edge.

Analytic Traditions

It is astonishing how varied a set of analytic traditions continues to flourish in electoral studies, in view of the fact that the field is widely believed to be strongly cumulative. These traditions differ in their basic method and choice of evidence. They are drawn toward quite different social and political factors. Indeed, they often diverge, at least implicitly, in their view of the purpose of inquiry.

The oldest belongs to the political historian or journalist or practicing politician who pieces together from a variety of sources the reasons for an election outcome. This sort of account is as old as liberal democracy itself and is splendidly illustrated in the recent past by Theodore White's interpretations of the results of American contests for the presidency from 1960 to 1972[1] or by the work of David Butler and his collaborators in the Nuffield series on British general elections since the Second World War.[2] Theirs is an eclectic art, and those who practice it consult widely different types of evidence. The content of appeals to the electorate can be sought in manifestoes, speeches, and campaign literature. The major issues or events can be

---

[1] See Theodore H. White, *The Making of the President, 1960* (New York: Atheneum, 1960), *The Making of the President, 1964* (New York: Atheneum, 1965), *The Making of the President, 1968* (New York: Atheneum, 1969), and *The Making of the President, 1972* (New York: Atheneum, 1973).

[2] See R. B. McCallum and A. Readman, *The British General Election of 1945* (Oxford: Oxford University Press, 1947); H. G. Nicholas, *The British General Election of 1950* (London: Macmillan, 1951); D. E. Butler, *The British General Election of 1951* (London: Macmillan, 1952); D. E. Butler. *The British General Election of 1955* (London: Macmillan, 1955); D. E. Butler and R. Rose, *The British General Election of 1959* (London: Macmillan, 1960); D. E. Butler and A. S. King, *The British General Election of 1964* (London: Macmillan, 1965); D. E. Butler and A. S. King, *The British General Election of 1966* (London: Macmillan, 1966); D. E. Butler and M. Pinto-Duschinsky, *The British General Election of 1970* (London: Macmillan, 1971); D. E. Butler and D. Kavanagh, *The British General Election of February 1974* (London: Macmillan, 1974); D. E. Butler and D. Kavanagh, *The British General Election of October 1974* (London: Macmillan, 1975); and D. E. Butler and D. Kavanagh, *The British General Election of 1979* (London: Macmillan, 1980).

sought in the mirror provided by the press and, more recently, by radio and television. The private motives and reactions of leaders and of individual voters can be sought in conversations or letters or diaries and related sources. The sociology and geography of the vote can be sought in the pattern of the election returns.

Our understanding of popular elections has been enriched by accounts of this sort more than we often recognize. In the hands of its most skilled practitioners this form has become a high art. But it has always been liable to criticism for leaps of inference about the nature of the electorate's response. Probing the decisions reached by exceedingly large, dispersed, and heterogeneous electorates, and recorded in confidence, puts a premium on skills of measurement and generalization possessed by few journalists or historians. The slenderness of the evidence with which they work has inspired the development of more rigorous approaches to the assessment of electoral motives.

A second tradition belongs to those who have brought the official election returns under far more intensive analysis. Popular elections yield as a byproduct enormous quantities of election statistics, which are tabulated by various geographic units about which a good deal else is known. For half a century varied statistical techniques, some of great subtlety, have been used to winnow judgments about the electorate's behavior from the aggregate returns. This tradition is as alive in the modern work of Allardt or Burnham or Rokkan as it was in the pioneering studies of Rice or Ogburn more than five decades ago.[3] This style of analysis has indeed both inspired and been strongly assisted in the recent past by the assembly of election returns in central data archives and published sourcebooks.[4]

---

[3] See Erik Allardt, "Patterns of Class Conflict and Working Class Consciousness in Finnish Politics," in *Cleavages, Ideologies, and Party Systems* (Helsinki: Proceedings of the Westermarck Society), vol. 10, pp. 97-132, 1964; Walter Dean Burnham, "The Changing Shape of the American Political Universe," *American Political Science Review*, vol. 59 (1965), pp. 7-28, and *Critical Elections and the Mainsprings of American Politics* (New York: Norton, 1970); Stein Rokkan, *Citizens, Elections, Parties* (Oslo: Universitetsforlaget, 1970), and Stein Rokkan and Henry Valen, "Regional Contrasts in Norwegian Politics," in Erik Allardt and Stein Rokkan, eds., *Mass Politics* (New York: Basic Books, 1970); Stuart A. Rice, *Quantitative Methods in Politics* (New York: Alfred A. Knopf, 1928); William F. Ogburn and Nell S. Talbot, "A Measurement of the Factors in the Presidential Election of 1928," *Social Forces*, vol. 8 (1929), pp. 175-83.

[4] Among the most notable electoral archives are those of the Inter-University Consortium for Political and Social Research at the University of Michigan, the Social Science Research Council at the University of Essex, and the Zentralarchiv at the University of Cologne. Exceedingly valuable sourcebooks on voting behavior have been compiled by Richard Scammon. See Richard M. Scammon, ed., *America Votes*, 13 vols. (vols. 1-10 were published by the Governmental Affairs Institute of Washington, D.C., from 1956 to 1973; vols. 11-13 have been published

A special branch of the analysis of aggregate returns is the research of the electoral geographers, mostly French, who have followed in the footsteps of André Siegfried.[5] Their method is extraordinarily simple in concept, and their maps do at times yield insights that would have been missed by other techniques.

The disciplined analysis of election returns can remedy many of the deficiencies of a more impressionistic scan of the electorate's decision. But this type of work has limitations of its own. Voters, after all, reveal only a little of what is in their minds by marking a ballot, even where, as in the American system, they are presented with several choices at once. And the attempt to describe the behavior of individuals by analyzing data aggregated by electoral units faces technical difficulties that the pioneers of this approach did not foresee.[6] The need to surmount these limitations led to the rise of a third main tradition of analytic work, exploiting sample surveys.

Almost from the moment opinion polling came into widespread use in the 1930s, there was a keen appreciation of the value of gaining information from a microcosm of the electorate. Indeed, the desire to open this vista to the electorate's mind has helped to shape the sample survey in its modern form. Early in World War II this instrument was used by Paul Lazarsfeld and his associates in the first major academic study of voting behavior.[7] Soon after the war it was taken up by other academic analysts in Britain and America and rapidly became a standard tool of electoral analysis in the democratic world.[8]

---

by the Elections Research Center and Congressional Quarterly, Inc., from 1975 to 1980).

[5] See André Siegfried, *Tableau politique de la France de l'ouest sous la troisième république* [The political picture in the west of France under the Third Republic] (Paris: A. Colin, 1913); and François Goguel, *La politique des partis sous la troisième république* [Party politics under the Third Republic], vol. 1: 1871-1932, vol. 2: 1933-1939 (Paris: Editions du Seuil, 1946), and *Géographie des elections françaises de 1870 à 1951* [Geography of French elections from 1870 to 1951] (Paris: A. Colin, 1951).

[6] I have particularly in mind the classic critique of the analysis of the intercorrelations of aggregate variables offered by William S. Robinson, "Ecological Correlation and the Behavior of Individuals," *American Sociological Review*, vol. 15 (1950), pp. 341-57, and the subsequent work on this problem.

[7] See Paul Lazarsfeld, Bernard Berelson, and Hazel Gaudet, *The People's Choice* (New York: Duell, Sloan, and Pearce, 1944).

[8] Influential survey studies in the early postwar period were R. S. Milne and H. C. MacKenzie, *Straight Fight* (London: Hansard Society, 1954), and *Marginal Seat* (London: Hansard Society, 1958); Bernard Berelson, Paul F. Lazarsfeld, and William N. McPhee, *Voting* (Chicago: University of Chicago Press, 1954); Angus Campbell, Gerald F. Gurin, and Warren E. Miller, *The Voter Decides* (Evanston: Row Peterson, 1954); and Angus Campbell, Philip E. Converse, Warren E. Miller, and Donald E. Stokes, *The American Voter* (New York: John Wiley and Sons, 1960).

Survey studies are by now the primary means of probing the sources of electoral outcomes used by academics and the research units that serve the contestants for office. The data from these studies as well are frequently assembled in massive central archives, where they are available to a wide company of political analysts.

These broad methodological traditions are associated with important differences of focus. At one level, these differences turn on the choice of substantive factors most deserving of analysis. It is, for example, almost inevitable that the analysis of aggregate voting returns, including the work of the electoral geographers, should emphasize class or religion or ethnicity or other aspects of social structure that vary across the units for which the analyst has data. It is equally natural that polls and surveys should emphasize voter attitudes as survey questions tap an ever wider set of popular responses to issues, events, leaders, parties, and the governmental system itself.

Yet these differences of focus turn at another level on conceptions of what inquiry is for, and we may note an important shift of goals in the newer traditions. A robust interest in explaining the outcomes of elections as whole events moved the journalist or historian who synthesized such an account from a variety of sources. This interest is by no means alien to the analyst of aggregate returns or of sample surveys, and each of these approaches has greatly widened the circle of light around the electorate's decision.[9] But much of the work in these newer traditions has pursued other goals— important in themselves but quite different from revealing the sources of electoral outcomes in a comprehensive way. The election returns are at times treated more as a sociological census than as a key to the electorate's motives. And the data of sample surveys are frequently used to explore problems of individual or social psychology that bear only distantly on electoral outcomes. Although much of the resulting knowledge can help us describe the sources of these outcomes, as we shall note below, it must be explicitly turned to this end. Opportunities of this sort have been consistently missed.

These limitations are especially clear in survey studies that see the world through the eyes of the individual voter. This new sort of Ptolemaicism ignores the richer, more Copernican view of an earlier tradition in two ways. On the one hand, it loses sight of the fact that elections are shaped by both leaders and led and should be analyzed from the perspective of each. On the other, it loses sight

---

[9] William F. Ogburn's path-breaking analysis of the Hoover-Smith election in 1928 was directly motivated by the desire to assess the relative importance of religion and Prohibition in the election's outcome. See Ogburn and Talbot, "The Presidential Election of 1928."

of the fact that the whole electorate, rather than the molecular voter, makes the ultimate choice. There are important ties between individual behavior and collective choice, but the two are not the same. Electoral research is studded with examples of factors strongly associated with individual voting that benefit none of the rivals for power when summed across the whole electorate.[10] It is also replete with examples of how the rules of electoral systems loosen this relationship still further as they map individual decisions into collective choices in complex ways.[11]

The displacement of an earlier goal is richly evident in the development of comparative electoral studies. The desire to explain elections as whole events has rarely led electoral research across national frontiers. Rather, the comparative method has been used to deepen the understanding of particular aspects of social structure or ideological belief or party systems or economic impact or generational change or some other limited segment of a much wider terrain. Whereas the study of social class in Britain by McKenzie and Silver showed a keen appreciation of the role of "cross-voting" by the working class in the electoral ascendancy of the Conservatives,[12] Alford's comparative study of class alignments in the countries of the English-speaking world gave scarcely a nod to the role of this sort of voting in shaping electoral outcomes.[13] Similarly, Rokkan's important analysis of the relationship between center and periphery in the election returns from several countries has other end-variables in view than the direction of electoral judgments.[14] And cross-national comparisons of ideological structure are only tangentially concerned with electoral outcomes.[15]

[10] One of the most interesting illustrations of this is to be found in the earlier cited work of William F. Ogburn. His analysis showed that attitudes toward Prohibition were more strongly associated with voting choice than were religious attachments. But the nation was very nearly equally divided on Prohibition, which therefore benefited neither Smith nor Hoover on balance, whereas the nation was overwhelmingly Protestant. Hence, the religious issue, though less highly correlated with the choices of individual voters, contributed far more overall to Hoover's victory. See Ogburn and Talbot, "The Presidential Election of 1928."

[11] A trenchant statement of this viewpoint is offered by Richard Rose, "Comparability in Electoral Studies," in Richard Rose, ed., Electoral Behavior: A Comparative Handbook (New York: Free Press, 1974), pp. 8-10.

[12] See Robert T. McKenzie and Allan Silver, Angels in Marble (London: Heinemann, 1968).

[13] See Robert Alford, Party and Society (Chicago: Rand McNally, 1963).

[14] Rokkan, Citizens, Elections, Parties, pp. 181-248.

[15] The attention given the ideological structure of political opinion in different countries is illustrated by Bo Särlvik, "Mapping the Party Space: Distances, Evaluations, and Ideological Perspectives" (paper prepared for the International Political Science Association, Edinburgh, August 1976), and by Samuel H. Barnes, "Ideology and the Organization of Conflict: On the Relationship of Political Thought and Behavior," Journal of Politics, vol. 28 (August 1966), pp. 513-30.

Against this backdrop the volumes commissioned for the *At the Polls* series can be seen as an interesting exception. Because they are sharply focused on a particular election in a particular country, many of these volumes synthesize from the available evidence a fairly comprehensive account of the reasons for the election's outcome. Because they follow a common format they allow these judgments to be compared and generalized across a number of countries. The series is in fact an important effort to pursue on a cross-national basis a goal that has often been displaced in comparative work.

The At the Polls Series

The typical volume in the twelve published to date follows a straightforward formula.[16] It is centered on a single election in a single country, edited (all but four) by Howard Penniman, and comprises chapters written by specialists drawn from the international academic community or by observers from the site country. The volume is introduced by a general essay on the country and its political and electoral system and usually by a second essay on the immediate context of the election at hand. These chapters are followed by successive essays on each of the major parties and their campaigns, on the minor parties, on the mass media in the election, on opinion polling, and on the results and aftermath of the election. There is often a special essay on the role of foreign policy or some other subject, and typically a valuable statistical appendix by Richard Scammon.

Three of the volumes in the series lie radically outside this standard pattern. One, *India at the Polls*,[17] on the dramatic parliamentary elections of 1977, was written entirely by Myron Weiner according to a quite different chapter structure. A second, *Scandinavia at the Polls*,[18] edited by Karl Cerny, grew out of a conference on political trends in Denmark, Norway, and Sweden. The distinctive structure of this volume reflects both the need to encompass three nations at once and the decision to give more attention to recent social and economic developments in the Scandinavian countries and less to the institu-

---

[16] The volumes available to the author covered the national elections in Australia in 1975 and 1977, Britain in February and October of 1974, Canada in 1974, Denmark in 1973, France in 1974, Germany in 1976, India in 1977, Ireland in 1977, Israel in 1977, Italy in 1976, Japan in 1974, Norway in 1973, and Sweden in 1973. For a complete list of the titles in print, see the back of this book.

[17] Myron Weiner, *India at the Polls: The Parliamentary Elections of 1977* (Washington, D.C.: American Enterprise Institute, 1978).

[18] Karl H. Cerny, ed., *Scandinavia at the Polls: Recent Political Trends in Denmark, Norway, and Sweden* (Washington, D.C.: American Enterprise Institute, 1977).

tionalized framework of their elections. A third volume, *Japan at the Polls*,[19] is edited by Michael Blaker and deals with the 1973 election to the House of Councillors, the upper chamber of Japan's bicameral national legislature. It consists of three essays, one on the House of Councillors itself, one on the 1973 campaign for the upper house, and one on the election outcome. This volume is also unique in treating an election that could not determine the control of the government.

Each volume in the series does a number of things, and none should be regarded only as an effort to fathom the sources of the election's outcome. But almost all treat the electoral decision as a central event to be explained, and this orientation colors most of the chapters—not only the chapter that deals directly with the election results and aftermath. The series therefore provides a new, comparative investigation of what has decided recent national elections across a significant part of the democratic world.

Issues of method raised by this investigation are examined later in this chapter. But it is worth pausing to consider the adequacy of the coverage of countries, forms of democratic government, and periods. The issue of coverage ought not to be regarded as a standard problem of sampling, since the idea of a universe of democratic politics is too elusive to be of help. The nations in the series include all of the main countries of democratic Europe and four of the smaller European democracies as well. They include two of the older democracies of the British Commonwealth, one of which shares the American continent with the United States. They include the major power in East Asia that emerged with a democratic constitution from occupation after World War II. They include the South Asian country that seemed to be restored to its role as the world's most populous democracy by the election of 1977. And they include the beleaguered Near Eastern country that was created by the dream of a Jewish homeland and has clung to democratic forms for a full generation. The list omits many of the countries of the world, including the United States, where democratic traditions are secure, and many more in which important elements of the democratic system are present. But the coverage of nations is hardly to be faulted for lack of breadth.

Perhaps more troublesome is the balance of countries adhering to the two main forms of democratic government. Of the thirteen nations included in the series, only one, the French Republic, is presidential in form, although the office of chancellor in the Federal Republic of Germany has acquired powers beyond those normal for a pre-

---

[19] Michael K. Blaker, ed., *Japan at the Polls: The House of Councillors Election of 1974* (Washington, D.C.: American Enterprise Institute, 1976).

mier minister. All of the rest are parliamentary democracies. The French volume deals with the election of a president, rather than of a parliament, and therefore focuses on the decision of the electorate that most directly disposes of the power of the state. In the parliamentary democracies with bicameral legislatures, all but the Japanese volume deal with the election of the house on which the government depends for its tenure in office—what the Australians call the "governing" house, in a phrase that events there have edged in irony, as we shall see.

Most problematic of all is the question of period. It would clearly be wrong to suppose that the recent experience of these nations is representative of popular democracy in all eras. They have in certain respects reached their current state through a common historical development. And they will in the future respond to changes in their global environment which they experience in common, as their politics today show the stresses on the world economy. All that can really be said is that the material set forth in these volumes is a faithful collective portrait of democratic elections in the recent past.

These accounts necessarily accept a good deal as given as they review the sources of election outcomes. They are indeed in good company in this respect. No analysis of influences on an election result can begin as if with a clean slate and build up a fully comprehensive account of all the social and political factors in the result. Few of the major events in the life of a democratic country—or, for that matter, of the international system of which it is part—do not in some way impinge on its national elections. Some studies have sought to impose a degree of conceptual order on the full array of factors that might enter a result.[20] But none has dealt with more than a finite range of influences.

The classic means of restricting the range is to focus on change. This approach allows the analyst to select as a benchmark the situation at some earlier point in time, such as the prior election, and say what has induced the change observed from one time to the next—dealing only selectively with stable influences present at both points. This expedient is widely used by the contributors to the *At the Polls* series. They have in general limited their view to what has led an election outcome to differ from the one that preceded it, or from the position at the beginning of the campaign, and so on—and have dealt only sparingly with influences that were present throughout the period under review. The briefer the period, the more they could regard as given.

---

[20] See Campbell et al., *The American Voter*, chap. 2.

We will in the main take the same stance and lay greatest stress on a fairly short-term dynamic of electoral outcomes as we generalize the findings to be gleaned from these volumes. But it will be useful first to lengthen the perspective and consider the more enduring bases of electoral decision in the demographic composition of the electorate and stable alignments with party, especially those rooted in the social structure. If the view is sufficiently long, each of these things too can be a source of electoral change.

Bases of Electoral Decision

The electoral politics of a country may be profoundly altered by changes in the composition of its electorate or in the voters' basic alignments with its rival parties. Moreover, these changes may be linked by the fact that substantial turnover in the electorate can weaken an older set of political attachments and open the way for new alignments. Typically these changes are gradual or widely spaced, with demography and traditional identifications usually cast in the role of substrata on which electoral outcomes are partly based.

Political Demography. Demography can be of immense importance for a country's politics if the boundaries of the state are substantially redrawn. This is very clear in the experience of several of the nations under review. The politics of the Federal Republic of Germany would have been vastly different if the Protestant lands of Prussia, Saxony, and other areas to the east had not been absorbed into the German Democratic Republic after World War II.[21] The decision by the founders of Israel to accept the partition of Palestine was designed to create a state in which Jews would be in the majority, and the politics of that country have been shaped by accessions of land and people in successive wars.[22] The politics of India and of Ireland have also been fundamentally altered by partition and the removal of substantial minorities from their electorates.[23]

---

[21] See Gerhard Loewenberg, "The Development of the German Party System," in Karl H. Cerny, ed., *Germany at the Polls: The Bundestag Election of 1976* (Washington, D.C.: American Enterprise Institute, 1978), p. 9.

[22] See Frank W. Notestein, "A Partial View of the Development of American Demography to the Late 1960s," in Donald E. Stokes, ed., *The Uses of Basic Research: Case Studies in Social Science* (Washington, D.C.: National Academy of Sciences, 1980).

[23] The electoral politics of these countries would in two senses have been transformed if they had not been partitioned. Vastly enlarged minorities—of Moslems in India and Protestants in the Irish Republic—would have been part of their electorates. And the political life of each country would have been much more sharply focused on the cleavage between the majority and this minority element.

Even where frontiers are fixed, immigration or emigration may alter the demographic base of politics. Australia furnishes an interesting example. The shock of World War II left Australia with a keen sense of the need to strengthen its population base, and it reached out in the postwar years to attract substantial numbers of immigrants from eastern and southern Europe, as well as from the British Isles. The policy worked well enough that a fifth of the electorate had been born abroad by the 1970s. Repeating an experience familiar elsewhere, the new arrivals generally took the lower rungs on the occupational ladder, where they might have been expected to lend substantial support to the Labor party. But many of those who came during the long ascendancy of Sir Robert Menzies and his heirs were grateful to the right-wing government, whatever their station in the new land, and this political tendency was reinforced by the hostility they felt from many of Labor's trade union allies, who were bent on protecting their members' jobs. The benefit for the right was heightened by the tendency of native Australians of working-class background, who moved up the occupational ladder as the immigrants took the lower rungs, to shed their Labor identifications as they went. Under the leadership of Gough Whitlam, Labor mounted an intensive appeal to the new Australians and repaired part of the damage. But these background factors probably account for more of the Liberals' success during their long years in power than is commonly recognized.[24]

The electoral importance of immigration is starkly evident in the case of Israel. The country achieved statehood with a population dominated by immigrants from central and eastern Europe, and in Israel's first decades the leadership of the dominant Mapai party and later of the Labor alignment was consistently drawn from this group, which provided the core of Labor's electoral base. But the Jews seeking refuge in Israel after independence were drawn more from Asia and North Africa than from Europe, and, as a new generation of voters came of age, an increasing fraction of the electorate also was native born. As a result, Labor's electoral strength decayed with its demographic base, and the dominant alignment was engulfed in the

---

[24] See Leon D. Epstein, "The Australian Political System," in Howard R. Penniman, ed., *Australia at the Polls: The National Elections of 1975* (Washington, D.C.: American Enterprise Institute, 1977), pp. 4-5; and Don Aitkin and Michael Kahan, "Australia: Class Politics in the New World," in Rose, *Electoral Behavior*, pp. 437-80. The importance of immigration for the success of the Liberal-Country party coalition in the postwar era is most deeply explored in Michael J. Kahan, "Some Aspects of Immigration and Political Change in Australia since 1947" (Ph. D. diss., University of Michigan, 1972).

1977 election by the Likud alignment, which had mounted an appeal well matched to the country's demographic realities.[25]

Yet demography's most pervasive influence requires the boundaries of the state to be neither redrawn nor crossed. In every country and every period the demographic base of politics is changed by the fact that some voters enter the electorate by coming of age and others are removed by death. Only in the rarest case will these two groups be identical in size and political inclination. Where they are not, the processes of maturation and death alter the balance of party strength.

This exchange gains added significance from the fact that new entrants to the electorate are young and more open to the influence of current politics than they will ever be again, whereas those departing by death are generally old and relatively set in political ways formed decades before. Two special factors have enlarged this circulation in the recent past. One is the unusually large size of the entering cohorts as those born in the "baby boom" experienced by many countries after World War II have come of age. The other is the lowering of the voting age to eighteen in most of the world's democracies, which has swelled the tide of new electors.

This sort of exchange has altered the base of electoral decisions in a number of the countries included in the *At the Polls* series. It is clear that the cohort entering the German electorate in 1969 and 1972 —the "Brandt generation"—has retained a strong attachment to the SPD/FDP alignment and that support for the center-left coalition is only slightly less strong among those who entered the electorate in 1976, whereas the oldest cohorts in the German electorate strongly favor the CDU/CSU alignment.[26] It is also clear that there has been a fairly steep gradient by age in the support for the Communists and Christian Democrats in the Italian electorate of the 1970s.[27] But other countries, such as Ireland, show scarcely any differential in party support by age in the recent past.[28]

The evidence on these questions set out by the *At the Polls* series is tantalizingly sparse. This is partly due to the complexity of this sort

[25] See Daniel J. Elazar, "Israel's Compound Polity," in Howard R. Penniman, ed., *Israel at the Polls: The Knesset Elections of 1977* (Washington, D.C.: American Enterprise Institute, 1979), pp. 1-38.

[26] See David P. Conradt, "The 1976 Campaign and Election: An Overview," in Cerny, *Germany at the Polls* (Washington, D.C.: American Enterprise Institute, 1978), pp. 54-55.

[27] See Giacomo Sani, "The Italian Electorate in the Mid-1970s: Beyond Tradition," in Howard R. Penniman, ed., *Italy at the Polls: The Parliamentary Elections of 1976* (Washington, D.C.: American Enterprise Institute, 1977), p. 120.

[28] See Richard Sinnott, "The Electorate," in Howard R. Penniman, ed., *Ireland at the Polls: The Dáil Elections of 1977* (Washington, D.C.: American Enterprise Institute, 1978), p. 64.

of analysis. It is by now recognized that a profile of party support by age at a single election is a slender foundation on which to rest judgments about past or future changes in the base of party support. It is particularly difficult to disentangle the "generational effects" that reflect the varied impressions retained by successive cohorts from their earliest experience of politics and the "life cycle effects," especially the widely assumed tendency of voters to shift to the right with advancing age.[29]

The concept of political generation embraces more than distinctive patterns of party support. There is in the *At the Polls* series at least a trace of the "postmaterialist" or "postindustrial" generation that is thought to have emerged in the late 1960s and early 1970s. The rising affluence of the Western countries after World War II may, it is said, have produced a generation for which the goal of relieving material wants no longer held the appeal it had for their forebears. The belief that such a trend, if real, was irreversible has been dealt with roughly by the shocks to the Western economies in the middle and late 1970s.[30]

Voter Alignments. In any democratic country, each election is the latest in a sequence that may extend far into the past, and every election builds upon prior alignments. The campaign gives many voters the opportunity to express again a "standing decision" they formed long before. These individual loyalties, although they are by no means rooted only in the country's social structure, also express the traditional alignments that form between the rivals for power and various social classes and castes, religious, ethnic, racial, and language groups, and regions and local areas.

The very continuity of these alignments means that they are likely to be discounted by reports of how the ebb and flow of party support led to a particular election result. Nonetheless, the evidence of their importance is richly apparent in the *At the Polls* series. Some element of the "democratic class struggle" can be found in the politics of almost every country under review. Political cleavages by class are overlaid by religion or strength of religious attachment in Australia,

---

[29] The literature dealing with these several factors is by now vast. Many of the complexities involved are evident in the independent effort to unravel their effects, in one of the countries of the *At the Polls* series, that is found in David Butler and Donald Stokes, *Political Change in Britain* (New York and London: St. Martin's Press and Macmillan, 1969), pp. 44-64.

[30] One of the most influential analyses of the emergence of a "postindustrial generation" appears in Ronald Inglehart, "The Silent Revolution in Europe: Inter-Generational Change in Post-Industrial Societies," *American Political Science Review*, vol. 65 (December 1971), pp. 991-1017.

France, Germany, and Italy. Religious, ethnic, and language differences are closely interwoven in the politics of Canada, and this weave is made still more intricate by the politics of caste in India. Beyond these differences, almost every country exhibits longstanding differences between regions or between the urban centers and the countryside.

Traditional alignments would hardly deserve the name if they were brief and evanescent patterns. But they will of course grow or weaken with the passing of the years, and in periods of marked realignment they are associated with major short-term change. The physical replacement of the electorate plays a dual role in this. Migration may alter the social composition of the electorate, as the inflow of Asian and North African Jews altered Israel's political alignments over recent decades. And the substitution of younger for older cohorts will remove the generations that felt most deeply about the issues associated with the existing alignments. The passing of an older generation has removed from the Italian electorate those most likely to see the Christian Democrats and Communists as starkly different in religious and ideological terms. And the succession of cohorts in Britain has introduced into the electorate a generation whose regional and nationalist loyalties are less likely to be constrained by the overriding class loyalties of an earlier era. Although the politics of a given election will build on the base of existing alignments, these politics and the physical replacement of the electorate will alter the base itself over time.

The Conduct of Elections

Elections evoke a remarkable array of organized activities in the democratic countries. Some of these, especially the myriad efforts of the parties and candidates to staff election organizations, formulate programs and project leaders, prepare and disseminate campaign literature, and mobilize mass support, are meant to be influential in the highest degree. Others, especially the coverage of the election by the mass media, may have important, if unintended, effects on the outcome. Even the system of laws that structures the competition and channels the result can be an important factor in the election outcome. Although the roles played by party organization, the mass media, and election systems are more fully explored in other chapters, we should consider their influence on the results of modern elections.

Party Organization. Assessing the influence of campaign activities is partly a problem of choosing benchmarks. Students of elections have generally been skeptical of the importance of campaigns and party organization. But they do not imply by this that the party organizers could spare themselves the effort and go on holiday for the weeks of the campaign without losing ground. Rather the studies are skeptical that relative success in the normal organizational aspects of competitive campaigns weighs very heavily in the balance between the parties. Yet even this limited negative reaches well beyond the evidence. Who is to say that the effectiveness with which Japan's ruling Liberal Democratic party has used its *jiban* system to mobilize support is not a key to the party's long series of victories? Or that organizational skill is not a key to the Italian Communists' gain in relative strength over a long series of elections?

All we can say with confidence is that the proofs of the efficacy of campaign organization adduced by the *At the Polls* series are few. These volumes do, however, report isolated cases in which the organization and timing of campaigns were widely thought to have paid off. Research on the triumph of Willy Brandt and his coalition partners in the German election of 1972 suggested that their head start in campaign advertising, and the greater willingness of the SPD/FDP partisans to speak out, had created a "spiral of silence" among their CDU/CSU rivals that led the undecided to believe the country stood solidly behind the governing coalition. This variant of the "bandwagon" theory convinced a new CDU/CSU leadership that they should turn the tables by being the first into the field in 1976, and they felt this tactic helped to reverse the tide of the two prior elections, although not strongly enough to relieve the SPD/FDP coalition of office.[31]

It was also widely believed in Canada that superior campaign organization played a major role in returning the government of Prime Minister Trudeau to power in 1974. Trudeau's relations with the press were bitterly hostile in the election of 1972, which he barely won, in marked contrast with the "Trudeaumania" the press had helped to create in the Liberal sweep of 1968. As a consequence, the Liberals organized the 1974 campaign to keep the prime minister away from reporters, while the government issued a series of policy statements that would constitute hard news and the party fed the media background "color" on the leader and his wife. The opposition leader, far more exposed to the reporters but with nothing new to say in policy terms, was forced onto the defensive, and he and his party fell steadily back during the campaign. The electoral outcome seemed

---

[31] See Conradt, "The 1976 Campaign," pp. 40–41.

to confirm the correctness of the Liberal stratagem for organizing the campaign.[32]

It is, however, notoriously difficult to disentangle the effects of this sort of factor from the influence of the issues that come to dominate an election. It is all too easy after the fact to attribute to strategy and organization the shifts of party strength that are due to broader conditions prevailing in the country. Indeed, we have in this case a clear interplay of issues, organization, and the contribution to electoral outcomes made by the media themselves.

Mass Media. The influence of the media on electoral outcomes within a single country can be complex enough. The analyst of Italy's media notes in the *At the Polls* series that "the variables are too many, solid evidence too slight; there are more leaps of faith than determinations of causality."[33] It may seem folly to search for generalizations that could fit the politics of countries with media as widely varying as those included in our background series. Yet the volumes of the *At the Polls* series typically devote a full chapter to describing the role of the media in the campaign. What insight do they give into the media's influence on election outcomes?

These essays present, to begin with, a fascinating account of the evolution of the mass media in the democratic countries since the war. We see reflected here the decline of two older models of a political press. In the English-speaking world the tradition of newspapers held by freewheeling proprietors who seek to impose their political views on their readers has given way to a more neutral and professional treatment of politics by the press—partly out of the papers' need to serve readers of differing views when they find themselves in a monopoly position within local markets. Against this trend, the Australian election of 1975, with its open warfare between a left-leaning Labor party leadership and the right-wing barons of the popular press, seems like a throwback to a former age. But in Continental Europe the tradition of a politically differentiated press that is closely aligned to particular parties and stridently attuned to narrow bands of political opinion has also given way to a more detached and professional treatment of politics and elections. Parts of the Continental press, such as the provincial papers in France, have also experienced the neutralizing effect of monopoly position.[34]

---

[32] See Frederick J. Fletcher, "The Mass Media in the 1974 Canadian Election," in Howard R. Penniman, ed., *Canada at the Polls: The General Election of 1974* (Washington, D.C.: American Enterprise Institute, 1975), pp. 253-54.

[33] See William E. Porter, "The Mass Media in the Italian Elections of 1976," in Penniman, *Italy at the Polls*, p. 259.

[34] See Alfred Grosser, "The Role of the Press, Radio, and Television in French

Still more dramatically reflected by these essays is the rise of television as the main source of the electorate's information about politics. In all of the industrial democracies the penetration of the new broadcast medium is by now virtually total. The logic of monopoly position seemed at first to dictate neutrality in political tone, although television has often had a measurable slant toward the government where it was a tightly controlled state agency. But the colorlessness that initially came with neutrality has in recent years given way to more experimental and attractive programming that has made television's political coverage more appealing to its mass audience.

Nothing in the more recent findings would require us to modify the conclusion from the early studies that the partisan press is far more effective in reinforcing existing opinion and mobilizing the faithful than it is in making new converts.[35] Everyone recognized that the press, supplemented by word-of-mouth communication, was the means by which the electorate learned of new issues and events that could sharply alter the strength of the parties. But the limited capacity of the press to convert, coupled with the fact that the broadcast media are legally forbidden from trying, has seemed to limit the influence of the media on election outcomes.

This view almost certainly understates the media's current role in two respects. The first is the capacity of mass communications to set the agenda of political discussion. If the media are unable to tell their audience what to think, they are, as the expression goes, able to tell their audience what to think *about*.[36] There is no clearer example of this than the case in which investigative reporting discloses scandal in government or the political parties, as the Israeli press disclosed the prime minister's illegal bank holdings abroad before the 1977 election. But over a far wider range the media are only partially constrained by audience interest or other limits in choosing the issues and events they will place on the agenda of public discussion. It is indeed likely that the Israeli electorate was more powerfully influenced in the 1977 campaign by having its attention drawn to domestic conditions, on which the government's record was weak, rather than foreign issues,

---

Political Life," in Howard R. Penniman, ed., *France at the Polls: The Presidential Election of 1974* (Washington, D.C.: American Enterprise Institute, 1975), pp. 210-11.

[35] This finding, which has been reconfirmed in an astonishing variety of settings, goes back to the early research by Lazarsfeld, Berelson, and Gaudet in *The People's Choice*.

[36] This felicitous phrase was coined in Bernard C. Cohen, *The Press and Foreign Policy* (Princeton: Princeton University Press, 1963).

on which the Labor alignment continued to enjoy the basic confidence of the electorate.[37]

The second enlargement of the media's influence is their role in moderating political differences. This role is difficult to demonstrate with firm evidence. But the tendency seems clear, especially with the rise of television and the greater activism of its political coverage. In an earlier period, the adherents of the Communist and Christian Democratic parties in Italy could draw their information about politics solely from a partisan press and from word-of-mouth communication in the workplace and church and village square. But the role of these sources was decisively modified by the rise of a medium that would expose the partisan voter to neutral or positive information about other parties and their leaders. Television's new programming for the 1976 election was superbly designed to convey intimate, reassuring images of the party leaders to a broad spectrum of the Italian electorate. Berlinguer, the Communist leader, was only the most skilled of the several leaders in using this medium to moderate the fears of those who adhered to the other parties.[38]

There is evidence in a number of these essays on the media suggesting that an effect of this sort has helped to shape the politics of many of the democracies, loosening the hold of an earlier, more strident partisanship, eroding established cleavages, amplifying the flows of mass support between the parties. It seems probable that all of this has worked to create an opening for the effective competition of rival, broadly based alignments that is so prominent a part of the recent experience of the democratic countries. In doing so, it has helped to establish the primacy of current political issues, to which we turn in a moment.

Electoral Systems. The thirteen democracies included in the *At the Polls* series conduct their electoral business under a remarkable diversity of institutional arrangements. Britain stands at one sort of pole with its pure system of single-member parliamentary constituencies and election by simple plurality (called "first past the post" by a country fond of racing horses). Britain's example is faithfully repeated by two of the Commonwealth countries included in the series, Canada and India. A third, Australia, uses single-member constituencies but eschews election by simple plurality in favor of the "alternative vote," an arrangement that requires the voter to rank the candidates seeking

---

[37] See Judith Elizur and Elihu Katz, "The Media in the Israeli Elections of 1977," in Penniman, *Israel at the Polls*, pp. 244-50.

[38] See Porter, "The Mass Media in the Italian Elections," p. 277.

a parliamentary seat. France also has single-member constituencies but requires election by absolute majority, if necessary in a runoff between the candidates who led in the first election. It applies this pattern to elections of a president, with the nation serving as a grand constituency, as well as to elections for the National Assembly.

At an opposite pole stands Israel, which elects its Knesset by proportional representation with the entire nation a single district and the voter choosing only among party lists. Variants of proportional representation are used by Ireland and Italy, but with a number of multimember constituencies in order to give the members of the Dáil and Chamber of Deputies a greater sense of identity with parts of the nation. In Italy's case the deputy's links to a support cadre are reinforced by the casting of "preference votes," which allow the voter to alter the precedence of candidates on the party list.

Two other countries in the set use practices that are still more intricately mixed. The Federal Republic of Germany chooses half the members of the Bundestag from single-member constituencies and the remaining half from national party lists in a way that matches the party's share of seats to its share of the national vote—except that no party is seated with less than 5 percent of the national vote. The Japanese have used a deceptively simple device to create a system that is unique and perhaps the most intricate of all. Members of the Diet are chosen from districts with three to five seats. But each voter is allowed to vote only for a single candidate, making general elections an arena of conflict both between the parties and among the candidates of opposing factions within the same party.

It is impressive how deeply these systems are woven into the consciousness of the countries that use them. Both political leaders and the electorate assume the persistence of these arrangements as they think about the political future, and the arrangements become increasingly insulated from change. In Italy, for example, few elements of the political system now enjoy a wider consensus between left and right than the existing electoral system. But a case for reform is of course heard from time to time. Among the nations under review, Britain and Israel have witnessed such a challenge. In Britain the aggrieved party is the Liberals, who pay the price for attracting support from a geographically dispersed minority under a single-member, simple-plurality system. The discount applied to their voting strength can be considerable: in the February election of 1974 the party received one vote in five across the country but only one seat in fifty in the new House of Commons. Hence, the Liberals have repeatedly pressed the two larger parties for some form of proportional representation. In Israel the cause of electoral reform was taken up in the 1977 elections by the Democratic Movement for Change, which split off from the dominant Labor alignment, and after the election the DMC won from the new Begin government agreement "in principle" to electoral reform; actually the details would be worked out by a committee on which coalition members could vote as they wished—and the DMC would be outvoted.[39]

Participants in the electoral process are exquisitely sensitive to the ways in which the electoral arrangements may lead to party advantage. But the most striking conclusion to be drawn from the recent experience of these nations is that an effective competition for power can emerge under the most diverse electoral systems. In particular, little in the experience of these countries supports the familiar thesis that proportional representation is more likely than the single-member, simple-plurality system to fragment the party system. The fact is that an effective competition of rival alignments has emerged almost everywhere, despite the sharp differences in electoral systems. Israel, with the purest of proportional representation systems, saw the broadly based Likud alignment wrest control from the Labor alignment, whereas Britain, with the purest of single-member, plurality-election systems, witnessed at least a mild degree of fragmentation of its party system. Apart from these countries, more effective rivalries between two major alignments emerged in France, in Germany, in Italy, in India, and in Norway and Sweden, and strong rivalries were sustained in Australia, Canada, and Ireland. In this whole list of democratic countries, different judgments would perhaps be entered only for Denmark and Japan.

The Primacy of High Politics

The evidence from these countries is likely to revise sharply the view of anyone who believes that elections count for little in the life of democratic nations. It is also likely to erode the view of anyone who believes that elections are dominated by long-established alignments. In perhaps two of thirteen countries the elections mainly expressed a "routine" politics in which customary alignments renewed a government's hold on power or ushered in a fresh period of parliamentary bargaining that would make and unmake governments with

---

[39] See Avraham Brichta, "1977 Elections and the Future of Electoral Reform in Israel," pp. 48-57, and Efraim Torgovnik, "A Movement for Change in a Stable System," pp. 147-71, both in Penniman, *Israel at the Polls*. The Social Credit party in New Zealand is another third party that has pushed for electoral reform: in the 1978 election it won 16.1 percent of the popular vote and 1.08 percent of the seats in Parliament.

little input from the electorate. In all of the others the elections dealt with issues grave enough to be called "constitutional," with issues that were reshaping the party system, or with issues that would turn out of power a government that had lost the confidence of the electorate. These issues were in all cases of critical importance for the outcome, and in virtually all, the electoral process seemed able to sustain the intense pressure that issues of this magnitude placed upon it.

Constitutional Politics. In three of the countries the electorate wrestled with fundamental issues about the nature of the constitutional system. The first was Australia, where the election of 1975 served in effect as a constitutional court of first resort after the sensational dismissal by the governor general of a prime minister who enjoyed majority support in the more popular house of the Australian Parliament. Nothing like this had happened in Australia since federation at the turn of the century—or, for that matter, in any of the older countries of the English-speaking world that adhered to the Westminster model of government.

The roots of the constitutional crisis went deep into Australia's past and owed a great deal to two elements of the constitution adopted in 1901. On the one hand, the framers of that document specified powers for the governor general that mainly repeated the formal powers the British sovereign was understood to have, although it was also understood at the time that the monarch could constitutionally exercise most of these powers in Britain only on the advice of ministers who enjoyed the confidence of the House of Commons. Equally, Australia's new constitution was largely silent on the powers of the prime minister and cabinet and other essential elements of the Westminster system. In other words, the operation of Australia's government, even when it was new, depended on many of the unwritten traditions of British parliamentary democracy, and not only on its written constitution. In particular, it was clear to everyone that control of the popularly elected House of Representatives, and not the will of the queen's representative, would decide who should form a government.

Three-quarters of a century after its adoption, a second feature of the Australian constitution led a desperate governor general to ignore this unwritten premise. The plan of the new Commonwealth created an upper house of Parliament, a Senate, with powers that were limited but far from negligible—certainly greater than those retained by the House of Lords at Westminster after its power to veto legislation was broken before World War I. Although it was never intended that the Senate should be able to drive a government from office—only the "governing" House of Representatives could do that—the constitution could be read as allowing the Senate to withhold the "supply," or appropriations, on which all governments depend. The opposition coalition of the Liberal and Country parties seized on this ambiguity in 1977 to try to force an unpopular Labor government into an early election by blocking supply in the Senate. To everyone's astonishment, the governor general undertook to break the impasse by dismissing Gough Whitlam, the Labor prime minister, and inviting Malcolm Fraser, the opposition leader, to form a caretaker government on the understanding he would immediately seek the dissolution of Parliament and allow the issue to be taken to the electorate.

The ensuing election was therefore of high constitutional significance. However heatedly Whitlam and his party disputed the governor general's right to act as he had, they and their adversaries recognized that the people would decide. Polls during the campaign and the months of the impasse showed how visible the constitutional issues were to the country. But sympathy for Whitlam's constitutional position was overwhelmed by the electorate's feeling that the Labor government's performance, especially on key economic issues, did not justify its return to power. As a result, the election was won by the Liberal/Country party coalition in a landslide, and the constitutional issue, for the moment, was resolved.[40]

Even more ominous constitutional issues faced the Indian electorate in March 1977. Twenty-one months before, Indira Gandhi, the prime minister of India, had responded to the challenges to her authority within and outside the Congress party by declaring a state of emergency, imprisoning large numbers of her opponents, severely restricting freedom of the press, and placing under direct rule by the central government a group of Indian states where opposition parties were in power. During the period of the emergency she and her allies took a number of added steps to consolidate her authoritarian rule. And then, almost miraculously, she announced in January 1977 that she would suspend the emergency, release her jailed opponents, unshackle the press, and let the country decide its future in free elections.

It is by no means clear why she so abruptly changed course. But there is no doubt the wraps came off for the period of the

---

[40] See Penniman, *Australia at the Polls,* especially Patrick Weller and R. F. I. Smith, "The Rise and Fall of Whitlam Labor: The Political Context of the 1975 Elections," pp. 49-76; Don W. Rawson, "The Labor Campaign," pp. 77-102; Colin A. Hughes, "The Electorate Speaks—and After," pp. 277-311; and David Butler, "Politics and the Constitution: Twenty Questions Left by Remembrance Day," pp. 313-36.

campaign and the electorate was given a genuine opportunity to choose. A key to the eventual outcome was the success of many of Mrs. Gandhi's adversaries in forging a new opposition coalition, the Janata party, which proved a far more effective opponent for her Congress party, under India's first-past-the-post electoral system, than its separate components had in earlier elections. The electorate, especially of North India, seized the opportunity given it to turn Mrs. Gandhi out of office in favor of her opponents. The Janata party and its allies formed the new government, and the constitutional crisis was, for the moment, over.[41]

Describing as constitutional the issues facing the Italian electorate in 1976 requires only a degree of license. The postwar history of Italian democracy can be divided into three eras. The first of these was a period of dominance by the Christian Democratic party. The party's success, especially in the election of 1948, in beating back the challenge of the Communist party established constitutional democracy in Italy and ushered in an extended period of economic growth. But the eventual decay of the Christian Democratic majority in Parliament had by the early 1960s forced the party to rule as the leading member of shifting center and center-left coalitions, with the Socialists as their major partners. Throughout this second era the Communists were excluded from effective power at the national level. But the Communist party sought to signal to the electorate its support of constitutional democracy, increased its share of the vote and of seats in the Chamber of Deputies in successive parliamentary elections, and gained an ever wider degree of power at the municipal and regional levels. Eventually the Christian Democrats found it necessary to govern with the tacit support of the Communists, and this ushered in the third era in Italy's postwar experience of democracy.

The election of 1976 was a major gateway to this third period. For seventeen months prior to the election Christian Democratic governments were sustained in office only by the tacit willingness of the Communists not to vote them down—indeed, to lend them legislative support. The Communists entered the campaign as a party avowedly committed to the constitutional order and prepared to accept the responsibility that would go with participation in a "government of national unity."

The election sharply increased the Communists' share of the popular vote and of seats in the Chamber of Deputies—by a margin exceeding the cumulative gains in five preceding parliamentary elec-

---

[41] See Weiner, *India at the Polls*, especially chaps. 1-3 and 6-8.

tions. The Christian Democrats maintained their ground in an absolute sense by attracting support that had hitherto gone to smaller parties of the center and right. Indeed, three-quarters of the electorate now supported the two main parties, and the stage was set for a strengthening of the uneasy, arm's-length alliance of the Christian Democrats with the Communists, with whom they were united in support of the prevailing constitutional order.

Although survey evidence is fragmentary, it is clear that such a constitutional result was wanted by wide segments of the electorate. The terrorism of the time created a keen public sense that the existing order was under attack from both the left and the right. In the face of this attack the electorate sustained the strength of the party that was the author of the constitutional system while it gave new strength to the party of the left that had identified itself with the system and offered the program and leadership many voters thought could save it.[42]

Reshaping Party Systems. Elections within four of the countries in the series helped to transform their party systems. In the Federal Republic of Germany the election of 1976 extended two related trends that had together restructured the party system over a period of years. One was the accretion of support for the two dominant party groupings, the Christian Democratic Union/Christian Social Union alliance and the Social Democratic party/Free Democratic party ruling coalition. The other was the clarity with which the FDP committed itself in advance to a particular candidate for chancellor in the new Bundestag, rather than deferring its choice until the votes were in, as it had after the election of 1969.

Each of these developments was encouraged by the safeguards written into the postwar federal constitution against the fragmentation of the party system. So deadly had fragmentation been in Weimar days that the framers of the new constitution required a party to poll 5 percent of the vote before it received any seats in the Bundestag under the system of proportional representation. This provision blocked the growth of several small, extreme parties over the years, especially the neo-Nazi National Democratic party (NDP). But it also lent a further urgency to the electoral position of the FDP, close to the line at which it would vanish from the federal parliament. And

---

[42] See Penniman, *Italy at the Polls*, especially Joseph LaPalombara, "Italian Elections as Hobson's Choice," pp. 1-39; Giuseppe Di Palma, "Christian Democracy: The End of Hegemony," pp. 123-53; Stephen Hellman, "The Longest Campaign: Communist Party Strategy and the Elections of 1976," pp. 155-82; and Samuel H. Barnes, "The Consequences of the Elections: An Interpretation," pp. 327-51.

this in turn reinforced the FDP's willingness to commit itself in advance to a coalition partner in order to avoid losing the support of those who wanted to know how their votes would be counted when it came time to choose the new chancellor.

But it would be wrong to see either of these developments as the simple result of constitutional language—as the last comment suggests. The German electorate has used its ballots over the years to legitimize the whole system of government that emerged from the postwar occupation, and its commitment to the major party groupings that operate within this system has been sustained and deliberate. The importance of the electorate's intentions is indeed illustrated by the pressure on the FDP to declare itself in advance of the election. The party might, after all, have felt there were more votes to be gained by projecting itself as able to moderate the CDU or SPD if it emerged from the election with the balance of power and were free to bargain with the larger parties. This was the FDP's situation after the election of 1969, when it turned its back on the CDU and formed a coalition with the SPD. But the party had gotten the message: those who preferred the SPD to the CDU would give their votes to the SPD directly if they were unsure how a vote for the FDP would ultimately be counted in the choice of a new chancellor.[43]

Yet Germany's neighbors to the north furnish the clearest examples of electoral pressures reshaping the party system. Denmark, Sweden, and Norway all held national elections in the autumn of 1973. All of these contests proved to be strong solvents of established party alignments. This result is the more remarkable since each of these countries seemed a textbook example of Lipset and Rokkan's maxim that party systems in the older democracies will be dominated by alignments formed at the time of the last major extension of the franchise.[44]

The Danish result was the most spectacular. Five new parties took the field in 1973, doubling the number that had sought the electorate's support at the prior election. The new entrants proved astonishingly successful, corralling together one-third of all the votes cast and making one of the new parties overnight the second largest in Denmark.[45] But the pressures on the existing party system

---

[43] See Cerny, *Germany at the Polls*, especially Conradt, "The 1976 Campaign," pp. 29-56; and Heino Kaack, "The FDP in the German Party System," pp. 77-110.
[44] See Seymour Martin Lipset and Stein Rokkan, "Cleavage Structures, Party Systems, and Voter Alignments: An Introduction," in Seymour Martin Lipset and Stein Rokkan, eds., *Party Systems and Voter Alignments* (New York: Free Press, 1967), pp. 1-64.
[45] See Ole Borre, "Recent Trends in Danish Voting Behavior," in Cerny, *Scandinavia at the Polls*, pp. 3-37.

were almost as strong in Norway, where the Labor government had relinquished power a year before after losing a special referendum on the entry it had negotiated into the European Economic Community. Support for the Labor party in 1973 plummeted by more than ten percentage points, the largest change seen in decades, and new parties fragmented the electorate on both left and right.[46] There was least disruption of the prevailing party system in Sweden. But the ruling Social Democratic party suffered major losses there as well, emerging from the election dead even with their opponents in seats in the Riksdag. They were then kept in power only by the reluctance of some of their adversaries to force an early election and were driven from office by the new coalition of bourgeois parties at the election of 1976.[47]

In each of these northern countries the electorate seized on emergent elements of the party system to channel feelings that were not well matched to the existing system. The worsening economic conditions of the 1970s induced the electorate to turn a fresh and baleful eye on the edifice of the welfare state erected by social democratic governments over several decades of secure control; steeply progressive tax systems looked quite different as inflation drove almost everyone's income into higher brackets. Beyond this, the issue of membership in the European Economic Community was strongly divisive within parties of left and right in both Denmark and Norway and left a considerable wreckage behind. As a result, a high politics of party realignment dominated the elections in these northern lands.[48]

Control of the Government. No one could review this sample of modern elections without sensing the importance of the electorate's knowing that it could force a change of government. In Australia and India and Italy this was accompanied by an awareness that major constitutional issues hung in the balance, in Germany and the Scandinavian countries by an awareness that the party system could itself be changed. But control of the government gave meaning to the election even in the five countries where the constitutional and

---

[46] See Henry Valen and Willy Martinussen, "Electoral Trends and Foreign Politics in Norway: The 1973 *Storting* Election and the EEC Issue," in Cerny, *Scandinavia at the Polls*, pp. 39-71.

[47] See Bo Särlvik, "Recent Electoral Trends in Sweden," in Cerny, *Scandinavia at the Polls*, pp. 73-129.

[48] See Cerny, *Scandinavia at the Polls*, especially Erik Allardt, "On Welfare, Happiness, and Discontent in the Scandinavian Countries," pp. 155-80; C. G. Uhr, "Economic Development in Denmark, Norway, and Sweden," pp. 219-48; and Göran Ohlin, "The Changing Role of Private Enterprise in Sweden," pp. 249-65.

party systems were relatively stable;[49] and in four of them the electorate used its power to force a change:

• The British electorate in February 1974 turned down the request of the Conservative government for a new mandate to face the defiant miners and gave decisive support to Labour and the lesser parties on other grounds.[50]

• The French electorate in the presidential contest of 1974 shifted the standard of the center and right from the Gaullists to Valéry Giscard d'Estaing, who then marshaled a narrow majority against François Mitterrand in the runoff election.[51]

• The Irish electorate in 1977 turned its back on the economic performance of the Fine Gael government and made Fianna Fáil the government once more, with an unprecedented number of seats in the Dáil.[52]

• The Israeli electorate in 1977 exacted from Labor the price of the wounds from the 1973 war and of scandal and economic dislocation at home by shifting power to Menachem Begin's Likud party.[53]

In these countries too it is impossible to understand electoral outcomes apart from a high politics of issues that moved the electorate strongly; indeed, strongly enough to transfer the power of government between the rival contestants. Major forces of change have been channeled through the elections of the democratic world in the recent past.

Sharpening the Analytic Edge

How real is the first of the roles assigned to popular elections, on the evidence of this comparative survey? The recent experience of this group of democracies shows how deeply the ballot has allowed the electorate to intervene in the affairs of state. The electoral interaction

---

[49] For evidence that the possibility of a turnover of governments was real enough in Canada too, see Penniman, *Canada at the Polls*, especially John Meisel, "The Party System and the 1974 Election," pp. 1-28, and William P. Irvine, "An Overview of the 1974 Federal Election in Canada," pp. 29-55.

[50] See Howard R. Penniman, ed., *Britain at the Polls: The Parliamentary Elections of 1974* (Washington, D.C.: American Enterprise Institute, 1975), especially Anthony King, "The Election That Everyone Lost," pp. 3-31.

[51] See Penniman, *France at the Polls*, especially Jean Blondel, "The Rise of a New-Style President," pp. 41-69, and Jean Charlot, "The End of Gaullism," pp. 71-112.

[52] See Penniman, *Ireland at the Polls*, especially Sinnott, "The Electorate," pp. 35-67, and Brian Farrell and Maurice Manning, "The Election," pp. 133-64.

[53] See Penniman, *Israel at the Polls*, especially Elizur and Katz, "The Media in the Israeli Elections," pp. 227-54, and Asher Arian, "Conclusion," pp. 283-302.

of leaders and led has made and unmade governments, reshaped party systems, helped to resolve basic constitutional issues. It would be difficult to question the primacy of this high political content among the forces shaping electoral outcomes.

This assessment from thirteen of the world's democracies is the more remarkable since only one, France, adheres to the presidential form and refers the choice of the executive directly to the people. In almost all of the parliamentary democracies, judgments by the electorate led immediately to the formation of governments rather than draining away into the sands of parliamentary bargaining. Indeed, there were notable cases—Sweden, Israel, and India, for example—where the emergence of a broadly based opposition alignment gave the electorate an effective opportunity to remove a party long in power.

It is problematic how well the intervention of the electorate in the affairs of the state helps to realize symbolic and material values that enjoy wide support—and thereby to enhance the legitimacy of democratic regimes. With the end of the long years of economic expansion that followed World War II, a new and darker commentary on the condition of democracy has come into fashion. The support accorded democratic regimes that could pay for egalitarian social measures from the economic surplus cannot, it is said, long be sustained. These measures must now either be paid for by inflation or be repealed, with dangerous implications for democratic politics in either case.

Few of the impressions gained from the *At the Polls* series would warrant a dark pessimism. There is scant evidence here of the legitimacy of democratic regimes sinking to disastrous levels or of electorates alienated by the futility of electoral choices. There is, to be sure, ample evidence of the new economic context of politics. But this has in the main reshaped the programs and choices offered the electorate, forcing at times substantial change in the party system, as it has in the Scandinavian countries. The impression conveyed by electorates in this recent era is that they acted as if they believed significant values turned on the choices they were asked to make at the polls.

The impressions gained from this comparative survey make the fingers itch for more. A great deal that is here is genuinely revealing, as I have said. But a great deal is also left out. Gaps could be identified under each of the main headings we have used for the substantive findings. Few of these countries are the site of rigorous and continuing analysis of the demographic and social change that lies at the base of electoral decisions. In very few is the descriptive knowledge of party organization and the mass media linked very satisfactorily to electoral outcomes. Indeed, it might also be said that the frameworks by which we understand the influence of leaders and issues on electoral politics are still in remarkable disrepair in view of the primacy of the high political content of electoral outcomes.[54]

No single group of analysts, certainly not those who will extend the *At the Polls* series, is solely responsible for sharpening the edge of analysis in all of these respects. The opportunity is one that confronts generally an international community of political analysts. If it is grasped, the gaps as well as the insights seen in this comparative survey will inspire the studies that are needed to set an exceedingly valuable form of historical description on foundations that are theoretically and empirically firm.

Bibliography

Butler, David, and Stokes, Donald. *Political Change in Britain.* 2d ed. New York: St. Martin's Press, 1974.

Campbell, Angus; Converse, Philip E.; Miller, Warren E.; and Stokes, Donald E. *The American Voter.* New York: John Wiley and Sons, 1960.

Lipset, Seymour Martin, and Rokkan, Stein, eds. *Party Systems and Voter Alignments: Cross-National Perspectives.* New York: Free Press, 1967.

Mackie, Thomas T., and Rose, Richard. *The International Almanac of Electoral History.* New York: Free Press, 1974.

Nie, Norman H.; Verba, Sidney; and Petrocik, John R. *The Changing American Voter.* Cambridge, Mass.: Harvard University Press, 1976.

Rokkan, Stein. *Citizens, Elections, Parties.* Oslo: Universitetsforlaget, 1970.

Rose, Richard, ed. *Electoral Behavior: A Comparative Handbook.* New York: Free Press, 1974.

Tufte, Edward R. *Political Control of the Economy.* Princeton: Princeton University Press, 1978.

White, Theodore H. *The Making of the President, 1960.* New York: Atheneum, 1960.

---

[54] Two interpretive biases seem to me symptomatic of how unsure the understanding of electoral issues continues to be. Observers tend both to assimilate too wide a range of "position" issues to overarching ideological frameworks and to overstate the importance of "position" issues relative to "valence" issues. For a discussion of these problems in a comparative context, see Butler and Stokes, *Political Change in Britain,* rev. ed. (New York and London: St. Martin's Press and Macmillan, 1974), especially chaps. 14 to 18.

12

What Do Elections Decide?

Anthony King

The last chapter was primarily concerned with explaining the out-comes of elections. In this chapter, we turn to considering in greater detail their consequences. What do elections decide? Do they matter? If so, to what? And straightaway we have to acknowledge a simple fact. The political science literature on electoral systems and electoral behavior is vast; by contrast, the political science literature concerned with the consequences of elections scarcely existed until very recently. The index of the average political science textbook typically contains a large number of entries such as "Elections, and corruption," "Elections, and exclusions from," and "Elections, role of social class in." But it almost never contains entries like "Elections, and political leadership" or "Elections, and the determination of public policy." Fortunately, in recent years political scientists have begun to interest themselves in the consequences of elections, and we shall consider their findings later in this chapter. We shall also note in passing some of the reasons why this central "So what?" used to be so largely neglected.

In trying to answer the question, What do elections decide?, we could pursue two strategies. The first would be to compare the universe of countries that do have democratic elections with the universe of countries that do not have them. We would be interested in trying to find out what difference it makes to a country whether it has elections or not. Suppose that two countries were very similar in most respects, except that elections took place from time to time in one of them but not in the other. Comparing the two countries, we might discover that their patterns of public policy differed quite sharply: that taxes were higher in one country than the other, that welfare spending was higher in one country than the other, that criminals were treated with much greater leniency in one country than in the other, and so on. We might wish to attribute these differences to the holding, or not holding, of free elections. Alternatively, we might discover that, in many respects, the two countries' patterns of policy were strikingly similar; in both countries, people were taxed heavily but also received substantial pensions. Despite these similarities, we might still want to argue that democratic elections do make a difference, if not always to specific policy outcomes, then to the quality of a country's political life. The differences between dictatorships and democracies are not, after all, to be measured solely in narrow policy terms.

The second strategy available to us is quite different. It does not compare countries with elections and those without them. Rather, it concentrates on the universe of countries that do have democratic elections and asks of them what part the holding of elections plays in the larger political order. Whereas the first strategy is concerned with the existence of elections, the second is concerned with their effects. Do elections in fact decide who shall form a country's government? What influence, if any, do they have on the contents of a country's public policies? It is this second strategy that we shall pursue here. This second strategy is in no way more important than the first; but it is more in keeping with the subjects dealt with elsewhere in this volume, and it will enable us to draw on the findings of some interesting, and significant, recent research.[1]

One other point needs to be made at the outset. It must be obvious that to discuss the effects of democratic elections on the political systems in which they occur is rather like discussing the effects of skyscrapers on New York or of Judaism on Israel. Each is typically defined in terms of the other; it is almost impossible to imagine either in the absence of the other. In this chapter we shall mainly be dealing with fairly close relationships between the holding of specific elections, or series of specific elections, and some of the

---

[1] The first strategy remains important all the same. Anyone studying the history of, say, Germany, Italy, and Japan in this century would be bound to admit that which party wins democratic elections in these countries is far less important than whether or not they have such elections. Militarism, the suppression of human rights, and the suppression of free trade unions characterized all three countries when they were dictatorships; they no longer characterize any of the three. Democracies and nondemocracies really are different. For some evidence on the similarities and differences between patterns of public policy in countries that do and do not have free elections, see Alexander J. Groth, *Comparative Politics: A Distributive Approach* (New York: Macmillan, 1971); Frederic L. Pryor, *Public Expenditures in Communist and Capitalist Nations* (London: George Allen and Unwin, 1968); Gaston V. Rimlinger, *Welfare Policy and Industrialization in Europe, America, and Russia* (New York: John Wiley, 1971); and Richard L. Siegel and Leonard B. Weinberg, *Comparing Public Policies: United States, Soviet Union, and Europe* (Homewood, Ill.: Dorsey Press, 1977).

more or less specific effects that they have. But the reader should bear in mind that, in democratic countries, elections exert their influence everywhere and all the time. Style, substance, timing, policies, personnel, the whole warp and woof of democratic politics are determined by the holding of free elections, past, present, and future. It follows that in this chapter we shall be dealing with only a few aspects, albeit important ones, of a subject that is in fact a great deal larger.

Elections and the Formation of Governments

Let us begin at the beginning. Whatever else they are about, elections are widely believed to be about deciding who shall govern. The principal purpose of elections, it is said, is to enable the electors of a country to choose that country's government. In fact, however, the world is more complicated, and less "democratic," than such a formulation implies.

In the first place, although the electorate in all twenty-eight of the countries under consideration in this volume determines the composition of some element or elements of government, in no case does it determine them all. Governments are traditionally said to consist of three more or less separate branches: the executive, including the civil and military services, the legislature, and the judiciary. Yet in none of our twenty-eight countries is the electorate given the opportunity to decide who will man the upper echelons of the civil bureaucracy, let alone who will command the armed services as generals, admirals, and air marshals; and in no country are judges at the national or federal level elected, though judges are chosen in this manner in more than half of the fifty American states.[2] Perhaps more important, in only six of our twenty-eight countries—Sri Lanka, Colombia, Venezuela, the Dominican Republic, the United States, and France (since the institution of popular elections for the presidency in 1962)—are voters given any direct say in the composition of the executive branch. Moreover, even in these six countries the electorate

---

[2] The reference above is to direct elections in the strict sense: to the filling of specific offices directly by the electorate. But, of course, in all democratic countries the electorate's influence extends a good deal further. Voters in Britain vote directly for parliamentary candidates; but they know that, if enough of them vote Conservative, the Conservative leader will become prime minister. Similarly, the election of a Democratic or Republican president in the United States leads to the making of hundreds of other more or less partisan appointments, some of them, given time, to the Supreme Court. On the direct election of judges in the American states, see Herbert Jacob and Kenneth N. Vines, eds., *Politics in the American States: A Comparative Analysis*, 2d ed. (Boston: Little, Brown, 1971), chap. 8.

is permitted only to determine whom it wishes to head the executive branch; not even in the ultrademocratic United States are voters asked whom they wish to form the president's cabinet.[3] In short, the norm in democratic countries is for the electorate to choose directly only the members of the legislature or representative assembly. This is a very restricted choice; it certainly does not amount, in itself, to choosing the country's government.

In the second place, the connection between the outcomes of elections to representative assemblies or legislatures and the subsequent formation of governments or administrations is a good deal less close than is often supposed. To be sure, in countries like Australia, West Germany, or the United Kingdom, with either dominant two-party systems or a stable pattern of interparty alliances, there is a fairly straightforward one-to-one relationship between the outcome of a national election and who subsequently takes power in the executive branch. If the Social Democratic and Free Democratic parties in West Germany between them gain a majority of seats in the Bundestag, then a coalition government is formed, with the leader of the larger party becoming chancellor; likewise in Britain, if the Conservative party wins a majority of seats at a general election, the party's leader forms a government, and that is that.

But in many democratic countries the holding of an election does not lead straightforwardly to the formation of a government; it merely makes possible, or more probable, the formation of one kind of government rather than another. In the end, it is bargaining among the political parties, rather than the election itself, that is decisive. In the France of the Fourth Republic, for example, the counting of the ballot papers was scarcely more than a preliminary to the serious business of party maneuvering within the National Assembly. Following the elections of June 1951, the Gaullists, Socialists, and Communists were the three largest parties in the assembly; but, after Radical and Conservative nominees for the premiership had been defeated, it was René Pleven, the leader of the tiny UDSR, who finally took office—without the support of the Communists and with the Socialists refusing to accept seats in the cabinet.[4] In January 1956, the two groups that gained most in the elections were the Poujadists and the followers of Pierre Mendès-France; but the Poujadists were

---

[3] They are, however, in a large number of states given a chance to vote directly for members of the executive branch in addition to the governor. In more than forty, for example, the attorney general and state treasurer are popularly elected. For details, see Jacob and Vines, *Politics in the American States*, chap. 6.

[4] Philip M. Williams, *Crisis and Compromise: Politics in the Fourth Republic* (London: Longmans, 1964), pp. 38-39.

denied office completely and Mendès-France was relegated to an insignificant ministry without portfolio from which he shortly resigned.[5] In Italy the same discontinuity between electoral outcomes and the interparty discussions leading to the formation of governments has been evident since shortly after the end of World War II. As Di Palma has put it, "Elections [in Italy] are not called to decide whether to change personnel and policies, but as if to decide whether the regime shall be preserved."[6] So far it has been, if only just.

Table 12–1 seeks to list those countries in which, as in West Germany and Great Britain, the outcome of each national election is directly reflected in the formation of the nation's government, and those countries, like Fourth Republic France, Italy, Belgium, and Denmark, in which the relationship between the vote of the people and the subsequent formation of a government is more tenuous.[7] The allocation of countries to one list or the other is in a few cases somewhat arbitrary, and it is perhaps too early to say in the cases of newer democracies like Portugal and Spain what the long-term pattern will be; but most of our twenty-eight countries fall fairly readily and neatly into one category or the other. No one will be surprised to learn that the more political parties a country has, the more likely it is that its elections will be indecisive in terms of the formation of its government.

---

[5] Williams, *Crisis and Compromise*, pp. 48-49. It goes without saying that, although bargaining among the parties determines the final outcome in cases like these, the election itself will have determined the framework within which the bargaining takes place. Even so, the outcome can sometimes be paradoxical. Take the fate of the Poujadists in 1956 referred to above. The Poujadists did well in the election, and were denied office precisely because they had done well: the older, established parties in effect formed a defensive alliance against them. Much the same thing happened in Denmark in 1963. The Progress party of Mogens Glistrup became almost overnight the second largest party in the Danish parliament, but the established parties saw to it that Glistrup and his followers were kept out of the government. On this last episode, see Ole Borre, "Denmark's Protest Election of December 1973," *Scandinavian Political Studies*, vol. 9 (1974), pp. 197-204, and Karl H. Cerny, ed., *Scandinavia at the Polls: Recent Political Trends in Denmark, Norway, and Sweden* (Washington, D.C.: American Enterprise Institute, 1977), chap. 1.

[6] Giuseppe Di Palma, *Surviving without Governing: The Italian Parties in Parliament* (Berkeley, Calif.: University of California Press, 1977), p. 248.

[7] In France and Italy, the relationship between election results and the formation of governments is somewhat closer than it would be otherwise because of the existence of strong antiregime parties, notably the Communists, whose presence has the effect of restricting the proregime parties' room for maneuver. The fit between election results and the subsquent composition of governments is especially loose in countries like Belgium, Denmark, Finland, and the Netherlands, which have a large number of parties, almost all of them supportive of the regime.

TABLE 12–1

Election Outcomes and Formation of Governments

Countries in Which Electoral Outcomes Normally Determine Composition of Government	Countries in Which Interparty Bargaining Following Elections Normally Determines Composition of Government
Australia	Belgium
Austria	Denmark
Canada	Finland
Dominican Republic	Italy
France	Netherlands
West Germany	Portugal
India	Turkey
Ireland	
Israel	
Japan	
New Zealand	
Norway	
Spain	
Sri Lanka	
Sweden	
Switzerland	
United Kingdom	
United States	
Venezuela	

NOTE: Two countries covered in this volume have been omitted from the table: Colombia and Greece. Both countries underwent substantial changes in their political systems in the 1970s. The French Fourth Republic, if it still existed, would clearly belong in the column on the right.

SOURCES: Arthur S. Banks, *Political Handbook of the World 1978* (New York: McGraw-Hill, 1978); Chris Cook and John Paxton, *European Political Facts 1918-1973* (London: Macmillan, 1975); Chris Cook and John Paxton, *Commonwealth Political Facts* (London: Macmillan, 1979).

A related point also needs to be made: the formation of a new government, especially in a parliamentary system, need not be related to the holding of elections at all. If the existing government falls as the result of the defection of one or more of the parties that hitherto supported it, parliament may be dissolved and new elections held; but, more commonly, parliament remains in being and negotiations among the parties merely lead to the formation of a new government. The people's votes at the preceding election merely set the parameters within which the parties negotiate. Table 12–2 sets out for selected

TABLE 12–2

NUMBERS OF ELECTIONS AND GOVERNMENTS, 1945–1977

Country	Number of Elections	Number of Governments
Australia	14	4
Austria	10	3
Belgium	11	14
Canada	10	3
Denmark	14	17[a]
Finland	10	33[a]
France (Fourth Republic)	3	19
France (Fifth Republic)	7	1
West Germany (since 1949)	8	5
India (since 1947)	6	2
Ireland	9	7
Israel (since 1948)	9	2
Italy (since 1947)	8	10[a]
Japan (since 1947)	13	1
Netherlands	10	9
New Zealand	11	6
Norway	9	5
Sri Lanka (since 1947)	7	7
Sweden	10	2
Turkey (since 1950)	9	11[a]
United Kingdom	11	5
United States	8	5
Venezuela (since 1958)	4	3

[a] In these four cases, the number of governments given is necessarily arbitrary, depending on the meaning given to the phrase in the text "substantially altered partisan composition." In the case of Italy, for example, the total number of new governments during the 1947-1977 period was thirty-five; but in only ten cases, at most, does it seem reasonable to say that the partisan composition of the government was substantially changed.

SOURCES: Banks, *Political Handbook of the World 1978*; Bertold Spuler, *Rulers and Governments of the World*, vol. 3, 1930-1975 (London: Bowker, 1977); Cook and Paxton, *European Political Facts 1918-1973*; Cook and Paxton, *Commonwealth Political Facts*; and Thomas Mackie and Richard Rose, *International Almanac of Electoral History* (London: Macmillan, 1974). The data in this last volume are regularly updated by Mackie and Rose in the *European Journal of Political Research*.

countries the number of elections that have been held since 1945 (or since the country became a democracy) and the number of new governments that have been formed, a new government being defined as one with a substantially altered partisan composition. As can readily be seen, in a number of cases the number of governments exceeds the number of elections. With regard to countries in this position, it is clearly a gross oversimplification to say, without qualification, that popular elections decide who shall rule.

Elections, then, determine the memberships of legislatures and sometimes who shall be chief executive. What, we need to go on to ask, is their influence on what governments actually do?

Elections and the Formation of Public Policy

The relationship we have been considering so far is fairly straightforward. One looks at the outcomes of elections. One looks at the formation of governments. One sees how close the fit between the two is. But when we come to consider the relationship between elections and the formation of public policy, matters are anything but straightforward. Indeed we are wading into a conceptual and empirical minefield. No wonder that political scientists, with a few intrepid exceptions, have steered clear of it.

The relationship between elections and public policy is bound to be complicated partly because the voters in an election are not being asked—or at any rate are not being asked explicitly—to determine issues of public policy. They are being asked, rather, to say which person or persons, or which party, they wish to return to the national legislature (or, in a few cases, to the presidential palace). If in choosing people and parties the voters are also choosing policies, the connection between the two is, at most, an indirect one. It is only in referendums that citizens are given an opportunity to pronounce directly on policy issues.[8] Elections in the first instance are about electing, neither more nor less.

Three other problems present themselves, two conceptual, the other more empirical. The first is simply the familiar problem of what would have happened under other circumstances—the problem of "counterfactuals," as historians like to call it.[9] Suppose that party A wins and forms the government. Suppose further that party A now proceeds to adopt and implement policies x, y, and z. One might be tempted to say that there was a causal link between A's

---

[8] For what is in a sense a companion volume to the present one, see David Butler and Austin Ranney, eds., Referendums: A Comparative Study of Practice and Theory (Washington, D.C.: American Enterprise Institute, 1978).

[9] On counterfactuals, see Robert W. Fogel, Railroads and American Economic Growth (Baltimore, Md.: Johns Hopkins Press, 1964); Robert W. Fogel and Stanley L. Engerman, Time on the Cross: The Economics of American Negro Slavery (Boston: Little, Brown, 1974); and Jon Elster, Logic and Society (New York: John Wiley, 1978).

victory in the election and the adoption of the three policies in question. But of course it is open to another observer to claim that the adoption of policies x, y, and z really had nothing to do with the election, because if party B had been elected it would have adopted exactly the same policies. Perhaps the country's economic and social circumstances required such policies; perhaps its international creditors did. As a matter of historical fact, the election of Franklin Roosevelt and the Democratic congresses of the 1930s did lead to the New Deal; but might not Herbert Hoover or Alf Landon have found himself forced to adopt similar policies if he had been in the White House? Answers to such questions are, of course, a matter for judgment; such judgments are by no means always easy to make.

The second problem has more to do with the way in which one uses words. The question, What do elections decide?, is of the same grammatical form as, What do voters decide?—but in one sense of the word "decide," of course, political procedures cannot "decide" anything; only people can. Elections not being directly related to the determination of public policy, it is perfectly possible for an election result to lead to the adoption of a specific policy without any individual elector's having voted for the winning party because it was advocating that policy; on the contrary, the majority of voters, even the majority of voters for the winning party, may have been opposed to it. The Conservative party's election victory of May 1979 in Britain can reasonably be said to have led directly to the raising of value-added tax to 15 percent, since it is most unlikely that a Labour chancellor of the exchequer would have acted similarly. Yet it may be misleading to say that the raising of value-added tax to 15 percent was "decided" by the election, since a majority of voters would almost certainly have been strongly against such a steep increase in VAT if they had been asked for their views during the election campaign— which they were not.[10] In short, even when the results of elections clearly have led to the adoption of some policies rather than others, one must beware of attributing any set of policy preferences to the electorate itself.

---

[10] The *Economist*'s leading article discussing the budget in which value-added tax was increased to 15 percent (June 16, 1979) was headed: "It's what you voted for." This may have been true in the sense that most voters who voted Conservative in the election only a few weeks before approved of the Conservatives' broad economic approach and were probably aware that the Conservatives intended to bring about a substantial shift from direct to indirect taxation; but they did not know, and probably in most cases did not suspect, that a Conservative chancellor would raise VAT by such a large amount. Voters take decisions. Elections have consequences. The connection between the two in any given case is an empirical matter.

The third problem is the empirical one. As we remarked at the beginning of this chapter, political scientists have had precious little to say until recently about the consequences—especially the policy consequences—of election outcomes. The problem of counterfactuals is daunting; the number of relevant variables is enormous; data are often hard to come by. It may also be that many American political scientists are deterred from tackling the subject by the fact that in the United States the separation of powers between the presidency and Congress makes it particularly difficult to relate a candidate's campaign promises to his subsequent performance in office.

At any rate, one result of the dearth of relevant research is that in much of the rest of this chapter, instead of presenting large amounts of data about a large proportion of our twenty-eight countries, we shall be forced to present a scattering of data about a considerably smaller number of countries. Since the data are scattered, and since few of them are comparable across more than a few countries, our presentation will of necessity focus as much on the academic literature as on the real world that the literature purports to describe. Three significantly different approaches to the study of the relationship between election outcomes and the content of public policies have, in practice, been adopted by scholars. They can be labeled, albeit somewhat crudely, the longitudinal, the "promise/performance," and the correlational. We shall say a word about each in turn.

The Longitudinal Approach. This approach is, in conception at least, the simplest of the three. One takes a single country, or a series of single countries. One takes a single policy area, or a series of single policy areas. One then looks to see whether changes in policy in each of the policy areas have coincided (allowing for leads and lags) with changes in the party or parties in power in the given country or countries. Suppose that, with regard to a specific field of public policy, there is a sharp ideological difference between parties A and B. Party A favors policy x; party B favors policy z. The aim of the longitudinal approach is to discover whether, when party A is in power, policy x is in fact pursued, and whether, when party B is in power, policy z is in fact pursued. In other words, the question, What do elections decide?, is asked in the form, Does it make any difference which party is in power?

Although the longitudinal approach is, in some ways, the most straightforward of the three, it has seldom been employed, for reasons that are not hard to discern. For the longitudinal approach to be worth attempting, no fewer than six separate conditions have to be fulfilled:

1. The researcher needs to be able to identify the party or parties in power. This may rule out, for example, the United States when the presidency and Congress are controlled by different parties.

2. The parties in the country need to have adopted reasonably explicit policy positions, so that there is some reason to suppose that policy will in fact change over time depending on which party is in power. This does not rule out countries in which politics is dominated by reasonably stable interparty coalitions, tendencies, or blocs, but it does effectively rule out countries in which the parties typically do not adopt distinctive policy positions, and also those in which government is carried on (insofar as it is carried on) by a congeries of rapidly shifting multiparty coalitions.[11]

3. The researcher must confine himself to policy areas that remain reasonably stable over time; issues that have a very short life span are not of much use. This rules out most "crises." Using this approach, one cannot ask whether Democratic and Republican administrations would have handled, say, the Cuban missile crisis differently.

4. The researcher needs to confine himself to countries in which the party system has remained reasonably stable over time. For these purposes, the stability of parties can also include the stability of interparty coalitions and blocs. Even so, it might prove difficult to study, say, France, since there have been so many and such radical changes in the French party system in almost every decade since World War II.[12]

5. More than one party or coalition needs to have been in power long enough to have had a chance to effect changes in policy. Ideally, there should have been some fairly frequent alternation of parties or coalitions in power. This rules out countries like Greece, Portugal, and Spain, where the partisan composition of the government in power has not changed significantly since these countries became democracies; and it might make the researcher a bit dubious about studying, say, Italy, where the Christian Democrats have been the dominant party in every coalition since the war.

6. Finally, having satisfied himself that the policy area he wishes to study has remained reasonably stable over time (that is, that the

---

[11] It is perhaps worth adding that, even in such countries, it is often possible to identify any given coalition's general political orientation. If so, and if the country is generally governed by coalitions of this type, however often their partisan composition may change, then the longitudinal approach may still be worth attempting.

[12] On the scale of the changes in the French party system, compare Williams, *Crisis and Compromise*, with, for example, Vincent Wright, *The Government and Politics of Modern France* (London: Hutchinson, 1978), chaps. 6-7.

issues raised in the policy area are, in some meaningful sense, "the same" issues), the researcher must find some means of measuring, or at least identifying, changes in policy, so that he will know when a policy change has occurred that is worth counting as such for purposes of analysis.

It goes without saying that not many combinations of countries and policy domains fulfill all of these conditions. In practice, the researcher is confined to countries with stable two-party systems in which the two parties have alternated in power, or to countries with a reasonably stable pattern of opposing coalitions, and also to parliamentary systems or to presidential systems in which the president and the legislature are usually or always in the hands of the same party. In practice, too, the researcher is likely to feel most comfortable dealing with policy areas in which changes in policy can fairly easily be quantified—areas such as public expenditure and taxation.

One further point should be made about the longitudinal approach. It does not assume the traditional model of "party government."[13] On the contrary, it can be used to test it. It can be used to ask whether the party formally in power really is in power. If parties A and B advocate opposing policies x and z in a given area of public policy, but if each of the two parties, when in office, pursues the other party's policy or some entirely different policy, or if changes in policy typically do not take place at all, then the researcher is entitled to suppose that some factor or factors other than party policy are crucial in determining public policy in that area. By the same token, sharp changes in policy in the direction predicted by the governing party's stated policy position are at least consistent with the hypothesis that the traditional party-government model holds for the country in question, at any rate with regard to the policy domain being studied.

Not much research has so far made use of the longitudinal approach; but the little research that has been done has produced some interesting, nontrivial findings about the United States and several Western European countries and strongly suggests that the approach ought to be used more often, in a wider variety of national settings.

Klein, in an important article published in 1976, set out to consider the determinants of levels of public expenditure in Great

---

[13] The literature on party government, and especially "responsible" party government, is vast. Most of the important issues are raised in Richard Rose, *The Problem of Party Government* (London: Macmillan, 1974), esp. chaps. 1-5 and 15-16.

Britain.[14] In particular, he was interested in finding out whether the rate of growth in public expenditure, both in general and in connection with specific categories of expenditure, owed anything to whether a Conservative or a Labour government was in power. He found that, for the period 1952–1973 at least, there was almost no relationship between rises in the overall level of public spending and the political complexion of the government of the day. Public expenditure began to rise quite rapidly during Harold Macmillan's Conservative administration, especially between 1960 and 1963; it rose even more rapidly in the first years of Harold Wilson's first Labour administration, between 1964 and 1968. But then it actually fell in 1969 and 1970 following the devaluation of the pound; it fell still further in the first two years of Edward Heath's Conservative government, only to rise to record levels in 1973 and 1974.

Even with regard to specific categories of expenditure, there appeared to be no very consistent relationship between spending levels and which party was in power. Spending on social security and on the National Health Service tended to increase rather more under Labour governments; but spending on education and housing tended to grow more rapidly when the Conservatives were in power. Klein cautions against a simplistic interpretation of his findings; he points out, for example, that some small spending programs, especially ones that are "both financially modest and politically sensitive," may be liable to extreme fluctuations depending on which party is in power.[15] All the same, his findings are generally negative. Taken by themselves, they would suggest that, as regards public spending in Britain at least, it does not matter greatly which party is in power; elections do not decide very much.

The findings of other researchers, however, complicate the picture. Cowart, in research reported in 1978, was concerned to identify the main determinants of monetary and fiscal policy in seven Western European countries: Britain, West Germany, France, the Netherlands, Austria, Sweden, and Italy.[16] He wanted to find out, among other things, whether social democratic and bourgeois governments typically

---

[14] Rudolf Klein, "The Politics of Public Expenditure: American Theory and British Practice," *British Journal of Political Science*, vol. 6 (October 1976), pp. 401-32. See also Frank Gould and Barbara Howeth, "Politics and Public Spending," *Political Quarterly*, vol. 49 (April-June 1978), pp. 222-27.

[15] Klein, "The Politics of Public Expenditure," p. 425.

[16] Andrew T. Cowart, "The Economic Policies of European Governments, Part I: Monetary Policy," *British Journal of Political Science*, vol. 8 (July 1978), pp. 285-311, and "The Economic Policies of European Governments, Part II: Fiscal Policy," *British Journal of Political Science*, vol. 8 (October 1978), pp. 425-39.

pursued different monetary and fiscal strategies. He hypothesized that social democratic governments would be more likely than bourgeois governments to maintain high interest rates (since low interest rates may be thought to benefit the rich), and also that social democratic governments would be more likely than bourgeois governments to pursue active fiscal policies, especially in the interests of reducing unemployment.

For our immediate purposes, Sweden and Italy can be ignored since the partisan composition of their governments did not change substantially during the period covered by Cowart, 1950–1975. That leaves us with five countries instead of the original seven. And in four of the five, according to Cowart, either the disposition to use monetary policy at all as a weapon of economic management, or the specific ways in which it has been used, have varied considerably depending on the type of government in power. Monetary policy has been most sensitive to changes of government in West Germany and the Netherlands:

> Officially set discount rates have been higher in the Federal Republic under Christian Democratic rule and higher in the Netherlands under Labour/Catholic coalitions than under majority Catholic rule with no Labour participation; this pattern holds regardless of the differences in economic conditions which those governments have faced.[17]

In Britain and Austria, social democratic governments have tended to maintain interest rates at higher levels than bourgeois governments, other economic fluctuations aside; in the same two countries, bourgeois governments have shown a greater disposition than social democratic governments to use monetary policy as a means of combating unemployment.[18] Only in France has the conduct of monetary policy remained relatively immune to partisan political forces.[19]

Cowart's findings with regard to fiscal policy are broadly similar.[20] Governments in France and Austria, whatever their political complexion, have not made use of fiscal policy to any significant extent to combat either rising prices or rising unemployment. But in Britain fiscal policy has been used in response to rising unemployment, and in West Germany and the Netherlands it has been used extensively

---

[17] Cowart, "Economic Policies of European Governments, I: Monetary Policy," p. 307.

[18] Ibid., p. 308.

[19] Ibid. Even in the case of France, according to Cowart, there is some evidence of greater responsiveness to unemployment under center-to-left coalitions during the Fourth Republic than under the Gaullist coalitions of the Fifth Republic.

[20] Cowart, "Economic Policies of European Governments, II: Fiscal Policy."

in response to both rising unemployment and rising prices. In all three countries, governments of the left have been readier than governments of the right to use fiscal policy for purposes of economic management. Cowart's conclusions, with regard to both monetary and fiscal policy, are worth quoting: "Governments of the left have distinguished themselves from governments of the right by (1) their significantly greater levels of response to changing macroeconomic conditions and (2) their diversity in the types of policy instruments chosen to deal with those macroeconomic changes."[21] These conclusions hold for West Germany and the Netherlands and, to a lesser extent, for Britain and Austria. In other words, in a number of polities it does matter which party is in power; elections do decide something of importance.[22]

Hibbs also made use of the longitudinal approach in studying macroeconomic policy in Britain and the United States, and arrived at conclusions quite similar to Cowart's.[23] Hibbs's hypothesis was that Labour and Democratic administrations, drawing their electoral support largely from the working classes, would give the task of reducing unemployment a higher priority than the task of fighting inflation, while Conservative and Republican administrations, drawing their support disproportionately from the middle classes, would emphasize the fight against inflation and would not be so concerned about the numbers of people out of work. Hibbs found that governments in the two countries did indeed behave in the way hypothesized. "Government-induced" unemployment levels in Britain were higher under Conservative than under Labour governments; in the United States, the difference between Democratic and Republican administrations was, if anything, even greater. Hibbs calculates that in the United States the interadministration difference in government-induced unemployment levels between 1948 and 1972 was on the

---

[21] Ibid., p. 438 (italics deleted).

[22] Moreover, Cowart's data cover the period from roughly 1950 to 1975, when all of the countries he deals with were enjoying unparalleled prosperity. It is possible that under conditions of greater economic and political stress the differences between right- and left-wing parties, both in and out of office, may become more marked. The recent experience of Britain certainly suggests that this may be so; the economic policies pursued by the Conservative government elected in 1979 differed sharply from those of its Labour predecessor—and almost certainly differed from the policies that the Labour party would have pursued had it remained in office.

[23] Douglas A. Hibbs, Jr., "Political Parties and Macroeconomic Policy," *American Political Science Review*, vol. 71 (December 1977), pp. 1467-87. See also Henrik J. Madsen, "Electoral Outcomes and Macro-Economic Policies: The Scandinavian Cases," in Paul Whiteley, ed., *Models of Political Economy* (Beverly Hills, Calif.: Sage Publications, 1980).

order of 2.36 percentage points—a very substantial figure given the long-run level of unemployment in the United States. Hibbs remarks:

> Macroeconomic outcomes . . . are not altogether endogenous to the economy, but obviously are influenced to a significant extent by long- and short-term political choices. The real winners of elections are perhaps best determined by examining the policy consequences of partisan change rather than by simply tallying the votes.[24]

The "Promise/Performance" Approach. One way of trying to determine what, if anything, elections decide is, as we have seen, to explore the relationship over time between the policies of governments and the partisan coloration of those same governments. Another is to compare the promises that political parties make before elections with the performance of those same parties when, and if, they are returned to power. Do political parties keep their election promises? If they do, we can at least entertain the possibility that elections have policy consequences. We can also entertain the possibility that the traditional party-government model has some validity. Cautious phrases like "entertain the possibility" have to be used because, of course, the fact that a party keeps its promises—or indeed does not keep them—in itself proves nothing about what would have happened if the other party had won. The problem of counterfactuals is ever present.

As in the case of the longitudinal approach, several conditions have to be fulfilled before the promise/performance approach can meaningfully be employed:

1. The political parties in the country being studied must make promises prior to elections, and these promises must be reasonably specific, so that it is possible afterward to say with some degree of confidence whether the winning party's promises have been fulfilled or not.

2. The researcher has, as before, to be able to identify the party or coalition in power. If a coalition government is based upon a substantial level of prior agreement among the parties making it up, then there need be no problem; but if a coalition has been patched together ad hoc without reference to the election promises of the parties composing it, then any comparison between the various coalition partners' election promises and the subsequent performance of the government in question may prove futile.

3. This condition, unlike the others, is not strictly necessary; but

---

[24] Hibbs, "Political Parties and Macroeconomic Policy," p. 1487.

in practice the researcher may be more confident in dealing with the counterfactuals problem if the parties competing at elections not merely make promises, but make different promises. If parties A and B both promise to pursue policy x, the fact that the winning party subsequently pursues policy x leaves open the possibility that the losing party, if it had won, would have done the same thing—that in policy terms the election would have decided nothing. If, however, one party promises to pursue policy x and the other policy y, and if the winning party proceeds to fulfill its promise, the researcher may, depending on the circumstances, feel more confident in saying that the election did indeed make a difference.[25]

Despite these conditions, one might have supposed that the promise/performance approach would have been widely employed. After all, the three conditions are fairly frequently met in the real world; and one might have thought that it would be of considerable intrinsic interest to know whether political parties, either in general or in particular cases, did or did not fulfill their pledges. In fact, however, this approach has been employed in a systematic way only very rarely. Perhaps political scientists are too afraid of appearing partisan; perhaps they are overly cynical about the bona fides of politicians; possibly they underestimate the importance that political parties in many countries attach to their platform and manifesto commitments.

Two studies that have been undertaken of the fit between partisan promises and partisan performance suggest that, contrary to widespread belief, the relationship between what political parties say they will do if elected and what they actually do (or attempt to do) is quite close. Political parties are "reliable" in this sense, even in the United States.

Pomper undertook a detailed examination of 1,399 platform pledges made by the Democratic party, or by the Republican party, or by both, between 1944 and 1964 (his study was published in 1968).[26] Predictably, the pledges made by both parties were the most

---

[25] Strictly, if the aim is to assess the promise/performance model rather than to see whether it makes any difference which party is in power, then party A's promise and its success or failure in fulfilling that promise should be compared, not with party B's promise and with what party B would or would not have done, but rather with how party A would have behaved if it had either made no promise in the relevant field or else promised the opposite of what it did. In other words, the relevant counterfactuals concern party A rather than any comparison between parties A and B. For this reason, the promise/performance model has to be used with care if the aim is to assess the influence of elections and parties.

[26] Gerald R. Pomper, *Elections in America: Control and Influence in Democratic Politics* (New York: Dodd, Mead, 1968), chap. 8. For a similar study of election

likely to be fulfilled; 85 percent of them were. But even the pledges made only by the party that subsequently captured the White House were far more likely to be fulfilled than not; the winning party's success rate indeed approached 80 percent.[27] Fulfillment of campaign pledges varied considerably by policy topic; performance was notably poor in three areas: labor, government (such matters as electoral college reform and home rule for the District of Columbia), and civil rights. Even so, Pomper was able to conclude that "voter endorsement of one party in presidential elections . . . makes a significant difference in future policies."[28]

I have made a comparable, though much less thoroughgoing, study of the promise-keeping performance of recent governments in Britain.[29] I extracted a number of the more important specific promises made by the Conservatives in the general election campaign of 1970 and by the Labour party in February 1974. I found that in almost every case a serious attempt had been made to fulfill the promise, even if the attempt was not in every case successful. Predictably, the Conservative and Labour governments both succeeded most often when their success or failure depended on their own actions and not to any significant degree on the actions of others. Thus, the Conservatives between 1970 and 1974 were able to abolish selective employment tax, as they had promised, making use of their overall majority in the House of Commons; but they were not able to reform the trade unions, since the success of trade union reform ultimately depended on the willingness of the unions themselves to cooperate, and their cooperation was not forthcoming.

The practical difficulties in the way of adopting the promise/performance approach are evident. Political promises are often highly unspecific; it is often very hard to know what, precisely, is to count as "fulfillment"; the promises that are the most specific, and the easiest therefore to deal with in research terms, are often not the most important. Nevertheless, this approach, like the longitudinal approach, seems to offer a so far neglected means of helping to answer the question, What do elections decide?

---

promises and subsequent legislative performance, see Richard C. Elling, "State Party Platforms and State Legislative Performance: A Comparative Analysis," *American Journal of Political Science*, vol. 23 (May 1979), pp. 383-405. The Elling article deals with Illinois and Wisconsin and contains a number of useful references to the literature in this field, at pp. 384 and 403-5.

[27] Pomper, *Elections in America*, p. 187.

[28] Ibid., p. 189.

[29] Anthony King, *Governing against the Odds: The British Political System in the 1980s* (Harmondsworth, England: Penguin Books, forthcoming).

The Correlational Approach. This approach is the one that has been employed most often. One takes one or more policy areas. One takes a number of countries (or states or provinces or local government units). One identifies a number of factors that might be expected to influence the policies adopted by the countries in each of the policy areas. One then tries to decide which of the factors thus chosen does the best job of explaining any variation that exists among the countries' policies. The notion of "explanation" in this kind of analysis is often construed statistically, and the correlational approach is usually associated with the use of quantitative techniques, though this need not be so, as we shall see.

The requirements of the correlational approach are quite straightforward in principle, even if they are often hard to meet in practice. At least four such requirements have to be met if the aim is to decide what difference it makes, in policy terms, which political party or coalition of parties is in power:

1. As in the case of the longitudinal and promise/performance approaches, the researcher needs to be able to identify which party or coalition of parties is in power at the moment or moments of time in which he is interested. It may be difficult to deal with constantly shifting coalitions in parliamentary systems and with presidential systems in which partisan control is divided between presidency and legislature.

2. The researcher needs to be able to sort the parties into two or more ideological or other categories so that variation among the parties in power can be related to variations in policy.

3. The policy areas and indeed the policies adopted must be comparable across the countries under study. Just as it would make little sense to compare health policy in one group of countries with foreign policy in another, so it would be misleading to compare policies that, while superficially similar in a number of different countries, were intended to serve quite different purposes and had very different consequences.[30]

4. The researcher, not least, has to be able to find, or generate, data that are relevant, accurate, comparable, and complete.

Needless to say, the practical difficulties of meeting this last requirement are often formidable, occasionally insuperable.

---

[30] For example, it would clearly be inappropriate to compare expenditure on highway construction in two countries if in one country highways were built to expedite the movement of tourists and freight while in the other they were built close to the country's frontiers solely for purposes of national defense.

We remarked a moment ago that the correlational approach is the one that has been employed most often. In fact, however, it is very doubtful whether it is the most suitable approach if one is trying to find out what elections decide, or what the relationship is between the political complexion of governing parties and the policies they adopt.

In the first place, all of the usual problems raised by the use of correlation techniques arise in a particularly acute form in this field. Much (though not all) correlational research focuses on a particular moment in time; but the moment chosen may for some reason be atypical or inappropriate. The countries chosen for study, possibly on the basis of the availability of data, may skew the findings or make them hard to interpret. The data themselves may be faulty, or may not measure what they purport to measure. Above all, the need for good data, and the desire of most researchers to study policy areas in which quantification is possible, may result—indeed have resulted—in a narrow concentration on certain policy areas at the expense of others. On occasion, very large conclusions have been based on very small quantities of data, like elephants dancing on the head of a pin.[31]

The second reason for doubting whether the correlational approach is as suitable as either the longitudinal or the promise/performance approach is, if anything, the more fundamental. The question, What do elections decide?, can really only be asked on a country-by-country (or state-by-state) basis: What do elections decide *in that country or in that state?* Similarly, the question, What difference does it make which party is in power?, is a question that is, or ought to be, country-specific. It is only in individual countries that elections take place and that parties or coalitions of parties govern. Suppose that a correlational analysis indicated that the proportion of GNP that a range of countries devoted to pest control varied as a function of GNP and was, in statistical terms, unaffected by the political complexion of the governments in power in those countries. Suppose further, however, that in country M the amount of money that should be spent on pest control constituted the major single point of controversy between the two major political parties, and that party A had a consistent record over time of spending large amounts on pest control, while party B equally consistently reduced the pest control budget. It would not be of much use to the people of M to tell them that they should ignore the issue of pest control when deciding how to vote on the ground that levels of spending on

---

[31] The temptation to name names will be resisted, but one writer concluded, in sweeping terms, that elections have little influence on public policy on the basis of only two studies both of which dealt with a very restricted range of policy variables.

pest control really had nothing to do with the politics of the party in power and were determined by GNP. Nor would it do them much good to be told that, although the political debate over pest control might be crucial at the moment, it was of no great long-term significance since the pest control policies of all of the major industrial countries would have converged by the year 2000. In other words, the scope and generality of correlational analysis are its greatest weaknesses as well as its greatest strengths.[32]

Be that as it may, the findings of correlational research are interesting—and, as it happens, the direction in which they point is not at all what it is widely imagined to be.

The largest single body of correlational literature concerns politics and policy in the American states. We shall not examine this literature in detail here, since *Democracy at the Polls* is primarily concerned with comparisons among countries rather than among subdivisions of countries.[33] But the central thrust of the literature is both

---

[32] The line of argument in the paragraph above has an important corollary. Given the great differences between different countries, and even between many American states, there is no particular reason to expect a good fit between, say, ideological positions in a number of countries and government spending in those countries. The British Conservative party is not the West German Christian Democratic Union is not the various conservative and Gaullist formations in France. The same .goes for the Democratic and Republican parties in different American states. Low correlations across countries, and even states, are therefore to be expected. If the correlations in fact turn out to be reasonably high, they deserve to be taken that much more seriously. By contrast with the correlational approach, the longitudinal (intertemporal) approach largely avoids this problem.

[33] Some of the more important contributions to the literature, in chronological order, are Richard E. Dawson and James A. Robinson, "Inter-party Competition, Economic Variables, and Welfare Policies in the American States," *Journal of Politics*, vol. 25 (May 1963), pp. 265-89; Thomas R. Dye, *Politics, Economics, and the Public: Policy Outcomes in the American States* (Chicago: Rand McNally, 1966); Richard I. Hofferbert, "The Relation between Public Policy and Some Structural and Environmental Variables in the American States," *American Political Science Review*, vol. 60 (March 1966), pp. 73-82; John H. Fenton and Donald W. Chamberlayne, "The Literature Dealing with the Relationships between Political Processes, Socioeconomic Conditions and Public Policies in the American States: A Bibliographical Essay," *Polity*, vol. 1 (Fall 1968), pp. 388-404; Ira Sharkansky, *Spending in the American States* (Chicago: Rand McNally, 1968); Charles F. Cnudde and Donald J. McCrone, "Party Competition and Welfare Policies in the American States," *American Political Science Review*, vol. 63 (September 1969), pp. 858-66; Brian R. Fry and Richard F. Winters, "The Politics of Redistribution," *American Political Science Review*, vol. 64 (June 1970), pp. 508-22; Gary L. Tompkins, "A Causal Model of State Welfare Expenditures," *Journal of Politics*, vol. 37 (August 1975), pp. 392-416; Michael S. Lewis-Beck, "The Relative Importance of Socioeconomic and Political Variables for Public Policy," *American Political Science Review*, vol. 71 (June 1977), pp. 559-66; and Edward T. Jennings, Jr., "Competition, Constituencies, and Welfare Policies in American States," *American Political Science Review*, vol. 73 (June 1979), pp. 414-29.

clear and very well known. Despite all of the qualifications and nuances that have been introduced into it, its central message is that the policies adopted by an American state, in a wide variety of policy fields, can be predicted far better by a knowledge of the state's economic and social structure than by a knowledge of its politics, whether its level of electoral participation, its degree of party competition, or the partisan composition of its legislature or executive. As Dye has written of his own work in this field, "I concluded that on the whole economic resources were more influential in shaping state policies than any of the political variables previously thought to be important in policy determination."[34]

The findings of the American state politics literature have been reinforced—or appear to have been reinforced—by the cross-national work of Cutright and his successors.[35] Cutright, Wilensky, and others have sought to determine the correlates of social policy in a large number of countries, seventy-six in the case of Cutright, between sixty and fourteen (depending on the specific focus of his analysis) in the case of Wilensky. Cutright took as his dependent variable a scale of national social security programs; Wilensky took "social security

[34] Thomas R. Dye, *Policy Analysis: What Governments Do, Why They Do It, and What Difference It Makes* (University, Ala.: University of Alabama Press, 1976), p. 29 (italics deleted). See also Thomas R. Dye, *Understanding Public Policy* (Englewood Cliffs, N.J.: Prentice-Hall, 1972), pp. 275-80.

[35] Phillips Cutright, "Political Structure, Economic Development, and National Social Security Programs," *American Journal of Sociology*, vol. 70 (March 1965), pp. 537-50; Harold L. Wilensky, *The Welfare State and Equality: Structural and Ideological Roots of Public Expenditures* (Berkeley, Calif.: University of California Press, 1975); Robert W. Jackman, *Politics and Social Equality: A Comparative Analysis* (New York: John Wiley, 1975); Ghulam M. Haniff, "Politics, Development and Social Policy: A Cross-National Analysis," *European Journal of Political Research*, vol. 4 (December 1976), pp. 361-76; Robert W. Jackman, "Socialist Parties and Income Inequality in Western Industrial Societies," *Journal of Politics*, vol. 42 (February 1980), pp. 135-49. Heidenheimer and Peters are the main contributors to a related literature that deals with a relatively small number of countries over a considerable period of time. See Arnold J. Heidenheimer, Hugh Heclo, and Carolyn Teich Adams, *Comparative Public Policy: The Politics of Social Choice in Europe and America* (New York: St. Martin's Press, 1975); Arnold J. Heidenheimer, "The Politics of Public Education, Health, and Welfare in the USA and Western Europe: How Growth and Reform Potentials Have Differed," *British Journal of Political Science*, vol. 3 (July 1973), pp. 315-40; B. Guy Peters and David Klingman, "Patterns of Expenditure Development in Sweden, Norway and Denmark," *British Journal of Political Science*, vol. 7 (July 1977), pp. 387-412; B. Guy Peters, "Social Change, Political Change and Public Policy: A Test of a Model," in Richard Rose, ed., *The Dynamics of Public Policy: A Comparative Analysis* (London: Sage Publications, 1976); B. Guy Peters, "Income Redistribution: A Longitudinal Analysis of France, Sweden and the United Kingdom," *Political Studies*, vol. 22 (September 1974), pp. 311-23; and B. Guy Peters, "Economic and Political Effects on the Development of Social Expenditures in France, Sweden and the United Kingdom," *Midwest Journal of Political Science*, vol. 16 (May 1972), pp. 225-38.

effort" as measured by the proportion of gross national product devoted to social welfare. Both writers concluded that economic and social factors were of overriding importance and that political factors mattered, if at all, only in influencing the timing of the introduction of new social welfare programs. Thus, Cutright: "The degree of social security coverage of a nation's population is most powerfully correlated with its level of economic development."[36] Similarly, Wilensky: "Over the long pull, economic level is the root cause of welfare-state development. . . . Ideology has no effect."[37]

In our present context, the work of Cutright, Wilensky, and their followers is open to five objections—which objections suggest that, at the very least, their work should not be taken to show more than it actually does. First, their research deals solely with social welfare provision: it tells us nothing about other aspects of public policy. Second, phrases like "over the long pull" should give us pause; the analyses of Cutright and Wilensky might have looked quite different if they had been related to, say, the period 1900–1920 instead of to, roughly, the 1950s. Third, neither Cutright nor Wilensky is concerned with the timing of policy innovations; but of course other writers might think that this was an issue of considerable importance: the fact that state medical insurance was introduced in Britain in 1911 but not in the United States till 1965 may not loom large in 1980, but it might have seemed quite important at any time between 1911 and 1965. Fourth, Cutright's and Wilensky's emphasis on the importance of economic and social factors is almost certainly in part an artifact of the very wide range of countries they chose to study, ranging in Cutright's case from the United States to Honduras and Jordan, in Wilensky's from the Netherlands to Nicaragua; their results might well have looked quite different if they had focused on countries at roughly similar stages of economic and social development.[38] Finally,

---

[36] Cutright, "Political Structure, Economic Development, and National Social Security Programs," p. 537.

[37] Wilensky, *Welfare State and Equality*, pp. 47, 45. Jackman in *Politics and Social Equality* sought to determine the correlates of social equality, defined in material terms, in sixty countries. On the basis of his measure of socialist party strength, he concluded (p. 200) that, "while countries where these parties are moderately strong tend to be more egalitarian than those where they are very weak or nonexistent, there is little difference in terms of social equality between the former and countries where socialist parties are very strong if not dominant." It looked, however, as though the socialist parties' apparent influence merely reflected the influence of strong labor unions. It does little violence to Jackman's findings to say that, like Cutright and Wilensky, he attaches relatively little importance to partisan (and, by implication, electoral) forces.

[38] This point is made by Francis G. Castles and R.D. McKinlay in "Public Welfare Provision, Scandinavia, and the Sheer Futility of the Sociological Approach to Politics," *British Journal of Political Science*, vol. 9 (April 1979), pp. 165-66,

if we are concerned with the political complexion of the party in power, and more specifically with elections, then Cutright's and Wilensky's conclusions may need to be qualified, since both writers dealt with a considerable number of countries that do not in fact have elections. The researches of Cutright and his successors in some ways resemble photographs taken from high-flying aircraft; the main features stand out, but much detail is lost—and the lost detail may be important.

In fact, contrary to widespread belief, most recent research into the correlates of public policy, within the universe of democratic states, does not support the findings of the American states literature or of the Cutright-Wilensky literature. On the contrary, it strongly suggests that it can matter a good deal which political party or coalition of parties is in power; it can matter who won the last election.

Hibbs, in the article already referred to, analyzes data from twelve Western European and North American nations in order to find out whether, as might have been predicted, socialist and labor governments, electorally dependent on working-class support, tend to pursue policies leading to relatively high inflation and low unemployment, while center and conservative governments, more dependent on the middle classes, tend to pursue policies leading to lower inflation and higher unemployment.[39] Hibbs's data, relating inflation and unemployment in the period 1960–1969 to the percentage of years during which socialist or labor parties participated in the executive between 1945 and 1969, broadly confirm this relationship.[40] For example, the four countries with both higher than median inflation and lower than median unemployment—Denmark, Finland, Sweden, and the Netherlands—were among the five countries with the longest postwar experience of socialist government, while the four countries with both higher than median unemployment and lower than median inflation—Britain, Belgium, the United States, and Canada—were among the seven countries with the least (if any) experience of socialist government since the war.[41] Hibbs observes: "The general conclusion of the study is

and Frank Castles and Robert D. McKinlay, "Does Politics Matter?: An Analysis of the Public Welfare Commitment in Advanced Democratic States," *European Journal of Political Research*, vol. 7 (June 1979), p. 184, n. 11.

[39] Hibbs, "Political Parties and Macroeconomic Policy," pp. 1468-75.

[40] See the scatterplots on pp. 1472-74. As so often in comparative analyses of this kind, Finland, Sweden, Norway, Denmark, and the Netherlands form a cluster, standing apart to a considerable extent from the other countries.

[41] Norway had a long history of postwar socialist government and lower than median unemployment, but also slightly lower than median inflation. In France and Italy, socialist parties formed part of the executive for less than half the 1945-1969 period, and, as predicted, they had unemployment above the median; but they also suffered from inflation somewhat above the median. With regard

that the macroeconomic policies pursued by left- and right-wing governments are broadly in accordance with the objective economic interests and subjective preferences of their class-defined core political constituencies."[42]

Castles and McKinlay went over somewhat the same ground as Cutright and Wilensky but came to strikingly different conclusions from them.[43] Castles and McKinlay, too, were concerned with social policy, but defined it rather more broadly than Cutright and Wilensky and included measures of infant mortality and spending on education as well as a measure of social welfare in the traditional sense. They also constructed a composite welfare index.[44] They took as their independent variables per capita gross domestic product and a number of political variables, including whether a secular or religious right-wing party had held office for more than half the period 1950–1974. On the basis of data from twenty-one advanced democracies, Castles and McKinlay conclude that the partisan coloration of governments is a factor of considerable policy significance:

> States characterized by an ideological dominance of the Right have significantly lower levels of performance on each of the four public welfare attributes. . . . Also, holding constant type of political structure and per capita gross domestic product, states without a dominant Right have higher levels of public welfare than those where there is such a dominant ideology.[45]

Two other studies have yielded similar findings with regard to the issue of social and income equality. Hewitt sought, for twenty-five modern industrial nations, to determine the sources of differences in the extent to which governments redistributed income, in the extent of actual income equality, and in the extent of social opportunity, measured by the availability of access to higher education.[46] One of his

---

to the one country remaining, Hibbs observes (p. 1471): "The principal exception to these generalizations is West Germany, which has been governed for most of the postwar period by the conservative CDU party and has experienced both low unemployment and low rates of inflation."

[42] Hibbs, "Political Parties and Macroeconomic Policy," p. 1468.

[43] Castles and McKinlay, "Does Politics Matter?" pp. 169-86.

[44] The index was constructed by standardizing and adding the authors' measures of the three other variables: total public education expenditure as a percentage of gross domestic product; total general government transfer payments (pensions, unemployment benefits, etc.) as a percentage of GDP; and infant mortality per thousand live births. "Does Politics Matter?" p. 172.

[45] Castles and McKinlay, "Does Politics Matter?" pp. 177, 179.

[46] Christopher Hewitt, "The Effect of Political Democracy and Social Democracy on Equality in Industrial Societies: A Cross-National Comparison," *American Sociological Review*, vol. 42 (June 1977), pp. 450-64.

independent variables was socialist party strength, measured as the annual average percentage of seats in the national legislature held by socialist and radical left-wing parties over the first twenty postwar years.[47] Hewitt also controlled for level of economic development and rate of economic growth. He concluded:

> The data do not support the argument that the relationship between socialism and equality is a spurious one when economic factors are taken into account. Socialism is consistently and positively related to government redistribution and a lowering of the share of the top income groups, regardless of the economic control being considered. . . . Strong socialist parties acting within a democratic framework appear to have reduced inequality in industrial societies.[48]

Dryzek, in another recent study, asked much the same questions and arrived at much the same answers.[49] He found no relationship at all between development and social equality within a universe of twenty advanced Western societies, and quite a strong relationship between equality and a class-politics factor that included a measure of socialist party strength akin to that employed by Hewitt.[50]

Most of the correlational literature, as we have seen, deals in one way or another with issues of equality and social welfare. Cameron, however, addresses himself to a different and in some ways broader question.[51] It is well known that government revenues and expendi-

---

[47] Note that this measure differs from those used by most other writers, being concerned with socialist party strength in the legislature rather than socialist participation in the executive. On the face of it, socialist participation in the executive would seem the more appropriate indicator; Hewitt himself (p. 451) refers to the election of "socialist governments." On the other hand, he defends his use of socialist strength in the legislature on the grounds "that socialist parties may have an impact even when in opposition as the non-socialist parties try to forestall the appeal of the socialists by adopting some of their policies" (p. 458).

[48] Hewitt, "Effect of Political Democracy and Social Democracy," p. 460.

[49] John Dryzek, "Politics, Economics and Inequality: A Cross-National Analysis," *European Journal of Political Research*, vol. 6 (December 1978), pp. 399-410.

[50] Dryzek concludes (p. 407): "The findings of this paper concerning the association of development (incorporating both economic and political development) with social equality within a universe of advanced Western societies are unequivocal: there is none. With respect to the impact of the class politics factor the results are more positive; they are consistent with the findings of Hewitt, who concluded that social democratic parties have had a positive impact upon social equality." Both Hewitt and Dryzek use measures of socialist strength over time that allow for the possibility of a cumulative socialist impact. Even if no single election makes a difference, a continuing socialist presence may.

[51] David R. Cameron, "The Expansion of the Public Economy: A Comparative Analysis," *American Political Science Review*, vol. 72 (December 1978), pp. 1243-61.

tures have expanded dramatically in recent years in all of the advanced capitalist states; but it is also true that their expansion has been much greater in some countries than in others. Cameron asks why this should be so, and considers seven possible explanations. Some of them are economic, such as the different countries' differing rates of economic growth, their varying degrees of reliance on indirect taxes and social security payments for revenue-raising purposes, and the varying degrees to which their economies are dependent on international trade and capital movements; others are political, such as the frequency of elections in a country and the extent to which its government is dependent on the support of left-wing political parties.[52] Cameron found that two factors were far more important than the others in explaining what he calls "the expansion of the public economy." One was the degree to which a country's economy was exposed to the world economy. The other, yet again, was the partisan makeup of the country's government:

> Contrary to the skeptics' view, politics is important in influencing the scope of the public economy. The partisanship of government is associated with the rate of expansion, and whether a nation's government was generally controlled by Social Democrats (and their leftist allies), or by nonleftist parties, provides a strong clue to the relative degree of change in the scope of the public economy.[53]

Finally, Field has shown that a correlational style of analysis can be used perfectly appropriately even when the dependent variable cannot (or need not) be quantified.[54] She studied the abortion policies of twenty-nine nations (including several with Communist regimes) and found that, among democratic countries, the greater the strength of leftist, non-Communist parties, the more liberal were policies on abortion, and that, again among democratic countries, liberal policies on abortion were more frequently adopted by socialist parties than by other parties. "Is there reason," Field asks, "to attribute some developmental or independent role to Socialist parties rather than to label the Socialist/policy correlations spurious?" She answers her question in the affirmative:

---

[52] Cameron's measure relating to partisanship is again different from that used by most other writers (see n. 47 above). Cameron's measure is "percent of government's electoral base composed of Social Democratic or Labor parties" (p. 1252; see p. 1248, n. 12).

[53] Cameron, "Expansion of the Public Economy," p. 1251.

[54] Marilyn J. Field, "Determinants of Abortion Policy in the Developed Nations," *Policy Studies Journal*, vol. 7 (Summer 1979), pp. 771-81.

Historical data about the types of political parties which have presided over legislative policy changes during the period 1920–74 suggest that the latter interpretation is too conservative. More radical abortion policies . . . have in seven out of ten instances been adopted by Socialist governments whereas the four changes limited to pure health grounds have all occurred under governments not controlled by Socialists.

In the mid-1970's, three countries with substantial Catholic populations liberalized their abortion policies. Two, Austria and Germany, had relatively new Socialist dominated governments. In the third, France, Socialists lost the election preceding law change by a small margin following a campaign in which abortion law reform was a prominent, Socialist-supported issue. The liberalization in France was more limited than that in Germany or Austria.[55]

Too much should not be made of the findings discussed in the last few paragraphs; they cover a limited number of policy areas, and some of them are open to the general objections lodged earlier to the correlational approach. Nevertheless, they are a powerful antidote to the view that economic and social factors in effect determine public policy, and that the influence of elections and political parties can therefore be safely ignored. It should be evident by now that they cannot.

Conclusions

The latter part of this chapter has dealt with a variety of the ways in which democratic elections influence the policies pursued by democratic governments. We have dealt chiefly with broad patterns of public policy in a number of countries over time. But we should never forget that specific elections may be crucial to the political life of the countries in which they occur. As Stokes pointed out in the last chapter, the 1975 federal election in Australia determined that one view of the Australian constitution should prevail over another; the 1977 election in India ended a period of increasingly authoritarian rule.[56] Going back further in time, we can easily identify other elections that brought the countries in which they occurred to a fork in the road: the 1860 presidential election in the United States, which resulted in the election of Lincoln and led directly to the Civil War; the two general elections of 1910 in Great Britain, which finally established the

---

[55] Ibid., p. 776.
[56] See chap. 11.

supremacy of the House of Commons over the House of Lords.[57] More generally, as Stokes also pointed out, election outcomes can determine the shape of a country's party system and therefore the structure in that country of political debate and controversy.[58]

In addition, it is important to remember that elections exist not just in retrospect but in prospect. We have concentrated on the consequences of elections, in the sense of what occurs after they have taken place. But of course politicians frequently act knowing in advance that their actions may have electoral repercussions. Years ago Miller and Stokes showed that congressmen's roll-call votes were, in many cases, powerfully influenced by their perceptions of their constituents' attitudes.[59] More recently, Tufte and others have argued that the periodic occurrence of elections gives rise to the phenomenon of the "political business cycle," as politicians in office seek to manipulate the economy to their own or their party's electoral advantage.[60] The mine that Miller and Stokes and Tufte have quarried is still rich in ore; much remains to be discovered about the relationship in democratic politics between electoral calculations and political, including governmental, decisions.

What do elections decide? Up to a point, we do not really know; or, more precisely, we do not know enough. We can list without difficulty the offices open to democratic election in various countries; and we can identify those countries in which elections lead more or less directly to the installation in office of one party or coalition rather than another. But we are not in a position to say with any confidence, in general terms, what the connections are between elections and their

---

[57] On the 1910 elections in Britain, see Neal Blewett, *The Peers, the Parties and the People: The General Elections of 1910* (London: Macmillan, 1972).

[58] Election outcomes can also send signals to those in power. The rise of the Poujadists in France, of the Glistrup party in Denmark (see n. 5 above), and of the Scottish National party and Plaid Cymru in Great Britain all had the effect of forcing those in government to take notice of widespread popular demands, even though none of the parties in question came anywhere near winning a majority of seats in the legislature.

[59] Warren E. Miller and Donald E. Stokes, "Constituency Influence in Congress," *American Political Science Review*, vol. 57 (March 1963), pp. 45-56.

[60] An enormous amount has been written, and is being written, about the political business cycle. Among the more important contributions to the debate are Edward R. Tufte, *Political Control of the Economy* (Princeton, N.J.: Princeton University Press, 1978); Bruno S. Frey, *Modern Political Economy* (New York: John Wiley, 1978); William D. Nordhaus, "The Political Business Cycle," *Review of Economic Studies*, vol. 42 (April 1975), pp. 169-90; C. Duncan MacRae, "A Political Model of the Business Cycle," *Journal of Political Economy*, vol. 85 (April 1977), pp. 239-64; Bruno S. Frey and Friedrich Schneider, "An Empirical Study of Politico-Economic Interaction in the United States," *Review of Economics and Statistics*, vol. 60 (May 1978), pp. 174-83; and Bruno S. Frey and Friedrich Schneider, "A Politico-Economic Model of the United Kingdom," *Economic Journal*, vol. 88 (June 1978), pp. 243-53.

consequences for public policy. In what types of democratic systems are elections and parties most likely to be influential? Which areas of public policy are most likely to be open to their influence? Under what circumstances are their interventions most likely to be crucial? We cannot answer these questions yet. For example, it may be that for many purposes it is sequences of elections and not just single elections that are important. Twenty consecutive years of social democratic, or right-wing, dominance may have far more important consequences than twenty nonconsecutive years that are interspersed with victories for the other side.

Of the three approaches to these issues discussed in this chapter, the longitudinal and the promise/performance appear, for the reasons given, to be the most promising. Both present difficulties, of course, and these have been set out at some length; but the difficulties have often been overcome in practice, and the gap between the amount of research that has been done using these approaches and the amount that could be done is enormous. Twenty-eight countries are under discussion in this volume. No work at all of this kind has been undertaken in connection with more than twenty of them.

So much is true. We do not know enough. Yet it would be quite wrong to end on so tentative a note. In recent years, many political scientists have rather pooh-poohed the place of competitive elections in the democratic political order. Elections are widely thought to be a defining characteristic of democracy, yet to be oddly lacking in practical consequences. This view has undoubtedly been reinforced by the comparative literature on the American states and by the work of writers like Cutright and Wilensky. Elections as major determinants of political outcomes have been discounted. If, however, one firm conclusion can be drawn from the last two chapters of the present volume, it is that elections count for a very great deal in the life of democratic nations. They frequently settle major constitutional issues; they influence, even determine, the structure of party systems; they can force changes of government; their results have a far greater impact on the content of public policy than is often supposed. Indeed the present volume, taken as a whole, should have the effect of vindicating the amount of attention that political scientists have paid ever since the 1940s to the forces shaping electoral choice. Academic observers may occasionally discount the importance of democratic elections. Politicians never do.

This chapter and the last have discussed what determines electoral outcomes and what is determined by them. In the final chapter of *Democracy at the Polls*, Jeane Kirkpatrick assesses the role of elections in democratic politics as a whole.

Bibliography

Cameron, David R. "The Expansion of the Public Economy: A Comparative Analysis." *American Political Science Review* 72 (December 1978): 1243–61.

Castles, Frank, and McKinlay, Robert D. "Does Politics Matter?: An Analysis of the Public Welfare Commitment in Advanced Democratic States." *European Journal of Political Research* 7 (June 1979): 169–86.

———. "Public Welfare Provision, Scandinavia, and the Sheer Futility of the Sociological Approach to Politics." *British Journal of Political Science* 9 (April 1979): 157–71.

Cowart, Andrew T. "The Economic Policies of European Governments, Part I: Monetary Policy." *British Journal of Political Science* 8 (July 1978): 285–311.

———. "The Economic Policies of European Governments, Part II: Fiscal Policy." *British Journal of Political Science* 8 (October 1978): 425–39.

Cutright, Phillips. "Political Structure, Economic Development, and National Social Security Programs." *American Journal of Sociology* 70 (March 1965): 537–50.

Dryzek, John. "Politics, Economics and Inequality: A Cross-National Analysis." *European Journal of Political Research* 6 (December 1978): 399–410.

Elling, Richard C. "State Party Platforms and State Legislative Performance: A Comparative Analysis." *American Journal of Political Science* 23 (May 1979): 383–405.

Field, Marilyn J. "Determinants of Abortion Policy in the Developed Nations." *Policy Studies Journal* 7 (Summer 1979): 771–81.

Frey, Bruno S. *Modern Political Economy.* New York: John Wiley, 1978.

Groth, Alexander J. *Comparative Politics: A Distributive Approach.* New York: Macmillan, 1971.

Haniff, Ghulam M. "Politics, Development and Social Policy: A Cross-National Analysis." *European Journal of Political Research* 4 (December 1976): 361–76.

Heidenheimer, Arnold J.; Heclo, Hugh; and Adams, Carolyn Teich. *Comparative Public Policy: The Politics of Social Choice in Europe and America.* New York: St. Martin's Press, 1975.

Hewitt, Christopher. "The Effect of Political Democracy and Social Democracy on Equality in Industrial Societies: A Cross-National Comparison." *American Sociological Review* 42 (June 1977): 450–64.

Hibbs, Douglas A., Jr. "Political Parties and Macroeconomic Policy." *American Political Science Review* 71 (December 1977): 1467–87.

Jackman, Robert W. *Politics and Social Equality: A Comparative Analysis.* New York: John Wiley, 1975.

Klein, Rudolf. "The Politics of Public Expenditure: American Theory and British Practice." *British Journal of Political Science* 6 (October 1976): 401–32.

Pomper, Gerald R. *Elections in America: Control and Influence in Democratic Politics.* New York: Dodd, Mead, 1968.

Siegel, Richard L., and Weinberg, Leonard B. *Comparing Public Policies: United States, Soviet Union, and Europe.* Homewood, Ill.: Dorsey Press, 1977.

Tufte, Edward R. *Political Control of the Economy.* Princeton, N.J.: Princeton University Press, 1978.

Wilensky, Harold L. *The Welfare State and Equality: Structural and Ideological Roots of Public Expenditures.* Berkeley, Calif.: University of California Press, 1975.

13

Democratic Elections, Democratic Government, and Democratic Theory

Jeane J. Kirkpatrick

The reality of political liberty consists in the details and the substance of actual institutions.

ERNEST BARKER, *Reflections on Government*

. . . as soon as the electoral process obtains a structural underpinning—the minute and multiple structural conditions that make for free voting—electoral multifunctionality rapidly comes to an end. If the voter is offered alternatives, if the candidates are free to compete, if fraudulent counting is impossible, then free elections do serve—everywhere—the purpose of allowing an electorate to select and dismiss officeholders.

GIOVANNI SARTORI, "Concept Misinformation in Comparative Politics"

Each language is a tradition, each word a shared symbol, and what an innovator can change amounts to a trifle.

JORGE LUIS BORGES, *Dr. Brodie's Report*

Democratic government, held in rather low esteem in most times and places in history, has never enjoyed as much prestige as it does today when its vocabulary and symbols are invoked by rulers of all kinds. Because the term "democratic" has become a counter in an ongoing political struggle for exceedingly high stakes, discussions of democratic government and democratic theory have been complicated and obfuscated almost beyond repair by the confusion of definition and norms, ideas and practices. Like so many of the key terms with which political scientists must deal, "democracy" can be approached descriptively, analytically, normatively, and polemically. To sort out

325

and decide among these uses, one must pass through a tangled semantic thicket.

It is conventional to begin considerations of the meaning of democracy with a bow to etymology—noting that *demokratia* was Greek for rule by the people. If taken seriously, this ritual bow introduces into the discussion a degree of constraint—it tells us that democratic government vests power in the people but leaves unanswered most of the important questions about what democracy is and is not. "The people" do not literally or directly rule, nor can anyone conceive a sensible scheme by which they might. Thus the etymological approach leaves us with a myth of ancient lineage: the myth of direct, popular democracy, which is no help at all in distinguishing among the many contemporary claimants who seek to appropriate the term for their preferred vision of a polity or to reap political benefits by appropriating to themselves the reputation of, in some sense, representing the people. Political scientists have not helped as much as they might.

Many of the difficulties surrounding the discussion of democracy in contemporary Western political science derive from different approaches to definition. One approach to defining democracy is descriptive and empirical. It begins with actual institutional practices and follows the logic of the empirical sciences, asking, What shall we call governments whose leaders are selected in periodic, competitive, inclusive elections? It answers, Such governments are termed "democratic." Practiced by persons gifted at seeing interconnections, the descriptive approach can illuminate whole systems by revealing the structures, functions, and interactions of all their parts. Carl J. Friedrich's *Constitutional Government and Democracy*,[1] Herman Finer's *Theory and Practice of Modern Government*,[2] E. E. Schattschneider's *Party Government*[3] are examples. This book and the others in the *At the Polls* series are products of the descriptive or empirical approach.

The second approach stems from the question, What is democracy?, which is usually interpreted to mean, What is real democracy? It answers by referring to such abstract norms as equality, majority rule, and self-fulfillment. This second approach is normative not because of a concern with ethics or values but because it postulates

---

[1] Carl Joachim Friedrich, *Constitutional Government and Democracy* (New York: Harper and Brothers, 1937).

[2] Herman Finer, *The Theory and Practice of Modern Government*, 2 vols. (London: Methuen and Co., 1932).

[3] E. E. Schattschneider, *Party Government* (New York: Farrar and Rinehart, 1942).

norms against which institutions can be measured, *ideas* of the good life or the good theory or the good institutions. It is "rationalist" or "intellectualist" in the sense that it regards concepts as appropriate measuring rods for reality. Peter Bachrach's *The Theory of Democratic Elitism*[4] and David Braybrooke's *Three Tests for Democracy*[5] are examples of books that define democracy in terms of moral ideals against which concrete institutions are measured. Robert Dahl's *Preface to Democratic Theory*[6] is an analytic variant of the rationalist approach. Bachrach and Braybrooke identify democracy with their vision of the perfect society; Dahl identifies it with the perfect theory.

So far this book has been primarily concerned with descriptions of institutions. In this chapter I propose to delineate these two approaches and to consider their implications for the discussion of the various institutions described in the earlier chapters.

The Descriptive Approach

The descriptive approach uses the word "democracy" as a symbol for specific patterns of behavior of persons in political contexts. The theory resulting from this approach is based on descriptions of electoral systems, legislative processes, interest groups, administrative behavior, voting behavior, political parties, and related institutional practices. The descriptive theory of democracy is a "middle range" theory about how specified institutional practices fit together to produce (roughly) predictable consequences. Like all other empirical theories, it consists of generalizations derived from the painstaking observation and description of institutional practices in various political contexts. The centrality of particular institutions to the definition reflects broad consensus about which practices are most crucial—across systems—to the observed pattern. There is broad consensus that elections are a central institution to one pattern of government, that most often termed democratic by empirical theorists.

J. S. Mill, for example, wrote, "The meaning of representative government is that the whole people or some numerous portion of them, exercise through deputies periodically elected by those the ultimate controlling power—which in every constitution, must reside

---

[4] Peter Bachrach, *The Theory of Democratic Elitism, A Critique* (Boston: Little, Brown, 1967).

[5] David Braybrooke, *Three Tests for Democracy: Personal Rights, Human Welfare, Collective Preference* (New York: Random House, 1968).

[6] Robert Dahl, *Preface to Democratic Theory* (Chicago: University of Chicago Press, 1956).

somewhere."[7] R. M. MacIver held the same view of the centrality of elections:

> Democracy, then, cannot mean the rule of the majority or the rule of the masses. . . . Democracy is not a way of governing, whether by majority or otherwise, but primarily a way of determining who shall govern by referring the question to public opinion and accepting on each occasion the verdict of the polls.[8]

And Joseph Schumpeter wrote: "The democratic method is that institutional arrangement for arriving at political decisions in which individuals acquire the power to decide by means of a competitive struggle for the people's vote."[9]

More recently Huntington and Moore observed: "Democracy exists where the principal office holders of the political system are chosen by competitive elections in which the largest part of the population can participate."[10] And Giovanni Sartori noted that elections are "the institution through which is operationalized the principle that legitimate power flows only from below."[11]

Of course, there are elections and elections. In some elections there is only one candidate or slate, and no choice; some elections feature several candidates or slates, and no choice; some offer several candidates all of whom are chosen by the incumbents; some provide limited choice and limited electorates (and exclude from participation some groups—ideological, racial, or other—not deemed worthy of participation); some elections are determined by fraud, some by violence.[12]

---

[7] John Stuart Mill, *On Representative Government* (London: J. M. Dent and Sons, 1910), p. 228.

[8] R. M. MacIver, *Web of Government* (New York: Macmillan, 1947), p. 148.

[9] Joseph Schumpeter, *Capitalism, Socialism and Democracy* (New York: Harper and Brothers, 1942), p. 269.

[10] Samuel P. Huntington and Clement H. Moore, "Conclusion: Authoritarianism, Democracy and One-Party Politics," in Samuel P. Huntington and Clement H. Moore, *Authoritarian Politics in Modern Society: The Dynamics of Established One-Party Systems* (New York: Basic Books, 1970), p. 509.

[11] Giovanni Sartori, *Democratic Theory* (New York: Praeger, 1967), p. 24. See also J. Roland Pennock, *Democratic Political Theory* (Princeton: Princeton University Press, 1979), and H. B. Mayo, *An Introduction to Democratic Theory* (New York: Oxford University Press, 1960). For a rather different perspective by a recent writer, see John Plamenatz, *Democracy and Illusion* (London: Longmans, 1973).

[12] For a recent treatment, see Guy Hermet, Alain Rouquie, Juan J. Linz, *Des elections pas comme les autres* [Different elections] (Paris: Presses de la fondation nationale des sciences politiques, 1978).

The authors cited above—Mill, MacIver, et al.—are not talking about just any process in which people put ballots in boxes or pull levers on machines. They are describing *competitive, periodic, inclusive* elections in which the chief decision makers in a government are selected by citizens who enjoy broad freedom to criticize government, to publish their criticisms, and to present alternatives. These defining characteristics of democratic elections distinguish them from other processes in which persons drop into boxes small pieces of paper bearing the names of living persons. Each of these characteristics has important consequences for the character of the process. *Periodic* elections limit the tenure of those elected and guarantee that before they or their group can continue in office, they will be required to submit themselves once again to the voters for approval or disapproval. *Competitive* elections are elections in which opposition and criticism of government and governors are permitted and alternative leaders compete for office, under conditions of free speech, press, and assembly on matters concerning public policy. *Inclusive* elections are those in which large proportions of adults are authorized to participate. *Definitive* elections are those whose outcomes largely determine the partisan composition of the resultant government.

According to descriptive theory, the elections that define democratic government are not merely symbolic legitimations or collective affirmations, they are the institution through which the adult members of a society select and empower certain persons and reject others to represent them in a specified and therefore limited role—as president, as congressman, as state legislator—for a specified and therefore limited period of time. It is noted that in democratic elections voters cast ballots as citizens of a territorial unit rather than in some more limited capacity (manager, producer, Catholic, father, woman).

The elections that figure so importantly in democratic theory command attention because of their role in the formation and duration of democratic governments, and not because of their position in a normative theory of democracy. There is here an important distinction: a democratic *government* is not a theory, it is not a set of ideas about how power and other values ought to be distributed in a society, it is not a whole social system. A government is a particular organization of offices and powers—that is, of institutions—whose incumbents make rules for a whole society and enforce them by using coercion whenever necessary and authorized. When the persons who make and enforce (by way of severe sanctions) rules for the whole society are chosen by democratic elections, the resulting government is termed "democratic" and the whole is called a "democracy" by political scientists and others employing an empirical approach to defining these terms.

"Democracy" becomes a category in a taxonomy based on how, by whom, and for how long rulers are chosen. It implies nothing about how government is organized or conducted beyond the fact that those who make authoritative decisions binding on the whole should be selected by the citizens under conditions of free competition and choice for limited terms. Descriptive democratic theories do not *prescribe* what the relations should be or must be between executive and legislative branches or how any branch of government should organize itself. However, descriptions are offered of the various ways that governments whose rulers are chosen in democratic elections do, in fact, organize themselves to carry out the basic functions of government.

These descriptions do not consist of observations only, but also of generalizations based on observed regularities, which may in turn be presented as empirical theories about the various types of governments based on competitive elections. Examples of such models of democracy are the "responsible party" model of parliamentary government, the theory of "consociational democracy," and the "Madisonian" or separation of powers model. Each of these models describes ways that power is organized in an actual system based on democratic elections.

The responsible party model postulates a parliamentary system in which two strong programmatic parties vie for electoral support with it understood (1) that the leader of the victorious party will become the head of government, (2) that the program of the victorious party will become the policy of the next government, and (3) that at a subsequent election the voters will hold those elected "responsible" for fulfilling the program mandated by the electorate. Whatever its accuracy or its subsequent polemical or normative uses, this model derived from descriptions and generalizations concerning British government.[13] The Madisonian or separation of powers model is a description of American government as a federal system in which power is divided vertically (among people, state, and nation) and horizontally (among the legislative, executive, and judicial branches of government), with decision-making power over constitutionally authorized subjects vested jointly in popularly elected executive and

---

[13] There is a large literature on this subject. Two especially notable works are Austin Ranney, *The Doctrine of Responsible Party Government* (Urbana, Ill.: University of Illinois Press, 1956), and Evron M. Kirkpatrick, "Toward a More Responsible Party System: Political Science, Policy Science or Pseudo Science," *American Political Science Review* (December 1971).

legislative officials who represent various constituencies.[14] The consociational model, offered as a description of how policies are actually made by elected representatives of the multiple parties of the Netherlands, Austria, Switzerland, and Belgium, describes a variant of legislative-executive relations and decision making in which a grand coalition is formed with parties represented according to their strength in the electorate, with the understanding that each party will have a veto on matters of principal concern to its constituency.[15]

These and other empirical models of democratic government describe how policy is made in systems which differ in their patterns of political cleavage and organization but have in common the selection of their chief decision makers through periodic, inclusive, competitive elections in which citizens enjoy broad freedom to criticize the government, to publish, and to organize.

Because these theories are derived from observation of actual governments, it is possible to "test" their truth content or accuracy, that is, to determine whether actual governments are organized and operate in the indicated manner. Because all the key terms in this definition have empirical referents, it is possible to determine whether the qualities in question are present in specific governments.[16] As long as democracy is thus defined, there is no problem in distinguishing democratic governments from others at either the analytical or the existential level.

Those who reject this usage of the term "democracy" do not deny that in some countries rulers *are* chosen in such elections. They only deny that this should be the criterion for deciding whether a government is democratic. They propose different definitions, which yield different conclusions about who is and is not democratic.

Ideas, Ideals, and Analytic Systems: The Rationalist Approach

The descriptive approach begins from the practices of persons, but the rationalist approach begins from ideas about how things ought to be.

---

[14] See especially Dahl, *Preface.*

[15] Arend Lijphart, *Democracy in Plural Societies: A Comparative Exploration* (New Haven: Yale University Press, 1977). Also, Eric A. Nordlinger, *Conflict Regulation in Divided Societies,* Occasional Papers in International Affairs, no. 29 (Cambridge, Mass.: Center for International Affairs, Harvard University, 1972); and Val R. Lorwin, "Segmented Pluralism: Ideological Cleavages and Political Cohesion in the Smaller European Democracies" *Comparative Politics,* vol. 3, no. 2 (January 1971), pp. 141-44.

[16] See especially Sartori, *Democratic Theory,* p. 24, and also Giovanni Sartori, "Concept Misinformation in Comparative Politics," *American Political Science Review,* vol. 64, no. 4 (December 1970), pp. 1033-53.

For observation and description, it substitutes speculation and ratiocination. Its central concern is normative rather than descriptive.

The rationalist (or intellectualist) approach to thinking about politics, government, or anything else involves measuring reality against concepts drawn not from experience but from speculation. The essentials of the procedure are the same whether the abstractions involve moral or analytical concepts. Either type of concept can function as a norm.

It is more than ironic that a political science that is often described as value free and ethically neutral should have spawned such a profusion of normative writing on democracy, and so many definitions which introduce into considerations of democratic government elaborate analytical and normative standards and rationalist habits of thought.

The literature of contemporary political science abounds in studies demonstrating the failure of some existing institution to approximate some postulated abstract standard. "Political equality" may be postulated as a requisite of democracy and defined as requiring exact mathematical equality in influence on elections or the composition of governments or the shape of policy. Specific electoral systems are examined to determine whether they achieve the goal of one man, one vote, or specific cabinet systems are scrutinized to see if each vote counts the same in determining the government's composition. Should the electoral system be anything other than a pure proportional system with one national constituency and no minimum number of votes required for representation, it will be concluded that the system does not ensure the closest possible correspondence between the percentage of votes cast and the percentage of seats won. Should a cabinet be found not to be the mathematically exact reflection of an electoral majority, or should it turn out not to have clearly articulated or implemented its program, it will be said to be unrepresentative. It will be argued that because institutions violate the principle of political equality and representation, they cast doubt on the government's claim to represent the people. So common are such arguments that one observer commented: "It is the specific nature of the electoral system and how well it approximates these ideal prescriptions which forms the bulk of the academic electoral system literature."[17]

Whole systems as well as specific institutions may be measured against analytical models of democracy. A good example of an analytical model of a whole system is Robert Dahl's *Preface to Democratic Theory*, which he describes as "to some extent an essay in definition."

[17] Louis J. Cantori, *Comparative Political Systems* (Boston: Mare, Holdbrooke Press, 1974), p. 238.

In that book Dahl provides three models of democracy: the Madisonian, the populistic, and the polyarchal. All three models consist of normative "requisites" constructed by "the method of maximization" whose strategy "is to specify a set of goals to be maximized." This strategy, Dahl tells us, permits democracy to "be defined in terms of the specific governmental processes necessary to maximize these goals or some among them."[18] The goal of the Madisonian model, Dahl asserts, is the "non-tyrannical republic"; the goal of the "populistic model" is the "maximization of popular sovereignty and political equality."[19] Having postulated these goals, Dahl proceeds by geometrical method, formulating axioms and corollaries, stating inferences, deriving conclusions, building models of what a Madisonian or a populistic democracy would "really" look like. Sometimes Dahl writes as though he were attempting to formulate an empirical theory, whose truth value could be established by "testing" key hypotheses. Thus, discussing the Madisonian model, he sets down two hypothetical conditions for "protection against factions and therefore against tyranny." He goes on:

> Because, as we have seen, the terms "factions" and "tyranny" have been given no specific meaning, as they stand these two hypotheses also have no specific meaning; i.e., no conceivable way exists by which we can test their validity. Hence they remain mere untestable propositions.[20]

Eventually, Dahl rejects Madison's theory, concluding that "as political science rather than as ideology the Madisonian system is clearly inadequate"[21]—in part because historical experience does not conform to the theory.

Other times he suggests that his models are purely analytical. When discussing the populistic theory of democracy, Dahl comments, "the theory of populistic democracy is not an empirical system. It consists only of logical relations among ethical postulates. It tells us nothing about the real world. From it we can predict no behavior whatsoever."[22] The theory, Dahl says, is "no more than an exercise in axiomatics, it tells us nothing about the real world."[23] Before constructing his third model, polyarchy, Dahl puts a new question: What are the necessary and sufficient conditions for maximizing democracy

---

18 Dahl, *Preface*, p. 2.

19 Ibid., p. 63.

20 Ibid., p. 27.

21 Ibid., p. 31.

22 Ibid., p. 63.

23 Ibid., p. 51.

in the real world?[24] By the time he has identified three "operationally meaningful" characteristics and some eight "conditions," Dahl is ready to conclude that the specified conditions exist nowhere. He proposes, therefore, to treat these conditions as norms—as the end of a continuum[25]—with "polyarchies" defined as organizations that rate high. Polyarchy is to be the real world variant of democracy, which Dahl defines as *"perfect* attainment of political equality and popular sovereignty."[26] Democracy is relegated to the realm of pure ideas. But polyarchy turns out to concern society rather than government, and the scene is set for replacing the demand for a perfect government with a still less attainable demand for a perfect society. Actual societies no more closely conform to abstract ideas than do actual political institutions.

The range of possible redefinitions of democracy or of any other word is almost boundless. Most often democracy is redefined to conform to a vision of ideal government. Socialists usually define democracy as involving socialism and reject nonsocialist theories or practices as not democratic. Peter Bachrach, for example, rejects descriptive definitions of democracy as "elitist" and identifies democracy with "self-realization" through active citizenship in a socialist community. For Bachrach, democracy is determined not by how rulers are chosen or by the legal limits on their powers but by governments' moral ideals and policy outcomes. Bachrach invokes "classical" democratic theory to support his argument that only if government has as its "paramount" objective the "maximization of the self-development of every individual"[27] should it be called "democratic." Yet it is hard to see how what is normally called the classical tradition in political theory could be stretched to cover this new demand.[28] For Bachrach, "The crucial question therefore is not whether the democratic method is open in a particular interpretation, but for whom it is open, and for what purposes."[29]

In Bachrach's view it matters little how a government is chosen or whether its powers are limited if the "many" remain preoccupied with their private lives while the "few" tend to the public business. Democracy, he asserts, depends on the quality and quantity of popu-

---

[24] Ibid., p. 64.

[25] Ibid., p. 75.

[26] Ibid., p. 63. Emphasis added.

[27] Bachrach, *Democratic Elitism*, p. 24.

[28] Bachrach's notion of "classical theory" seems to derive from Schumpeter, *Capitalism, Socialism and Democracy*, and the French Enlightenment and not at all from the Greek and Anglo-Saxon classics of political philosophy.

[29] Bachrach, *Democratic Elitism*, p. 23.

lar participation in politics, and both depend on the scope of popular control. Real democracy requires that the economy and large portions of the society be brought under the control of an active people. For Bachrach and allied thinkers, such as Christian Bay, Michael Parenti, and C. B. Macpherson,[30] democracy is identified with an idealized version of socialism in which egoism, self-interest, alienation, injustice are transcended in a just and happy community of autonomous, fulfilled, self-respecting individuals. Democracy, then, is a term reserved for the best *conceivable* form of government.

However, if democracy is defined in terms of ideals rather than institutions, any ideal will do. In his recent book on democratic government, for example, David Braybrooke poses three criteria or "tests" for evaluating "acceptable" democratic governments. "Passing all these tests," he asserts, "is a necessary condition of a government's being accounted fully acceptable in a democrat's eyes."[31] Braybrooke's postulated tests require that government respect the rights of citizens, provide for their welfare (including food, safety, clothing, shelter, medical care, education, congenial employment, and companionship),[32] and respect their "collective preferences" (defined as being "more fundamentally concerned with relating collective preferences to policies than with relating them to the choice of representative 'rulers' ").[33]

The arguments of Bachrach and Braybrooke differ in important respects, but they share the same fundamental methodology. Each postulates a vision of what a more moral society would be like. Though Bachrach purports to derive his conception from "classical political theory" and Braybrooke to ground his in the views of "advocates of democracy," both postulate abstract speculative standards of moral perfection realized nowhere and probably incapable of realization through any institutions that exist now or have ever existed. Because they propose as criteria by which a government should be classified democratic or nondemocratic moral *ideals* without empirical referents, it is a foregone conclusion that no government will be classified as democratic. There will only be varieties of nondemocracies.

Like most contemporary authors of prescriptive definitions, neither Braybrooke nor Bachrach makes a serious effort to justify the

---

[30] Christian Bay, *The Structure of Freedom* (Stanford: Stanford University Press, 1958); C. B. Macpherson, *The Real World of Democracy* (Oxford: Clarendon Press, 1966), and *The Life and Times of Liberal Democracy* (Oxford: Oxford University Press, 1977); and Michael Parenti, *Democracy for the Few* (New York: St. Martin's Press, 1974).

[31] Braybrooke, *Three Tests*, p. 150.

[32] Ibid., p. 143.

[33] Ibid., p. 152.

moral principles he postulates as the defining characteristics of democ-racy or seriously to inquire whether or how they might be institutiona-lized. Instead of undertaking the sort of inquiry into the claims of alternative ends with which Plato began the *Republic*, contemporary ethical prescriptivists tend to write as though their goals—self-realization, equality, or welfare—were universally shared, for self-evident reasons.

Braybrooke, who has empirical aspirations even in this book, claims to base his theory on "how real people use certain terms of ordinary language and what they would agree on as accurately de-scribing the implications with which they use them."[34] But he acknowledges that no survey of real people—not even of real British philosphers—would confirm his description of the views of the "advo-cates of democracy."

Other Rationalist Critiques. The range of rationalist theories of democracy is wide. One related but not identical view holds that elections, even if they are competitive, periodic, and inclusive, have only symbolic consequences because the "real" locus of power is determined by the unequal distribution of wealth in society. An un-ambiguous statement of this radical Marxist view is provided by Albert Szymanski, who asserts:

> The general belief in the sovereignty of the masses as exer-cised through voting is an effective tool for securing the sovereignty of the capitalist class—which is all the more secure by being founded on the consent of the governed. The act of voting every several years acts to legitimate the rule of the capitalist class as firmly as did the coronation of emperors or popes in the past.[35]

There are many variations on the theme that elections and parliaments do not "decide" anything important because important decisions are vested elsewhere—frequently in an economic elite. C. Wright Mills, for example, argues that regardless of the outcomes of elections or the composition of parliaments, "big" decisions are made by a unified "power elite" of powerful men who ultimately control the political, economic, and military domains.[36] Herbert Marcuse insists that the institutions of liberal democracy are part of a system of "repressive

---

[34] Ibid., p. 7.

[35] Albert Szymanski, *The Capitalist State and the Political Class* (Cambridge, Mass.: Winthrop, 1978), p. 121.

[36] C. Wright Mills, *The Power Elite* (New York: Oxford University Press, 1956), p. 228.

tolerance" which induces a false consciousness that blinds the masses to their true interests and precludes popular control over government.[37]

Though they differ on many questions, the authors of such analyses have in common: (1) some vision of what "real democracy" would be like; (2) a conviction that existing governments based on competitive, periodic elections do not conform to the vision of what a real democracy would be like; and (3) a desire to reserve the terms "democracy" and "democratic" for ideal systems for which there are no empirical referents, no examples to which they can point to illustrate their conception. There are only perfect ideals and imperfect institutions. Frequently, the otherworldly quality of these discussions is compounded by neglect of serious consideration of how the postulated ideals *might* be embodied in real institutions—discussion comparable, for example, to Plato's plan for the ideal state.

The Case against Rationalism. In contemporary political science the search for the good institution—defined as one which conforms to an analytical model—is almost as widespread as the concern with the good society in an earlier age. The proclivity of contemporary political scientists for building models of reality against which reality can be measured testifies to the powerful rationalist bias of much contemporary social science. Karl Popper, T. D. Weldon, Giovanni Sartori,[38] and others have argued that there are good reasons why measuring institutions against abstract standards is a bad practice. There are at least three important reasons why it is inappropriate and misleading to define democracy (or any other form of government) by way of abstract ideas or models for which there are no empirical referents: first, because the relationship of the ideal (whether a moral ideal or an intellectual construct) to the real is such that empirical indicators cannot be specified for the ideals and thus have no fixed, knowable meaning; second, because abstract ideas and ideals inevitably result in the devaluation of actual values and actual institutions; and third, because abstract models without empirical content distort and frequently falsify the relations among values and institutions. The requirements of logic and of governments are not at all identical.

The Absence of Empirical Referents. Pure ideas provide no standards for their own measurement. They only seem to. There are no empirical referents by which we can recognize pure equality or perfect

---

[37] Herbert Marcuse, *One Dimensional Man* (New York: Beacon Press, 1964).

[38] Karl Popper, *The Open Society and Its Enemies*, 2 vols. (Princeton: Princeton University Press, 1966); T. D. Weldon, *The Vocabulary of Politics* (Baltimore: Penguin Books, 1955); and Sartori, *Democratic Theory*.

democracy or self-realization. How, for example, can one determine whether a person has "realized" or "fulfilled" himself? By asking him? Usually observers who propose this standard do not accept subjective evaluations as evidence of self-realization. After all, the subject may be confused. He may only *think* he has been fulfilled. Peter Bachrach suggests that we can identify the extent of self-realization by the degree of participation in the life of the community, but that is problematic. How do we know that all persons are fulfilled in active citizenship? What about those who prefer solitary activities? Are they too alienated to know their own true will? And what about participation that is forced, or unthinking? Is all participation equal? In the absence of empirical referents, disagreements about true and false participation can only be resolved arbitarily—by force and fiat.

Because no indicators link them to recognizable practices, relating abstract ideals to real institutions becomes an arbitrary exercise in stipulation and assertion. One can, to be sure, stipulate whatever one can conceive, but one cannot realize anything that one can conceive. Measuring the actual against the conceivable implies that the conceived standard is relevant to reality, but there are no grounds except faith for supposing that ideals or models which do not exist can be created. For this reason, Sartori asserted: "It is not my purpose to talk about something that does not exist, and I am unable to judge what exists by using a yardstick which in its turn does not exist."[39]

Using abstract standards to measure real institutions and political systems is sometimes defended on grounds of the superior "clarity" of analytic categories, which are said to illuminate relationships and characteristics that may be obscured by the greater ambiguity of empirical reality. But it is impossible to be sure what is being "clarified." Moreover, most social scientists find it difficult to bear in mind that their purely analytical models are devoid of existential relevance and slip into assuming that "pure" participation or equality or majority rule is a norm against which it is useful to judge the adequacy of reality.

"Forms" and Substance. Thinking about politics and society independently of actual systems is almost always misleading. Real values exist in contexts and derive their substance at least partially from those contexts. Dahl's search for the "meaning" of tyranny in the Madisonian system is a case in point. His efforts at abstract definition lead him to conclude that the concept "seems to have no opera-

---

[39] Sartori, *Democratic Theory*, p. 46.

tional meaning in the context of political decision-making" and further, "if tyranny has no operational meaning then majority tyranny has no operational meaning."[40] But tyranny has a meaning in Madison's arguments: the meaning it had for Madison and his contemporaries. It is only the effort to abstract the concept of tyranny from its concrete context and render it a universal form that deprives it of meaning.[41] This kind of concept stretching and the theories built upon it have been incisively analyzed by Sartori.

Ideas and Institutions. Since the world has not arrived at Hegel's promised end where the rational becomes the real and the real, the rational, there exists no experience with the realization of abstract ideas in society. Many ideas can probably never be realized. Not everything that can be conceived can be created. One can conceive a unicorn, describe it, destroy whole forests in a determined effort to find one, and still finally fail. Since institutions exist not in the minds of philosophers but in the habits and beliefs of actual people, they can be brought into existence only as people are persuaded or coerced into conforming their thoughts, preferences, and behavior to the necessary patterns. History and recent experience indicate that some kinds of goals and plans cannot finally be implemented, no matter how much persuasion or coercion is employed. Moreover, in the absence of experience there is no way to estimate accurately the feasibility, the costs, even the concrete desirability of an idea or ideal.

In actual societies, political principles do not exist in isolation; they interact, and the effort at maximization begins at some point to undermine itself. These dynamics are well known to political philosophy. They are one source of the famous "mixed" constitutions which Plato advocated in the *Laws* after he had rather reluctantly concluded that a constitution based on the maximization of some one principle would fail. A constitution based on either liberty or aristocracy would, he concluded, lack some important elements. But by combining in a single constitution the principles of democracy and aristocracy, Plato thought it would be possible to secure the values of both liberty and wisdom.[42]

---

[40] Dahl, *Preface*, p. 24.

[41] On the problems involved in just such "concept stretching," see especially Sartori, "Concept Misinformation." The Declaration of Independence, the debates of the Congresses, and a great many other public decrees spell out the indicators of tyranny which Madison had in mind.

[42] Plato, *The Laws*. Plato probably never abandoned the view that rule of a true philosopher king would be preferable, but experience persuaded him that "there is no such mind anywhere," and that this being the case, the best of all actual constitutions would *not* be based on the principle of maximizing the imperfect wisdom of an actual man, but on mixing principles which would limit one another.

Instead of clarifying the relation of values to regimes, analytical models and definitions based on maximizations of "pure" ideas falsify the actual relations. For example, it is not likely that a system that realized "pure" majority rule or political equality would be equal or superior to regimes where these desired qualities exist in less "pure" form. Probably a government that seriously attempted to maximize a single principle, such as majority rule, would rather quickly self-destruct. A government whose only value was the maximization of popular sovereignty could not preserve free speech or assembly against a majority that desired to silence an opposition; by failing to protect minority rights, it would destroy the possibility of realizing the principle it set out to maximize. A single-minded effort to maximize political equality in the adoption of policies (another of Dahl's hypothetical conditions) would likewise lead to the destruction of democracy by destroying leadership and liberty.

The pursuit of the perfectly (mathematically) just electoral system which would ensure that each vote had precisely the same weight as all others in determining the composition of a legislature has more than once illustrated the pitfalls of trying to maximize one value in one institution without adequate appreciation of the consequences for other values expressed in other institutions such as parties, legislatures, cabinets, and stable governments. Most of the constitutions written since World War II display better understanding of the interaction of value-oriented institutional practices than did the founding fathers of the Weimar Republic, who wrote into their constitution a "pure" system of proportional representation in the belief that it would make for purer democracy. But even though it is generally understood today that electoral systems influence the character and organization of cleavages in societies and legislatures and affect the capabilities and stability of governments, among political scientists there remains a powerful tendency to judge electoral arrangements in the abstract on the basis of whether they maximize some one value also considered abstractly. The current debate on the American electoral college, for example, has produced a plethora of articles demonstrating the consequences of the electoral college for the principle of one man, one vote. One widely cited study demonstrates that given certain rather elaborate (and dubious) assumptions, a vote cast in New York has 3.312 times the weight in determining the outcome as one cast in the District of Columbia.[43] Such inequalities tend to be regarded as a prima facie case for abolition of the offending institution.

---

[43] John F. Banzhaf III, "One Man, 3.312 Votes: A Mathematical Analysis of the Electoral College," *Villanova Law Review*, vol. 13 (Winter 1968), pp. 304-31.

A further consequence of measuring real institutions against "pure" principles is that it leads almost inevitably to devaluation of the real, as actual regimes fail to measure up. Actual institutions deviate from the abstraction much as actual triangular objects deviate from the definition of a triangle. Since actual institutions never very closely resemble ideas—being too complex, too varied, too multifunctional, too unpredictable and uncontrollable—they never conform to ideals or analytical constructs. No regime ever achieves the total control over society, culture, and personality postulated by the concept of totalitarianism,[44] no king's personal power ever equaled that of the ideal absolute monarchy, no hereditary nobility ever conformed fully to the conception of aristocracy. Curiously enough, the practice of measuring actual institutions against abstract norms that is the very essence of rationalism in political thought leads to the conclusion that the institution is faulty rather than to reexamination of the standard. Reality is always deficient; the analyst is always right. This relation between pure ideals and adulterated realities explains the affinity of "analytical" social science and utopianism.

Words and Experience: The Case for a Descriptive Definition of Democracy

There is no law against giving new meanings to old words, but it rarely facilitates communication or clarifies arguments. It is sometimes possible to strengthen an argument by stating it in very abstract language or by redefining old terms. The argument for "popular rule" of the economy, for example, seems more attractive if presented as a return to "classical democracy" than as a demand for socialism; the theory is more appealing than a concrete plan for the confiscation of property and the use of coercion to impose equality. But such distinc-

---

[44] See among others, Carl J. Friedrich, Michael Curtis, Benjamin R. Barber, *Totalitarianism in Perspective: Three Views* (New York: Praeger, 1969). Note however, that the concept of totalitarianism has been criticized on precisely those grounds. The problem of moving from the abstract to the empirical domain is, of course, as old as philosophy itself. There is an interesting and suggestive tendency among contemporary social scientists to be willing to rely on imperfect or gross measurements to solve the problem. The result is a model which relies on an impure measurement to relate the pure ideal to the real. Dahl provides an interesting example of this juxtaposition of purism and pragmatism in his *Preface to Democratic Theory*, when after an exhaustive examination and painstaking statement of the eight "conditions" of democracy he notes that there is "at present no known way of assigning meaningful weights" to them but adds that "even without weights" it might be useful to "metricize" the scales, establishing thereby "arbitrary, but not meaningless classes of which the upper chunk might be called 'polyarchies' " (pp. 73-74).

341

tions, though the key to successful propaganda, have no standing in scientific discourse.

The most important reason for preferring a descriptive definition of democracy is that it leaves us talking about real governments run by real people in the real world. A closely related reason for preferring a descriptive definition of democracy is that it conforms to the traditional usage in our civilization. Yet another related reason is that empirical referents for key terms can be provided. We can know what we are talking about.

Using language in familiar ways and using concepts which can be referred to specific experiences facilitates communication and understanding; and though that is a great advantage (especially as compared with the alternatives), it is not the only reason, or even the most compelling reason, why the familiar usage is to be preferred in the discussion of political, social, and economic matters such as democracy. The most important reason for preferring conventional usage is that a term like democracy has a history, and conveys that history. Sartori emphasizes this point when, in his distinguished study of *Democratic Theory*, he asserts, "the term democracy is a carrier of historical experience whose meaning is stabilized."[45] Its meaning is rooted in specific events and processes, and it is not possible to define away this historical content merely by stipulating this or that new meaning for the word. To quote Sartori again, "A word like democracy acquires a definite, helpful and usable meaning only if we remember that it is an abbreviation summarizing the acquisition and values of a civilization. Since all this is only *implied*, it is easily forgotten."[46]

The historical content of what empiricists call democracy is inextricably bound up with the long struggle against arbitrary power—with the notions of liberty, individual rights, consent, and representation in terms of which that struggle against church, state, and guild was carried out. Modern democratic institutions had their origins not in the forests of Germany but in the persistent efforts of Englishmen to limit the power and jurisdiction of their kings. These efforts began before a reluctant King John was persuaded to sign the Magna Carta early in the thirteenth century, but even though dramatic progress was registered in the Bloodless Revolution, it was not until the eighteenth century that the outlines of modern democracy began to emerge in new doctrines of legitimacy that made just government dependent on the consent of the governed (and suggested thereby that legitimate

---

[45] Sartori, *Democratic Theory*, p. 221.
[46] Ibid., p. 224.

power flowed only from the "people"); in doctrines of contract that not only attributed natural rights to the people but asserted that the protection of these rights was the very purpose of government; in doctrines of representation that claimed each was entitled to speak for himself about "where the shoe pinches" and how laws affect him.

The organization of offices called democratic government became possible only as the triumph of liberalism established the credibility of claims that individuals had interests and rights distinct from those of any collectivity, that legitimate governments must respect these rights and take cognizance of these interests, and that the best way of ensuring this is to make rulers representatives chosen by and responsible to the citizens. The actual history of democratic governments definitively establishes that the expansion of individual liberty, the rise of popular rule through institutions of representation, and the institutionalization of limits on government's power occurred together. From the beginning, then, relations among individual liberty, limited government, and popular rule existed in fact as well as in theory, and this existential relation gives the notion of "liberal democracy" a substantive content which is neither arbitrary nor capable of being defined away.

Practices and Values. So far I have emphasized two approaches to defining democracy, the descriptive, which calls democratic any political system characterized by certain stipulated practices, and the normative or rationalist, which begins from a vision—analytic or moral—that has no base or analogue in experience. Because people are value maximizers and political institutions are stabilized (structured) patterns of value-oriented interactions,[47] the descriptive approach involves one in consideration of values; and because visions of the good life are realized only through institutions, the rationalist approach involves one in the consideration of institutions.

However, the descriptive and rationalist approaches to relations among values and institutions differ markedly. Here too, the descriptivist and the rationalist start from different questions. The former asks, What values are embodied in and maximized through characteristic democratic practices? The rationalist asks, What institutional practices would most effectively maximize the stipulated values? The descriptivist works from institutions, the rationalist from ideas about

---

[47] Here and throughout the following discussion I utilize the conception of value-institutional practices developed by Harold D. Lasswell, to whom my debt is large. The most comprehensive presentation of these is found in Harold D. Lasswell and Abraham Kaplan, *Power and Society* (New Haven: Yale University Press, 1951).

what institutions should be. The descriptivist moves from the concrete to the abstract, the rationalist from the abstract to the concrete. Naturally these two approaches yield very different results. The derivation and function of values in the rationalist approach are clear; the remainder of this chapter deals with the derivation of values and standards of value in descriptive analysis.

The point of departure is the identification of values and value processes in functioning institutions. Any serious effort to identify the values present in the various institutions of a political system readily illuminates their *multiplicity, diversity, interrelation,* and *complexity.* These characteristics are the key to a descriptive approach to evaluation and prescription.

In his structural-functionalist phase, Gabriel Almond emphasized that political institutions are multifunctional: each institution is involved in the performance of several functions in the political system. The point was not only that courts are involved in legislating and implementing as well as adjudicating, or that legislatures are involved in implementation and adjudication, but that multiple functions essential to government are performed in, through, and around each political institution. Thus, political parties perform the functions of leadership recruitment, socialization, screening, communicating, and structuring the electorate, as well as the more explicit functions of nominating candidates and articulating political orientations; and electoral systems perform the functions of aggregating opinions, building consensus, reinforcing or fracturing parties and coalitions as well as establishing rules for counting votes and distributing seats. Observation of political institutions establishes not only that any given institution performs multiple functions but also that multiple values are involved in those functions and that the functions and values occur in endlessly complex webs of goals, habits, and rules.

The values pursued through an electoral system may include:

• *participation,* because the electoral system is a vehicle through which masses take part in decisions affecting who shall rule and to what broad ends

• *representation,* because an electoral system is the mechanism through which voters may choose (normally among specified alternatives) the persons they regard as most likely to "represent" in their decisions, the voters' views and values

• *equality,* because an electoral system is a mechanism for weighting the influence of various kinds of persons in specified political decisions

- *consensus,* because in specifying the levels and units in which votes will be aggregated and the rules for translating votes into seats, an electoral system may encourage alliances or reward divisions
- *stability,* because an electoral system may enhance the stability of governing coalitions by encouraging or discouraging fragmentation, by making governments more or less vulnerable to schism and defeat
- *majoritarianism,* or popular rule, because an electoral system can strengthen and clarify or weaken and obfuscate links among candidates, programs, and parties, thus facilitating or discouraging the participation of masses in decisions on policies
- *strong government,* because an electoral system can encourage or inhibit construction of coalitions capable of confronting difficult issues without falling apart or being toppled

Further complicating the relations among institutions and values is the fact that each of these values is integrally related to other values. Representation, for example, is valued because of its relation to government by consent, responsiveness, limited power, and participation. Participation is valued because of the relation to community, polity, and citizenship. Equality is valued because of its relation to beliefs about the natural (and equal) dignity of man (and woman) and about democracy and justice. Stability is valued because of its relations to social peace, safety, and strong government, which last is valued because of its relations to safety, effectiveness, majoritarianism, and so forth.

But though these and other values are involved in democratic electoral systems, they are not equally involved. The primary functions of an electoral system are to provide a vehicle for mass participation in decisions and to implement one stage of the representative process. However, secondary values and functions are also important because of their involvement with the primary functions and with the total system. Representation, for example, depends not just on casting and counting votes, but on some institutionalized practice through which candidates are designated and labeled, on a campaign that features publicity, discussion of public problems, a free press and free assembly, on opportunities for communication, and on the periodicity of elections, which provides the electorate an opportunity to throw the rascals out. An electoral system which offers voters a wide range of alternatives increases the electorate's opportunity of voting for someone with whom they are in nearly perfect agreement but greatly complicates the task of building a stable majority coalition—that is, it decreases the likelihood of a government's emerging which will be capable of translating majority views into public policy or otherwise responding to problems. The dynamics of these interrelationships make it impossible for all values to be maximized equally. When an electoral law is adopted or amended, choices are present—whether or not the participants are aware of them. Should equality be maximized at the expense of consensus, stability, and the capacity to govern? Should representation of all opinions be maximized even if the means will permit or encourage the proliferation of parties and undermine the potential for majoritarianism and stability? Should majoritarianism be given priority over equality and representation of all points of view?

How can and should such questions be resolved? On what basis can we prefer one value to others? Can one who has described democracy in terms of existing practices decide that a given institution that exists as part of a democratic system should be reformed to emphasize some other value? Does the descriptive approach lead inevitably to the conclusion that whatever is, is right? How can we move from describing value-institutional practices to criticizing or reforming them? And if all value choices entail choosing among values on grounds other than that they exist, do the descriptive and rationalist approaches merge at the crucial point where one must stand to create a regime or improve an existing one?

If the descriptive approach does not yield a definite basis for judging the adequacy or desirability of any institutional practice, then it cannot help us judge the merits (the value) of alternative ways of nominating candidates, organizing electoral systems, utilizing media, participating in a polity.

There is, of course, a more basic question: whether the descriptive approach can ever provide definitive grounds for preferring a democracy to a monarchy, a theocracy, or a revolutionary totalitarian regime. This is a more difficult problem, though I believe that experience provides us grounds for choosing. However, once the choice of a democratic system is made, the descriptive approach provides a distinctive perspective on questions about which is better, proportional representation or single-member districts, programmatic or nonideological parties, candidate selection vested in party leaders or ordinary voters, basic access to media on the basis of ability to pay or on governmental regulation, and so on. Criteria for making such decisions are present in the descriptive perspective. That perspective is characterized by:

- an appreciation of the extent to which context shapes practices, and practices contexts
- an appreciation of the multiplicity of values involved in apparently simple institutional practices

- an appreciation of the existence and importance of unplanned, unintended patterns of interaction that grow up around formal institutions and their vulnerability to changes in rules and formal structures
- some understanding of the interaction among the relevant values and practices
- some understanding of the impact of various institutional practices on who is attracted into the political arena and who is successful in it

Because the descriptive approach focuses attention on the *constellation* of values involved in institutional practice and never on a single value, it assumes always that variations in one aspect of a value-institutional process will affect other values. It anticipates that variations in rules have consequences for the surrounding and supporting extralegal associational life and attempts to anticipate the effects of their interactions. It affects both questions and answers about value-institutional practices. Institutions and values are never considered in the abstract but always in specified contexts. One does not ask, What is the best electoral system? but rather, Assuming that one desires to produce a popularly elected stable government that represents a majority, is responsive to it, has leaders capable of governing, a capacity for action, and a degree of continuity in a nation with complex social cleavages, weak parties, and a tradition of regime instability, what is the best electoral system? Just such considerations of previous experience, patterns of social and regional cleavages, and goals guided the architects of the Federal Republic of Germany, France's Fifth Republic, and the contemporary Spanish government in designing their electoral systems.

From the descriptive perspective no single value is absolute, and none has absolute priority. The total process of democratic government has priority. The value of each aspect of the process depends on its contribution, in its actual context, to the desired outcome. An institution is therefore never judged on the basis of a single value.

As equality never becomes *the* criterion for judging which is the best electoral system, turnout or participation never becomes *the* criterion for judging the best democratic system. Each is important, but each is only one dimension of a democratic system, only one of a constellation of values present in any system in which rulers are chosen in periodic, competitive, inclusive, and definitive elections.

Obviously, the descriptive approach requires wide comparative knowledge of value-institutional practices in diverse regimes. Only comparative knowledge makes it possible to identify the contextual factors and the institutional configurations associated with a given institutional practice, the practices and values that fit a given pattern of candidate selection or party organization or popular participation or media rules. The great contribution of this volume and, indeed, of the various studies in the *At the Polls* series is to provide precisely this: the information required to make sound judgments, realistic evaluations, and effective reforms.

Bibliography

Bachrach, Peter. *The Theory of Democratic Elitism, A Critique.* Boston: Little, Brown, 1967.

Barker, Ernest. *Reflections on Government.* London: Oxford University Press, 1942.

Burke, Edmund. *Reflections on the Revolution in France.* Edited by Thomas H. P. Mahoney. New York: Liberal Arts Press, 1955.

Dahl, Robert. *Pluralist Democracy in the United States: Conflict and Consent.* Chicago: Rand McNally, 1967.

————. *Preface to Democratic Theory.* Chicago: University of Chicago Press, 1956.

Friedrich, Carl J.; Curtis, Michael; and Barber, Benjamin R. *Totalitarianism in Perspective: Three Views.* New York: Praeger, 1969.

Hamilton, Alexander; Madison, James; and Jay, John. *The Federalist Papers.* New York: New American Library of World Literature, 1961.

Mayo, H. B. *An Introduction to Democratic Theory.* New York: Oxford University Press, 1960.

Mill, J. S. *Considerations on Representative Democracy.* Edited by Currin V. Sheilds. New York: Bobbs-Merrill, 1958.

————. *On Liberty.* Edited by Aubrey Castell. New York: American House Publications, 1947.

Orwell, George. "Politics and the English Language." *A Collection of Essays.* Garden City, N.Y.: Doubleday, 1957.

Pennock, J. R. *Democratic Political Theory.* Princeton: Princeton University Press, 1979.

Plamenatz, John. *Democracy and Illusion.* London: Longmans, 1973.

Popper, Karl. *The Open Society and Its Enemies.* 2 vols. Princeton: Princeton University Press, 1966.

Sartori, Giovanni. "Concept Misinformation in Comparative Politics." *American Political Science Review* 64 (1970): 1033–53.

————. *Democratic Theory.* New York: Praeger, 1967.

de Tocqueville, Alexis. *Democracy in America.* Edited by Phillips Bradley. 2 vols. New York: Vintage Press, 1958.

————. *The Old Regime and the French Revolution.* Translated by Stuart Gilbert. Garden City, N.Y.: Anchor, 1955.

Weldon, T. D. *The Vocabulary of Politics.* Baltimore: Penguin Books, 1955.

Contributors

DAVID BUTLER, an adjunct scholar of the American Enterprise Institute, has been a fellow of Nuffield College, Oxford, and senior author of the Nuffield studies of British general elections since 1951. He is coauthor (with Donald Stokes) of *Political Change in Britain* and coeditor (with Austin Ranney) of *Referendums: A Comparative Study of Practice and Theory*. He has written and broadcast widely on politics in Great Britain and Australia.

IVOR CREWE is director of the SSRC Survey Archive and codirector of the British Election Study, both at the University of Essex. Editor of the *British Journal of Political Science* since 1977 and coeditor of *Party Identification and Beyond*, he is also coauthor of *A New Conservative Electorate?* (forthcoming).

LEON D. EPSTEIN, Bascom Professor of Political Science at the University of Wisconsin–Madison, was president of the American Political Science Association in 1978–1979. A contributor to *Australia at the Polls: The National Elections of 1975*, he is also the author of *Politics in Wisconsin, Political Parties in Western Democracies*, and *British Politics in the Suez Crisis*.

DENNIS KAVANAGH is at the University of Manchester in England and spent the first six months of 1979 at the University of California, San Diego. A specialist in British politics and elections, he is the author of *New Trends in British Politics* (with Richard Rose) and *The British General Election of 1979* (with David Butler).

ANTHONY KING, an adjunct scholar at the American Enterprise Institute, is editor of *The New American Political System* and author of *Britain Says Yes: The 1975 Referendum on the Common Market*. He is professor of government at the University of Essex and comments on elections for the British Broadcasting Corporation and the London *Observer*.

JEANE J. KIRKPATRICK, a resident scholar at the American Enterprise Institute and Leavey Professor of Government at Georgetown University, has written widely on democratic political culture and insti tutions. She is the author of *The New Presidential Elite, Political Woman,* and *Leader and Vanguard in Mass Society* and a frequent contributor to journals of opinion.

AREND LIJPHART was appointed professor of political science at the University of California at San Diego in 1978 after holding the chair in international relations at the University of Leiden for ten years. He was editor of the *European Journal of Political Research* from 1971 to 1975 and is the author of *Democracy in Plural Societies.*

KHAYYAM ZEV PALTIEL is professor of political science at Carleton University in Ottawa. A former research director of the Canadian Government Advisory Committee on Election Expenses and secretary of the International Study Group on Political Finance, he is the author of *Political Party Financing in Canada* and chapters in both *At the Polls* studies of Canadian elections.

HOWARD R. PENNIMAN, general editor of the *At the Polls* series, is codirector of the program in Political and Social Processes at the American Enterprise Institute and an election consultant to the American Broadcasting Company. The author of several books on politics and government in the United States, he has served as an official observer of elections in developing countries, including the 1979 and 1980 elections in Zimbabwe-Rhodesia.

AUSTIN RANNEY, a former professor of political science at the University of Wisconsin–Madison and a former president of the American Political Science Association, is codirector of the program in Political and Social Processes at the American Enterprise Institute. His recent works include *Participation in American Presidential Nominations, The Federalization of Presidential Primaries,* and *Referendums: A Comparative Study of Practice and Theory.*

ANTHONY SMITH, director of the British Film Institute, has participated in numerous studies of the media and politics. He is the editor of *Television and Political Life: Studies in Six European Countries* and the author of *Goodbye Gutenberg: The Newspaper Revolution of the 1980s.*

DONALD E. STOKES is professor of politics and public affairs and dean of the Woodrow Wilson School of Public and International Affairs at Princeton University. His books on voting and elections include *The American Voter* and *Political Change in Britain,* of which he is coauthor.

Index

353

Britain at the Polls, 1979
A Study of the General Election

Edited by Howard R. Penniman

This study describes the election that gave Britain its first woman prime minister and a Government more committed to private enterprise than any since World War II. Although the Callaghan Government had succeeded in halving the inflation rate between 1974 and 1979, its supporters' confidence in Labour's ability to handle the economy was broken by a winter of industrial strife. This compounded a secular erosion in support for Labour's fundamental principles and brought a decisive swing to the Conservatives among the working class.

The chapters in this book explain the British electoral system and analyze the economic context of the election, the campaigns of the Labour, Conservative, and Liberal parties, the role of the opinion polls, the financing of the campaign, the participation of women in British politics, and the causes of the Conservative victory. The authors are Austin Ranney, Anthony King, Dick Leonard, William S. Livingston, Jorgen Rasmussen, Richard Rose, Michael Pinto-Duschinsky, Monica Charlot, and Ivor Crewe. In an appendix, Richard S. Scammon gives a regional breakdown of the election returns. *1981/Political and Social Processes Study/3406-3   Cloth $16.25/3402-0   Paper $8.25*

Available from
American Enterprise Institute for Public Policy Research
1150 Seventeenth Street, N.W., Washington, D.C. 20036

AEI's *At the Polls* Studies

Australia at the Polls: The National Elections of 1975, Howard R. Penniman, ed. Chapters by Leon D. Epstein, Patrick Weller, R. F. I. Smith, D. W. Rawson, Michelle Grattan, Margaret Bridson Cribb, Paul Reynolds, C. J. Lloyd, Terence W. Beed, Owen Harries, and Colin A. Hughes. Appendixes by David Butler and Richard M. Scammon. (373 pp., $5)

The Australian National Elections of 1977, Howard R. Penniman, ed. Chapters by David Butler, David A. Kemp, Patrick Weller, Jean Holmes, Paul Reynolds, Murray Goot, Terence W. Beed, C. J. Lloyd, Ainsley Jolley, Duncan Ironmonger, and Colin A. Hughes. Appendix by Richard M. Scammon. (367 pp., $8.25)

Britain at the Polls: The Parliamentary Elections of 1974, Howard R. Penniman, ed. Chapters by Anthony King, Austin Ranney, Dick Leonard, Michael Pinto-Duschinsky, Richard Rose, and Jay G. Blumler. Appendix by Richard M. Scammon. (256 pp., $3)

Britain Says Yes: The 1975 Referendum on the Common Market, Anthony King. (153 pp., $3.75)

Britain at the Polls, 1979: A Study of the General Election, Howard R. Penniman, ed. Chapters by Austin Ranney, Anthony King, Dick Leonard, William B. Livingston, Jorgen Rasmussen, Richard Rose, Michael Pinto-Duschinsky, Monica Charlot, and Ivor Crewe. Appendixes by Shelley Pinto-Duschinsky and Richard M. Scammon. (345 pp., cloth $16.25, paper $8.25)

Canada at the Polls: The General Election of 1974, Howard R. Penniman, ed. Chapters by John Meisel, William P. Irvine, Stephen Clarkson, George Perlin, Jo Surich, Michael B. Stein, Khayyam Z. Paltiel, Lawrence LeDuc, and Frederick J. Fletcher. Appendix by Richard M. Scammon. (310 pp., $4.50)

France at the Polls: The Presidential Election of 1974, Howard R. Penniman, ed. Chapters by Roy Pierce, J. Blondel, Jean Charlot, Serge Hurtig, Marie-Thérèse Lancelot, Alain Lancelot, Alfred Grosser, and Monica Charlot. Appendix by Richard M. Scammon. (324 pp., $4.50)

The French National Assembly Elections of 1978, Howard R. Penniman, ed. Chapters by Roy Pierce, Jérôme Jaffré, Jean Charlot, Georges Lavau, Roland Cayrol, Monica Charlot, and Jeane J. Kirkpatrick. Appendix by Richard M. Scammon. (255 pp., $7.25)

Germany at the Polls: The Bundestag Election of 1976, Karl H. Cerny, ed. Chapters by Gerhard Loewenberg, David P. Conradt, Kurt Sontheimer, Heino Kaack, Werner Kaltefleiter, Paul Noack, Klaus Schönbach, Rulolf Wildenmann, and Max Kaase. Appendix by Richard M. Scammon. (251 pp., $7.25)

India at the Polls: The Parliamentary Elections of 1977, Myron Weiner. (150 pp., $6.25)

Ireland at the Polls: The Dáil Elections of 1977, Howard R. Penniman, ed. Chapters by Basil Chubb, Richard Sinnott, Maurice Manning, and Brian Farrell. Appendixes by Basil Chubb and Richard M. Scammon. (199 pp., $6.25)

Israel at the Polls: The Knesset Elections of 1977, Howard R. Penniman, ed. Chapters by Daniel J. Elazar, Avraham Brichta, Asher Arian, Benjamin Akzin, Myron J. Aronoff, Efraim Torgovnik, Elyakim Rubinstein, Leon Boim, Judith Elizur, Elihu Katz, and Bernard Reich. Appendix by Richard M. Scammon. (333 pp., $8.25)

Italy at the Polls: The Parliamentary Elections of 1976, Howard R. Penniman, ed. Chapters by Joseph LaPalombara, Douglas Wertman, Giacomo Sani, Giuseppe Di Palma, Stephen Hellman, Gianfranco Pasquino, Robert Leonardi, William E. Porter, Robert D. Putnam, and Samuel H. Barnes. Appendix by Richard M. Scammon. (386 pp., $5.75)

Japan at the Polls: The House of Councillors Election of 1974, Michael K. Blaker, ed. Chapters by Herbert Passin, Gerald L. Curtis, and Michael K. Blaker. (157 pp., $3)

A Season of Voting: The Japanese Elections of 1976 and 1977, Herbert Passin, ed. Chapters by Herbert Passin, Michael Blaker, Gerald L. Curtis, Nisihira Sigeki, and Kato Hirohisa. (199 pp., $6.25)

New Zealand at the Polls: The General Election of 1978, Howard R. Penniman, ed. Chapters by Stephen Levine, Keith Ovenden, Alan McRobie, Keith Jackson, Gilbert Antony Wood, Roderic Alley, Colin C. James, Brian Murphy, Les Cleveland, Judith Aitken, and Nigel S. Roberts. Appendix by Richard M. Scammon. (295 pp., $7.25)

Scandinavia at the Polls: Recent Political Trends in Denmark, Norway, and Sweden, Karl H. Cerny, ed. Chapters by Ole Borre, Henry Valen, Willy Martinussen, Bo Särlvik, Daniel Tarschys, Erik Allardt, Steen Sauerberg, Niels Thomsen, C. G. Uhr, Göran Ohlin, and Walter Galenson. (304 pp., $5.75)

Venezuela at the Polls: The National Elections of 1978, Howard R. Penniman, ed. Chapters by John D. Martz, Henry Wells, Robert E. O'Connor, David J. Myers, Donald J. Herman, and David Blank. Appendix by Richard M. Scammon. (287 pp., cloth $15.25, paper $7.25)

Referendums: A Comparative Study of Practice and Theory, David Butler and Austin Ranney, eds. Chapters by Jean-François Aubert, Austin Ranney, Eugene C. Lee, Don Aitkin, Vincent Wright, Sten Sparre Nilson, Maurice Manning, and David Butler. (250 pp., $4.75)

Studies are forthcoming on the latest national elections in Belgium, Canada, Colombia, Denmark, Greece, India, Italy, Japan, the Netherlands, Norway, Spain, Sweden, and Switzerland and on the first elections to the European Parliament.

A NOTE ON THE BOOK

*The typeface used for the text of this book is
Palatino, designed by Hermann Zapf.
The type was set by
Hendricks-Miller Typographic Company, of Washington.
BookCrafters, Inc., of Chelsea, Michigan, printed
and bound the book, using Glatfelter paper.
The cover and format were designed by Pat Taylor,
and the figure was drawn by Hördur Karlsson.
The manuscript was edited by
Claudia Winkler, of the AEI
Political and Social Processes Studies staff, and
by Gertrude Kaplan, of the AEI Publications staff.*

SELECTED AEI PUBLICATIONS

Public Opinion, published bimonthly (one year, $12; two years, $22; single copy, $2.50)

Britain at the Polls, 1979: A Study of the General Election, Howard R. Penniman, ed. (345 pp., paper $8.25, cloth $16.25)

Venezuela at the Polls: The National Elections of 1978, Howard R. Penniman, ed. (287 pp., paper $7.25, cloth $15.25)

How Democratic Is the Constitution? Robert A. Goldwin and William A. Schambra, editors (150 pp., paper $5.25, cloth $12.25)

The Presidential Nominating Process: Can It Be Improved? Jeane J. Kirkpatrick, Michael J. Malbin, Thomas E. Mann, Howard R. Penniman, and Austin Ranney (27 pp., $3.25)

Vital Statistics on Congress, 1980, John F. Bibby, Thomas E. Mann, Norman J. Ornstein (113 pp., paper $5.25, cloth $12.25)

Presidents and Prime Ministers, Richard Rose and Ezra N. Suleiman, eds. (347 pp., $8.25)

Democracy and Mediating Structures: A Theological Inquiry, Michael Novak, ed. (216 pp., paper $7.25, cloth, $13.25)

Future Directions for Public Policy, John Charles Daly, mod. (38 pp., $3.75)

Prices subject to change without notice.

AEI ASSOCIATES PROGRAM

The American Enterprise Institute invites your participation in the competition of ideas through its AEI Associates Program. This program has two objectives:

The first is to broaden the distribution of AEI studies, conferences, forums, and reviews, and thereby to extend public familiarity with the issues. AEI Associates receive regular information on AEI research and programs, and they can order publications and cassettes at a savings.

The second objective is to increase the research activity of the American Enterprise Institute and the dissemination of its published materials to policy makers, the academic community, journalists, and others who help shape public attitudes. Your contribution, which in most cases is partly tax deductible, will help ensure that decision makers have the benefit of scholarly research on the practical options to be considered before programs are formulated. The issues studied by AEI include:

- Defense Policy
- Economic Policy
- Energy Policy
- Foreign Policy
- Government Regulation

- Health Policy
- Legal Policy
- Political and Social Processes
- Social Security and Retirement Policy
- Tax Policy

For more information, write to:

AMERICAN ENTERPRISE INSTITUTE
1150 Seventeenth Street, N.W.
Washington, D.C. 20036